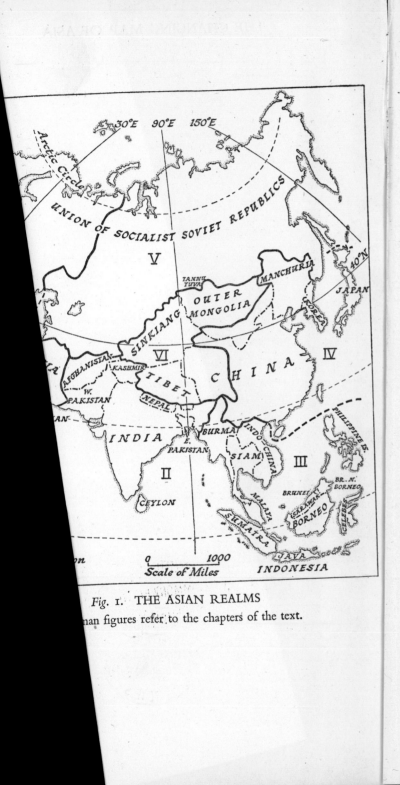

Fig. 1. THE ASIAN REALMS

man figures refer to the chapters of the text.

The Ro

THE CHANGING MAP
OF ASIA

A Political Geography

Edited by

W. GORDON EAST
Professor of Geography in the University of London

and

O. H. K. SPATE
Reader in Geography in the University of London

It is often said that geography does not change. In truth the geography changes as rapidly as ideas and technologies change; that is, the meaning of geographical conditions changes.

DR. ISAIAH BOWMAN

WITH 34 MAPS

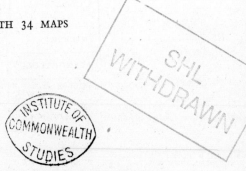
LONDON: METHUEN & CO. LTD.
NEW YORK: E. P. DUTTON & CO. INC.

1950

First published in 1950

CATALOGUE NO. 4253/U (METHUEN)

PRINTED IN GREAT BRITAIN

PREFACE

WHILST in its social texture Asia retains so much that is traditional and slow to change, its economy, long subjected to the powerful alien forces of the world market and of modern industrialism, has now embarked, in many areas, upon a more autonomous development. Moreover, during this last decade of war and revolution, spectacular changes have been wrought in its political structure, changes strikingly displayed on the political map. The destruction of the Japanese Empire; the abandonment by Britain of imperial and mandatory responsibilities in India, Burma, Ceylon, and Palestine; the partition of the Indian sub-continent and the mediatization of most of the congeries of states which lived in the favour of the British Raj; the clash of cultures in the Levant and in Malaya, with the incalculably significant emergence of the state of Israel in the former area; the planned development of Siberia; new forms and phases of the perennial conflict between the old and the new, between localism and integration, in China; the stormy struggles of nationalism in Indo-China and Indonesia—these are some of the dramatic political changes now working themselves out in this greatest of continents.

Behind these events lies the impulse to build up independent economic power, an impulse manifested in the almost universal demand of Asiatic publicists for planned industrialization. More fundamental, perhaps, are those acute agrarian problems from which hardly any country of Asia is free. While some of the older colonial powers are still struggling, and perhaps not without success, to retain their old dominion, other extraneous interests find a large field for manœuvre and conflict in Asia which, with its wealth of raw materials or war materials, cannot remain aloof from the great contention which divides the world in our time of troubles. Asia is re-shaping against a geopolitical background in which the Soviet Union and the United States are engaged in a many-fronted contest.

Since Asia includes within its borders over half of mankind, its problems are clearly of vital importance to the world as a whole. But these infinitely serious and complex problems are too often discussed in terms of political personalities and popular movements only, against but a vague and shadowy background of landscape and resources. This book seeks to present the setting of the stage, to give a fuller content to those names of peoples and of places which too often remain mere names in the headlines. It brings together contributions by authors who have studied the environmental problems of Asia either at first hand, or in their academic or war-time work, or in a combination of these activities. So far as may be political narrative is eschewed, and the attempt is made to survey broadly the political geography of Asia and its major divisions as a basis for closer study of the complex internal and international problems of the continent. The several authors have, however, naturally interpreted their terms of reference with reasonable latitude. It would be futile to attempt to write political geography without touching on current politics; hence in some sections matter not inherently geographical has been discussed where that seemed essential to attain clarity and coherence. This book however is but complementary to the many interesting discussions of the Asian revolution which have appeared, especially in the United States, in recent years; and while it strives to be comprehensive, it makes no attempt to be encyclopædic.

It is a truism that each age, as it asks new questions, must evaluate anew past history. It appears no less imperative that, as political forces re-fashion the map, and as new means of communication and new weapons of open or ideological warfare re-act on the world as a whole, the new politico-geographical structure of this major fraction of the earth's surface and population should be appreciated at its true significance. For while Asia starts a fresh phase of history in proximity to mighty neighbours whose not altogether disinterested activity may well have determinative effects, it must also be recognized that, should this immense reservoir of man-power develop an external energy comparable to its numerical pre-ponderance, the reaction upon the western world will not be less profound for being largely incalculable. Yet some efforts towards an assessment must be made; and this book seeks to assemble the more significant geographical data bearing upon this vast and fascinating problem.

W.G.E.

London, March 1949   O.H.K.S.

ACKNOWLEDGEMENTS

The Editors wish to record their thanks to colleagues who have helped them in the preparation of some of the maps for this book. Miss E. M. Timberlake, B.Sc., of Bedford College, computed the projection for Figure 16, Miss E. M. J. Campbell, M.A. and Dr. H. C. Brookfield of Birkbeck College, prepared Figures 34 and Figure 29 respectively. We are grateful also to Professor R. O. Buchanan, Ph.D., for the use of Figure 4. Thanks are also due to Miss A. M. Bailey of Birkbeck College for the preparation of the Index.

THE CHANGING MAP
OF ASIA

A Political Geography

Edited by

W. GORDON EAST

Professor of Geography in the University of London

and

O. H. K. SPATE

Reader in Geography in the University of London

It is often said that geography does not change. In truth the geography changes as rapidly as ideas and technologies change; that is, the meaning of geographical conditions changes.

DR. ISAIAH BOWMAN

WITH 34 MAPS

LONDON: METHUEN & CO. LTD.
NEW YORK: E. P. DUTTON & CO. INC.

1950

First published in 1950

CATALOGUE NO. 4253/U (METHUEN)

PRINTED IN GREAT BRITAIN

PREFACE

WHILST in its social texture Asia retains so much that is traditional and slow to change, its economy, long subjected to the powerful alien forces of the world market and of modern industrialism, has now embarked, in many areas, upon a more autonomous development. Moreover, during this last decade of war and revolution, spectacular changes have been wrought in its political structure, changes strikingly displayed on the political map. The destruction of the Japanese Empire; the abandonment by Britain of imperial and mandatory responsibilities in India, Burma, Ceylon, and Palestine; the partition of the Indian sub-continent and the mediatization of most of the congeries of states which lived in the favour of the British Raj; the clash of cultures in the Levant and in Malaya, with the incalculably significant emergence of the state of Israel in the former area; the planned development of Siberia; new forms and phases of the perennial conflict between the old and the new, between localism and integration, in China; the stormy struggles of nationalism in Indo-China and Indonesia—these are some of the dramatic political changes now working themselves out in this greatest of continents.

Behind these events lies the impulse to build up independent economic power, an impulse manifested in the almost universal demand of Asiatic publicists for planned industrialization. More fundamental, perhaps, are those acute agrarian problems from which hardly any country of Asia is free. While some of the older colonial powers are still struggling, and perhaps not without success, to retain their old dominion, other extraneous interests find a large field for manoeuvre and conflict in Asia which, with its wealth of raw materials or war materials, cannot remain aloof from the great contention which divides the world in our time of troubles. Asia is re-shaping against a geopolitical background in which the Soviet Union and the United States are engaged in a many-fronted contest.

Since Asia includes within its borders over half of mankind, its problems are clearly of vital importance to the world as a whole. But these infinitely serious and complex problems are too often discussed in terms of political personalities and popular movements only, against but a vague and shadowy background of landscape and resources. This book seeks to present the setting of the stage, to give a fuller content to those names of peoples and of places which too often remain mere names in the headlines. It brings together contributions by authors who have studied the environmental problems of Asia either at first hand, or in their academic or war-time work, or in a combination of these activities. So far as may be political narrative is eschewed, and the attempt is made to survey broadly the political geography of Asia and its major divisions as a basis for closer study of the complex internal and international problems of the continent. The several authors have, however, naturally interpreted their terms of reference with reasonable latitude. It would be futile to attempt to write political geography without touching on current politics; hence in some sections matter not inherently geographical has been discussed where that seemed essential to attain clarity and coherence. This book however is but complementary to the many interesting discussions of the Asian revolution which have appeared, especially in the United States, in recent years; and while it strives to be comprehensive, it makes no attempt to be encyclopædic.

It is a truism that each age, as it asks new questions, must evaluate anew past history. It appears no less imperative that, as political forces re-fashion the map, and as new means of communication and new weapons of open or ideological warfare re-act on the world as a whole, the new politico-geographical structure of this major fraction of the earth's surface and population should be appreciated at its true significance. For while Asia starts a fresh phase of history in proximity to mighty neighbours whose not altogether disinterested activity may well have determinative effects, it must also be recognized that, should this immense reservoir of man-power develop an external energy comparable to its numerical pre-ponderance, the reaction upon the western world will not be less profound for being largely incalculable. Yet some efforts towards an assessment must be made; and this book seeks to assemble the more significant geographical data bearing upon this vast and fascinating problem.

W.G.E.

London, March 1949   O.H.K.S.

ACKNOWLEDGEMENTS

The Editors wish to record their thanks to colleagues who have helped them in the preparation of some of the maps for this book. Miss E. M. Timberlake, B.Sc., of Bedford College, computed the projection for Figure 16, Miss E. M. J. Campbell, M.A. and Dr. H. C. Brookfield of Birkbeck College, prepared Figures 34 and Figure 29 respectively. We are grateful also to Professor R. O. Buchanan, Ph.D., for the use of Figure 4. Thanks are also due to Miss A. M. Bailey of Birkbeck College for the preparation of the Index.

THE CHANGING MAP OF ASIA

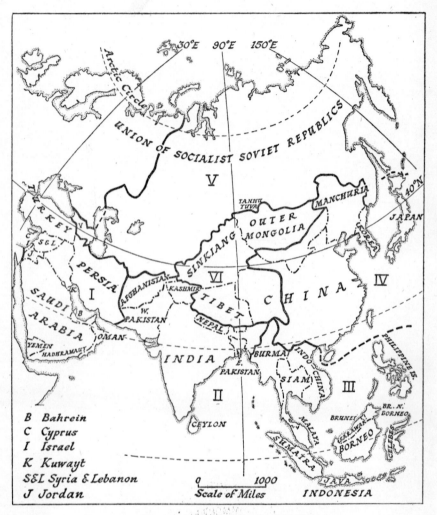

B   Bahrein
C   Cyprus
I   Israel
K   Kuwayt
S&L Syria & Lebanon
J   Jordan

Fig. 1. THE ASIAN REALMS

The Roman figures refer to the chapters of the text.

CONTENTS

INTRODUCTION: THE ASIAN BACKGROUND

By the Editors

I SOUTHWEST ASIA

By Walter Fogg, M.A.

*Senior Lecturer: Department of Geography and Anthropology,
University of Wales, Aberystwyth*

II INDIA AND PAKISTAN

By O. H. K. Spate, M.A., Ph.D.

III SOUTHEAST ASIA

By Charles A. Fisher, M.A.

*Senior Research Officer, Institute of Colonial Studies,
University of Oxford*

IV   THE FAR EAST

BY H. J. WOOD, PH.D. (Econ.)

Lecturer in Geography, King's College, University of London

V   SOVIET ASIA

BY W. GORDON EAST, M.A.

VI   HIGH ASIA

BY R. R. RAWSON, B.SC.

Lecturer in Geography, The London School of Economics and Political Science,
University of London

EPILOGUE: THE UNITY OF ASIA?

BY THE EDITORS

Short Booklists and Tables will be found at the end of each Chapter

MAPS

ix

TABLES

INTRODUCTION

THE ASIAN BACKGROUND

Love if you will your roses and your nightingales,
Those mountains neighbour to the sky,
Those microcosms meshed in silk and stone,
Those intricate fossil thoughts too old to die;

But remember the rivers bone-dry and their shingle spread like ash,
The cattle gasping in the fragmented fields,
The vultures wheeling down from the brazen sky
And the usurer's pious text as he counts his yields—

The one and the other Asia. . . .

A GENERAL SURVEY

THE PHYSICAL SETTING

THE primary, and the most significant, geographical fact about the
continent of Asia is simply the obvious one of its size. Its area of about
17 million square miles is no less than one-third of the land surface of the
globe. Asia extends over 164° of longitude and 85° of latitude; no other
continent spans all zones from strictly Arctic to strictly equatorial, and the
next in longitudinal extension, North America, has only 115°, and that
in its far north only. To assess fully the extreme continentality of Asia
we must remember that its longitudinal extension runs through the heart
of the continent, and we must add another 36° for its peninsular projection, Europe.

This difference in scale as compared with the lesser continents is indeed
so great as to produce qualitative differences. Apart from all the peninsular and insular appendages, the main mass of Asia (within the quadri-
lateral Basra-Hanoi-Angarka-gulf of the Ob) has itself an area of 11 or
12 million square miles, which roughly equals that of Africa, the next
largest continent. The innermost parts of this quadrilateral, around Lake
Balkhash and Dzungaria, are some 2000 miles from the sea north and
south, and considerably further than that east and west; and the nearest

seas are the frozen Arctic or are walled off by the loftiest and most massive mountain barrier on the face of the earth. Mere distance is thus associated with a unique massiveness of build.

The main physical components of Asia are the great northern lowlands; the vast wedge of central plateaus and their border ranges; the southern peninsulas and the complicated area in the east where the central mountain masses break down through great river-basins to the marginal seas and island-arcs of the Pacific.

The core consists of a series of great plateaus and mountains, forming a belt some 5000 miles long and at its widest 2000 miles across, trending roughly southwest-northeast across the continent. Some half a million square miles in Tibet lie at an altitude of over 13,000 feet, while less than 400 miles to the north (no great distance on an Asiatic scale) the Turfan depression sinks below sea-level. The Andean plateaus rival this roof of the world in altitude, the African in extent; but in height and area together there is no comparable mountain mass in the world. Incomparable also is the scale of its border ranges: the Himalaya-Karakoram could be wrapped around the Alps, whose loftiest peaks would barely peep over many of the notches in the Asiatic ramparts. Of the 94 peaks in the world which exceed 24,000 feet, all but two are in the Himalaya-Karakoram; the two are in the Trans-Altai. At the other end of the orographic scale the Asiatic northwest forms the greater part of the largest lowlands in the world, and includes in the Caspian depression the largest area of dry land below sea-level. The appendages to the main mass are themselves almost continental in build: the Arabian peninsula covers about 1,000,000 and that of India, outside its mountain girdle from Baluchistan to Burma, about 1,300,000 square miles, while the Indonesian archipelagoes, including western New Guinea but excluding the Philippines, extend an eighth of the way around the globe—from 95° to 140°E.—and some 10° N. and S. of the Equator, this sea area about 3000 miles long by 1200 miles wide containing over 800,000 square miles of land. Again at the opposite extreme, we may note that the total area of interior drainage in Asia, which contains seven of the longest rivers of the world, is no less than 5 million square miles.

These statistics of bigness are intended to make concrete the impression of the vastness of the physical background, the radical characteristic of this continent. This background controls the regional climates, and they in turn influence the daily and the secular life of man in Asia not perhaps more profoundly, but certainly more directly, than in industrialized Europe. With so large an area, and such immense topographical differentiation, it is natural that the climates also should be extremely varied.

But in the broad there is one cardinal division, formed by the plateau-core from Iran to Mongolia. North and west the most important climatic influences are those of the temperate westerlies, very greatly modified, of course, by extreme continentality, but preserving typically temperate régimes of rainfall and temperature relationships. South and east are the monsoon lands, under the domination of the great seasonal changes of temperature and pressure in the interior: cold winters with dry out-blowing winds, succeeded in summer by in-blowing winds as great low-pressure systems are set up over the intensely heated Punjab and Gobi regions.[1] Consequently the summer is the rainy season almost everywhere between the Indus and the Hwang-ho, 75–90% of the annual precipitation falling from June to October inclusive, except in some few coastal areas where the lie of the land produces a reversal of phase: the west of Japan, the east of Annam and of southern India; while in the East Indies local variations of aspect and of position north or south of the Equator account for numerous very local anomalies. But, apart from these restricted equatorial regions, the exceptions are rather variations on the theme than fundamentally different régimes. More important are the differences in the actual yearly rainfalls, from 10–15 inches in the Indus plains to as much as 200–400 around the head of the Bay of Bengal; the extreme variability in areas of small amount, such as Western Pakistan and the landward margins of the Hwang-ho plains; and the concentration of rainfall into less than half the year, and in many areas into a few torrential downpours. This last feature facilitates soil erosion in those too numerous areas where deforestation, over-grazing, and shifting agriculture have given it a start.

The vegetation cover is also extremely complex in detail and, especially in the densely peopled monsoon lands, it has been greatly altered—over large areas indeed practically destroyed—by the work of man and his symbiotes, especially the goat. But two major forest realms are discernible, corresponding to the major climatic division, and separated by the great belt of steppes and barren plateaus and basins, enclosed by or flanking the ranges of the central core. The northern forest, the *taiga*, sweeps right across Siberia in what is probably the largest broadly homogeneous forest block in the world. The tropical and sub-tropical

---

[1] It is an obvious over-simplification to think of a homogeneous interior alternating between high and low pressures, as shown on small-scale atlas maps. The differences in latitude, and hence in summer insolation and winter radiation, between the Punjab and the Gobi go far to explain the reversal in the strengths of the winter and the summer monsoon winds as between India and China, the latter having the stronger winter and the weaker summer winds. Modern airmass meteorology uses more refined modes of analysis and expression, but the broad facts remain as stated, though it must not be thought that there are no obscurities about the mechanism of the monsoons.

monsoon lands are also essentially a forest realm, but with far more variation than is found in the *taiga*, variations both in species within a given forest-type and in the types themselves. These range from the broad-leaved evergreen rainforest and tidal mangroves to the very open and stunted acacia scrub of western India. Moreover in such regions as the Indo-Gangetic and Hwang-ho alluvial plains millennia of close agricultural settlement have reduced the original forest to scattered groves and riverine strips—themselves much altered ecologically—in a sea of arable; or, as in the Deccan, produced over large areas an aspect strongly reminiscent of savannah.

ASIAN ENVIRONMENTS[1]

Such then, in broadest outline, is the physical setting: vast, complex, cast in heroic moulds. Only Europeans, seized of its continentality, dared, in Classical antiquity, to give Asia its name, and thereby to suggest a unity to which it is, perhaps, only formally entitled. There are indeed many Asias—the long ramparts of the Himalayas towering above the alluvial monotony of the Gangetic plain, the dwarf birches of the tundra and the giant dipterocarps of the rainforest, the cold desolation of the high plains of Tibet and the smiling Burmese countryside, the tilled steppe lands of Siberia and the shifting seas of sand in the Tarim basin. Corresponding to these almost infinite varieties of milieu are many not less distinct societies: Veddahs and Sakais leading an almost prehistoric life in their jungles; the immemorial complexities of the Hindu and the Chinese civilizations; varieties within the Muslim world from the tough fundamentalism of Saudi Arabia to the sophistication of Persia; fossil relics of once mighty faiths, such as the Parsees and the Syrian Christians of Malabar; the Levantine cosmopolitan cities with their roots striking deep to the very beginnings of urbanism, and their analogues born yesterday, Shanghai and Singapore; and the other new creations of ideology and industrialism, Tel Aviv, Jamshedpur, Karaganda, Komsomolsk. In India alone the economic historian might study at first hand laboratory specimens, as it were, of every stage in human organisation, from that of tribes not much above a chalcolithic level to that of monopoly capitalism.

Yet, violent as the contrasts of modern Asia are, there are recurrent motifs: only in this century has the superior mobility of the air and of motor transport finally and fatally weighted the balance between nomadic

[1] Nationalist leaders in Asia seem to dislike the word "Asiatic", which like "native" may be used, or interpreted, in a depreciatory sense. Their preference for "Asian" suggests a shade of difference in the meaning of the two words; we have taken advantage of this to use "Asian" when looking from Asia outwards, "Asiatic" when adopting an external view.

and sedentary cultures in the latter's favour; and still the rhythm of the monsoonal year weaves the pattern of work and festival, its uncertain bounty spells food or famine, for nearly half the human race. There are also underlying similarities of environment which foster gradual transitions on the margins of the great cultural realms. From the Levant through Iraq and Iran to the Punjab ways of life are not really dissimilar: the datepalm and the well, the flocks of sheep and goats, the camel, the flat-roofed house with blank outer walls built round an enclosed court— these leading features of the picture are strikingly alike in all these lands, related to an environment predominantly arid but with favoured oases and great caravan towns; related also to the Islamic cultural pattern. Across India the transitions are subtle: somewhere in the Ganges valley the flat-roofed mud houses give way to bamboo and thatch, with gables to shed the rain; but their frontier is a wavering and indefinite zone, and in a whole day's rail journey the traveller needs a trained eye to detect much difference between the morning and the evening landscape, though on the second morning he looks out upon a different world. Moving eastwards we see but little change in the physical earth and in farming practice between the deltas of the Ganges and the Kistna and that of the Irrawaddy. The patterns of Burma recur in Siam, Cambodia, Annam, with a difference of scale even in Malaya: the organized kingdoms in the great paddy-deltas, the shifting agriculture and tribal society of the wilder jungly hills, and between these two the semi-feudal congeries of petty principalities on the open plateaus. Again, through all the wetter monsoon lands the line of villages on the neutral ground—lateritic aprons, diluvial terraces—between the waterlogged paddy plains and the forested mountains is one of the most constantly recurring settlement patterns. This is common ground; yet if in Burma the Indian elements in culture fundamentally prevail over the Chinese, Annam is 'Little China', a miniature edition of the Celestial Empire. Beirut to Shanghai—there are few abrupt changes, yet the ends of the series are distant in every sense, except that, if we look to these cities merely and not to their hinterlands, both are cosmopolitan ports with all their implications of culture contacts and plural societies.

Continental as it is, Asia is no exception to the general rule of greater peripheral development; indeed it may be held that the only exception is Europe, and Europe is a land merely marginal to Asia, comparable in size and population to either India or China. The Asiatic œcumene is indeed restricted and very unequally exploited. More than 1200 million people live in Asia, but of these three-quarters are in India (including Pakistan), China, and Japan; indeed the monsoon lands alone account for nearly half of mankind. But the rest of Asia is thinly peopled, with ribbons and scattered pockets of closer settlement. It is the monsoon lands which are the essential Asiatic Asia as distinct from "the Asia which seems to merge so imperceptibly into Europe that of the two great countries, Russia and Turkey, it is difficult to say whether they are indeed European or Asiatic."[1] These two correspond to the fundamental climatic and vegetational divisions already noted, and between them, along the arid and/or mountainous barrier zone, lies a third broad division: the steppe and desert lands. From these, whatever the ultimate causation, have come those great movements of nomadic peoples whose actions and reactions with the settled populations of European Europe and Asiatic Asia have been the reagents of very much of the historic process. Looked at from another angle, Russian Asia represents a civilization essentially the result of recent European colonisation, and reminiscent in some respects of North America a century ago, an extrusion of the European œcumene; leaving aside all questions of ideology, such at least is its technical cast. The simple division between Asiatic Asia and this northern realm is, however, much blurred in the southwest whence, as Datta puts it, the Semitic faiths of Christianity and Islam arose to reinvigorate the Hellenistic civilisation implemented and spread, or at least defended, by the Roman and Byzantine Empires. This blurring of the Euro-Asiatic cultural divide has been in recent centuries largely a matter of the Islamic cultural pattern, which extends far into both the greater realms, of the northern lowlands and of the monsoon lands. But it goes deeper than that, for Southwest Asia is a steppe and desert land in the main, but with very significant oases on a scale large enough to foster the earliest civilizations. On the definitely Asiatic side of the steppe and mountain zone monsoon Asia has been the cradle, if not of Civilization, at least of civilizations of high achievement, self-conscious and self-regarding and of very notable stability; India and China are in fact exceeded in this respect by Egypt only, whose civilization spanned a period longer than has ensued since its fall. And Egypt itself lay partly in Asia as Herodotus conceived it.[2]

THE ASIAN REALMS

The broad realms into which Asia may be divided, with due attention to the facts both of physical environment and of social evolution, are

[1] S. K. Datta, *Asiatic Asia* (1932), p. 9.
[2] How far the considerations discussed in this paragraph correlate with the currently fashionable "Heartland" concept may be worked out by the student. Valuable as shorthand (and as a slogan), the concept appears to be a drastic over-simplification of an exceedingly complex historical reality. But see below, pp. 357-9.

fairly generally accepted, and are implied in the very selective survey above; the scheme of treatment adopted in this book conforms in essentials to the divisions of common usage (Fig. 1, frontispiece). These are:

I SOUTHWEST ASIA: lands of purest Islamic culture, yet shot through with strands going back to the beginnings of history; largely a desert and steppe environment with important agricultural pockets and mountain belts; at once a bridge and a barrier between East and West, so that positional factors are of great importance and, with the oil resources of these lands of backward technique, are responsible for the conflict of interests of great external powers in this area—interests which restrict the real independence of the several small states into which it is divided.

II INDIA AND PAKISTAN: "India" is still the most convenient geographical expression for the sub-continent between the Himalayas and the Indian Ocean; Western Pakistan has strong environmental and cultural affinities with SOUTHWEST ASIA, but Eastern Pakistan is, apart from religion, purely Indian in character; and the Partition is too recent for much divergence in the structure of government and of economic activity to have taken place, other than the difference inherent in the industrial poverty of Pakistan. With these two Dominions of the British Commonwealth the smaller Dominion of Ceylon and the buffer-state of Afghanistan are briefly considered.

III SOUTHEAST ASIA: the old names Further India and the Indo-Chinese Peninsula (in the broader sense) express much of the quality of the mainland area, which is peculiar in being an (at least relatively) under-peopled monsoon area. Malaya and Indonesia form a distinctive maritime realm which has, however, much in common with the peninsula to the north. Including the Philippines there are four definitely independent (but weak) states, and although European control has been much weakened since 1941, it is still stronger here than elsewhere in Asiatic Asia.

IV THE FAR EAST: the sphere of Chinese civilization and the peculiar oriental-occidental hybrid developed in Japan; this realm impinges upon HIGH ASIA and is impinged upon by SOVIET ASIA, with some consequent blurring or overlapping. Since the 19th century it has been a region of outstanding international interest, as a field of investment and trade for alien commercial powers and as the base of Japanese imperialism. Like Europe, it is now an ideological borderland: Allied-occupied Japan faces a Communist China.

V SOVIET ASIA: essentially the northern macro-region already noted in structure, climate, and vegetation; politically a part of one federated state, technologicaly a European extrusion into Asia. It is a pioneer land endowed with considerable resources, now being energetically exploited, in a rigorous physical environment. There is some overlap into HIGH ASIA, and in the northeast and southwest marchlands with the FAR EAST and SOUTHWEST ASIA.

VI HIGH ASIA: the plateau and mountain core of the continent, a great and

2

generally negative tract separating the two great macro-divisions, Euro-Asia to the north and Monsoon or "Asiatic Asia" to the south; politically also a marchland between the continental and the oceanic worlds.

The old terms Near and Middle East are avoided altogether; always ambiguous, they are now confounded beyond any possibility of clarification by the official wartime usage of Middle East to cover an area practically coterminous with the older acceptance of the Near East, except for the latter's indefinite protrusions in North Africa and the Balkans.[1] Southwest Asia is clear and unmistakable in import. The use of Middle East for the old Indian Empire (including Burma) was never very common and has now less than nothing to recommend it. The Far East was sometimes taken to include everything east of Singapore, but it is safe to say that the concept is generally taken as equivalent to China and Japan, with Korea and Manchuria, and its use here in this restricted sense does not seem likely to cause ambiguity.

THE IMPACT OF THE WEST

The political geographer, concerned as he is primarily with place and space relations, cannot ignore the human realities which give uniqueness to the many Asiatic societies and condition their politics. The broad and massive physical outlines which we have sketched break down, of course, into a more subtle mosaic when seen in greater detail; and similarly, although Asiatic empires have on occasion brought immense tracts of land under one rule, and although Asia still includes, in China, Soviet Asia, and India, some of the largest political units in the world, its history and social texture present more intricate designs, designs immensely complicated by the long-standing intrusion of the West. Some review of the historical and social factors is therefore necessary for the disentangling of the more important interlaced patterns.

THE LINKS BETWEEN EAST AND WEST

In the history of civilization as a whole one of the most significant and most permanent factors has been the struggle of the westerners to keep open the trade-routes between the great foci of occidental and oriental civilization. Easterners, in contrast, little felt this urge; their world was

[1] On these terminological inexactitudes, see W. B. Fisher, "Unity and Diversity in the Middle East", *Geographical Review* XXXVII (1947), pp. 414-435. Fisher rejects Near but accepts Middle East, which latter term may have a limited use when it is desired to discuss Egypt with her partners of the Arab League.

large and varied enough to meet their commercial needs: as the famous reply of the Chinese Emperor to Lord Macartney's embassy in 1793 put it, "Our Celestial Empire possesses all things in prolific abundance. . . . There is, therefore, no need to import the manufactures of outside barbarians"; and this was then simple truth. It is true that the maritime activities of the Arabs, the Indians, and the Chinese, were not negligible, though very generally neglected: "Up to about 1400 the peoples of Asia followed the sea in far greater numbers than Europeans and navigated their ships over a far wider extent of the earth's surface."[1] Indians colonized Further India, Chinese fleets sailed to the Persian Gulf. Yet, as the Celestial Emperor unkindly pointed out, Europe needed Asia much more than Asia needed Europe, and hence most of the commercial initiative came from the west, although, until the Portuguese voyages, the actual routes east of the Levant were worked predominantly by Asiatics, and had of course been so worked for centuries.[2] After 1500 this was no longer true; the social shift implied was perhaps as important as the locational.

These routes fall into two groups, the landways flanking the central Asian plateaus and deserts, the seaways from the Mediterranean to Ceylon, beyond which the trade with the Indies was more purely intra-Asian. In either case Southwest Asia held the keys, since all routes but the northermost (by the Black Sea and the Volga) had somehow to cross or skirt the lands between the Caspian and the Red Sea. From the days of the caravan cities of Petra and Palmyra and the Roman and Byzantine struggle against Parthians and Sassanids, down to Napoleon's invasion of Egypt and imperial Germany's *Drang nach Osten*, political control of the Levantine portages and terminals has been a major preoccupation of European powers, a preoccupation weakened by the maritime discoveries of the Renaissance but resuscitated by the opening of the Suez Canal (1869) and by the development of airways.

The drain of precious metals to the East in exchange for silks, spices, and other luxuries, a persistent complaint of Roman publicists, is attested by finds of Roman coins in southern India; but that merchandise did not

[1] Sir J. T. Pratt, *The Expansion of Europe into the Far East* (1947), p. 40. There is perhaps some exaggeration here, and Sir John implies less than justice to the Vikings, for instance. But see "Chinese Voyages in the Indian Ocean in the Early Fifteenth Century," *Geographical Review* XXIV (1934), pp. 672–4.

[2] "This vision of Classical Imperialism as the pioneer . . . is in conflict with Herodotus' sober opinion that Darius was the discoverer of the greater part of Asia. In point of fact, rice, ginger, and pepper all appear in classical Greek under their proper Indian names, indicating close mercantile contacts of long standing. . . . The coincidence of the Greek and Sanskrit for 'tin' seems to be due to a Sanskrit borrowing." K. de B. Codrington, "A Geographical Introduction to the History of Central Asia," *Geographical Journal* CIV (1944), pp. 27–40 and 73–91.

pass only from the East is shown by the recent discovery near Pondicherry of warehouses of Roman pottery. During the early centuries of our era this sea-trade was most active; the 'discovery' of the monsoons by Hippalus (about A.D. 45) is a commonplace of historical geography; but of course they must have been well known to Arab seamen for centuries. Aden and Ceylon (normally the meeting place of Græco-Roman and Chinese traders) were great centres of exchange, and a Byzantine official stationed near Suez yearly visited India. The continuous interference of Persia and later the Islamic conquests caused a shift of interest to the northern routes; the Nestorian monks who brought the silkworm eggs to Justinian came by the 'Silk Road', from the land of the Seres (China) via the Tarim basin to the Caspian shores. It may be noted that under the expansionist Han dynasty (202 B.C.–A.D. 226) Chinese armies reached the Caspian, and for a short time the Roman and the Chinese frontiers were only 600 miles apart.[1]

After the Dark Ages the active role was taken up by the Italian republics and especially by Venice, whose cynical diplomacy diverted the Fourth Crusade to the capture of Constantinople (1204), in an endeavour to secure this great European entrepôt of eastern trade; and although the Byzantine emperors emerged from their sixty years' exile at Nicea they were never able seriously to reassert themselves in the two centuries of existence left to them. The Seljuk Turks were a far more serious menace to the West than were the Saracens, and in the search for an ally for western Christendom the Mongols, earlier regarded quite literally as diabolical baby-eaters, became assimilated in European imagination with the fabulous Christian kingdom of Prester John, perhaps originally some local Nestorian potentate.[2] In the 13th century several diplomatic missions were sent from the Pope and the King of France to the courts of the Mongol Khans; William of Rubruck, an admirable man and a remarkably good observer, has left a fascinating narrative of life in nomad camps and Mongol courts. Rubruck's mission (1253–55) took the northern route, to Karakoram, the Mongol capital, from the Volga north of the Caspian, Aral, and Balkhash to Dzungaria; the Polos (from 1271) went out by land through Asia Minor, Persia, and the Tarim; but Marco Polo returned 25 years later by sea. After these journeys the northern routes were well known and, thanks to their grip on the Aegean

[1] On these topics see: H. G. Rawlinson, *Intercourse between India and the Western World . . until the Fall of the Roman Empire* (1917); E. H. Warmington, *The Commerce between the Roman Empire and India* (1928); J. Poujade, *La Route des Indes et ses Navires* (Payot, Paris, 1946); S. Runciman, *Byzantine Civilisation* (1933) Ch. VII.

[2] The cynical may find a parallel in 1941 and another yet more recent. The later shift of the Prester John legend to Abyssinia (in Byzantine times an important trader with India) played a large part in motivating Portuguese activities in the Red Sea.

and Constantinople, well exploited by Genoese and Venetians. It was their stranglehold, and not the Ottoman conquests, which provided the economic incentive to the Portuguese voyages, which had pushed down the West African coast as far as Cape Verde by 1445, whereas Constantinople did not fall to the Turks until 1453 and Alexandria, after Constantinople the great entrepôt, until 1518.

Vasco da Gama reached India in 1498, and thenceforward the transformed seaway was supreme; the caravan routes and the trade of the Mediterranean cities declined, though the Syrian or the Egyptian portage was used on occasion for rapid messengers, or when the sea-routes were exposed to dangers.[1] Before the Suez Canal was built there were many portage-projects—railways across the isthmus, or to connect with steamer navigation on the Euphrates; but the Canal, if it left the caravan cities more decayed than ever, brought new life to the Mediterranean. Interest in the land-routes remained lively, if on the whole ineffective, as a result of Russo-British rivalry in central and southwest Asia; the construction of the Trans-Siberian (1891–1903) and the projection (and much-delayed completion) of the Berlin-Baghdad-Basra railways gave new orientations to the ancient problem. We may mention for the sake of completeness the new northern sea route by the Arctic shores, but this is an intra-Soviet matter and even so limited in its use by obvious physical difficulties.

To-day the great airway to the East follows essentially the old seaway with its Levant-Persian Gulf portages, and the old caravan tracks of the Syrian Desert have their successors in half a dozen motor roads. Terminals, way-stations, turning-points—Cairo, Lydda, Rutba Wells, Habbaniyah, Basra, Bahrein, Sharjah—may alter, but the fundamental route is still there. Further east the Malay-Indonesia arc, formerly only a barrier with its breaches guarded by Malacca, Batavia, Singapore, is now also a bridge for airlines to Australia. The peninsular extremities, Colombo and Singapore, retain their great importance as nodes on shipping lines; and although the airways at present take a more northerly course, the great arc Karachi-Calcutta-Rangoon-Singapore-Darwin may be cut across by direct flights from Colombo to Port Hedland, a long hop not infrequently made during the war. Rangoon, a steamer backwater, is likely however to remain an air junction for lines diverging to China, Indo-China, and Indonesia. North of the plateau core the old routes by Sinkiang (the Tarim basin) and across the Gobi were used for motor transport to China during the war, and with increased Soviet activity they

---

[1] Ironically enough it was the Portuguese who, as a consequence of the Dutch blockade of Goa, were first compelled to fall back upon these routes. See the extracts from the admirable narrative of Manuel Godinho's journey of 1663, in C. D. Ley (ed.), *Portuguese Voyages 1498–1663* (1947), pp. 331–360.

may well be revitalized. The negative significance of the massive mountain barrier, however, persists, since apart from the obvious navigational
risks the technical difficulties of take-off in the rarefied atmosphere of the
high plateaus, if not insuperable, will at least remain strong inhibiting
factors for some time to come.

But the lower plateaus of Mongolia, with their strong nodality on
great circle routes between America and Asia, may well become a great
crossways of the air.[1]

Such were and are the links between the Orient and the Occident.
It remains to discuss the nature of the societies which were so profoundly
affected, if not subverted, by over four centuries of western influence, and
the stages in the expansion and regression of European power.

ASIAN SOCIETIES

The naïve view that Asiatic history is a mere monotonous record of
dynastic wars and palace revolutions is fallacy and nothing more. Yet,
despite their rich diversities of ideology and organisation, it is safe to say
that the more developed classic civilizations of Asia had two broad
features in common: in comparison with Western civilization since the
Renaissance, they had a pronounced non-secular cast; and the family
has been the strongest form of association to a degree not paralleled in
Europe. The spirituality of the East has indeed been exaggerated by some
Asian writers, in a natural reaction, beyond the possibilities of parody, and
still more grotesquely, with less excuse, by European and Californian
neophytes. In many cases the repudiation of materialism is all too
obviously a psychological compensation for the lack of wordly power and
goods; a similar tendency can be seen in other nations which have fallen
from their high estate, e.g. Spain and Portugal, nor are its incipient signs
wanting in France and Britain to-day. Moreover the fullest development
of the acquisitive instinct appears to be a matter of family duty and even
of religious sanction to Hindu banking and money-lending castes and to
Chinese traders; the Jains, who will not wittingly take the life of an
insect, will take interest to a most exorbitant extent. There is no question
of Western corruption here; the 17th century Dutch were notoriously
hard businessmen in their own day, but Pelsart stands aghast at some
forms of exploitation of man by man which were native to the
Asian scene.[2] The glittering façade of imperial courts dazzled the early

[1] See O. Lattimore, "The Inland Crossroads of Asia", in H. W. Weigert and V. Stefansson
(eds.), Compass of the World (1945), pp. 374-94.
[2] See W. H. Moreland, From Akbar to Aurangzeb (1923), pp. 198-201, 294.

European adventurers, setting the note of legendary riches summed up by Milton—

> *High on a Throne of Royal State, which far*
> *Outshon the wealth of Ormus and of Ind,*
> *Or where the gorgeous East with richest hand*
> *Showrs on her Kings Barbaric Pearl and Gold. . . .*

But that too was based on the most ruthless and sordid exploitation of the peasant masses, checked only in the smaller princedoms by the more intimate connections of the ruler with his people, in China by the good sense of the imperial tradition which allowed the check of rebellion, in India by customary usage and the occasional enlightened self-interest of a Sher Shah or an Akbar. These were precarious mitigations.

Probably much more important than this alleged spiritual etherealization (in Toynbee's phrase) was and is the strength of loyalty to the family, and to associations such as Indian castes, Chinese guilds, and Japanese clans; these have definitely hampered the functioning, if not the sense, of national solidarity, although in China to some extent, and with more spectacular success in Meiji Japan, these narrower group loyalties were overcome by the careful fostering of an Imperial mythos. Nevertheless, while monarchy in Asia has been absolutist to an extent very rarely paralleled in Europe (perhaps only by the Italian despotisms), this social fragmentation, and the difficulties of effective control over vast interiors, kept Asiatic state structures so weak as to enable numerically tiny, but far more cohesive, European groups to undermine and eventually to overthrow powers in appearance infinitely stronger, and initially not greatly inferior in military technique and equipment. It is questionable whether religious 'other worldliness' also enfeebled secular power; religious sanctions were often, perhaps usually, enlisted in support of the powers that were. This religious conservatism acted on the one hand as a strong preservative of the more intimate cultural *mores*; on the other it tended to an ossification of thought which inhibited the assimilation of, or rapid *autonomous* adjustment to, the expansive forces of the West. Thus attempts to borrow European techniques, e.g. of military organization, often produced a mere façade which could not take any real strain, lacking as it did the basis of long tradition. Even Japan is perhaps no exception in this sphere.

Finally it may be noted that in contact with the Mogul and the Chinese Empires the intruders at first walked with extreme circumspection; among the petty rajahs of the Indian littoral or Indonesia they carried themselves with brutal arrogance, but at Agra and Peiping they approached as suppliants glad of the crumbs of imperial favour, in the form of severely restricted rights of residence and trade. But by the 18th century the Mogul dynasty, by the 19th the Manchu, were in dissolution or at least decadence; India fell completely, and China survived, after a fashion, perhaps more by reason of internecine European rivalries than of its own strength.

As for how the intruders looked to Asia, we have a unique document, which needs no comment but the remark that it might well describe Indian (and Indo-British) reactions to the arrival of American forces in 1942. This is a letter addressed in 1505 by the captain of Colombo to his King at Kandy, reporting the coming of the Portuguese:

> "There is in our harbour of Colombo a race of people with fair skins, but sufficiently comely; they wear hats of iron and jackets of iron; they rest not a minute in one place; they walk up and down all the time; they eat hunks of stone [ship's biscuit] and drink blood [good Madeira, with luck]; they give two or three pieces of gold or silver for one fish or one lime. . . ."

The captain of Colombo was a perspicacious man. His last observation is much to the point: "but their guns are very good."

THE EUROPEAN INTRUSION: EARLY PHASES

Within twenty years of da Gama's arrival at Calicut in 1498 the astonishing audacity and geopolitical insight of Afonso de Albuquerque, and a generation of only less notable captains, had laid the foundations of Portuguese domination from Mozambique to Malacca and beyond: a chain of fortified naval bases centred on Goa, and a Carthaginian ruthlessness in sweeping rival shipping from the seas, warranted Dom Manuel's assumption of the lofty title *Senhor da Conquista, Navegação, e Comércio da Etiópia, Arábia, Pérsia, e India.*

A definitive analysis of the causes of the rapid Portuguese decline remains a prime desideratum of historical geography; the matter is too complex for discussion here, but we may hazard the view that the root cause is largely summed up in the fact that Portuguese society was still essentially 'late medieval' at the time of the Discoveries, and was unable to adjust itself to revolutionary economic changes as did the 'early modern' bourgeoisies of Holland and England. On the other hand, this very archaism, and the strong religious element in Portuguese culture, fitted more naturally into the Asiatic environment than did the straightforward commercialism of the Dutch and English East India Companies.

The latter were far more efficient instruments of economic infiltration and exploitation than the always cumbrous and generally corrupt Portuguese royal monopoly; but in areas such as Ceylon and the Bombay littoral, where Portuguese influence existed for a comparable period to that of the Dutch and English, its cultural effects have been more intimate (in several senses) and more lasting at least than that of the Dutch.[1]

The dynastic accident by which Portugal became subject to Philip II of Spain in 1580 made her possessions the legitimate prey of the Dutch and English, working at first in an uneasy and slippery alliance. The Portuguese showed a notable capacity for almost incredible unpreparedness, redeemed morally but not materially by gallant last-ditch defences: the fall of Ormuz to the English and Persians in 1623, of Malacca and Colombo to the Dutch in 1641 and 1656, virtually extinguished Portuguese power,[2] and the stage was clear for bitter Anglo-Dutch rivalry. In the event the English remained dominant in India, the Dutch in the Indies. French intervention, not uncharacteristically based on local power-politics at the courts of the Deccan and of Indo-China (including Siam) rather than on the solid commercial organization of their northern rivals, produced less tangible returns,[3] being vulnerable to shifts in palace politics at both ends. The Napoleonic wars saw the occupation of the Dutch possessions by the British; Ceylon was retained, and the post-Napoleonic settlement left Malaya as a definitely British sphere, although only Penang, Malacca, and Singapore were really held. Similarly in the Indies only Java, Madura, and some smaller posts and islands in the Outer Provinces were effectively occupied by the Dutch. Full and rigid control of Malaya and Indonesia waited until the increasing demand for raw materials in the later 19th century gave these equatorial lands a new value. But by 1800 the lineaments of the two greater imperialisms, in India and Indonesia, were beginning to take decisive form. (Fig. 2 (a)).

LATER PHASES: INCREASING INTERDEPENDENCE OF ASIATIC PROBLEMS

European expansion in the three-quarters of a century before 1914 is

[1] ". . . even as late as 1828, the Indian commandant of the little Danish settlement at Serampore submitted his daily report to its Norwegian Governor" in Portuguese. L. S. S. O'Malley, *Modern India and the West* (1941), p. 47.

[2] Spain however retained the Philippines until the war with the United States in 1898.

[3] Other countries to take a hand were Sweden, Austria (the Ostend and Imperial Companies, 1722–44 and 1781–84), Prussia (the Emden Company), and Denmark. The Danes continued their courageous but pathetically inept attempts to colonize the Nicobars well into the 19th century; their settlements at Tranquebar (Madras) and Serampore (Bengal) were not sold to Britain until 1845; the Dutch ceded Chinsura in 1825. Culturally the Danish settlements, especially Serampore, were important as centres of European missionary activity (largely by English and Americans) at a time when the E.I.C. frowned on Christian zeal: Tranquebar remains the seat of a Lutheran bishopric.

dominated by five major themes, of which one, and that probably the most important, is by way of an Asiatic reaction against the intruders, although this did not become fully clear until the Russo-Japanese War of 1904–05 proclaimed it beyond mistaking. These themes are: (i) renewed interest in the Southwest Asia portages; (ii) the extension of Russian power; (iii) the *mise-en-valeur* of Southeast Asia; (iv) a more serious attack on the Far East; and (v) the reaction of Japan (Fig. 2 (b-d)). By 1900 the problems of all Asia are for the first time interlinked: British, French, German, and Russian interests clash in Southwest Asia; China becomes the scene of a free-for-all struggle of intrigue, enormously complicated by the Japanese intervention; Russo-British rivalry in Persia and in the innermost parts of Asia contributes to the Anglo-Japanese alliance of 1902, which makes possible the sequel of 1904–05; and the Japanese victory is the catalyst for the super-saturated solution of Asiatic nationalism, which then begins to crystallise out. The interdependence of Asiatic problems, however, is by no means the same thing as the unity of Asia.

(i) The problem of Southwest Asia cannot be separated from more purely European questions; the '(Near) Eastern Question' and the 'Turkish Question' of 19th century diplomacy were the same thing.[1] The protagonists on the ground, Turkey and Russia, both controlled large and contiguous areas in both continents; although after 1878 the buffer-states of Bulgaria and Romania were interposed in Europe. Other strands in a most complex pattern were the traditional French influence and interest in the Levant; British preoccupation with the security of the Suez route; and the dynamic German exploitation of the political potentialities of the 'Berlin-Baghdad-Basra' slogan (cf. pp. 85–86 below). After the Russo-British agreement on spheres of influence in Persia (1907) an uneasy equilibrium prevailed, but the whole area was involved in the 1914–18 war. The consequent collapse of the Ottoman Empire left its non-Anatolian lands as a congeries of British and French mandates and client-states, but attempts on the part of France, Italy, and Greece to obtain footholds in Anatolia itself failed before the emergence of a strong Turkish national state.

(ii) The Russians had pushed out along the Siberian steppe in the later decades of the 16th century and by about 1650 they had discovered Kamchatka and the Bering Strait. Their advance to the lower Amur was checked for two centuries by the Manchu power, but the Russian-American Company[2] established trading outposts in Kamchatka, Alaska,

[1] It must be remembered that until 1878 the Ottoman Empire extended nominally from Tunisia and the Danube to the Persian Gulf.
[2] Founded 1799, it was even active in Hawaii.

and (by 1820) far down the American coast, almost to San Francisco and so within the Spanish 'farthest north' around Vancouver Island. But all these lands were thinly held and exploited; Alaska was sold to the United States in 1867. Between 1859 and 1884, however, the Caucasus, long within the Russian orbit but containing wild mountain principalities incapsulated rather than assimilated, was finally subjugated, and the central Asian Muslim khanates, of which the chief were Khiva and Bokhara, were annexed. This latter expansion was one factor, probably the most important, in British intervention in Afghanistan and the annexation (1876) of Baluchistan to the Indian Empire. On the Far Eastern wing the Amur Province was secured from China in 1858. The construction of the Trans-Siberian Railway (1891–1903) gave Russia an obvious interest in controlling the chord of the great Amur arc, the short-cut from Chita, east of Lake Baikal, to Vladivostock, and from 1900 she occupied Manchuria. Her expulsion by the Japanese in 1905 left her with the Chinese Eastern Railway, the chord of the arc, though its economic value was greatly diminished by the Japanese occupation of Port Arthur and Dairen and the South Manchurian Railway from those ports, while Russia lost security on the short route to Vladivostock, as well as military prestige.

(iii) The motives of the three powers which between them secured all Southeast Asia (except Siam, the Philippines, and Portuguese Timor) were interestingly differentiated. The earlier mercantile imperialism was interested simply in trade in indigenous products, and especially spices. In the 17th century the Dutch secured a position too strong for them to be easily dislodged; in the 18th France and Britain were engaged in a power-conflict in India. The Dutch were thus left in practically undisputed control of the Indies, except during the Napoleonic phase, but until the early 19th century their dominion (outside Java) was mainly a matter of trading stations securing the spice trade by highly unequal treaties with the local sultanates. Later they became the European continental entrepreneurs for tropical products such as sugar, tobacco, and coffee, but these were still produced by native cultivators, bound to the Dutch commercial system by tenures which compelled them to raise large quantities of these products, and incidentally fostered a very rapid increase of population in Java. The first British annexations in Burma, those of Arakan and Tenasserim in 1824, were purely political and strategic, and these territories were almost completely neglected; the annexation of Lower Burma in 1852 brought no fundamental change, for its rise as the granary of southern Asia awaited the stimulus of European demand for rice after the opening of the Suez Canal. In Indo-China

France protected or annexed Cochin-China and parts of Cambodia in 1863–8 but little interest was taken in these holdings until the 'eighties, and there was always a marked element of political opportunism; Ferry's imperialism was largely a matter of compensation for enforced acquiescence in German pre-eminence in Europe.

All these areas were, of course, markets as well as suppliers, but in the former respect they could not be compared with the vast populations of India and China. Towards the end of the 19th century the increasing demand for tropical products, especially vegetable oils and later rubber, gave an obvious new value to these relatively thinly peopled lands in which, in contrast to India and China, there was room for an expansion of non-indigenous and non-subsistence agriculture: the era of plantations, in the stricter modern sense, had begun. Mineral wealth also, especially tin and oil, attracted attention, and as the vast potentialities of the Chinese market were appreciated grandiose railway schemes for entering by the backdoor, through Yunnan, were mooted in France and Britain. The results were an expansion and an intensification of direct European control: in Malaya the various petty sultanates were brought under definite British suzerainty in 1874–95; France occupied Annam and Tonkin in 1884 and nine years later pushed into Laos, thus coming into direct contact with Siam and with Upper Burma, the old kingdom of Ava which had been annexed by Britain in 1886–87, in all probability to forestall imminent French penetration. In the Indies the Dutch strengthened their hold on the hitherto largely neglected Outer Provinces, not without a desperate resistance in Bali and especially in the north of Sumatra, where the Achinese War dragged on from 1873 to 1903. Siam alone remained independent; gravely threatened by the French advance in Cambodia in 1904–07, her immunity was due in part to an adroit reliance on more than one of the smaller European countries for necessary capital and technical assistance, but probably in larger part to her position as a buffer between French and British holdings. As it was she suffered erosion on the east and the south.

(iv and v) The old 'trading factory' system lasted longer in China than elsewhere; in the first half of last century the Celestial Empire still had sufficient cohesion for something like face value to be allowed to the magnificent arrogance with which it repulsed the embassies of the barbarous traders in idle curiosities.[1] The first crack came with the Opium War of 1839–41 and the resulting cession of Hong Kong and opening of five Treaty Ports. Two decades later France and Britain

---

[1] See above, p. 9.

together enforced the opening of further ports, in which foreigners
possessed extra-territorial rights; in some cases, as at Shanghai, these tiny
enclaves became virtual free republics. Almost simultaneously (1854) the
American Commodore Perry secured rights of entry into Japan, which
after an interesting period of intercourse with European nations in the
17th century had decided, quite correctly, that this was incompatible with
her own standards, and had thereupon enforced for over two centuries a
policy of seclusion paralleled only in Tibet, geographically as well fitted
for seclusion as Japan was for intercourse. But while the overthrow of the
feudal shogunate by the Meiji dynasty was in effect a revolution, with all
that that implies in the release of national energy for great and dynamic
tasks of reconstruction, the Manchu dynasty and its bureaucracy proved
utterly incapable of adjustment. Japan succeeded in canalising and harness-
ing to her own purposes the powerful currents of western influences;
China lost even fiscal autonomy. The contrast was dramatically pointed
by the easy victory of Japan in the war of 1894–95—a victory once again
of cohesion over unorganized bulk. In the resultant scramble Japan was
elbowed out—for the time—by the European powers, who seized the
vital gates to the north China plain: in the Liaotung peninsula Russia
secured Port Arthur and Dalny (Dairen), in Shantung Tsingtao fell to
Germany and Wei-hai-wei to Britain. So precarious seemed the continued integrity of the great empire that incipient spheres of influence were
mooted; Manchuria actually fell under Russian occupation for five years,
and later the exploitation of its major non-agricultural resources was
dominated by Japanese or Russian railway and mining corporations. The
task of consolidation was beyond the powers of the revolutionaries who
overthrew the Manchu dynasty in 1911. The outer territories became
virtually, and to some extent even formally, independent: for many years
no Chinese writ has really run in Tibet or Sinkiang, though local factions
may make tactical use of the central government's real or alleged approval;
Outer Mongolia has hardly been Chinese even in name, and in the
extreme north the republic of Tannu-Tuva has reached its logical destiny
of incorporation in Soviet Asia. Japan, which had taken Formosa
(Taiwan) in 1895, ended the farce of Korean independence in 1910, and
profited by European preoccupations in 1914–18 to secure a dominating
position. The great Kuomintang campaigns of 1927 seemed to offer the
promise of a revolutionary unity and energy; but internal social and
personal conflicts and the renewed Japanese onslaught which began with
the seizure of Manchuria in 1931 were too strong, and the political unity
of China is not yet, though it may be approaching in an unexpected
fashion.

This sketch of political history provides a background to the territorial pattern of the inter-war years (*Fig.* 2(e)). To sum this up: the entire north was occupied by Soviet Asia, and Soviet influence remains strong on the northern glacis of High Asia, whose western outlets are in Soviet Central Asian territory. In the Southwest there was one reasonably strong national state, Turkey; a Soviet outwork in Caucasia; a group of British and French mandates or client states in the Levant and Mesopotamia; a British holding, Aden, and the Hadhramaut protectorate, in the extreme south of Arabia, and British suzerainty or paramount influence over the petty shaykdoms of Muscat, Oman, Bahrein, Kuwait, and the Trucial Coast. The interior of Arabia remained a haven of an Islam undefiled, though not unappreciative of such modern devices as motor vehicles, radio, and the lighter armaments. Riza Shah's Iran displayed the semblance, but the semblance only, of a united national state, but was overshadowed by Russia in the north and by British oil interests in the south; Afghanistan under Amanullah went through the motions of modernism and later settled down to a respectable but modest independence as a Russo-British buffer. Thailand (Siam) excepted, the whole vast area from Baluchistan to the South China Sea, including the islands, was under direct European control, British, Dutch, or French; the Philippines, under American tutelage, were approaching a quasi-independence. Only the heart of Asia, the deep interior of China, and Japan were really free from alien domination; for to littoral and riverine China Japan represented an intruder essentially western in technique and equipment.

Thus Asiatic Asia had only three states of any real independence and weight in the world: Turkey, China, and Japan; and some six or eight independent states either essentially archaisms or with no real freedom of action: Saudi Arabia, Yemen, Iraq, Iran, Afghanistan, Tibet, Siam (re-named Thailand), possibly Sinkiang and the Philippines. Of the three truly independent, Turkey had perforce to follow modest aims; China was, and still is, deeply divided, and even when engaged in a deadly struggle with Japan hardly attained more than nominal unity; Japan was openly, if not frankly, imperialist and had bettered her instructors in the arts of aggression and exploitation. The whole north then was Soviet, almost the whole south directly or virtually dominated by Europe. Asia herself was left with the deserts of Arabia and the barren plateau core, with Anatolia, with a China in disruption, and with one explosively dynamic power, Japan.

On the eve of the late war European economic and political power in Asia had reached its height; on its morrow it was everywhere (except in

Soviet Asia) in retreat, if not rout, and the vast and populous Indian
sub-continent had been politically if not economically abandoned (*Fig.* 2
(e-f)). American interests have now infiltrated into the Southwest and
the Southeast and are dominant in Japan itself; and in Korea the American
and the Soviet worlds made direct contact along the 38th parallel. In
five years, from 1942 to 1947, the pattern had thus been radically changed
in many important areas, though rearguard struggles, whose final success
cannot yet be evaluated, secured local success in Indonesia and Indo-China.
To begin to understand this gigantic reversal in human affairs it is necessary to examine the Asian reaction (including some intangibles) to the
long history of European conquest.

THE DISINTEGRATION OF LOCAL SOCIETIES

Contemplation of the formidable energy and efficiency displayed by
the occidental intruders in all the more material aspects of living, in the
mobilization and deployment of capital, of human labour, and not least
of armed force, could not fail to act as a powerful solvent of traditional
thought. Those least affected by this aspect of the intrusion were naturally
the great peasant masses; yet even among them, the ever-increasing importance of a money economy, and of contractual relationships as against
customary status, could not fail to introduce new outlooks. In many
respects indeed the impact of the west was disastrous to agrarian societies.
If, in British India at any rate, the share of produce demanded by the
state was less than that usually taken by indigenous rulers, the administration was far more tightly organized and impinged more directly on
individuals, and that generally in a restrictive manner: grazing rights,
for example, might be subordinated to a forest policy which might well
be in the national interest, but the peasant was inhibited by the narrowness
of his geographical and social horizons from seeing that, and little or
nothing was done to help him to see it. The unspeakably atrocious
private war of the post-Mogul anarchy was suppressed; but the rule of
law too often meant that for the right of the strong and lawless was
substituted the right of the rich and literate, and the hold of the middleman and the moneylender, previously restrained by custom and on
occasion by the most direct action, came to be sanctioned by pedantically
legalistic courts and enforced by an efficient police. The myriad 'village
republics' of India, which had maintained for millennia a humble
autonomy so long as they paid their taxes, and had preserved the structure
of society, if on a lowly plane, through dynastic wars and anarchies,
became subverted by an all-powerful bureaucracy. The flood of western

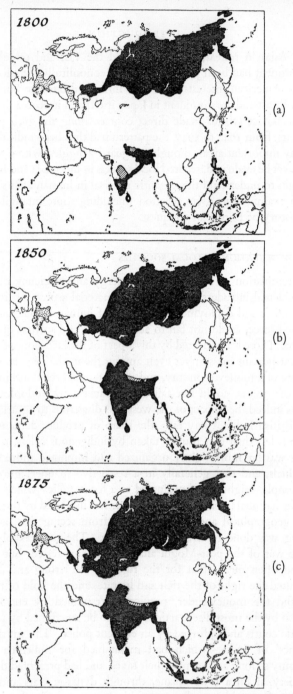

Fig. 2. THE EXPANSION AND REGRESSION
Black and shaded areas indicate full legal and virtual European (or
lines indicate Russian and British spheres in Persia, British and French
is indicated in (e) and (f).

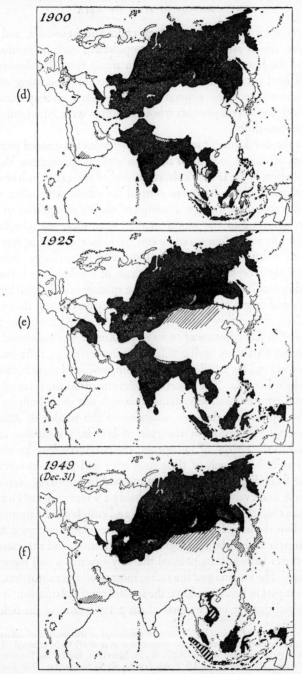

OF EUROPEAN TERRITORIAL POWER IN ASIA
American) control; dotted, Asian control in Europe. In (d) broken
in Siam; in (f), Japanese conquests in 1942. The Chinese Eastern Railway

3

manufactures ruined flourishing cottage crafts and industries, and even the artisanate which naturally follows population, such as smiths, carpenters, and the like, suffered severely. In many cases the demand for payment of land revenue in cash contributed to the weakening of subsistence economy, and the general trend towards a money economy placed a heavy burden on peasants whose resources were liquid only once a year, at harvest-time.

Such was the development in India; in other areas the general picture is similar, with of course individual modifications, as for instance the fine art of exploitation of the Dutch 'culture system' of the early 19th century. In areas not under direct European control the effects were often worse still, since the economic ravages consequent on the integration of these agrarian economies into the world market were there not checked or mitigated by efficient administration and by justice at least in intention even-handed. Admission of the general justice of these charges does not, of course, imply acceptance of the hypothesis of a golden age before the European domination, an hypothesis whose sponsors rarely attach a date to their mythical reigns of plenty, and, when they do commit themselves, usually adduce remarkably unconvincing evidence. Although in many cases a society in fair adjustment to its environment was subverted, "we must not forget that these idyllic village-communities . . . restrained the human mind within the smallest possible compass", and there is much to be said on the other side. The material achievements in the form of great irrigation and communication systems, although not often built by pure altruism, do represent undeniable additions to the wealth of Asia; the almost universal subversion of the rule of law by corruption cannot fairly be laid to the charge of Europeans; the peasantry may be insecure and maladjusted, but much of their insecurity and abject poverty is a result of the fecundity with which they respond to improved conditions of production, and even so they have probably a wider range of comforts and amenities than they had under so great and enlightened a monarch as Akbar, let alone the megalomaniacs who not infrequently occupied Asiatic thrones.[1] In recent decades also legislation, education, and the extension of social services have at least pointed the way towards a real increase of social welfare. The cinema and the radio, most of all the motor-bus, have played a great part in breaking down the squalid rural isolationism: it must be remembered that the best weapon of the petty tyrants of the fields has

[1] All these matters are of course highly controversial, and as the sources of information are scrappy and difficult to evaluate no final judgment is ever likely to be attained. Diverse points of view may be found in such books as W. H. Moreland, *India at the Death of Akbar* (1920); Lin Yutang, *My Country and My People* (1936); K. S. Shelvankar, *The Problem of India* (1940); Guy Wint, *The British in Asia* (1947).

been their monopoly of information. A hundred years ago Marx himself bore witness to the unintentionally revolutionary action of the British in breaking the iron cramps of Indian traditionalism; in which he was paradoxically at one with Macaulay.

THE REVOLT OF THE CLERKS

In despite of its own natural conservatism, one of the chief agents of change in all directly European-controlled territories has been a powerful bureaucracy. The strong tradition of paternal government—perhaps most marked in the whole tenor and symbolism of Chinese ethics and government—and, in early days, the immense difference in technical intellectual equipment between the governors and the governed, favoured legislation by edict and authoritarian regulation of many departments of life. In matters of religion and the more intimate social *mores* indeed the general rule was non-intervention; it was only after long hesitation, and in response to urgent pleas from an active Indian minority, that the British prohibited suttee. Moreover, the direct economic agents of the European powers were initially monopolistic chartered corporations of traders; *laisser faire* came late to the East, was generally construed to the benefit of Europeans only, and departed early. The areas and populations controlled were vast, their peoples divided into innumerable groups with complex systems of customary law, speaking strange and difficult tongues. All these factors called for an immense administrative and judicial machinery, which obviously could be staffed only in small proportion by Europeans. Yet the language and technique of administration were European. For all these reasons an army of subordinate officials was necessary, and it had to be trained to at least a minimum competence in western methods of business.

Western education, in this limited sense, proved all too successful. The willing recruits were soon too many for any possible establishment, and an educated, or at least literate, clerical and intellectual proletariat came into being. The composition of this army was badly balanced. The indigenous educational tradition had been, for many generations at least, almost entirely lacking on the scientific and technical side; such technical education as existed was in the form of craft apprenticeship, with the excellencies and defects of that system. As a result there was an enormous excess of arts and legal students, while scientists and technicians, as well as doctors, have been in short supply, or (in the last case) over-concentrated in some parts of some towns only. Unemployed lawyers have often been catalysts in radical political movements, not always with happy results.

There are deeper issues than these. Too often this alien knowledge has not itself been assimilated, and yet has destroyed or warped the old adjustment to the old society. Whole generations of the professional and clerical classes wandered between two worlds and belonged to neither.[1] Together with the economic anxieties of a merciless struggle for existence within the overcrowded professions, and constant political frustration, this schizophrenia fostered the deep-seated malaise which all observers have noted as one of the most persistent features of the Asian social scene. All European possessions and, with natural differences, China, have suffered from this disease of the body politic, while it has even been alleged as the most fundamental factor in the Japanese psychological situation. In any case, the revolt of the clerks is part of the standard pattern of imperialism and the nationalist reaction to it; it may be seen to-day in an incipient form in Africa; and it leaves to the newly independent Asiatic countries a difficult problem of social maladjustment.

INDUSTRIALISM AND NATIONALISM

If the clerks, and especially the lawyers, were the spearhead of nationalism, weight was given to the attack by the rising indigenous trading and industrial classes; and at intervals large masses of the peasantries have been drawn in to provide a more massive backing. Speaking generally, however, these last have not played an initiatory role, which indeed could hardly be expected, and it is difficult to resist the conclusion that they have been not infrequently exploited by more articulate and adroit classes. More important has been the role of the industrial workers. In many cases their links with the villages are still strong, and labourers returning to the fields after a spell in the factory have provided at least the rudiments of political ideas and organization in the countryside; soldiers returning from the wars have also played their part. A true industrial proletariat is in its infancy in most Asiatic countries, but its increasing self-consciousness foreshadows the break-up of the 'Popular Fronts', such as the Indian National Congress, into parties with coherent programmes based on defined group interests. This is probably the next stage after the first turmoil of independence has settled down, and is at least an improvement on the factional intrigues and personal cliques within the general framework of nationalistic demands, which provide much of the machinery of politics to-day.

The general pattern has been leadership from the intellectuals, the sinews of war from the new industrialists, stimulated by the example of

[1] Similar, but more tragic, is the position of Eurasians.

theWest but hampered in their development either by open discrimination in favour of metropolitan industry or by the strong position it had secured before the rise of indigenous modern industry. The rank and file of mass movements has been provided by the young men of the middle classes and by the town workers. In the earlier phases the boycott has been a favourite weapon, especially in India and China, accompanied by non-co-operation and strikes by the workers. With the attainment of fiscal autonomy (in India in 1921, in China as late as 1928) there was naturally a very strong bias to protectionism; the Indian sugar and steel industries were built up behind tariff walls. In these matters the political and the economic wings of the nationalist movements have worked together, and this tendency has been carried on into the new conditions of independence. Practically political groups (with the exception of the more sentimental followers of Mahatma Gandhi) accept industrialization as a major objective of the state, the usual more purely economic arguments in its favour being rein-forced by old resentment of alien economic domination and a natural reluctance to remain dependent on outside powers for technical cadres and equipment. It is not too much to say that there is even a bias towards autarky in less responsible circles; impossible of attainment even in India and China, this aim becomes grotesque in some of the lesser states, whose resources in raw materials, labour, technical skill, capital, and markets are not enough to support large-scale heavy industry. The most promising line of advance in countries like Pakistan and Burma is through a con-centration on ancillary agricultural industries, but this is understandably not very acceptable for political reasons, although the logic of geo-graphical facts will probably compel it.

Japan of course is *sui generis*. There was no antithesis between govern-ment and indigenous economic expansion, and indeed in the early stages of the Japanese industrial revolution the real drive came from the state, which initiated enterprises later transferred to private hands. But the close contacts of the great industrial families with politics, and the con-sistent atmosphere of preparation for war, meant continued state direction of the major lines of industrial expansion. In Southeast Asia, again, industrialization on any large scale, if conceivable at all, is hardly con-ceivable without governmental mobilization of capital and training of technicians, with the corollary of control.

For widely different reasons, therefore, there is a strong tendency to state action in the economic field; the necessity for expensive hydro-electric and irrigation works is also an important factor in this tendency. And where much of the large-scale enterprise of a country is in alien hands, nationalization will obviously be a popular slogan. At the same time the nationalist movements were largely financed by private capitalists, and it is not to be expected that these will not look for their reward, in the form largely of tariffs, subsidies, and bounties. There is room for a wide variety of economic-political relationships.

From the western point of view, it is important to remember that the movement for political independence has been largely motivated by the desire of the new bourgeoisies of colonial (or semi-colonial) territories for economic independence. Technical and financial assistance will be needed, but on terms less favourable to the West. Although it is on the whole unlikely that, in any readily foreseeable future, southern or eastern Asia will be industrially developed to the same degree as northwest Europe or the United States, the possibilities are undoubtedly large and their full exploitation will involve a very great readjustment of world trade movements. The Japanese experience has relevance: although Japanese industry did make inroads on markets held by western powers (e.g. in cheap cotton goods), it also created entirely new markets by producing such wares as rubber shoes and light metal goods at prices low enough for purchase by many who had never been able to buy such things before.[1] The appallingly low purchasing power of the Asiatic and African peasant masses is perhaps the chief limiting factor (in the long run) to Asiatic industrialization.[2] It is essential to the economic health of Asia that it should be raised, and if this can be done the vast size of the Asiatic market would provide full employment for eastern industries for a long time to come, without making extensive inroads on markets at present held by the West; and indeed it is possible that the general increase of wealth and welfare, and the increased demand for machine tools and production goods of all kinds, would actually mean increased markets for both Europe and Asia. Beyond this point it is fruitless to speculate; and before it is reached there is the practical problem of how to increase Asiatic purchasing power. This problem is of overpowering complexity, and no one solution is possible; but it is at least clear that the solutions, if they are found at all, will depend largely upon the maintenance of a healthy balance between agriculture and industry, between the country-side and the city; and here too at least an overall control must be assumed by the state, which alone can deploy the vast expenditures necessary, expenditures not immediately productive of any very large direct cash

[1] Incidentally, the efforts of the metropolitan powers to restrict Japanese imports, at a time when the purchasing power of the masses was hard hit by the agrarian depression of the thirties, played no small part in stimulating nationalist agitation.

[2] The paradoxes involved in the possession of these potentially vast but actually desperately poor markets may be studied (by implication) in *A Plan for the Economic Development of India* (1945)—the Tata or Bombay Plan.

return. The returns in human welfare and in collective prosperity might
well be immense. But so desperate is the present agrarian crisis almost
throughout Asiatic Asia that only the most heroic measures have any
slightest hope of success.

THE DEMOGRAPHIC ASPECT

POPULATION GROWTH AND ITS SOCIAL IMPLICATIONS

To the political geographer the demographic position in Asia is of
fundamental importance. The existence of dense populations and their
distribution and growth are major background facts to politics, national
and international. Population numbers in Asia, since modern industrialization has not yet advanced very far there, express themselves in terms of
pressure on food supplies and thus on cultivable land. An ultimate result
of Asia's great and increasing millions may be the growth of its military
might proportionate to its numbers. But this is far off, if only because
Asia is politically fissured, industrially backward and dependent not a
little on outside powers; moreover its peoples are ill-fed and further
debilitated by disease. No less remote are visions of Asiatics swarming
out into the other continents. But in the short run the social organization
and political stability of Asiatic countries may be in jeopardy unless their
demographic problems are studied and resolutely met. For if population
pressure grows too intense, it threatens famine in the economic and civil
war in the political sphere.

During the last three hundred years, after a period of relative stability,
Europe's population grew five to six times, and most markedly in the
19th century. Asia's population similarly would appear to have grown
five-fold in these centuries and, in contrast to western Europe's, its
increase continues. In Asia, again in contrast to Europe, a falling death
rate was not until recent decades and then only sporadically a contributory
cause of population growth; nor was its apparent increase lessened as was
Europe's by large-scale emigration. The main cause of Asia's great
population was and remains the large unlimited family, i.e., its high
fertility rate. Behind the large family, and in part an explanation of it,
were the new incentives and opportunities, notably during the last
century, provided by international commerce and western capital. Now
that Western ideas on sanitation and preventive medicine are spreading
over widening areas, mortality rates should show steadily falling trends—
already characteristic of Japan, Ceylon and Formosa and less markedly of
India—and another factor making for population growth becomes

operative which as yet more than counter-balances self-imposed restriction of births. In the past those drastic 'positive checks' of which Malthus wrote—famine, pestilence and war—served, together with infanticide, to maintain equilibrium between population numbers and food supplies. During the last century these checks, although they have not been eliminated, have been to some extent controlled. Asia's population then should continue to grow and, if the harsh operation of 'positive checks' is to be prevented, new population policies will have to be thought out and applied. To find policies which will be effective and yet feasible given the immemorial social attitudes of most Asiatic countries, will not be easy.

DENSITIES AND DISTRIBUTION OF POPULATION

The number of Asia's population is not known. Many areas, and above all China proper, are statistically obscure, so that careful estimates may vary by as much as 10% or 100 millions. But the precise total does not affect the major distributions and problems of politico-geographical interest. Our table reaches a total of 1181 millions in 1940 out of a world total of 2155.[1] Thus Asia with one-third of the land surface of the earth contained rather more than half (55%) of its population. The relative crowding of this population is seen at a glance when it is noted that it carries an average density of 71 persons per square mile, the figure for the world being 43. Asia's average density of population is actually not much more than one-third of Europe's (71 as compared with 186), although densities greatly exceed Europe's over wide areas—in China, India, Japan and Java. But what is remarkable about the high densities in such Asiatic countries is the low ratio of capital, mineral production and technology to population. Moreover the application to Asia of the concept of average density of population per unit area is particularly unilluminating, for much the greater part of the continent consists of land which either forbids or discourages settlement—hot and cold deserts, high plateaus and mountains. In the distribution of Asia's population nothing is more striking than the great differentiation in densities, and this applies with equal force both to the broad pattern of continental distribution and to the smaller patterns within the most densely settled lands.

The main outlines of the demographic pattern of Asia in relation to land area are shown in the table below in which major compartments of the continent are distinguished.

[1] For a somewhat different total and analysis, see J. Lorimer, "Population Trends in the Orient", *Foreign Affairs*, vol. 23 (1944–45), pp. 668–674.

TABLE I

THE POPULATION OF ASIA IN 1940

Region	Land Area (million square miles)	Population (millions)	Population per square mile
SOUTHWEST ASIA*	2·5	55	22
SOVIET ASIA (1939)	6·3	41	7
INDIA AND CEYLON	1·7	394	232
SOUTHEAST ASIA	1·7	151	90
HIGH ASIA	2·8	17	6
FAR EAST†	1·7	523	308
ASIA	16·7	1181	71
WORLD	50·0‡	2155	43

* Including Afghanistan.
† Population of China proper, together with Manchuria, Korea and Taiwan, taken as 450 millions.
‡ Excluding Polar regions.

In the above table it is the concentration of population in the Far East (i.e., China and Japan) and in India which first leaps to the eye; that in Southeast Asia, too, stands out. Around these populous and largely insular or peninsular lands are ranged in contrast the vast and scantily peopled expanses of southwestern, high-central and northern Asia.

The relative crowding of population within India, Southeast Asia and the Far East cannot be explained simply in environmental terms. Fundamental physical factors are the monsoon régime which provides an abundance of water, long growing periods, and mighty rivers which create and renew alluvial deltas rich in plant foods. But such favourable opportunities are not available throughout these regions, nor when they occur have they been equally exploited, and the key to the demographic patterns of these regions must be sought in their peculiar cultural history. Superior, long established civilizations of peoples whose essential needs of food, clothing and shelter were met from crops and plants, made it possible for millions of peasants to find sustenance in lands which on the whole are not intrinsically rich and do not give high crop yields.[1] Thanks to their traditional forms of social organization, their ability both to live on little at or near bare subsistence level and, by intensive effort, to extract

[1] In terms of protein one hectare produces from a crop of wheat in Europe or the U.S.A. nearly three times as much as a crop of rice in Asia, but in some monsoon areas two (and in a few) three crops of rice are grown per year. See P. Gourou, *Les Pays Tropicaux*, 1947, p. 18.

the most from tiny plots of land, the peoples of monsoon Asia had already, long before the full impact of the western world was felt there during the last hundred years, achieved that dominant demographic position which they still hold. During the last century the provision of foreign capital for railways, irrigation, land reclamation, plantations and mining, the intensification of international commerce and industrialization, especially in Japan, so revitalized the economy of tropical Asia as to permit a remarkable swarming of population, above all in India, Japan and Java. And although many of these peoples exist at an extremely low standard of living, a standard which might be higher were their numbers less, this is probably higher generally than it was when their numbers were much smaller. The growth of cities, including 'millionaire' cities such as Calcutta, Canton and Shanghai, has helped to shape the demographic pattern, but it is the high densities of rural population engaged wholly in agriculture which most arrest attention. In the low alluvial plains of French Indochina, for example, some of which were brought into cultivation only during the last century, an area of 40,000 square miles supports 19 million people, i.e., at an average density of 720 per square mile. In the remaining mountainous or hilly part of this province, 2.6 million people are settled on 250,000 square miles, i.e., at 10 per square mile.[1] This glaring contrast is not of course exceptional: it has analogues in China, India, Japan and Java and elsewhere. The uneven spread of population, already noted as characteristic of Asia as a whole, is thus repeated within the monsoon lands, its most populous part.

Figures for population density per square mile of territory, while they broadly indicate distribution, are inadequate since they take no account of the unequal potentialities of the land. Figures for population per unit of cultivated land are much more revealing: they reflect the varying pressure of population on food supplies. The highest figure in 1940 is for Japan: 2850 persons per square mile; the figure for China—much less exact—may well have reached 1500; whilst that for British India approached 900. In contrast, for Soviet Asia (in 1939) the average figure was 370. In detail, such figures are difficult to interpret, for crops, yields and diets are not uniform throughout the continent. But by and large the cultivated area is given over to food crops, technical crops—vegetable fibres, tea, rubber, etc.—accounting for only a small proportion of the cultivated land. Moreover, before World War II, which adversely affected agriculture in many areas, the major regions of Asia were virtually self-sufficient in food, which meant above all grain, although some, like India, had a small net import, and others, notably Southeast and Soviet

[1] P. Gourou, op. cit., pp. 118–123.

Asia, a net export. The high average densities per unit of cultivated land, above all in Japan, but also in China and British India, in contrast to the lower figures characteristic of the other regions, illustrate not only the disequilibrium which existed there between population numbers and food supplies but also the ability of agriculture, and especially of 'wet' ricefields, to support (at low levels of consumption) remarkably high numbers. This disequilibrium is now more marked because of the widespread destruction caused by war and by civil disorders.

Hard by the congested lands of China, Japan, India and Java lie lands whose settlement is as yet by no means complete. The Indochinese lands—Burma, Siam and French Indochina—together with the Malay peninsula, contrast sharply in population density with the four congested lands: 73 persons per square mile as compared with 280. Their economic development is relatively recent and considerable expansion of the cultivated area and concomitant increases in industry and trade are to be expected. Their present numbers reach only about 60 millions, and at least a doubling of this can be confidently foreseen. These countries have already drawn a substantial part of their population from China and India, but the local peoples are virile, so that, even were there no political hurdles in the way of immigration, they cannot be expected to afford large-scale relief to India, China and Japan, the total annual increment of whose population almost certainly exceeds 10 millions. Again the outer provinces of Indonesia and of the new independent state of the Philippines, with average densities of 35 and 54 per square mile respectively, are yet clearer instances of under-settled lands. The fuller exploitation of their agricultural lands and considerable mineral resources should similarly allow for more than the doubling of their populations which together at present little exceed 40 millions. These opportunities for settlement have been fully appreciated for some decades, and the process of redistribution of population from Java to the Outer Provinces and within the Philippine group has already made headway. It seems likely that the in-filling of these regions will be largely a matter of controlled internal redistribution of population and that their doors will not be flung open to would-be immigrants from China, India and Japan.

AREAS OF SCANTY AND PIONEER SETTLEMENT

Exception made of Southeastern Asia and the Far East, there remains no less than two-thirds of Asia's area containing only one-tenth of its population. This totals 115 millions, half of which occupies Southwest Asia; the rest is unequally shared between Soviet Asia and High Asia, in both of which the average density reached or approached in 1940 only 7 persons per square mile. Here indeed would appear to be some of the wide open spaces of the world, but how far are they really open to settlement and to what extent will they be able to support increasing numbers? Aridity, and in Siberia prolonged cold, are the chief limiting factors to sedentary agriculture and thus to population numbers. Only very small proportions of each of the three regions are really inhabited lands. Nomadic life, related to natural pastures, and irrigated agriculture in oases have been traditional ways of life. But nomadism is fast declining and irrigation enlarges and can continue to enlarge the oases: both changes, by increasing the extent of sedentary agriculture, permit larger populations. Considerable resources of petroleum, coal, iron and non-ferrous metals offer scope for capital, industrial enterprise and trade of which advantage has been taken by the Western powers in Southwest Asia and by the Soviet Union in its Asiatic realm. Either on a short or a long view the demographic position of this scantily settled Asia is dynamic. For Russians, Siberia continues to be a pioneer land with mineral, timber and water power resources as yet little exploited; the several states of High Asia, with their mineral resources and scope for improvement in stock-raising and for irrigated agriculture may, with Soviet help, be able to develop their economies and so augment their populations considerably. Southwest Asia, where already over the last 150 years population has increased fourfold, has some large-scale possibilities for irrigation, notably in Iraq and Syria. The recent history of Palestine where, by the application of capital and western technique, economic advances have been made hand in hand with very rapidly increasing numbers, is not, of course, likely to be repeated in other countries of Southwest Asia. The economic and demographic development of Palestine is individual and a-typical: it received large inflows of labour and capital and its long-term economic stability may not be assured. But whilst clearly there is substantial economic room for the growth of population in Soviet, High and Southwest Asia, this expansion will be small in relation to Asia's numbers as a whole, and no immigration appears likely of the surplus populations from over-populated areas in China, India, Java and elsewhere. Soviet Siberia and Central Asia, notably the former, will continue to receive immigrants from Soviet Europe. High Asia, which has not as yet attracted any large influx of Chinese, is unlikely to do so as its economic development proceeds. And in Southwest Asia, where national states (mostly new) are characteristic and the rate of natural increase is very high, a growing need for labour, the more so as foreign capital develops its economy, can be met from within, particularly if the mortality is, as it could be, reduced.

In sum, two-thirds of Asia, in relation to their economic potentialities, are under-populated lands. But as their population-supporting capacity grows, they are unlikely to require or desire immigrants on any scale from the over-populated parts of the continent.

THE PROBLEMS OF OVER-POPULATION AND MIGRATION

With its congested areas and wide empty spaces, Asia thus affords glaring contrasts as a whole and in its parts. While the mass of the population in the more densely populated agricultural areas has been static, historically some groups have been remarkably mobile—nomads from Central Asia ever intruding into the agricultural plains of China, Indians and Chinese voyaging into Indonesia and Indochina, Slavs trekking into Siberia—so much so that its present so-called aboriginal peoples hold no ancient title to their lands. And war in recent years has caused some further large-scale shifts of population.[1] It is commonly and too simply said that Asia's population is distributed in general accord with the food-producing capacity of its various regions. This generalization obscures the degree to which, as control over environment grew, population has been differentiated and redistributed, in particular during the last hundred years. Population has reached or exceeded food-producing capacity in certain areas, especially China and Japan, while in others it still falls short of potential food supplies. Further, a number of regions —Manchuria, Siam, French Indochina and Burma—were before the 1941–45 war food exporters, mainly to Asiatic markets. Some Asiatic countries may be expected—perhaps optimistically—to solve their population problems, at least in the short run, as internal problems—by the expansion and improvement of agriculture, the establishment of industries and trade, and the better distribution of population within the state territories. But acute difficulties arise where over-population obtains. Over-population, in the strict sense, implies that the national income and standard of living are lower than they would be were population less; it is applicable without doubt to major components of the continent, namely China and India, as well as to Japan and Java.

The trend and total of China's population are unknown. Chinese enumerations have been usually very differently conceived and conducted from censuses in Western countries and 'China' too has been a remarkably variable geographical expression. Experts do not agree, for example, on

[1] The Sino-Japanese war (1937–45) and the World War (1941–45) enforced large-scale shifts of population. 42 millions were displaced from their normal abodes in China and several millions from Soviet Europe to Soviet Asia. Political partition in India has involved migrations of some 8 millions. *United Nations Economic Report*, Jan. 1948.

the likely trends even during the last hundred years, and a recent writer[1] finds no evidence of so marked an increase in population-supporting capacity as to justify some of the higher current estimates. Jaffe's suggested figure of 400 millions appears preferable to Lorimer's 468, but may be even too high. It appears probable, as Carr-Saunders suggested,[1] that the high fertility in China is virtually offset by its high death rate. Although China's industrial possibilities may be considerable, they have been little exploited and, under its existing economy, extreme and widespread poverty doubtless reflects a condition of over-population. The possible remedies, or at least reliefs, consist of economic re-organization, e.g., by flood control, road and railway construction, mineral exploitation and development of industries—of internal migration and of emigration. The settlement of Manchuria by millions of Chinese coolies after entry there was permitted in 1875, and especially in this century, afforded temporary relief and, when political conditions stabilize, Manchuria, as the industrial base of China, should still provide work and living room for a large number of immigrants. China officially estimated its nationals abroad at 8 millions. This is probably a maximum estimate, yet clearly a small number relative to China's population and shows how little emigration took place even when no impediments were offered to it by receiving countries. Chinese traders, industrialists, miners and labourers (2.6 million strong) form a big element in Malaya; there are similar numbers in Siam, smaller numbers in Indonesia, Burma and French Indochina, while farther afield Chinese are found in western North America, in Peru, the Soviet Far East, and elsewhere.

Emigration has played an even smaller part in relieving the population pressure felt in many parts of India, e.g., the Madras Presidency. Indians abroad are numbered at less than 4 millions, distributed as shown in Table II. About half this number are workers on plantations; some are traders, as in East Africa; others hold administrative and professional positions. (Cf. Fig. 16).

For the last twenty-five years emigration of Asiatics across international frontiers has been greatly restricted, notably by the United States and the British Dominions. Australia, for example, with a population density of 2·3 persons per square mile, only a third that of Soviet and High Asia, denies entry to emigrants from Asiatic countries, where average densities reach and exceed 500. Queen Victoria's proclamation as Empress of India that her Indian subjects should be free to travel and reside

---

[1] A. J. Jaffe, "A Review of the Censuses and Demographic Statistics of China," *Population Studies*, vol. I, no. 3 (1947).
[2] A. M. Carr-Saunders, *World Population* (1936), p. 289.

TABLE II

INDIANS OVERSEAS
(estimated)

						(in thousands)
Burma	..	..	..	..	..	1,000
Ceylon	..	..	..	..	..	750
Malaya	..	..	..	..	..	600
West Indies	..	..	..	..	..	450
South Africa	..	..	..	..	..	280
Mauritius	..	..	..	..	..	269
East Africa	..	..	..	..	..	126
Fiji	..	..	..	..	..	105
Indonesia	..	..	..	..	..	27
Siam	..	..	..	..	..	5
French Indochina	..	..	..	..	..	5
						———
						3,617

in any of her dominions has been rendered nugatory, although immigrants are still free to enter many colonial dependencies. The possibilities of international friction and dangers arising from population pressure unable to seek adequate relief through emigration spring not from any powerful urge by Indians and Chinese to emigrate. Indeed they share a rooted attachment to their native soil and, individuals apart, migrate only reluctantly when compelling circumstances—unemployment and the threat of starvation—force them to move. The dangers are rather psychological and for this reason the more serious. Exclusion from countries of immigration on ground of race and colour creates a sense of injustice and resentment and a powerful and rare unity of national feeling, not merely among Indians and Chinese but potentially at least amongst all Asiatics. The Indian problem in Natal raises an issue dangerous to the unity of the British Commonwealth.

Emigration from Japan was proportionately greater than from either China or India, but was scarcely an important means of relieving its pressure of population. The rapid growth of Japan's population—from 30 millions in 1868 to 73 millions in 1940 and 78 in 1948—accompanied drastic changes in its social organization and economy. A policy of large-scale industrialization and international trade was vigorously applied and supported by an aggressive foreign policy. Indeed Japan was successful in achieving a standard of living appreciably higher than that of its less populous days, thanks to the food, raw materials, fuel and metals derived from its dependent territories and to the markets which it won and served in China, the United States, the United Kingdom and elsewhere. Despite varied opportunities for emigration created by Japan's military successes, its nationals were reluctant to emigrate *en masse*. Although the Japanese population was increasing before the 1941–5 war at the rate of one million a year, Japan had only 2 million nationals overseas, widely distributed but, to the extent of three-quarters, settled or resident within its imperial territories. The main reasons for this relatively small emigration were first the strong attachment of the Japanese to their homeland, and second their unwillingness to emigrate unless they could achieve thereby a higher standard of living. But by waging and losing a world war Japan has lost completely the fruits of its fine achievement in the material sphere. With the loss of its empire, a disrupted economy, and enemy occupation, Japan must now appear clearly an over-populated land. Moreover, although its birth rate has been falling for some time, the fall has been too little and too late in comparison with that of the death rate, and its population continues to increase. Japanese projections indicate that the maximum population—of nearly 125 millions—may be reached at the end of this century.[1]

Finally, although the current political re-organization of the Netherlands East Indies threatens difficulties, some if not all the overflow population of Java may be expected to colonize areas of the Outer Provinces where already by 1930 a million Javanese were settled.

It is possible that, as in Western Europe, the more congested countries of Asia may, like Japan, decline in fertility, but the possibility of downward trends in the death rate, together with national desires to augment demographic stature, suggest that increasing populations will be the rule for some time to come.[2] This raises serious international problems, both in the short and the long run. In the short run, over-population breeds internal social disorders and political weakness and thus presents troubled seas in which outsiders can seek their own fish. China, preoccupied by its internal political problem and set between the continental power of the U.S.S.R. and the maritime power of the United States, and India, no longer a single political entity, illustrate such possibilities. Alternatively, population pressure in a world where immigration into under-settled lands is politically controlled, provides fuel for nationalist and imperialistic policies such as that pursued in this century by Japan. On the long view,

[1] The fertility rate continued to fall after 1920, largely as the result of the postponement of marriage, but it rose somewhat during World War II: see I. B. Taeuber and F. W. Notestein, "The Changing Fertility of the Japanese", *Population Studies*, vol. I, no. I (1947).

[2] Unless greater social stability and development of resources are attained, the tendency to a falling mortality rate due to the spread of Western hygiene and medicine will, of course, continue to be arrested in some areas (*e.g.* China) by the operation of the positive checks referred to above (p. 30).

imperialistic adventures by the major nationality groups of Asia—the Indian and the Chinese—with the former seeking a field for expansion in Indochina and the latter in Burma, Malaya and the Indian Ocean, are perhaps more than possibilities. With the collapse of Japanese imperialism and the large-scale abandonment of that of the United Kingdom, the stage is set for new political adventure. But the achievement of such ultimate possibilities would depend no less clearly on an industrial revolution in China and India and on the attitude of the Great Powers, not least on that of the United States, now interventionist not isolationist in its foreign policy and, in addition, mistress of the seas.

GEOPOLITICAL CONSIDERATIONS

ASIA'S CONTINENTAL POSITION

Only as a continent does Asia really appear a unit, so distinct and self-contained are its many physical and human environments. But as a continent, now that the full implications of its geographical position are being more clearly realized, it stands in ever closer relation to all the other continents. Given its sheer extent, Asia presents façades alike to the Old World, to the New and to the Arctic (*Figs.* 3 and 4). Its relative geographical position has changed during recent centuries and is changing still. It is not enough to visualize it, as did the first European cartographers, as forming the outer land areas beyond Europe and Africa—merely as part of the Old World Island, as Mackinder put it. It looks now across the Pacific and finds there increasingly significant relationships. It looks too, in the far north, across Arctic seas which no longer deny passage to modern aircraft. Modern scientific and technological achievements in the West, notably in transportation and communication, have created in a new sense the One World, as physically united as it is politically sundered, which Wendell Willkie demonstrated in his 36-hour world flight in 1942.

Now that imperialism in Asia is largely in abeyance, it would be simple to infer that the peoples of Asia will again revert to their one-time isolation and seek to work out their several destinies in seclusion. They can no longer live of their own, content as the Chinese and Japanese once were with their own civilizations and disinterested in those of outside peoples, designated as 'barbarians'. Demographically and economically, Asia is too important for the rest of the world to ignore. The Western world cannot dispense with its oil, its tin, its jute, its tea and much else; Asia itself cannot dispense with the capital, machine tools, manufactures, scientific and technological services which, at present, only the West can amply provide.

4

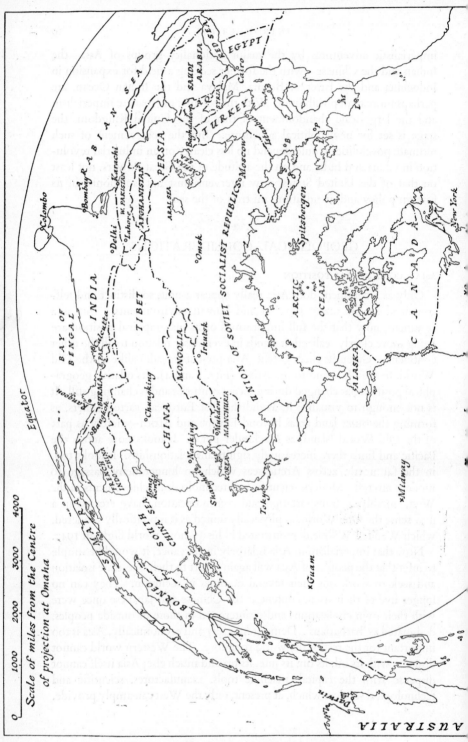

Fig. 3. ASIA: A TRANS-POLAR VIEW

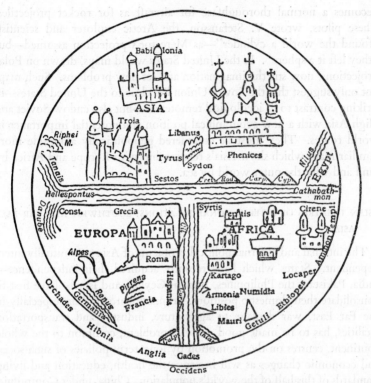

Fig. 5. ASIA ON A MEDIAEVAL WHEEL-MAP

Strategical considerations, too, no less forbid seclusion. Asia is so located geographically, contains so many strategical pawns, and lies so exposed to Soviet 'permeatism' that the organization of world peace or, for that matter, the pursuit of power politics, inescapably bind it to the rest of the world. As in world economy, so also in geopolitics, which studies the application of political geography to contemporary world politics in peace and war, Asia's position is clearly outstanding, although less easy to define now that it is politically changing so fast.

Each age must re-interpret its geography and make its own maps. For the medieval wheel-maps (*Fig. 5*) are now substituted geopolitical maps. Mercator maps, adequate to the purposes of oceanic navigation for which they were projected, have by their very familiarity obscured certain positional relationships which, in an air age, it is necessary to appreciate. The non-stop flight of Soviet pilots from Moscow to the United States in 1937 demonstrated that for aircraft at least the world has no necessarily negative areas: once technical requirements have been met, the Arctic becomes a normal thoroughfare for aircraft as for rocket projectiles. These pilots, wrote V. Stefansson, the Arctic explorer and scientist, "found the world a cylinder"—as Mercator's projection assumed—but "they left it a sphere". In the United States world maps, drawn on Polar projections, now stir the imagination and set new problems. Such maps not only suggest that the Soviet Union lies close to the United States—in striking contrast to its ideological remoteness—but also endow Soviet and High Asia with a new geographical position and potential importance in world routes. They must be considered geopolitically alongside more familiar maps which show Asia's relationship with Europe and Africa by land and with the outer world by sea.

ASIAN THEATRES OF INTERNATIONAL RELATIONS: SOUTHWEST AND FAR EAST ASIA

The internal and external political problems of Asia are mutually inter-dependent. States which have recently acquired their independence— India, Pakistan, the Philippines, Burma, Ceylon, and Israel—have first to consolidate their domestic positions. In many parts of Asia, especially in the Far East, war damage to agriculture, industry and transportation facilities, has to be made good. A vast problem, common to the whole continent, centres on the promotion by long-term policies of such social and economic changes as will improve the health, education and living standards of this half of the world's population. China, under Communist rule, now enters a phase of perhaps radical re-organization. And all these problems can be tackled only with the co-operation of the Great Powers which have so much to offer that Asia needs. But the Great Powers, who still hold establishments there, each with its own interests and policies, have no common agreed policy in Asia. Indeed this continent provides only too clearly theatres for the display of their divergent purposes.

Two main theatres are Southwestern and Far Eastern Asia. In its physical content Southwest Asia might appear deterrent rather than inviting to extraneous powers—so greatly is it dominated by desert, steppe, mountain and high and arid plateaus. Poverty and low educational standards characterize the great bulk of its peoples whose energy is sapped by disease. Yet it is a region of striking contrasts alike in its physical and cultural geography; a region, too, of remarkable interest in the cultural history of mankind. Cities and seaports situated amid 'sown' land, notably in the Levant where the interior plateaus descend to the Mediterranean, and modern oilfields under exploitation in south Persia, on the Persian Gulf, and at Kirkuk in Iraq, afford sharp contrasts with the pastoral husbandry and nomadism of the dry uplands. It is its geographical position, and also its resources of petroleum, that focus the attention of the Great Powers on Southwest Asia. There Asia narrows significantly and is deeply penetrated by the seas, and sea and air routes pass between populous Europe and monsoon Asia. The relation of Southwest Asia to the open seas and oceans inevitably attracts the leading trading countries as it affords scope for the exercise of sea power. The Suez Canal, the Persian Gulf, the Suez isthmus, whence routes confined between desert and sea pass westwards along the coast of North Africa and northwards to Palestine, Syria, Turkey and Iraq—all these have obvious strategical interest near the convergence of three continents. Nor, now that the end of major sources of oil in the Americas and the Soviet Union lies only a few decades ahead, is the interest of the Great Powers lessened in the wells of Persia, Iraq, and Saudi Arabia, whose mounting output has still a long lease of life. The political status of Southwest Asia, too, has international implications. Traditionally an imperial domain—we need only recall the Persian empire of Darius, the Macedonian empire of Alexander, the Byzantine and Ottoman empires—Southwest Asia now comprises, apart from some colonial areas, nine independent states, none of which by reason of man power and industrial resources is militarily strong and some of which are bound by treaties of alliance with the United Kingdom.

Already in two world wars Southwest Asia was inevitably involved, although in the second the defeat of German forces at Alamain and at Stalingrad halted a gigantic pincer movement directed respectively from Egypt and from the Caucasus. For the Western powers Southwest Asia affords strategically an extensive buffer zone between the U.S.S.R. on the one hand and Europe and Africa on the other, an important cross-ways of sea and air routes and a sphere of politico-economic interest to which, in time of war, a powerful enemy must be denied access. The United Kingdom enjoys special treaty relationships with Egypt, Jordan, Iraq and Persia, in accordance with which transport facilities, necessary for their defence in wartime, are made available. British troops still maintain guard in the Suez Canal zone; the Anglo-Egyptian Sudan, British-occupied Eritrea, Aden with its naval port, Socotra and Perim, Kuwait and Bahrein—all are located hard by the sea routes which flank Arabia to the west and east. South Persia, in which lie British-owned oilfields and also concessions recently granted to the United States, has long been recognized as a sphere of British interest, an outpost in the defence of the Indian sub-continent. North Persia, no less clearly, is recognized as a zone of special Soviet interest. France retains interests in her formerly mandated territories of Syria and Lebanon, and in the oil-pipe at Tripoli from which it derives its main source of oil. It holds also its naval base at Jibuti in Somaliland at the southern entry to the Red Sea. The United States, by acquiring oil interests in Persia and in Saudi Arabia and mindful of the strategical significance of Southwest Asia should it become again engaged in global warfare, has clearly a stake in this theatre —witness, for example, its financial support of Turkish rearmament, Lastly, the third Great Power whose territories lie on the threshold of Southwest Asia where they border Turkey, Persia and Afghanistan, cannot fail to estimate the importance of this region in either defensive or offensive strategy. It might appear that since the Caucasus ranges constitute naturally an excellent zone for military defence, the U.S.S.R. need not greatly concern itself with a militarily weak Southwest Asia. But the great city of Baku with its neighbouring oilfield lies on the southeastern side of the mountains—a veritable Achilles' heel, since it accounts for about two-thirds of Soviet oil production on which the mechanized agriculture, industry, air transport and the armed forces of the Soviet Union depend. And Baku, as aircraft fly, lies close to Iraq (where the plain of Mesopotamia is particularly suited to landing grounds)—only 500 miles from Mosul, 600 from Baghdad and 700 from Basra. Similarly, the Donetz coalfield, the ports and heavy industries of South Russia and the lower Volga waterway lie within similar ranges from Turkish territory. In Europe, High Asia and in the Far East, the U.S.S.R. has with marked success either acquired territory or more or less friendly and dependent neighbours, the better to insulate and secure its own territories. In Southwest Asia, in contrast, it has achieved neither of these objectives: indeed, as its post-war relations with Persia and Turkey have shown, it impinges there, not on malleable satellites, but on outposts of the Western powers.

The Far East, comprising China, Japan, Korea and the Soviet Pacific territories, has become in this century, like Southwest Asia, one of the conflict areas of the Great Powers. These were not attracted there in their search for oil, nor by world routeways through relatively undeveloped and scantily peopled regions. For the Far East contains rather more than a quarter of the human race, and landwards broad zones of mountain, high plateau, desert and steppe conspire with political conditions to minimize the potential importance of trade routes. To the great industrial states of Europe and to the United States the demographic status of the Far East pointed to the possibilities of large and expanding markets, while the technical backwardness of China promised a field for investment and its political weakness privileged positions for the strong. The completion of the Trans-Siberian railway to Vladivostok and Port Arthur and the meteoric rise of Japan as a military and naval power created in this century, a new situation both locally and geopolitically. It was one thing when Japan grew strong enough to be a useful check on Russian and German ambitions in the Far East; another when it occupied Manchuria and sought to subjugate China; yet another when it challenged America by its assault on Pearl Harbour, Australasia by its invasion of New Guinea, and Europe by its capture of French Indochina, the Netherlands East Indies, Singapore, Malaya and Burma. But the destruction of Japan destroyed the Far East as an 'autonomous power zone' in international relations, i.e., as a base from which attempts at world mastery might be launched by combined naval, military and air forces. A power vacuum has thus been created there which, as it re-fills, draws two of the Great Powers—the United States and the Soviet Union—into closer contact.

The United States now assumes the principal rôle in the Far Eastern theatre. It has set up the Philippines as an independent state, but remains, an occupying power, in Japan and until 1949 remained in southern Korea. Further, it has inherited from Japan those Pacific island groups—the Carolines, Marshall and Ladrones—which for over 2000 miles provide stepping-stones towards the Philippines. But it may well be asked what are the interests of the United States in the Far East, from which it is separated by 5000 miles of ocean, except in the far north where Siberia and Alaska draw close.

Before the Japanese assault on Pearl Harbour, for Americans "distant countries were words and pictures in a book, not territory and fields and culture systems and irreducible human diversities".[1] The successful assault on Pearl Harbour, though it lies over 2000 miles from the American mainland, threatened the United States for the first time on its Pacific flank; and the second world war necessitated a re-assessment of American defence and foreign policy. The policy of 'hemisphere defence' was clearly, on several grounds, impracticable, not least because the United States adhered to the doctrine of the 'free sea', i.e., the right of access to markets and sources of supply in all parts of the world. In the pursuit of peace and national security the United States can clearly not disinterest itself in Asia, least of all in the Far East, which commands the western Pacific, and southern Asia, on which it depends for strategical raw materials. Actual and likely increases in the range of aircraft and rocket projectiles and the atomic bomb, coupled by a new realization that the Arctic is no longer a complete shield, have fostered ideas (perhaps exaggerated) about the vulnerability of the American homeland. Having

[1] Isaiah Bowman, "The Geographical Situation of the U.S.A. in relation to World Policies," *Geographical Journal*, vol. CXII, April, 1949.

won the war, the United States appears determined to win the peace. The United Nations Organization offers one line of approach. Another seeks security by the creation of outer as well as inner zones of defence. "Bases which our military experts deem to be essential for our protection, and which are not now in our possession," said Mr. Truman (9.8.45), "we will acquire . . . by arrangements consistent with the United Nations Charter." The establishment of bases in the former Japanese islands of the Pacific, by lengthening the long arm of American sea power, protects supply routes, mans the outermost defences of the American mainland and, in some measure, helps to bring the prestige and influence of the United States to bear on the internal politics of the Asiatic mainland. But clearly no threat to the United States from Asia can presently be seen except perhaps from the Soviet Union which has substantially strengthened its position in the Far East.

Already before VJ day the United States government sensed potential danger from the assertion of Soviet power and policy in the Far East: indeed the dropping of the atomic bombs on Hiroshima and Nagasaki can possibly be interpreted as an American diplomatic coup to ensure that Japan capitulated to the United States and not to the U.S.S.R.[1] While it is difficult, in view of the great oceanic distances and the climatic difficulties and transport deficiencies of northeastern Siberia, to visualize Soviet attacks on America, except perhaps in Alaska, it is clear that American forces stationed in Japan occupy an advanced position *vis-à-vis* eastern Siberia and the Soviet Far East. And, it would appear, Americans, as the principal occupying forces, are there to stay, for, as Dr. Isaiah Bowman put it, "the present Allied beach head in the Orient is not one of the dilemmas of victory. It is to-day to our western mainland coast what Pearl Harbour was up to 1941 as a naval and air outpost". And if the future of Japan cannot yet be clearly discerned and if the extent of its democratization may be in doubt, it already unmistakably appears that the enemy of yesterday is to be industrially re-developed under the ægis of the United States as part of its system of global defence.

The resurrection of Japan, under due safeguards, would seem a likely result of the Communist ascendancy in China, which interests the United States as a field of trade, investment *and* humanitarian endeavour. China, too, after the end of the second world war interested the United States as a field for dollar diplomacy since, by supporting the Nationalist government, it seemed possible to hold Chinese Communism within bounds. But by the autumn of 1948 it became evident that the régime of General

[1] This thesis is argued by P. M. S. Blackett, *Military and Political Consequences of Atomic Energy*, 1948, Ch. X.

Chiang Kai-Shek could not withstand the Communist advance; indeed that it might not even survive. Further American support is scarcely to be expected, and a new political situation, in which the *deus ex machina* is a Communist China on friendly terms with the Soviet Union, has to be reckoned with.

By the Yalta agreement of 1945 the U.S.S.R. was richly rewarded for its promised last-minute entry into the war against Japan. For many years the presence of Japanese forces in Korea, Manchuria, Jehol, Inner Mongolia, Karafuto and the Kurile islands threatened Soviet Pacific ports and Far Eastern territories and necessitated the permanent maintenance there of armed forces. This defence problem remains only in so far as Allied-occupied Japan and Korea may be conceived by the U.S.S.R. as a potential spring-board for attack on itself. Even so, the Soviet frontiers are no longer immediately beset by a potential enemy but now possess many outer bastions of defence. In accordance with the Yalta agreement the U.S.S.R. won additional territory, recovered the naval base of Port Arthur and its specially privileged position in Manchuria, enjoys special relations with Outer Mongolia and until the end of 1948 occupied northern Korea. Further, the apparent triumph of Communism in China and the failure of the Allied-sponsored Nationalist régime give a favourable turn to the Soviet wheel.

For offensive operations in the Far East the U.S.S.R. has certain local positional advantages, although in a wider sense its geographical position is disadvantageous. Both from Chita and Vladivostok Manchuria and Korea lie directly open by rail, and in northern Korea the U.S.S.R. has already set up a 'democratic' Communist government to balance the 'democratic' liberal administration created under the American ægis in south Korea: the withdrawal of American forces, in view of the success of Chinese Communism, might threaten an early 'liquidation' of the south Korean administration. Further, the U.S.S.R. has always potential control of the strategical routeway between lake Baikal and the Yellow Sea (between Irkutsk and Peiping), the military use of which it efficiently demonstrated in 1945. In short, given its continental position and its military preponderance in Asia, the U.S.S.R. could always deploy powerful air and military forces in the Far East. But the as yet very limited development of heavy metallurgical industries in the regions east of lake Baikal as well as their low density of population would involve very heavy hauls of men, war material and supplies from major bases far away—notably from the Urals—and transport deficiencies would thus limit the scale and pace of military effort.

Southwest and Far Eastern Asia, both of which are directly accessible from the Soviet Union, which possesses the greatest army, and both of which are no less accessible to the Western sea powers which have economic and strategical interests there, clearly occupy in Asia the most prominent geopolitical positions.

Situated between Australia and the continental interior of Asia, the new states of Southern Asia are charting their uncertain courses in troubled seas. On their landward flanks they appear reasonably secure. Remarkable physical obstacles and the organization of the Northwest Frontier, which now devolves on Pakistan, may well, as during the last two centuries, protect the Indian sub-continent, despite the relative propinquity of one Great Power—the U.S.S.R. The landward advance of the Japanese into Southeast Asia in 1942 emphasized what had been forgotten, namely the limitations of defence based solely on sea power: but the preoccupation of China in its internal political problem, as indeed its usually friendly relations with India, should make for temporary stability. Seawards the balance of power has changed since the late war; indeed it had already changed before it. British sea power, which for so long effectively defended India, Burma, Australia, New Zealand and British dependencies in south Asia from bases strung out from Alexandria to Suez, Aden, Trincomalee, Singapore and Hong Kong, was overstretched before the second world war so that, as events proved, British territories east of India and Ceylon fell to the Japanese aggressor. The war against Japan brought American naval power to the western threshold of the Pacific and to the China Sea and, having acquired island bases, the United States intends presumably to maintain the naval supremacy there which it has inherited from Japan. It would not appear that British economic and defence interests in the Indian Ocean and its approaches have greatly changed as a result of the political changes in the status of India, Burma and Ceylon. A large share in the maritime defence of Australasia and the dominions of India, Pakistan and Ceylon must continue to fall on the United Kingdom, whose naval bases remain intact. The major change in the geopolitical setting is that the Indian subcontinent, with its enormous man power and its supplies, is no longer automatically available to the United Kingdom in time of war. Even so, the Indian Ocean would appear to remain a British lake, from which can be undertaken the maritime defence also of Southwest Asia and of Africa, to which increasing strategical interest now attaches. The other European states which still uneasily retain territorial emplacements in Southeast Asia—France, the Netherlands and Portugal—are not strong enough to affect the broad pattern of maritime control wielded by the United States and the United Kingdom.

THE HEARTLAND AND THE MONSOON COASTLAND

Finally geopolitical interest turns towards the U.S.S.R. which territorially and militarily occupies the commanding position in the continent. The vast area of Soviet Asia, rich in coal and minerals and in industrial potentialities, is in process of further colonization and of rapid economic development. Already it contains heavy industrial bases, nitrate factories, aircraft and automobile plants and a population which will soon have trebled that shown by the Tsarist census of 1897. Soviet Asia, we have seen, provides vantage points for military action in Southwest Asia and the Far East. It enjoys special political opportunities beyond its borders in Sinkiang and Outer Mongolia where its prestige stands high. Its Communist ideology provides, too, an insidious weapon which can be infiltrated at long range to create embarrassments for its opponents. In relation to the divergence of the policies of the Soviet Union and of the Western Powers, led by the United States, it is relevant to recall the geographical division of Euro-Asia made long ago by Sir Halford Mackinder. His two major divisions in Asia, separated by a transitional zone, were the interior, continental 'Heartland' and the outer 'Monsoon Coastland' (*Fig.* 32). In a struggle for world mastery, Mackinder argued, the dice would be heavily weighted in favour of the 'Heartland': the validity of this arresting conclusion we shall attempt later to assess.[1]

---

[1] See below pp. 357–359.

SELECT BOOK LIST

A. GENERAL GEOGRAPHIES

Élisée Reclus: *Nouvelle Géographie Universelle:* Tomes VI–IX, Paris, 1881–83
> Despite its date, can still be read with advantage by the advanced student for its remarkable grasp of fundamentals and powers of synthesis.

L. W. Lyde: *The Continent of Asia*, 1938.

L. D. Stamp: *Asia*, 8th ed., 1950.

P. Vidal de la Blache and L. Gallois (eds.), *Géographie Universelle*, Paris, 1928–32:
> Tome V: Russie d'Europe et d'Asie (P. Camena d'Almeida)
> VIII: Asie occidentale (R. Blanchard), Haute Asie (F. Grenard)
> IX: Asie des Moussons (J. Sion)

G. B. Cressey: *Asia's Lands and Peoples*, N.Y., 1944.

A. D. C. Peterson: *The Far East, A Social Geography*, 1949.

R. Linton (ed.): *Most of the World*, N.Y., 1949.

H. W. Weigert, V. Stefansson, and R. E. Harrison (eds.): *New Compass of the World*, 1949.

B. SPECIAL STUDIES

E. Dennery: *Asia's Teeming Millions*, 1931

S. K. Datta: *Asiatic Asia*, 1932.

R. K. Mukerjee: *Migrant Asia*, 1936.

I. Bowman: *The Limits of Land Settlement*, N.Y., 1937.

N. J. Spykman: *America's Strategy in World Politics*, N.Y., 1942.

P. Gourou: *Les Pays Tropicaux*, Paris, 1947.

F. B. Eldridge: *The Background of Eastern Sea Power*, 1948.

G. Wint: *The British in Asia*, 1947.

R. Payne: *The Revolt of Asia*, 1948.

P. Elken: *The Far East since 1500*, N.Y., 1948.

With these it is interesting to compare two books written by men of insight at the height of European optimism:
> A. T. Mahan: *The Problem of Asia*, 1900.
> M. Townshend, *Asia and Europe*, 1901.

CHAPTER I

SOUTHWEST ASIA

By Walter Fogg

THE GEOGRAPHICAL SETTING

SOUTHWEST ASIA is that part of the continent whose confines are washed by the five seas—the Mediterranean, Black, Caspian, and Red Seas and the Persian Gulf. In area nearly 2 million square miles—more than 24 times that of Great Britain—its total population is less than 55 millions, which is not much more than the United Kingdom's. Politically, it now includes nine principal states, namely (in order of population) Turkey, Persia,[1] Saudi Arabia, Iraq, Yemen, Syria, Israel, Lebanon, and Jordan, as well as several dependent territories, such as Aden, the Hadhramaut, Kuwait, Bahrein, and the Trucial Shaykdoms of the Persian Gulf, and the principalities of Oman and Muscat.

CONTRASTING PHYSICAL ELEMENTS

Southwest Asia presents sharp physical differences. In the rift valley of Palestine, and again along the shores of the Caspian, considerable areas lie well below mean sea level, as much as nearly 1300 ft. about the Dead Sea; while great lengths of mountains of Pyrenean and even Alpine magnitude, folded in the Tertiary era and with crests standing above 10,000 ft., form much of the framework of its northern and northeastern parts. Between these folded mountain chains, in Anatolia and Persia, lie expanses of high plateau land which recall the altitudes of the *meseta* of Spain, while in the confused and old volcanic parts of the convergence area of these chains, where lie the great high-altitude lakes of Van and Urmia, Mt Ararat, nearly 17,000 ft. high, climbs well above the summit level of Mont Blanc, the highest mountain of Europe, and in the Elburz Mts south of the Caspian Sea, Mt Demavend reaches some 2000 ft. higher still. To the south and southwest of these mountainous areas are vast

---

[1] The official name is Iran, which is used solely of their country by Iranian government officials among themselves. But English usage commends the name Persia, to the extent that even Iranian government officials use it in their official relations with foreign countries. Therefore in this chapter, both Persia and Iran are used.

expanses of gently-rising plateau land in Syria and Arabia which, structur-
ally related to the great plateaus of India and Africa, attain in Yemen
heights well above 10,000 ft. in several areas, with some peaks around
12,000 ft. Between the gently-inclined plateau of Arabia and the sharply-
rising mountain front of Persia, extends the low-altitude riverine plain of
Iraq, everywhere below 600 ft., for some 500 miles northwest of the Shatt
el-Arab at the northwest limit of the Persian Gulf.

The entire region lies within the thirty degrees of latitude between
42° N. and 12° N., and is thus largely sub-tropical by location. But great
ranges of altitude, along with geographical position between northeast
Africa, northwest India and Pakistan, southeast Europe and Soviet
Turkestan, combine to give the region a wide variety of climates. Fully
characteristic Mediterranean climates, with winter precipitation maxima
and summer drought are exemplified in all the coastal lands between the
island of Lesbos, off northwest Anatolia, and Gaza in southwest Palestine,
while attenuated Mediterranean climates prevail in much of inner southwest and south Anatolia and in interior Syria, Palestine, and north Iraq.
Around Izmir (Smyrna), annual precipitation is rather more than 25 ins.,
and northeast of Beirut it is more than 40 ins., but southwest of Gaza it
falls to less than 16 ins.

In northern Anatolia, exposed to winter influences from the cold south
Russian steppes, climatic conditions are more like those of east Central
Europe; northeast of Trabzon (Trebizond) precipitation reaches the high
figure of 120 ins. On the Anatolian interior plateaus winters are cold and
dry, and summers hot and dry, while in the highland areas of eastern
Turkey and northwest Persia, much snow lies in winter, whereas along
the south shores of the Caspian in northern Persia, moist warm sub-
tropical climate conditions prevail.

Roughly two-thirds of Southwest Asia form part of the hot desert
zone of the Old World, within which are included all of Arabia, much of
Iraq, and most of central and eastern Persia. Within these vast areas
precipitation is, in general, less than 4 ins. per year. In the great Rub el-
Khali of southern Arabia, there is unmitigated sand-desert where plant life
is practically non-existent, and in the Kavirs or saline basins of interior
Iran wide spaces are wholly devoid of plant and animal life. But even in
Arabia and interior Persia, there is much dry steppe, and in northern
Iraq and Syria the steppes of the plains are comparatively rich. In the
higher altitudes of the Zagros mountains of western Iran, and on those
of Kurdistan in southeast Turkey and northeast Iraq, as well as in
the Anti-Taurus mountains northeast of Iskanderun (Alexandretta), and
in the coastal mountains of northern Turkey, much forest of a north

temperate type is found; around Trabzon, and farther east, along the Caspian shores between Resht and Bandar Shah, the forest cover is often dense and rich. In the lands along the eastern shores of the Mediterranean and Aegean seas, there is much *maquis* and hard-leaved woodland, with even rich stands of cedar remaining sporadically in higher altitudes.

THE DISTRIBUTION OF POPULATION

Population distribution in Southwest Asia is remarkably uneven. A great part of the south and east of Arabia and Iran, remains either entirely unpopulated or extremely sparsely populated, while relatively high rural densities prevail in large areas of the west and northwest of Iran, and elsewhere in oasis and riverine lands. In Turkey, which includes about one-third of the entire population of Southwest Asia, relatively high densities of more than 200 per sq. mile characterize northwestern and western parts around Uskudar (Scutari) and Izmir (Smyrna), as well as Black Sea coastal lands around Trabzon; but interior areas such as those around Konya in the south and Erzurum in the northeast, have densities below 25 per square mile.

Persia, with some 13 million people, includes nearly one-quarter of the total population of Southwest Asia; its greatest densities are found in the northwest around Tabriz, in the north, along the favoured Caspian shores between Resht and Asterabad, and around Tehran, where densities greater than 64 per square mile are found. Further, in considerable areas of the west and southwest, for example between Hamadan and Isfahan, densities between 30 and 60 per square mile are recorded. On the other hand, large areas of the centre and east fall below 16 per square mile in continuation of the similar low-density dry lands of Baluchistan and Afghanistan. Syria, Lebanon, and Palestine, which include much of the so-called 'fertile crescent' have, together, about one-tenth of the total population of Southwest Asia, and include many well-populated rural areas of relatively high density, quite apart from closely-crowded oases. Iraq, with a total population of nearly five millions, and the more important part of the courses of the two principal rivers of Southwest Asia, namely Tigris and Euphrates, shows areas of densely-crowded population in irrigated riverine lands, such as those around Basra and Muntafiq in the south and around Karbala in the centre, sharply contrasted with more sparsely populated cultivated lands in the northeast around Mosul and Erbil, which depend directly on rainfall, and all but unpopulated areas in the uncultivated poor steppe-lands of the west.

Throughout the Arabian peninsula, apart from the well-populated terraced high-lands of the Yemen and relatively small total areas of oasis and wadi-valley elsewhere, population density is everywhere very low, and in the great sand desert areas of Rub el-Khali and Nefud, all but non-existent. Saudi Arabia alone occupies 700,000 square miles which form the home of less than eight million inhabitants, that is about four times the population of Palestine which has an area only one-seventieth that of Saudi Arabia.

It is true to say of all the countries of Southwest Asia that the major part of the population is rural, but there are also large and relatively numerous urban centres, although, in the main, widely separated. Of these, excluding Istanbul, which strictly is outside Southwest Asia on the European shore of the Bosporus, Baghdad, with a population approaching that of Manchester or Birmingham, and Tehran with nearly three-quarters of a million, are by far the largest. But, near the eastern end of the Mediterranean, are six large urban centres with populations between 140,000 and 350,000, namely Beirut, Aleppo, Damascus, Jerusalem, Haifa and Tel Aviv. In Persia, Tabriz and Isfahan exceed 200,000, as do Ankara in Turkey, and Mosul in Iraq, while Basra exceeds 180,000.

Even sparsely populated Saudi Arabia has Mecca with 150,000 per-manent residents, as well as Medina, Riyadh, and Jiddah with populations between 40,000 and 50,000.

THE VARIETY OF ETHNIC TYPES

Southwest Asia is occupied predominantly by three distinct ethnic groups, all of which have developed empires of much greater territorial extent in the past than the Southwest Asia homelands which they now occupy.

The Persian Empire, at its greatest extent about 500 B.C., extended east and northeast of modern Iran to the Indus in Pakistan and to the upper Syr Daria in Russian Turkestan. Westwards and southwestwards it extended from the Caucasus to Macedonia and western Egypt, including modern Turkey, Iraq, Syria, and Palestine, but not Arabia, and with the modern Persia as its heartland.

The Arab empire in the mid-8th century A.D., extended from its heart-land in Arabia, east and northeast to the Indus and Russian Turkestan, northwards to the Caucasus, and westwards throughout north Africa, and into Iberia and southeast France. It thus included modern Iran, Iraq, Syria, and Palestine, but not modern Turkey, which remained part of the Eastern Roman Empire.

The Ottoman Turkish Empire in the 17th century A.D., extended from its heartland in Anatolia northwestwards to Bosnia and Hungary, north-wards to the Crimea and southern Ukraine, southeastwards to the head of the Persian Gulf, and southwestwards to Egypt, Libya and Tunisia, with, in addition, shadowy control over western Arabia. Thus were included Palestine, Syria, and Iraq, but not Persia, and not the major part of Arabia.

These three empires, the last of which continued in decadent form in Southwest Asia until the first world war disrupted it, represented the politico-territorial effort respectively of each of the three major ethnic groups still found in Southwest Asia, namely Iranians, Arabs and Turks. A fourth ethnic group of Southwest Asia, namely the Jews, is of great importance, in that, although it did not develop a territorial empire with a heartland in Southwest Asia, it became far more widely distributed geographically than any one of the three aforementioned, and culturally, if not politically, the Jews can be said to have had their heartland in Palestine through all the centuries of their dispersion.

The Persians belong to the Irano-Afghan branch of the Mediterranean race which is the chief population element in the entire highland territory between eastern Iraq and western Pakistan. About one-quarter of the population of Persia is made up of transhuming tribesmen who depend mainly on flocks of sheep and goats with herds of cattle, and, as riding- and pack-animals, horses. They ascend from their modest fields of wheat and barley in spring, to the better pastures of the mountains in summer, and descend for the harvest, using as dwellings goat-hair tents mostly. In southeast Persia, camels and the date-palm provide local variants in food-supply. But there are virtually no true camel-herding nomads of the Arabian or Saharan desert type: the vast interior salt deserts of Kavir and Lut are virtually lifeless. The rest of the population of Iran are partly sedentary cultivators, and partly urban dwellers. The former live in many small and some large oases in valleys and plains between mountain ranges, or on the mountain slopes that descend to the main plateau or to the sea; in the lowlands of the Caspian provinces with their tea plantations and rice fields; in the Khuzistan plains with their date groves, which are a continuation of those of Iraq; and especially in the well-watered plateau lands of northwest Iran around Tabriz. The latter live in widely separated towns which are located mainly in the north, northwest, and southwest.

The Arabs proper, belong, almost without exception, to the most typical and most highly evolved form of the Mediterranean race. It is in the Arabian peninsula that lies the largest unified area within which this moderate-sized race-type is found in greatest purity, with, as far as is yet known, its purest nucleus in the Yemeni plateau around San'a. But, in the ethnic sense, the northern boundary of Arabia is a line skirting the southern edge of the so-called 'Fertile Crescent' that is, a line well to the north of the present political boundary of Saudi Arabia, and not coincident with any modern state boundary.

Among the Arabs are included bedawin, settled agriculturists, and urban dwellers. The bedawin, who are camel-herding nomads, dwell in goat-hair tents and migrate almost throughout the year, their movements being dominated by the opportunities provided by their desert and steppe environment for pasturing and watering their herds of breeding camels. They are particularly important in northern Arabia, Jordan, eastern Syria, and western Iraq, and are exemplified by the Ruwala and Shammar groups of tribes.

Arab sedentary cultivators are found especially on the fertile highlands of Yemen which support a large agricultural population, and in its continuation northwards in Asir, also a mountainous country occupied for the most part by Arab farmers. In the Hejaz, the Arab sedentary population is, in part, agricultural, and in Nejd also, some of the population, which, excluding negroid slaves, is entirely Arab, are sedentary cultivators. The urban dwellers live in almost purely Arab inland cities such as Riyadh and Haïl; in the coastal zone, trading- and pilgrimage-cities such as Mecca and Medina include a large proportion of greatly-mixed population, in addition to Arabs proper.

Although the inhabitants of the Arabian peninsula are predominantly Arabs, in some parts, notably Hadhramaut in the south, there is a large admixture of elements other than Arab, and the seafaring people who occupy the Arabian shores of the Persian Gulf, as also its Persian shores, conform but slightly to the Mediteranean-race Arab proto-type. Of these, the Omanis, the greatest sailors of all Arabia, have acquired much African blood; also in the farming villages and date groves of Oman, as on the Yemen coast, there is a large negro and negroid population.

Unlike the Iranians in Iran, or the Arabs in Arabia, the Turks in Anatolia can hardly be said to be indigenous, even though, as is known, they have absorbed much of the pre-Turkish peasant-farming population. The nomadic Turks came in great numbers from Russian Turkestan, in a long succession of immigrations of different kinds of Turks, over a long period, partly in search of new pastures; the Seljuk tribes started about A.D. 1070, the Osmanlis, who numbered but a few thousands, arrived in A.D. 1227. In some cases their original Central Asiatic way of life remained little changed until the rise of the Turkish republic after the first World War; for example, that of the pastoral nomadic Yuruks of Cappadocia on the western plateau.

The modern Turks have medium stature, and a body-build which is often thick-set. For the most part they are moderately broad-headed, with facial dimensions reminiscent of the Yugoslavs and Macedonians of southeast Europe. But, although markedly different from the Mediterranean Arabs and Iranians, the Anatolian Turks are in no sense Mongoloid; the epicanthic eye-fold typical of Mongols is almost unknown in Turkey. They are of Mediterranean race stock with admixture of Alpine race stock, the immigrant Turks from Central Asia having contributed roughly 25% and the previous inhabitants roughly 75%. They are Turks in speech and tradition rather than in race.

About three-quarters of the inhabitants of Turkey are rural-dwelling. On the central plateau of Anatolia, and in other parts where steppe vegetation is predominant, there are some pastoralists who are continuously migrant. But mostly, herding is done by tent-dwelling transhuming groups who migrate only between habitual lowland winter pastures and upland or mountain summer-grazing grounds. But the transhuming groups are usually members also of sedentary village-dwelling communities who cultivate fruit-trees and vegetables in gardens which often are irrigated from domestic wells.

Urban dwellers are located predominantly in the Black Sea and Aegean coastal zones, although several large centres are on the interior plateau or in the eastern highlands.

Although from their first dispersion until the present time, a period of more than 2500 years, the Jews can hardly be said to have been a political entity, through the endogamy enjoined by their religion they have always remained a powerfully cohesive socio-religious group, even though not territorially united. It is likely that the Children of Israel were nomadic Semitic-speakers from the desert borders of southern Mesopotamia, who moved north and west along the fringes of cultivation and finally into Palestine about 1200 B.C., where they founded a Jewish kingdom. Thereafter, they lived continuously and exclusively in Palestine until the capture of Jerusalem by the Babylonians in 586 B.C. and the initiation thereby of the first dispersion. In Palestine, they gradually absorbed earlier inhabitants, both racially and culturally, to the extent that the resulting composite group became eventually Hebraic. In physical type originally, the Children of Israel must have been brunet Mediterranean, like most Arabs and Mesopotamians, as were, for the most part, the peoples in Palestine whom they absorbed. According to Coon, the so-called Jewish face, and especially the Jewish nose, that is, high-bridged and convex in profile with a tendency to depression at the tip, are a part of the heritage of the entire Mediterranean-race population of Asia Minor, Syria, and Mesopotamia; hence it is a socially-induced quality of 'looking

Jewish' rather than measurable physical details which distinguishes the Jewish people physically from other Mediterranean-race population.

In Palestine, there is complete historical continuity of Jews since the time of Christ, but in recent times it is only since the first World War, that their concentration there has become so overwhelmingly predominant within Southwest Asia. Even so, in 1922, there were fewer than 84,000 Jews in Palestine, whereas, by the end of 1946 the number had risen to more than 608,000,[1] against some 35,000 in the neighbouring states of Syria and Lebanon.

In Central and Southern Arabia, Jews were numerous in the centuries immediately preceding Islam, and colonies were to be found in the urban centres of both the Hejaz and Yemen. But during the lifetime of Mohammed, they were expelled from the Hejaz to which they have not since been permitted to return. To-day, they are found in Arabia mainly in Yemen, where there is a large community of urban Jews as well as a considerable number even of rural and farming Jews, and in Aden, where there are some 7000.

After Palestine, Iraq with some 120,000 has the largest concentration of Jews, most of whom live in Baghdad. Strong Jewish colonies were founded in Mesopotamia with the captivity of the Jews in Babylon at the time of the first dispersion, and became even more numerous in later centuries, before the incoming of the Mongols. Turkey has nearly 79,000 Jews, and Persia more than a half that number.

WORLD RELIGIOUS SIGNIFICANCE

Southwest Asia is remarkable as the cradle of three of the six major world religions, namely Judaism, Christianity, and Islam. All three established their major shrines and centres of pilgrimage in the narrow strip of territory which borders the eastern shores of the Mediterranean and of the Red Sea: located there are Jerusalem, Bethlehem and Nazareth, Mecca and Medina. On these accounts, Southwest Asia holds a prominent place in the spiritual life of a very large proportion—probably no less than half—of the world's population; of Christendom, which includes Europe, North and South America, Australasia and South Africa, quite apart from Christianized groups in other parts of Africa and in Asia; of some three hundred million Muslims widely distributed in Africa and Asia, from Morocco and the Sudan through Pakistan to China and Indonesia; of the much smaller group of Jewry, now fewer than twelve millions strong, but widely distributed in a relatively small number of major urban centres of

[1] Statistics for years since 1946 are not published. The present number is nearer one million.

Europe, of North and South America, and of North and South Africa, as well as in a few widely separated urban centres of Asia, e.g., until recently 15,000 in Shanghai. The zealots of all three religious groups, wherever in the world they may dwell, are profoundly interested in, and concerned with, happenings in and concerning Palestine and Arabia.

GEOPOLITICAL IMPORTANCE

HISTORICAL FACTORS

The geographical position of Southwest Asia as the land link between Europe, Asia, and Africa, where also the Asiatic and African seas come closest to those of Europe, has exerted a powerful influence on the development of world history since the earliest recorded times.

Among the early aspirants to mastery of the 'world', as then known, the Assyrians felt the necessity to control shores both at the head of the Persian Gulf and on the Mediterranean; the Persians, when their empire was at its maximum extent about 500 B.C., bestrode most of the lands between the river Oxus (Amu Darya) and the Aegean, and between the Araxes (Aras) and upper Nile, with shores on all the five included seas of Southwest Asia; Alexander's conquests, during the latter half of the 4th century B.C., when the 'West' asserted its first recorded political supremacy over the 'East', spanned the whole of Southwest Asia, from Turkestan and the river Indus to Greece and lower Egypt; and even the Romans, in the 2nd century A.D., controlled not only the coast lands of the eastern Mediterranean and Black Seas, but also extensions as far as the western shores of the Caspian and the head of the Persian Gulf.

With the renewed struggle between East and West following the development of the Muslim World outwards from Arabia from the 7th century A.D., the successful Eastern power finally ousted the West from all of Southwest Asia, and dominated the latter completely; during the later centuries of bitter mutual hatred between Islamdom and Christendom, the whole of Southwest Asia, as the core of the wide-spreading Mohammedan lands, remained in the complete control of Muslim powers to the complete exclusion of the powers of Christendom.

But the rise of Napoleon saw the renewal of attempts by the West to gain access to, and control of, at least the strategically significant areas in Southwest Asia and, at the same time, the real beginning of the modern period of rivalry between political powers extraneous to Southwest Asia for control of this area, still vital for world power, even though of a greatly expanded 'world'. These were the rivalries, first between France and Britain expressed in the battle of the Nile of the early 19th century; later between Britain and Russia expressed in the Crimean War of the mid-19th century; still later between Germany and Britain expressed in the German *Drang nach Osten* and the two World Wars of the 20th century; and last of all, between Britain, the Soviet Union, and U.S.A., expressed in the 'cold war' now so hotly waged.

Britain is more vitally concerned with Southwest Asia than is any other of the extraneous powers. Yet her active interest in this part of the world goes no farther back historically than does that of several other powers. It can be said to have begun in the latter part of the 18th century and has increased constantly from that time, since, without strong or dominant influence in these lands, Britain could hardly have maintained herself as the centre of a great maritime empire.

In the beginning, after the development of the Indian Empire and of Far East interests by means of the Cape of Good Hope shipping route, since the Muslim Ottoman empire still closed Southwest Asia and the Suez Canal was not yet constructed, Britain was concerned with these lands mainly to ensure that powerful hostile influences be prevented from developing in parts whence her vital shipping links could be threatened. Thus the beginnings of British control were located in the coastlands to the west of what is now Pakistan and included south Arabian shores mainly, with the annexation of Aden completed by 1839. But, with the completion of the Suez Canal in 1869, the eastern Mediterranean was transformed from a relative backwater to a world highway and part of the main sea-lane to India, the Far East, and Australasia, all of which were of vital political and economic importance to Britain.

Thenceforward, therefore, all the lands near this highway acquired a new strategic meaning as bases within striking range of the new water life-line, and became a direct and vital concern of Britain, as a kind of keystone to the British Empire arch.

Hence, political stability in these lands became a vital British concern, and it was to ensure this that British policy aimed at prevention of the threatened disintegration of the Ottoman empire, which was based on, and included, a large part of Southwest Asia (*Fig.* 6). But from 1880 onwards, largely on account of pan-Islamic developments, with their repercussions among the Muslims of India, Britain became more restrained in her relations with Turkey, and it was in this period after the Franco-Prussian War had tended to weaken French activity there, that can be said to have begun the German penetration of Turkey and the German *Drang nach Osten*. The emphasis of the latter was on railway development from Berlin to Baghdad and the head of the Persian Gulf, and had obvious intention to compete with and circumvent the Suez water route, although later these aims were associated with the quest for oil.

The Ottoman Empire, whose Sultan in Istanbul besides being Khalif was the legal sovereign of all the northwestern parts of Southwest Asia,

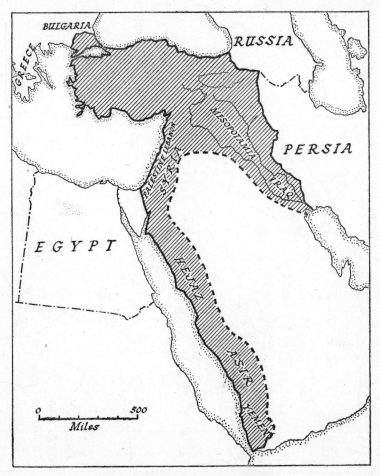

Fig. 6. THE OTTOMAN EMPIRE IN 1914

was able to maintain a semblance of order and surface stability in these lands until the onset of World War I. But on the collapse of the Ottoman Empire towards the close of that War, the unified political control of large parts of Southwest Asia came to an end and, in its place, followed political fragmentation, deliberately planned (*Fig.* 7).

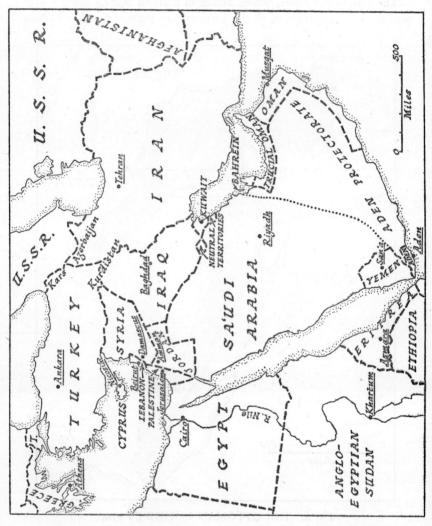

Fig. 7. SOUTHWEST ASIA. POLITICAL DIVISIONS AFTER
WORLD WAR I

The new state of Turkey emerged as an independent state mainly confined to Anatolia, and Persia remained much as before. But in the Arab lands to the south and southwest no less than eight new political entities were brought into being, six of them under British tutelage direct or indirect, and the remainng two in tutelage to France.

This new political fragmentation of the Arab lands of Southwest Asia on the basis of 'divide and rule', ensured to the French and British essential control in the place of the Ottoman Empire, and at the same time accorded with the new doctrine of national self-determination, with evolution, albeit at a deliberately-planned pace, towards ultimate independence at some indefinite date in the future.

During the inter-war period, rampant nationalism and a rising tide of anti-foreign feeling, partly fanned by German political agency with intention to stage a German 'come-back' to these lands, led to an orderly but constant retreat of both French and British political power. Even so, in the treaties with some of the new states, the great strategic significance to Britain and France of Southwest Asia was underlined by provisions for the maintenance of local French and British garrisons and for transport facilities in the event of war.

CURRENT PROBLEMS

With the outbreak of World War II, and its subsequent development in Southwest Asia, fragmentation was revealed as dangerous weakness. Consequently, a totally new programme was initiated with emphasis on 'unity is strength': support was given to the Arab unity movement, and the Arab League upheld in opposition to the nationalism of the new Arab States, with ultimate intention to evolve a confederation of states with British-Arab ties.

During World War II, and beginning with the joint British-Russian occupation of Persia, a series of events marked the re-establishment of the U.S.S.R. as a power in Southwest Asia. Likewise, it was mainly during World War II that the U.S.A. evolved a new interest in Southwest Asia, partly linked with oil, which is destined to last.

At least as much as any other factor, it was the likely threat to established British influence and interests in these lands that the incoming of these two 'new' powers presaged, which led to the new British support for unity of the local states through confederation.

Moreover it is partly because Britain must stay on as a power in Southwest Asia in order to survive as a world power, that other great powers developed their increased interest in Southwest Asia. German interest in Southwest Asia was partly motivated by the potentialities that the strategic position of these lands and the denial of oil offered for crippling the power of the British Empire; Soviet interest is motivated similarly, but relates also to defence strategy; the interest of the United States is based in part on her conviction that British power must be supported in these lands, against expanding Soviet power, if only in order that its own world power may be upheld.

Besides its enormous importance for reasons of strategy and communications, the positive value of its mineral oil resources has contributed greatly to the inescapable pull of Southwest Asia for Britain, the Empire, and the Commonwealth throughout this century, with ever-growing significance in proportion as air communications and air warfare have developed.

The U.S.S.R. is locationally much closer to Southwest Asia than is Britain, yet her interest therein is less vital, to the extent that the compact land-mass of the U.S.S.R. in Europe and Asia can intercommunicate easily without fear of interference of a foreign power by land, and the power of U.S.S.R. can survive regardless of these territories contiguous to her southern borders. None the less, its interest in Southwest Asia is just as intense as is that of Britain, and with much the same objectives, that is, facility of world communication, material resources, and strategic security. A great difference between them is that Britain is already in and well-established there, whereas the U.S.S.R. is as yet only on the fringes, even if determined to get in.

To the predominantly land-locked dominions of Tsarist or Soviet Russia, largely ice-bound in winter, this tri-continental land-bridge with warm water ports has been a magnet for decades, and always during that period Russia has been thwarted by Britain, already well-intrenched. In the past, control of the Bosporus and Dardanelles were Russia's more immediate concern. But World War II demonstrated very forcibly, by the rapid development of the overland motor-supply routes from sea-ports of the southern shores of Iran via Khanaqin and Birjand to the open plains of Turkestan in the very heart of Soviet Asia, how vital these lands could be from the point of view of its own security. Control of these lands by a rival great power could constitute a challenge which the new Russia, on its rising tide of world power, clearly intends to meet. On account of its territorial contiguity, the U.S.S.R. could readily obtain control over the stepping-stone approaches in eastern Turkey and northern Persia to this world crossroad. But it is also in parts of Southwest Asia, farther removed than these from Soviet territory proper, that it seeks control, or at the very least, a share in control.

Similarly Britain could view complete Soviet control or even shared control of these lands, only as the virtual end of the independence of the British Empire and Commonwealth, unless the vastly more difficult and circuitous mid-African land- and trans-African air-links between western seas and the Indian Ocean could be developed in substitute.

The oil resources of Southwest Asia are less directly vital to the Soviet Union than to Britain, or even to the U.S.A. since the former is well provided within its own territories, at least for some decades. But denial of these very resources to rival powers can be as great an incentive to the seeking of their control, as can be their exploitation by itself. Similarly, the rapid development of the new means of transport by air has given this inter-continental crossroads a vital new significance to the U.S.S.R., whether for defence or attack, or merely for commerce. Hence since 1944, when the change was well marked by the establishment of Soviet Lega-tions in Iraq and the Levant states, followed by a developing *crescendo* in 1945–46, the U.S.S.R. has practised a forward policy in Southwest Asia, in replacement of its earlier policy of watchful waiting. In this it is favoured for contacts and internal political manœuvres within Southwest Asia by having within its own territories some twenty-five million Muslims, already largely in autonomous Soviet republics, as well as many Jews. On the other hand, its brutal claims to Azerbaijan on ethnic grounds and, based thereon, her retention of troops there in 1945, along with peremptory claims for oil concessions east of Tehran, revealed only too clearly to the Arab World what to expect: absorption into the Russian politico-economic system through the creation of a chain of new Soviet republics, one by one, and one after the other in contiguity outwards from Soviet territory proper, Russian control spreading like a *tâche d'huile*. Hence, the attitude of the Arab world of Southwest Asia has rapidly become one of fear towards the U.S.S.R., with its corollary of a less hostile attitude to Britain. On the one hand, Arab Jordan, with its *cadre* of British military personnel and British treaty rights, and on the other, the contiguous state of Israel, with its large recent influx of Russian and East European Jews, can be taken as the locations of the centres of the Russo-British rivalry within Southwest Asia at the present time.

During the 19th century and until World War I the concern of the U.S.A. for Southwest Asia was predominantly religious and humani-tarian, and was expressed especially in and through the American university at Beirut. It was the discovery of oil in Southwest Asia that led to her more intensive practical interest in these lands. After World War I, and especially in the 1930's, American oil companies acquired important oil holdings in Iraq, but even then direct government participation was lacking. It was especially the prodigious drain on U.S.A. domestic·reserves of oil during World War II, to the extent that it is now estimated that, at the present rate of production, these are likely to be exhausted within a short period of years,[1] that led to the real beginning of the direct practical interest of the American government in the oil resources of Southwest Asia, with a view to ensuring an adequate future oil supply to meet, at least, the domestic needs of the U.S.A. Now, therefore, the U.S.A. is vitally concerned with Southwest Asia on account of its mineral oil. But, located in a continent other than the three which meet about Southwest Asia, and with no colonial empire or Commonwealth distributed about the Indian and Chinese seas, the direct strategic significance of the geographical position of these lands would appear far less to the U.S.A. than to Britain or the U.S.S.R. On the other hand, from the point of view of world communications, particularly air transport, U.S.A. is equally concerned with Britain and the U.S.S.R., in that it seeks to prevent these lands coming under the exclusive control of any one power which could thereby exercise a dangerous monopoly and power of veto over air movement in this major crossroad area of the Old World. Thus, initially oil and air communications, followed by a direct concern with maintaining world peace, which might well be broken by the Soviet-British conflict in these lands, have made U.S.A. one of the three world powers most vitally concerned with Southwest Asia.

But, in its turn, pushed by powerful Jewish interests in America, the U.S.A. government, through its early recognition of the newly-emerged State of Israel, has incurred the distrust of the Arab states, thus reinforcing their new tendency to turn to Britain on account of Soviet activities.

On account of oil, Saudi Arabia is too deeply involved with the U.S.A. economically, to be wholly free politically, but, as well as Egypt in Africa, at least Iraq, Syria, and Lebanon, in Southwest Asia, are now likely to seek new treaty relations with Britain, on the lines of the present British-Jordan treaty, which provides for mutual military help against aggression.

Just as, at the present time, the influence of the U.S.A. in Southwest Asia can be said to be waxing and likely to become second to none, so that of France, formerly second to none, is clearly waning. In the mid-19th century, before the completion of the Suez Canal, France was the most influential of the extraneous powers in Southwest Asia, particularly in Syria and Lebanon, and French influence there was at its peak about

---

[1] Statements of authorities give various estimates of the likely duration—12, 14, and 30 years. These estimates do not take account of recently located new oilfields in the U.S.A.

1860. In many ways for France, herself with shores along the western basin of the Mediterranean sea, a direct concern for lands at the opposite end of that sea would seem to be natural, and in fact, many centuries of purposeful cultivation of trading and cultural relations lay behind the special 19th century position of France in these lands. But after the Franco-Prussian War, France was obliged to yield ground in Turkey to Germany, while the completion of the Suez Canal, essentially a French enterprise, made the neighbouring territories a specially vital concern to the maritime power of Britain. After World War I, the French mandate in Syria was intended to serve the immediate strategic and economic interests of France in Southwest Asia, and to allow of the continued propagation of French culture and influence there. But the events of World War II, and finally the removal of French troops in 1946, virtually ended the long-sustained rôle of France as a major political power in Southwest Asia, until it was partially resuscitated by the joint guarantor's pact for Southwest Asia concluded in 1950 between U.S.A., Britain and France.

OIL IN RELATION TO INTERNATIONAL POLITICS

THE OIL WEALTH AND CONCESSIONS OF SOUTHWEST ASIA

The known oil-bearing areas of Southwest Asia lie predominantly within a zone aligned northwest-southeast, which extends from southeast Turkey through eastern and central Iraq, western Persia, and eastern Saudi Arabia. Their location and alignment are associated with the fractured and folded zone between the stable crustal block of Arabia and the mountain front of the Iranian plateau (*Fig.* 8). Apart from that located in this zone, little oil is as yet known to exist elsewhere in the vast extent of Southwest Asia, except on the flanks of the Elburz mountains, particularly around Samnan, east of Tehran, and in Sinai. But the fact that the existence of oil is not yet known does not preclude the possible discovery of other important fields.

Until very recently Turkey was not included among the known oil-bearing lands of Southwest Asia. But, in the Raman Dağ area, about the Tigris headstreams south of Lake Van in southeast Turkey, wells are now producing at a rate of 30,000–50,000 tons per year, and a conservative forecast is that Turkey will be self-sufficient in oil within a few years, that is, an annual yield of some 500,000 tons is likely. The disadvantage of this field is its remote inland location in mountainous terrain, which will present an exceptionally difficult transport problem: it will probably

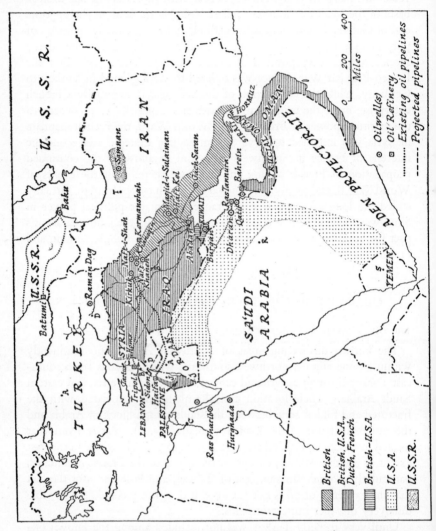

Fig. 8.   SOUTHWEST ASIA: OILFIELDS AND OIL CONCESSIONS.

For Damman read Dharan. For some 350 miles from Dharan the pipeline to
Sidon is already completed. There is also a pipeline between Dharan and Ras
Tannura.

take at least five years to construct a pipe-line to either the Mediterranean or the Black Sea. But its discovery places Turkey in an entirely new position among Southwest Asia lands, as a potential exporter of oil, instead of an importer of all oil requirements: in addition it makes Southwest Asia even more significant to the extraneous world powers. Under present political conditions, given the post-war financial difficulties of Britain, the mutual distrust and hostility between Turkey and the U.S.S.R., and the present financial and political support of Turkey by the United States, it seems likely that the last-named especially, will find here a further field for economic and technical activity, although oil concessions to foreign powers are not to be granted.

Iraq, with proved reserves in 1944 of approximately 714 million tons, ranked in 1939 eighth among oil-producing countries, although concessions were first granted only as recently as 1925. In 1927, the famous Baba Gurgur well near Kirkuk, in the foothills of the Sulaimaniya mountains of northeast Iraq, began its production of 860 tons per day.

The Kirkuk oilfield, some 60 miles long with an average width of two miles, is one of the largest single oil-bearing structures known, and has been proved to have vast potentialities. It is from this field that the 12- and 16-inch pipe-lines via Haditha (on the west bank of the Euphrates) have been laid to the Mediterranean seaports of Haifa in Israel and Tripoli in Lebanon. At present, it is only the capacity of the pipe-lines which limits the amount of oil exported from this field, but in 1938, through Tripoli alone, nearly $2\frac{1}{4}$ million tons passed in transit. The production from this field in 1948 was expected to be 4·5 million tons which is likely to become 14 million tons in 1951, that is an increase within three years of more than three-fold (but see Additional Table).

Large quantities of oil have been proved also in the northern parts of Iraq to the west of the Tigris, where more than sixty wells have been drilled. Exploitation there has hardly begun, but eventually a further pipe-line to transport a minimum quantity of one million tons per year from these parts is allowed for. More recently, concessions have been made for the exploration of the lands farther south—between Baghdad and Basra, with an expected production of a minimum amount of one million tons per year.

In the strip of land known as the 'transferred territories' along the Iraq-Persia frontier, northeast of Baghdad, oil from the Naft-Khaneh field is delivered through a twenty-five mile pipe-line to its refinery on the Alward river near Khanaqin, the output from which is consumed locally. Oil production in Iraq is controlled by British, Dutch, U.S.A., and French interests.

Persia with proved reserves of 930 million tons was the first of the Southwest Asia countries to make oil concessions to a foreign power: they date from the beginning of the present century, and are overwhelmingly British. The principal concession covers the vast area of about 100,000 sq. miles which extends in a zone roughly 100 miles wide along the eastern shores of the Persian Gulf, northwestwards from the Strait of Hormuz and beyond the head of the Persian Gulf to the lands northwest of Kermanshah. At present there are two major exploited parts of this zone, one to the northwest of Kermanshah, the other to the northeast and southeast of Abadan, which is on the Shatt el-Arab at the head of the Persian Gulf.

To the east of Abadan there are six fields in exploitation, the four most important being the Masjid-i-Sulaiman in the north, the Haft Kel in the centre, the Aghajari, and the Gach Saran in the south, all of which are connected by pipe-line to the refinery at the port of Abadan. Both the Masjid-i-Sulaiman and Haft Kel fields have produced already some 100 million tons each, and at present the Haft Kel oilfield is the second largest producing field in the world: Haft Kel is producing approximately 10 million tons per year from twenty-four wells, compared with the U.S.A. East Texas field which produces about 17 million tons from 240 wells. Most of the oil from these six fields is exported through the port of Abadan, and in 1949, the British-owned wells of Persia produced 26·8 million tons.

To the northwest of Kermanshah in the 'transferred territories', there are the two fields of Khanaqin and Naft Khanah, the latter of which is linked by a twenty-five-mile pipe-line to the refinery near Khanaqin, while that of Naft-i-Shah has pipe-line connection to the refinery at Kermanshah, which produces approximately 100,000 tons per year.

Saudi Arabian oil is under U.S.A. financial control and technical development, by concessions made in 1933 which cover 450,000 square miles. Exploration and drilling began only in 1935, but already in 1940 more than 700,000 tons per year were produced, and the rapid developments of the period of World War II have continued, resulting in an enormous increase in the post-war period. Thus, by the end of 1949, with an annual rate of production of over 23·0 million tons, Saudi Arabia was ranked as fifth world producer, that is after U.S.A., Venezuela, U.S.S.R., and Persia. Production is now in progress at three fields, namely Dhahran, Abqaiq, and Qatif, all in the coast zone along the Persian Gulf between the Qatar peninsula to the southeast and the Kuwait territory, southwest of Basra, to the northwest. A new 21-inch diameter pipe-line, the Trans-Arabian, is under construction from Dhahran to

Sidon in Lebanon. Negotiations are under way for the laying of a 24- or 26-inch diameter pipe-line, the Middle East, from Abadan and Kuwait to Tartus in Syria; this will be the largest in the world.

The Ras Tannura refinery, constructed during World War II on a spit near the Qatif field and with pipe-line connection to Dhahran, operates at a capacity of 13,500 tons per day. It has become the mainstay for the supply of naval fuel oil to the American navy in the Far East.

In Saudi Arabia, the U.S.A. now has control of what is probably the second greatest oil reserve in the world to-day. In 1945, De Golyer estimated the proved reserves at about 286 million tons, the indicated reserves at between 570 and 1290 million tons, and the possible reserves at about 2860 million tons. The significance of the latter figure can be the better understood when it is stated that it is also the usually cited figure for the proved reserves of the U.S.A.

At the head of the Persian Gulf, between southwest Iraq and northeast Saudi Arabia, lies the Shaykhdom of Kuwait, a further rich oil area with proved reserves of some 1286 million tons, that is a quantity greater than the present proved reserves of either Persia or Iraq. In this territory, control of the oil is shared equally by British and U.S.A. interests, and at the present time, the workings are at Burgan. In 1949, production from this field alone was 5.6 million tons a year.

In the Shaykhdom of Bahrein Island, off the Saudi Arabian eastern shore north of the Qatar peninsula, British since 1899, but recently—presumably with an eye to more oil royalties—claimed as an inseparable part of Persia, the concession for the rich oilfield is American. Production since 1939 has exceeded 1 million tons a year, and in 1948 reached 1.37 million tons.

In the Egyptian territory of Sinai a new oilfield has recently been located in the Assal district 10 miles south of Sudr on the Gulf of Suez, which although not yet properly proved, is said to be capable of producing over two million tons per year. The location of this field near the south end of the Suez Canal will give it peculiar strategic significance.

Thus, according to the available statistics for 1948, the countries of Southwest Asia were producing collectively about 54 million tons per year. Southwest Asia then accounted for 11·5% of the world total; by comparison the U.S.A. still produced over 60%. But whereas the latter fields are certainly decreasing in output, the former are increasing rapidly.

Taken together the Southwest Asia oil-producing countries took third place among world oil-producing areas, that is after U.S.A., and Venezuela, compared with which they produced nearly $\frac{1}{3}$ as much as

6

U.S.A., about $\frac{3}{4}$ as much as Venezuela, and nearly twice as much as the U.S.S.R.[1]

Thus, it may well be that within a relatively short period of years, Southwest Asia will overtake the declining production of U.S.A., eventually surpass it, and so become the major oil-producing area of the world. Even several years ago the proved reserves of Southwest Asia were officially reported as 3500 million tons, compared with the estimated U.S.A. reserves of 3000 million tons, and if estimates are realized, the output, collectively, of Persia, Kuwait, Iraq, Saudi Arabia, and Bahrein, may approach 100 million tons per year, within the next few years. The significance of the latter figure will be the better appreciated by comparing it with the world total production in 1947 of 445 million tons.

As expressed by the petroleum geologist De Golyer, the centre of gravity of world oil production is shifting from the Gulf-Caribbean area to Southwest Asia, and is likely to continue to shift until it is firmly established in the latter area.

POLITICO–ECONOMIC SIGNIFICANCE OF OIL

The politico-economic significance of this important oil area can be considered from the point of view both of the interested extraneous world powers, particularly Britain, U.S.A., and the U.S.S.R., and from that of the new states of Southwest Asia.

For Britain, although coal is still the key to her economic prospect, oil is only second to it in importance, that is, as a substitute fuel, particularly for shipping, and for industrial power in direct home consumption. Secondly, in exclusive fields of its own, that is, in motor road transport and in air transport, it is indispensable to the modern economic life of the country. Thirdly, for a country so largely dependent on exports, the rapidly increasing product of the vast new oil-refining industry being developed on the Clyde, Manchester ship canal, near Southampton,[2] and elsewhere in Britain, and dependent on Southwest Asia supplies of crude oil to be exported as refined oil to parts of Europe, to Africa, and to Asia, will effect an increasingly important contribution to the annual balance of payments: this will tend to make good the contribution thereto

[1] U.S.S.R.'s pre-war production (as in 1940) exceeded that of Southwest Asia but fell off sharply during the 1941–45 war.

[2] Under the provisional British four-year plan to achieve economic stability by the end of Marshall Aid seven oil refineries are to be built, capable collectively of treating nearly 20 million tons of crude oil in 1952, as compared with 2½ million tons in 1947. The new oil refinery to be completed in 1952 at Fawley will be the largest of its kind in Europe and exceeded in size only by a few of the very largest U.S.A. refineries: it is planned to produce 5,500,000 tons of petroleum products annually. Extensive new docks alongside will accommodate tankers of up to 37,000 tons where, on account of the double tides of Southampton Water, fully-laden ocean tankers will be able to berth at any hour.

which formerly was made by greater quantities than now of exported coal. Further the new refining industry, by drawing its crude oil supplies from Southwest Asia will lead to a curtailment in imports of refined oil from U.S.A., not only to Britain but also to parts of Europe, Africa, and Asia, which will thus avoid expenditure in the hard currency of dollars. It will also lead to a diversion of much British-controlled Caribbean oil, mainly Venezuelan oil refined in Curaçao and Aruba, to the U.S.A., which will yield dollars as payment. This consequent saving of dollar expenditure and receiving of dollar payments should contribute much to the renewal of the economic and political independence of Britain. Thirdly, should world war supervene yet again, victory or defeat might be determined by the mere possession or denial of these oil supplies.

For the U.S.A. the fundamental politico-economic interest in Southwest Asia oilfields is occasioned by the rapid dwindling of oil supplies at home and the consequent necessity, in the absence of a substitute, to ensure their access to large future supplies elsewhere. Hence, within the last fifteen years in particular, as already indicated, the U.S.A. has seen to it that they should hold a very substantial share of the new oil concessions of Southwest Asia, notably in Saudi Arabia.[1] But, on the one hand, Britain has in the past relied largely on oil from the western hemisphere, and has thereby conserved large oil supplies under her control in Southwest Asia. Hence, according to Speiser, in countless political details the U.S.A. must long remain under the shadow of British oil control, to the extent that an independent oil policy in Southwest Asia on their part is impracticable. Thus there is ever present political rivalry for the oil of Southwest Asia between Britain and U.S.A. On the other hand, it is to the overriding interest of the U.S.A. to ensure, in case of war with the U.S.S.R., not only supplementary oil supplies for themselves, but for Britain and other potential allies, which could come only from these fields. In ensuring these oil supplies for herself and potential allies, the U.S.A. is *ipso facto* involved in ensuring that they be denied to the Russians.

The new significance of these oil fields to U.S.A. is very clearly demonstrated by the use of the product of the Saudi Arabian Qatif oilfield, via the Ras Tannura refinery, for the U.S.A. navy in the Far East, as already indicated.

The Russians, who before the war produced 30 million tons of oil per year, even though, on account of war ravages and shortage of new constructional steel supplies, reduced to 25 million tons in 1945, are said

---

[1] Of the areas in Southwest Asia within which oil has been located, U.S.A. interests control 41% of the concessions, British and Dutch interests control 53%, and others control the remaining 6%.

to be well supplied for current needs from their Baku fields, and the newly developed Volga-Ural, Emba, Central Asia, and Sakhalin fields. Together these fields give her home access to about 6% of the world's total production. Even so, since her needs are large and growing, the U.S.S.R. has a keen interest in possible oil reserves in north Persia; witness her vigorous demands for an oil concession there in 1946–47, even though political infiltration may have been a joint motive.

But it is equally self-evident that in the event of World War III, the denial of the vital oil supplies of Southwest Asia to its major antagonists would be an even more urgent Soviet objective, quite apart from the achieving of the greater aggressive and defensive power that the possession undamaged of these oilfields would ensure.

No clearer indication of the great politico-economic significance to extraneous world powers of the oil fields of Southwest Asia could be given than the desperate, if vain, efforts made by Hitlerite Germany during World War II, by its tremendous drive southeastwards, to achieve control of these lands. Even remote Japan had tried, before World War II, to get an oil concession in Arabia, although as much with the ulterior motive of achieving a foothold in Southwest Asia, as for obtaining oil.

For the new states within Southwest Asia, it is not only royalties on oil production and the very large sums of money paid for concessions by the interested extraneous world powers that are of prime significance, but also the important modern industrial and cultural developments, and the introduction of modern economic amenities within their territories, which are consequent on the exploitation of the concessions. King Ibn Saud of Saudi Arabia was reported as stating in 1931, that is before the Saudi Arabian oil concessions were made, that practically the whole of the revenue of Saudi Arabia was derived from the dues paid and gifts made during the annual pilgrimage to Mecca. This had the great inconvenience of fluctuating widely from year to year in close relation to widely varying annual numbers of pilgrims. Thus, in 1929 along with some 5000 overland pilgrims there were nearly 90,000 from overseas, whereas in 1934, the number from overseas was only 25,000, and, after rising again in 1938 to nearly 64,000, the number from overseas again fell enormously in 1941 to fewer than 10,000, and during later war years Saudi Arabian revenue from Muslim pilgrims to Mecca declined to virtually nothing. Hence the large advances of money made by the American oil companies became even more important relatively.

At the rich oil dome of Jebel Dhahran where the first oil camp in Arabia was established, there is now a modern oil settlement, with the most up-to-date drilling machinery and tank storage accommodation, and some scores of millions of pounds are to be spent in developing its resources until its production is some hundreds of thousands of barrels[1] per day. It is from this site, too, that is to be laid the 1200 miles pipe-line to carry 40,000 tons of oil per day to the east Mediterranean coast. With modern industrial settlements come roads, railways,[2] schools, and hospitals, so that certain parts of this vast land of camel-breeding nomads are likely to have their geography changed in an entirely revolutionary way within a very short period of years.

What is likely in Saudi Arabia is already exemplified in Persia. When in 1911 the completion of the 130 miles of pipe-line from Masjid-i-Sulaiman to Abadan permitted the beginning of commercial production of oil, this part of Persia was barren high land annually traversed, back and forth, by transhuming Bakhtiari pastoralists. Now, modern industrial establishments extend over a total area of some 200 square miles around the inland termination of the pipe-line, where also there is a sedentary population of more than 40,000, with stone dwellings, gardens, club buildings, and sports grounds, at the town of Fields; while at the seaport end of the pipe-line, at Abadan, is located the largest oil refinery in the world with a production capacity of 25 million tons of crude oil per annum, and a town of almost purely British way of life. Labour is recruited mostly from the Bakhtiari nomadic tribesmen who become accustomed to sedentary life and work of regular hours, but only by means of a careful educational technique.

The number of Persians employed is considerable and includes not only labourers and craftsmen, but also, by means of the education and training provided by the oil company, a steadily increasing number of clerks, engineers, and administrators. There are elementary schools, workshop training schools, and modern hospitals.

Nevertheless, the rapid industrialization, and consequent crowding of native workmen alongside European administrative and technical staff, often occasions much social discontent; a situation which was recently exploited by the Russian-controlled Tudeh party. In attempts to ease the position, the oil company, in its turn, has been led to undertake better housing schemes and social amenity developments.

During World War II, even though it amounted to only a very small part of its profits, the oil company contributed in royalties and other payments, something like one-quarter of the entire revenue of the Government of Persia, quite apart from its contribution to the economic

[1] 70 barrels of 42 gallons each are equivalent to one ton.
[2] See below p. 90.

life of the country through employment of many thousands of Persian subjects.

In Iraq, there are proportionately high contributions by the oil companies to the state revenue, and similar industrial and urban developments around Kirkuk at the inland end of the pipe-lines to Tripoli and Haifa. Moreover, similar developments are to be expected in other parts of Iraq, and in Kuwait,[1] Dhahran,[2] and southeast Turkey, as well as in other parts of Southwest Asia not yet proved as important oilfields, but where exploratory drilling is in progress as, for example, in south Palestine near Gaza.

Finally, the oil and associated installations give the internal states of Southwest Asia a new power in relation to the extraneous great world powers; they are able to play off one power against another in order thereby to achieve greater modern economic and financial resources; they are able to use threats to destroy pipe-lines and oil installations, as a means to compel defence measures or military support against another great power or another internal state; they are able to withhold concessions from the companies of a powerful state in order to compel acquiescence to their will in great world political issues, as when, in 1945, on account of American support of the Zionist cause in Palestine, the Lebanese refused to approve the application of two American oil companies to construct oil refineries at the Tripoli terminus of the Iraq pipe-line. In time of war even between the Southwest Asia states themselves, as recently between Israel and Jordan, a pipe-line can be cut to deny the vital means of modern mechanical transport to the enemy: Haifa refinery was reduced to complete dependence on crude oil brought by tankers, and even these were refused entry to the Suez Canal by Egypt!

THE CROSS-ROADS OF SOUTHWEST ASIA

Apart from the native sailing craft on the Euphrates downstream of Baghdad, and the shallow-draught steamers on the Tigris, transportation by river is virtually absent from Southwest Asia. No long natural water-

---

[1] At Ahmadi in Kuwait, with a labour force of about 18,000, there is already a hospital, school, laundry, and sports ground, even though the entire water supply (500,000 gallons a day), as well as all food supplies, must come by ship from the Shatt el-Arab.

[2] Dhahran, 16½ miles from the small ancient seaport of Damman and the headquarters of the Arabian American Oil Company, was the first-established of the oil-settlements of Saudi Arabia. It houses about 1,200 Americans who direct the labour of several thousand local inhabitants. Besides extensive shops, offices, and storehouses, it has a hospital, steam-laundry, cinema, tennis courts, golf courses, swimming pool and baseball ground. Vegetables and fruit are provided from the Company's own farming project and from the native gardens of Al-Khabar and Damman, which have water supply from springs. (See below p. 90).

way, such as the Nile, Volga, and Yangtze Kiang, has contributed to the easy inter-communication and unification of the Southwest Asia lands. Further, apart from Roman, Byzantine, Seljuk, and Ottoman imperial roads between main settlements in certain of its northwestern parts, most of Southwest Asia was roadless until very recent times. Almost everywhere overland communication remained in the pack- and riding-animal stage, along merely trodden tracks, until the economic revolution of the late 19th and early 20th centuries brought a few railways, and some motor roads, to certain parts. Even so, a very large proportion of Southwest Asia is still dependent entirely on camel- or horse-caravan traffic, along widely separated animal-trodden tracks, and still to-day vast areas of Arabia, as also of Persia, lack even tracks (*Fig.* 9).

From the dawn of history, if not from long before, the seas and gulfs which border the lands of Southwest Asia have been important for local coastwise, and small-scale trans-oceanic, communication and transport; they were important even for inter-continental communication and transport, whether between East Africa and Southern Asia, as far as India and Malaysia, or between Europe and Asia by means of the intervening overland caravan connections from Red Sea to Nile, across the isthmus of Suez, or across the land bridge between the East Mediterranean and the head of the Persian Gulf.

Moreover the Bosporus-Dardanelles sea-water link between the Black Sea shores of Southwest Asia and, via the Aegean Sea, those of the East Mediterranean, has been of continuous commercial and political importance since the earliest recorded times.

After the expansion of European power into India and the Far East, among the earliest successful attempts to shorten the five to eight months' journey by sailing-ship between India and Britain, if only for transmission of letters, was the establishment at the end of the 18th century by the Indian government in agreement with the Ottoman government of a camel-caravan post-service, which survived for several years, from the head of the Persian Gulf across the Syrian desert to the Mediterranean. Several decades later, in 1831, the first modern road-river link between the Persian Gulf and Mediterranean was projected by Captain Chesney, but, contemporaneous in conception with the early development of railways in Britain, the project was abandoned in favour of the first ideas for a future railway-link between the two seas. Reconnaissance for a 'Euphrates Valley' railway having demonstrated its practicability, the project was favoured by the British government, in part to speed up communications with India, but also in part in opposition to the French-Egyptian project for the Suez Canal; but in the event this railway was not even begun.

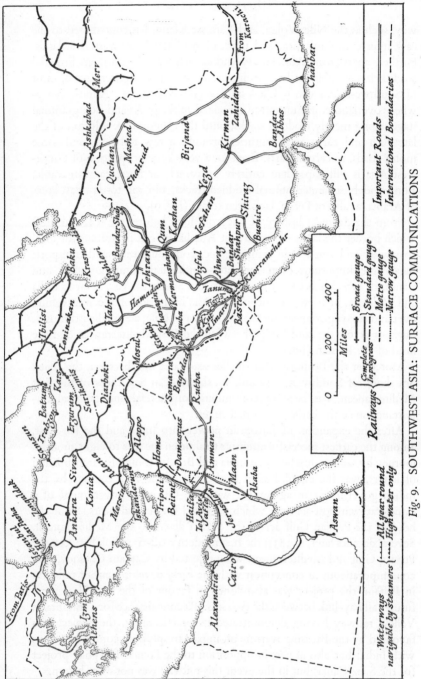

Fig. 9. SOUTHWEST ASIA: SURFACE COMMUNICATIONS

For the new Saudi Arabian line, see page 90.

With the coming of the steamship, the sea passage via the Cape of Good Hope was reduced in time by months, and had the advantage also of greater safety than the overland camel-caravan connections. But it was the completion of the Suez Canal, in November 1869, after nearly thirty years of diplomatic discussions concerning it among the Great Powers, which finally ushered in the modern era of inter-oceanic and inter-continental transport and communication through Southwest Asia, even though the canal is territorially within Egypt and therefore politically in Africa. Thereby these lands and their offshore seaways became finally invested with their world political and economic significance in the modern sense.

THE SUEZ CANAL

The Suez Canal, with a depth of 42 ft., permits vessels of up to 45,000 tons burthen[1] to pass directly from the Mediterranean to the Red Sea: even between London and Bombay the saving, as compared with the Cape route, amounts to nearly 4500 sea-miles. Hence, for all maritime world-powers, and most of all for Britain, the Suez Canal-Red Sea-Strait of Bab el-Mandeb waterway and its shores, along with those of their approaches, acquired in 1869 an incalculably increased politico-economic significance which has not waned even in the air age.

In its early development the canal was an expression of Franco-British rivalry. Even though the French government has no shares in it, the Canal company is French, and it was not until six years after the opening of the canal that the British government secured a quantity of the company's shares which, although large, yet remained less than a half of the total, that is 176,602 out of 400,000 or 44% of the total. Strange as it may now appear, at first the project for a French ship canal through Ottoman-Egyptian territory was met by the British government with strenuous hostility: it was viewed as a French threat to the British command of the seas, and as a renewed French attempt to gain influence in the Orient at the expense of, or in rivalry with, that of Britain; perhaps eventually a French protectorate over Egypt might result. British reactions included the strengthening of Malta, the re-occupation of Perim, and the declaration of a protectorate over Socotra.

But, from the outset, the canal proved to be of far greater significance to Britain than to any other power; economically, in that British ships have nearly always formed an absolute majority of those passing through;

[1] By the addition of a new by-pass canal of the same dimensions, near El Ballah (some 30 miles from Port Said), and deepening the existing canal by 20 inches throughout its length, the canal is to be improved within 5 years to allow greatly accelerated passage of ships up to 36 ft. draught.

politically in that the Commonwealth and dependent territories of Britain
east of Suez were, and have remained, far greater, whether areally or
demographically, than those of any other colonial power.

During the canal's first decade British and French tonnage, respectively,
formed rather more than 76% and little more than 8% of the totals,
followed by Dutch tonnage with about 4%. In the succeeding decade
although the tonnage of both countries was absolutely greater, their
percentages of the total tonnage declined, but the British portion has
rarely been much less than 50% and often nearer 70%. The tonnage of
other nationalities has reflected changes in their national economy
consequent on political changes. The acquisition of East Africa by
Germany greatly increased the amount of German tonnage through the
canal before World War I, and the conquest of Abyssinia by Italy greatly
increased Italian tonnage before World War II—in 1936 Italy's share,
previously 6%, rose to 18%. But throughout the history of the canal,
until World War II, U.S.A. and Russian tonnage have been comparatively negligible, though in 1905 a portion of the Russian Baltic Fleet
passed through to its destruction by the Japanese at Tsushima.

In 1938, the total nett tonnage through the canal amounted to nearly
$34\frac{1}{2}$ millions; of which, nearly 9 millions to and from India, Burma,
Ceylon, and Siam; nearly $8\frac{1}{2}$ millions to and from China, Japan, Philippines, and Indo-China; nearly $5\frac{3}{4}$ millions, largely tankers, to and from the
Persian Gulf; less than $3\frac{3}{4}$ millions to and from Malaya; while East Africa
and Australasia together claimed less than $2\frac{1}{4}$ millions. In 1948 the
number of ships increased to 8686 and the total nett tonnage to 55 millions.
The bulk of this traffic is still British, but America now holds second
place, owing almost entirely to the oil traffic from Saudi Arabia. Of the
daily average of 25 ships passing through, 14 are tankers.

During both world wars, the canal was of incalculable importance; in
World War I for supplies and men, especially from India and Australia,
to the forces in Arabia and Palestine engaged in shattering the enemy
Ottoman Empire in Southwest Asia and Southeast Europe; in World
War II, as a 'front-door' used from the back, for supplies and men from
Britain arriving via the Cape for the forces opposing Germany and Italy
in North Africa.

A contributory cause of World War II was the Italian fear that the sea
link with her East African empire might be severed at Suez. In acute
form, this dated from the time of the conquest of Ethiopia, when there
was sanctions talk of closure of this long-internationalized[1] waterway. It

[1] Use of the Canal by shipping of all nations, in peace and war, was agreed by the 1888
Convention of Constantinople.

was intensified by the stationing, under the Anglo-Egyptian Treaty of 1936, of British military and air forces in territory alongside the Canal. Moreover the Italians could hardly forget that French money and officials were dominant in the ownership, servicing, and administration of the Canal. Before World War II, Italy received through the Suez Canal roughly 17% of her supplies.

It is significant of the political place the Suez Canal still holds in men's minds that recently Britain was accused in Cairo of seeking the right to construct an outflanking ship canal via Gaza to the Dead Sea and thence to Akaba. Such accusations must be related to the approaching reversion to Egyptian control of the Suez Canal in 1968; to the new ties by treaty between Britain and Jordan; and the assumption that the Negeb will eventually form part of the state of Israel.

With the opening of the Suez Canal in 1869, earlier projects for overland links across the land-bridge between the Levant and the head of the Persian Gulf, whether by road or railway, fell temporarily into abeyance, but only to re-emerge as a new basis for acute international rivalry later in the century.

HIGHWAYS AND ROADS

In the 15th and 16th centuries the Ottoman Empire, including the northwestern parts of Southwest Asia, is said to have had one of the best road systems in the world, by which all principal towns were connected by well-engineered highways and good bridges, with posting-houses and inns for travellers. But, as the empire declined, so did the road system fall into decay and, already before the railway era, it was derelict.

Beyond the limits of the Ottoman Empire, in Persia, an internal route system with good bridges, and stone causeways across marshes, was in existence during the 16th and 17th centuries, but it was not maintained during the 18th century, and, by the end of the 19th century had become completely out-of-date. In Arabia, apart from an occasional freak, no roads at all were constructed until recent times.

In 1923, the new republican Turkey had only 4600 miles of road in Anatolia and Thrace together, most of which were in complete disrepair. But, already by the outbreak of World War II, there were more than 10,000 miles of roads, motorable except in bad weather, even though less than three-quarters were in a state of good repair. The new roads were planned to supplement the new railways, so as to form a grid of modern communication lines centering on the new capital, Ankara. Even so, many parts of the country were still quite inaccessible even by road. But a new programme of trunk-road construction was started in 1939, by which a further 20,000 miles of motorable roads were to be built in ten years.[1]

In Persia, a few short lengths of carriage road in and near principal towns were built during the latter half of the 19th century. But, apart from those in the oil-field areas of the extreme southwest, only during World War I did modern road construction really begin: highways for light motor traffic at all seasons were built, but mainly in the northwest and southwest. During World War II, British, American, and Russian engineers made many improvements, so that now there is a network which interconnects principal urban centres in all main parts of the country, including through north-south and through west-east roads, with general convergence on Tehran.

With the closure of the Mediterranean Sea access to Southwest Asia, the *coup d'état* in Iraq of Rashid Ali, and actual and threatened German activities in Persia, Britain and U.S.S.R. occupied respectively the south and north of Persia. Thenceforward several roads, in supplement to the one railway from the Persian Gulf, acquired great significance as 'back-door' supply routes to U.S.S.R. Particularly valuable were the following roads: from the port of Khorramshahr on the Shatt el-Arab, via Ahwaz, Dizful, and Qum to Tehran; from the port of Bushire on the Persian Gulf via Shiraz and Isfahan to Tehran; and from the port of Bandar Abbas on the Strait of Hormuz, via Yezd and Kashan to Tehran. From Tehran, roads across the Elburz Mountains provided links with the sea ports of Pahlevi and Bandar Shah, on the southern shores of the Caspian, whence inland sea transport could be effected to the Soviet railway system at Baku, at the eastern extremity of the Caucasus. In addition, although to a lesser extent, the road from the more easterly and smaller port of Chahbar on the Gulf of Oman, via Zahidan at the western termination of the railway from Pakistan, to Meshed, and thence to Ashkhabad on the Turk-Sib railway in Turkestan, was of importance. Immense quantities of British and U.S.A. supplies were transported along these routes for the Soviet armies operating on the Caucasus front and at Stalingrad.

In Syria, modern wheeled transport developed late, and until the end of the 19th century, apart from the carriage-road between Beirut and Damascus, even wagon roads were very few. But during World War I Allied military needs imposed the construction of new roads, so that by

---

[1] Recent reports place about 15,000 miles of roads under the jurisdiction of the Minister of Public Works, but only about half of this mileage can be used with safety by ordinary motor vehicles.

1918, for the first time since the Roman era, Syria had acquired the elements of a road system. Under French Mandate administration during the inter-war period, much road-building was carried out mainly to meet economic needs, so that now, except in very remote parts, transport is largely by road vehicles. Western Syria has three north-south trunk roads, parallel with the coast and major relief features, which connect with those of Palestine to the south and of Turkey to the north; they are inter-connected, at wide intervals, by west-east roads. Eastern Syria has no continuous metalled roads, but in the main, the desert tracks are suitable for motor traffic, and there is a regular desert motor-bus service between Damascus and Baghdad via Palmyra.

In Palestine, Roman roads were still in use in the Middle Ages, and in many places even until the end of the 19th century; in addition, a few so-called carriage roads were constructed after 1890. But at the beginning of World War I there were no first-class roads, and only the Jaffa-Jerusalem road was in fair condition. During World War I, for military reasons, and especially in the few years before World War II, for economic reasons, and afterwards during World War II, for both military and economic reasons, there was considerable improvement, so that now first-class roads connect all the principal towns and even many villages. There are two main south-north roads; the coast road from Gaza via Haifa to the Syrian coast road, and the interior road from Beersheba via Jerusalem to the Syrian central road. These are connected by several west-east roads in the manner of the West Syrian road system.

In Jordan there are very few metalled roads but a number of the desert tracks have been improved to take motor vehicles: the old north-south 'pilgrim route' along the edge of the desert has been improved to take light vehicles between Amman and Maan, and, some 10 to 20 miles to the west, a road to take heavy vehicles has been constructed between Amman and Akaba, at the head of the Gulf of Akaba, and a 'back-door' sea approach to Jordan, while from Jerusalem to Amman there is a first-class metalled road.

Finally, along the oil pipe-line, and marked by a succession of landing-grounds for aircraft, there is the new trunk road, fit for heavy lorries in almost all weather, from Haifa, via Amman to the water wells of Rutba in Iraq and so on to Baghdad. This, the modern fulfilment of pre-railway era projects to traverse by road the land-bridge between the head of the Persian Gulf and the Mediterranean, must be considered the principal *raison d'être* of the curious northeast extension of Jordan territory so as to form a contiguous frontier with that of the equally curious western extension of Iraqi territory, even at the expense of severing, except by the grace of rights of free passage, the age-old communication links between Nejd and Damascus. The intention is, through the close treaty ties of Britain, Transjordan, and Iraq, to ensure indirect British protection not only for the pipe-line, but also for the alongside road and air-corridor.

In Iraq, before 1900, there was an almost complete lack of wagon roads and permanent bridges, but during World War I military requirements led to many tracks being made passable for light motor-vehicles in dry weather, while during the inter-war period, more than 5000 miles of fair-weather motor-roads were constructed, even though only some 500 miles have a metalled surface. Main roads are, between Basra and Baghdad along both Tigris and Euphrates banks; between Baghdad and Mosul along the Tigris bank and via Kirkuk to connect with a Turkish road from Istanbul and Ankara at Nusaybin; between Baghdad and Khanaqin, to connect with the Kermanshah-Hamadan road to Tehran; between Baghdad and Rutba for Amman and Haifa. Therefore, Baghdad, as the centre upon which roads converge radially from widely separated important parts of Southwest Asia, is a land-route centre of major significance. A further important new road in Iraq is that from Kirkuk alongside the oil pipe-line to Rutba.

In Saudi Arabia, in general, roads are notably absent. The only metalled and asphalted roads are the short length in Western Arabia from the port of Jidda to Mecca, and in eastern Arabia, where the Arabian-American oil company has constructed good roads in the vicinity of the oil camp of Dhahran, and connected the latter with the neighbouring Persian Gulf sea ports of al-Khobar, Damman, Ras Tannura, and Jubail. There are un-metalled but motorable 'roads' from Mecca to Medina, and from Mecca to the Saudi capital Riyadh.

Moreover, in view of the frequent need on the part of oil-company and Saudi officials to travel between Riyadh, the oilfield, and the ports, and of the increasing amount of imports to Nejd via Persian Gulf ports, a similar motorable improved track has been established between Riyadh and Jubail. These provide a motorable route across the Arabian peninsula, between Jidda on the Red Sea, and Jubail on the Persian Gulf, passing via the holy city of Mecca and the Saudi capital, and thus of considerable strategic significance as a centrally located trans-peninsular land-route. In addition there are motorable tracks from Riyadh to Aden via San'a; from Jidda to Ma'an and to Aden; and from Medina to Baghdad and Basra.

Given the abundant production of petroleum within Arabia, it is likely that motor transport services will continue to develop rapidly in that country, which will thus skip directly from slow camel-caravan transport to rapid motor transport, supplemented, for long distances, by air transport. This change, along with the greatly increased amount and wide dispersion of modern material equipment of all kinds that the oil royalties will permit, is in process of effecting revolutionary changes in the economic and strategic significance of Arabia, with unpredictable political consequences.

RAILWAYS

When, soon after its submission to the British government in 1831, the project for a strategic road between the Mediterranean and Persian Gulf was considered abortive, a syndicate put forward proposals in 1836 for the 'Euphrates Valley' railway. But rivalry between the great European powers resulted in nearly twenty years delay before the Ottoman government granted any concessions for railways in its territory, and even these were for connection of the European parts of the Ottoman Empire to Istanbul. In its Asiatic parts, railway construction began only in 1871, at first solely with Ottoman government resources; the first line was that known as the Anatolian railway, from Haydarpasha on the eastern shore of the Bosporus opposite Istanbul, to Konya, with only a branch line to Ankara. By 1880 a concession for continuing the work was given to a British group, but, with the development of German influence in Ottoman government circles, the concession passed in 1889 to a German group. The line was completed to Konya in 1896, and thenceforward Konya was regarded as the starting point of the proposed 'Baghdad railway'; a line conceived largely for strategic and political ends, that is as a means of outflanking the British water-link to India via the Suez Canal, and as a means of extending the German zone of influence to the head of the Persian Gulf, as part of the German thrust towards Asia.

But it was not until 1902 that the concession was granted for a line from Konya across the Taurus Mountains and Amanus range to Nusaybin, Mosul, Baghdad, and Basra. An easier route, but in part seeming to head for the Caucasus, i.e. via Sivas and Harput for Diarbekr and Mosul, although favoured by the Ottoman government, was rejected, largely in deference to Russian opposition on strategic grounds. During the period 1903–14, several sections of the Baghdad railway were constructed, all single-track, including one from Baghdad northwest to Samarra on the Tigris. During World War I, apart from two difficult sections in the Taurus and Amanus mountains, the whole of the line from Konya to Resulayn, west of Nusaybin, was in use for the transport of supplies and reinforcements to the Ottoman armies on the Palestine and Mesopotamian fronts. For its part, the opposing British army had extended the Baghdad-Samarra section considerably to the north, that is to Baiji on the Tigris. Thus, at the close of World War I there remained two long uncompleted sections, one in northern Iraq, and southern Turkey between Resulayn via Mosul and Baiji, the other in southern Iraq between Baghdad and Basra. With the eclipse of German influence, and the collapse of the Ottoman government, the line was completed by the British civil administration in Iraq after World War I. But it was not until 1940, that is 44 years after its commencement at Konya, and 59 years after the start at Haydarpasha, that the last section was finally completed, and the whole line Istanbul-Baghdad made available without breaks: the first through train to the Bosporus left Baghdad in July 1940.

Conceived as an arterial route across the territory of a single political power, the line now traverses the territories of three states, Turkey, Syria, and Iraq, and also forms, from Nusaybin almost to Aleppo, the political boundary of Syria and Turkey, both states having reciprocal rights in the use of this section, including the transport of troops.

During World War II, the closure of the Mediterranean to Allied shipping diverted much traffic for Turkey to Basra and the Baghdad railway via Mosul, while the German advance through Southern Russia led to the concentration on Basra and the railway as far as Baghdad, of vast quantities, of military supplies for the 'back-door' trans-Iran route to U.S.S.R. via Khanaqin. Hence the capacity of the line was greatly increased by the addition of rolling-stock and passing loops.

The single-track narrow-gauge Hejaz railway, built exclusively by Moslem capital, served both pan-Islamic cultural and Ottoman strategic ends, in that while functioning as a pilgrim transit line, it also enabled the Ottoman government to hold Medina with troops and to send them from the railhead even to remote Yemen. For security reasons, at the expense of economic considerations, it was laid at some distance from the coast, so as to be out of range of naval guns, the major threat of the time. At only two points were there branch lines to the Mediterranean, that is, from Damascus to Beirut and from Deraya to Haifa, the latter being thereby transformed from an insignificant fishing village to a rapidly-growing seaport. The Damascus-Maan section was opened in 1904, and the remainder in succeeding years before the outbreak of World War I. During the latter war, the line was wrecked from Medina approximately to Maan in Jordan, and has not since been restored, so that it may finally be superseded by a motorable road, as already stated.

During World War I, to meet Allied military needs on the Palestine front, and in little danger from enemy naval guns, a single-track standard-

gauge line was built along the Mediterranean coastal plain, from the
Suez Canal at Al Qantara to Haifa. During the inter-war period this was
extended through Syria, via Beirut and Tripoli to Homs, where it joins
the interior line for Aleppo. From its inception, this line was much more
significant for world strategy than was the Hejaz line in that it was conceived as part of an inter-continental link between Africa, Asia, and
Europe, joining Alexandria and Cairo via Aleppo on the Baghdad railway
to Istanbul and the Orient line for Paris.

A further important line is projected, with substantially the same alignment as one proposed in 1836; it is to connect Haifa, passing north of
Amman via Rutba to Baghdad, crossing the Euphrates at Ramadi north
of Al-Habbaniya lake. But, for the present, this seems to be in abeyance
in favour of the existing pipe-line motor road via Rutba.

In 1923, when the Kemalist republican government of Turkey took
over, a vigorous policy of railway construction was adopted.[1] The
through line from Istanbul, via Ankara and Sivas to Erzurum, linking
west to east Turkey, was opened for traffic in 1939. From this, a line to the
southeast via Malatya and Diarbekr has been completed and is in course of
being linked with Mosul in northern Iraq; while there is a project to connect with the Persian railways by a train-ferry across Lake Van and eastward continuation north of Lake Urumiah. Two important lines, linking
seaports of the well-populated Black Sea coast zone to the interior plateau
lines, were completed to Samsun and Zonguldak in 1932 and 1937, but
Trabzon, nearer to the Soviet frontier, remains unconnected with the
Batumi terminus of the U.S.S.R. broad-gauge railways.

Between Erzurum and Leninakan (formerly Alexandropol) just within
the Soviet frontier southwest of Tbilisi (Tiflis), there is a line of three
different gauges. The Russian broad-gauge branch line of the Tbilisi-
Tabriz line, passes from Leninakan through Kars to Sarikamis, and thus
has a length within Turkey of 76 miles; between Sarikamis and Erzurum
is a narrow-gauge line completed in occupied Ottoman territory during
World War I by the Russians in 1916; while from Erzurum westwards
the line is standard-gauge. Lastly, in 1939, with the transfer of the Sanjak
of Alexandretta (Iskanderun) from Syria, the Turkish government took
over the important Iskanderun branch line linking the Baghdad railway
to the sea on the shores of the Gulf of Iskanderun.

All the lines in Turkey are single-track and standard-gauge, apart from
the narrow-gauge and broad-gauge exceptions to the east of Erzurum
already noted.

---

[1] During the last 25 years the railway mileage of Turkey has been doubled, and 1,400 miles
of entirely new railway are planned for construction in 1950–65.

7

Iran had virtually no railways until 1927. The principal exception was the extension during World War I, in 1916, of the broad-gauge Russian railway from the frontier at Julfa to Tabriz. But, after 1927, through the personal initiative of Riza Shah, standard-gauge lines were constructed, partly to tighten political control over the whole country by the central government in Tehran, partly to distribute more readily the agricultural products of the fertile northern lands to the more arid lands of the south, but also to make Iran less dependent in foreign trade on the two world powers with spheres of influence in Persia namely the U.S.S.R. and Britain.

With a view to circumventing Soviet control in the north and British control in the south, the important trans-Iran line was contracted mainly to Germans in the north and to Americans in the south, and was financed entirely by Persian capital. Begun in 1927, it was completed for traffic in 1938, as a single-track standard-gauge line, from the sea-port of Bandar Shahpur (on the Khor-Musa channel at the head of the Persian Gulf, and so well within Persian territory and far enough away from the Iraqi port of Basra), via Ahwaz and Andimeshk in the Ab-i-Diz valley, through the Bakhtiari country, to Qum and Tehran, whence it was continued via Garmsar to the Caspian seaport of Bandar Shah.

A second line from Tehran northwestwards via Kazvin and Mianeh to Tabriz was completed for traffic to Mianeh by the end of 1942, and is to have a western branch north of Lake Urumiah to join the Turkish system, as already mentioned. A third line eastwards from Garmsar was completed as far as Shahrud in 1941, and is to extend to Meshed, and eventually, thence to the Soviet Transcaspian railway, probably at Ashkhabad. Finally, a fourth line was constructed southeastwards from Qum via Kashan to Yezd, with likelihood, eventually, of continuation via Kirman to Bam, and possibly Zahidan to form connection with the Pakistan railway system. All these lines are single-track and standard-gauge, so that break of bulk is imposed at points of connection with broad-gauge lines, as at Tabriz.

During World War II, when Soviet and British military forces occupied Persia, the Trans-Iran railway immediately acquired great importance as a supply line for war material to the Soviet front. The capacity of this single-track line, therefore, was greatly increased by the provision of additional sidings, passing-loops, and water-storage facilities, and by a greatly increased number of wagons and engines brought from both U.S.A. and Britain. In addition, two new port-terminals were established on the Shatt el-Arab, namely Tanuma, in Iraq opposite Basra, with a new submersible road-and-railway bridge across the Shatt el-Arab, and Khorram

Shahr farther downstream, in Iran, both of which were provided with railway links to the Trans-Iran railway at Ahwaz. Thus, with its original terminal seaport of Bandar Shahpur, the trans-Persian railway now has three terminal ports directly accessible to sea-going craft. Very large quantities of war material passed along this line to the Caspian; in mid-1944 the annual rate was approximately 2 million tons.

In Iraq, besides the standard-gauge railway from Baghdad along the Tigris to Mosul and the Syrian frontier, the Baghdad-Basra line, constructed during World War I on different gauges as available material and the conditions of the advancing Allied front permitted, finally emerged in the inter-war period as a metre-gauge line along the Euphrates, considered sufficient for peace-time economic purposes. Break of gauge, therefore, takes place at Baghdad.

In the same period, a metre-gauge line was constructed from Baghdad northeastwards along the Diyala valley to Qaraghan, whence the main line continued northwestwards to Kirkuk and a branch line passed north eastwards beyond Khanaqin. Further, during World War II, a new metre-gauge line was laid from the river port of Kut al-Imara on the Tigris to near Baquba on the Baghdad-Khanaqin line to help increase the capacity of the Khanaqin line, beyond which 600 miles of road haulage via Kermanshah to Tabriz, were used in the effort to get supplies to the Soviet front. In addition to supplies for the Russian front, much traffic for the British forces in Palestine and Egypt passed along the line to Baghdad, to go thence by overland motor transport. Hence the capacity of this line was increased to the maximum, by every possible device.

In Syria and Lebanon, roughly two-thirds of the total are standard-gauge railways, the remainder being narrow-gauge, and the entire system is single-track. The earliest line was the Beirut-Damascus narrow-gauge line built under an Ottoman government concession to the French, and opened in 1895; next followed the Damascus-Amman section of the narrow-gauge Hejaz railway which was opened in 1904, and in 1906 its link to the coast from Deraa to Haifa. Completed in 1906 also, was the standard-gauge line from Rayak, on the Beirut-Damascus line, to Aleppo, where it was joined by the Baghdad line in 1914, while the standard-gauge line from the coast at Tripoli to Homs, on the line to Aleppo was opened in 1911.

During the inter-war French Mandate period, there was very little railway construction. But during World War II, after the military campaigns of 1941, the British government built the standard-gauge line from Haifa via Beirut to Tripoli, and so extended the coastal-plain line built by the British government in Palestine during World War I. This was connected with the existing line from Tripoli to Homs for Aleppo, thus completing the standard-gauge through line from Alexandria and Cairo to the Istanbul-Baghdad railway.

In Palestine and Jordan, as in Syria and Lebanon, all railways are single-track. The standard-gauge lines include, besides the main coastal-plain line, its branch lines from Lydda to the coast at Jaffa, and inland to Jerusalem. In addition, there is the narrow-gauge line from Haifa to Samakh on the Syrian frontier, which is continued thence to Deraa on the Hejaz railway south of Damascus.

In Jordan, the only railway is that part of the narrow-gauge Hejaz railway, south of the Syrian frontier at Nasib, to Maan, which was opened in 1904. Although greatly damaged during World War I, it was restored during the inter-war period as far as Maan. During World War II, with the closing of the Mediterranean route, when all the possible 'back-doors' of Southwest Asia accessible via the Cape sea route were exploited to the full, the seaport of Akaba, southwest of Maan, became one of the ports of entry and, to supplement its motor road to Maan, an extension of the railway from Maan as far as Akaba was in progress, but abandoned only half-completed after the Allied occupation of North Africa and the consequent re-opening of the Mediterranean sea routes.

Until recently, apart from the shattered Hejaz line, Arabia had no railways. Now, in Saudi Arabia, an American single-track standard-gauge line is already completed from the 7,000 metre pier at the oil-port of Dammam, via Dhahran to Abqaiq and Hufuf. It is being extended to Qurain, some 100 miles south of Riyadh, and thence to Riyadh itself, which it is expected to reach by the end of 1951.

Thus, political and economic circumstances have endowed Southwest Asia with a skeletal railway system which is single-track in its entirety, and within which four different gauges are in use, namely broad, standard, metre, and narrow. But much of it, especially in Iran, Iraq, Palestine and Syria, is oil-burning, and so both up-to-date and independent of fuel imported from overseas.

AIRWAYS

For the present, surface motor-transport and air transport are relatively more important than rail transport for inter-continental communications between Europe, Asia, and Africa. Surface motor transport is less advantageous economically and strategically than railway transport, but its mobility, adaptability, and cheapness of installation, are great advantages where railways are not already in existence. Even so, as a regular means of communication, surface motor-transport is more important in relation to relatively small areas, while aircraft, which cover vast distances in short times, are more important in relation to very large areas (*Fig.* 10).

In Southwest Asia, the pioneer air line was the regular postal-service established by British military authorities in 1921, between Cairo and Baghdad, by which, as a distant echo of the late-18th century camel-caravan post-service, the Persian Gulf was brought within one day's journey of the Mediterranean, and the as yet unfulfilled 19th-century project for a direct railway from the Persian Gulf to the Mediterranean, was anticipated. For some years this service, at first once a fortnight, then once a week, remained the only airline between Mesopotamia and the Mediterranean. After a few years operation by British military authorities, the service was handed over to Imperial Airways to run: it was routed from Egypt via south Palestine, Jordan, and the Rutba oasis, to Baghdad and Basra. In 1929 the service was extended northwestwards to London, and southeastwards to Karachi, whereby the long-pursued aim of fast communication between England and India was consummated, and Southwest Asia acquired even greater significance as a transit area for major communication lines of the Old World.

In 1930, the governments of Egypt, Iraq, and Saudi Arabia, began preparations for the establishment of air fleets of their own. Early in 1931, the French air route from Marseille to Beirut, in French mandated territory, and thence to Baghdad, was extended to India and Saigon, in French Indo-China. At about the same time, a German line was established from Baghdad via Tehran and Baku to Moscow. Thus, Franco-British-German rivalry in Southwest Asia was resurrected in a new form of great intensity, and command of the seas was revealed as no longer sufficient as a means of furthering and protecting British trading and diplomatic activities in the Orient.

With the contemporaneous development of the East African air route from Europe via Cairo to Cape Town, Cairo and Baghdad have emerged as the twin air *carrefours* of the Euro-Asia-Africa land bridge, and at present thirteen differently-located international air routes cross Arabia, making it a land of world passage instead of the land of isolation that it remained until yesterday. The political potentialities of these air-age changes in geographical values can be appreciated by reference to the recent denial by Pakistan, India, and Burma, of landing-ground facilities and air-passage to Dutch aircraft *en route* for the Indonesian 'police action' region. All the South West Asia countries but particularly the Arab states of Syria, Jordan, Iraq, and Saudi Arabia have analogous negative

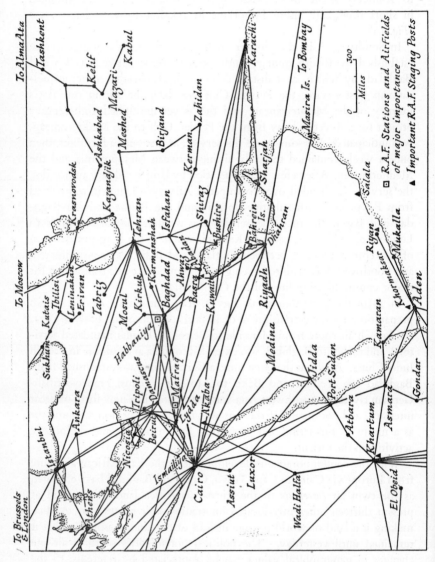

Fig. 10. SOUTHWEST ASIA: CIVIL AIR ROUTES

power of denial, which would be all the more effective if operated col-lectively, as might well be the case by Arab League collaboration.

Moreover, in view of the winter weather-conditions over Soviet Asia, quite apart from Soviet politics, it is readily seen that an all-season round-the-world air route is hardly practicable without the use of landing grounds in, or air-space over, Southwest Asia, so that even the Old World significance of the land-bridge is now greatly extended.

At the present time, regular civil air services interconnect many of the principal population centres of Southwest Asia, besides connecting these with the outer world. In Turkey, Istanbul and Ankara are the two centres principally served. In Persia, Tehran is the link centre between U.S.S.R. and the rest of Southwest Asia, Africa and the Orient, while a number of main towns along the Tehran-Meshed-Zahidan Isfahan-Tehran quadri-lateral have air-line connections; several international lines, between Europe and Karachi, cross or skirt southern Persia. In Arabia, Aden, besides being an important local air-route centre, is a starting-place for a number of services which connect, via Khartum, Addis Ababa or Mogadishu, and Kisumu, to the East Africa and Egypt lines, as well as via Port Sudan to Jidda and Medina; there is also a trans-peninsular service, from Jidda via the Saudi capital, Riyadh, to Dhahran near the Persian Gulf; in addition one international line from Cairo to Bombay passes via Dhahran, from which also, there are several important connections, for example, to Baghdad and Lydda; further, Jidda has a service via Medina to Cairo, while several international lines, from Cairo to Karachi and Bombay, cross the peninsula without making use of Arabian landing-grounds. Palestine, Syria, and Lebanon, enjoy a number of local services from Lydda, Beirut, Tripoli, and Damascus, along with important ser-vices to Europe, via Istanbul or Athens, and to North Africa via Cairo.

But, excluding Cairo, strictly in Africa, the Iraqi capital, Baghdad, must be considered the most important single air-route centre in that it is the main convergence and interchange-point of Southwest Asia, and as such, has more air routes to and from it than any other place in this region. Thus, the combination of transport facilities by air, rail, road, and river, makes this city, barely accessible but a few decades ago, the dominant communications centre within Southwest Asia, and therefore of vital politico-economic significance.

NEW STRATEGICAL CONSIDERATIONS

Denial to the Allies during World War II of the Mediterranean sea-access to Egypt and Palestine, and the threatened German advance

towards the Baghdad railway, along with the subsequent changed
political relationship to their former Soviet ally, the withdrawal of British
troops from Egypt (the Canal zone apart) in 1947, and the changed conditions in Palestine consequent on the cessation of the British Mandate,
have resulted in the adoption by Britain of new strategical measures in
relation to Southwest Asia, the Suez canal zone, and Egypt, all of which
are primarily concerned with communications.

Libya, including Cyrenaica, Tripoli, and Fezzan, is to be constituted
an independent State by 1952. But Cyrenaica, although already granted
a measure of autonomy, is to remain until then under British administration. It seems certain, therefore, that the important seaport of Benghazi,
the harbour and potential military base of Tobruk, and a number of airfields within reach of the east Mediterranean lands, will be not only
beyond the possibility of immediate control by a hostile power, but
available to British forces in case of need. In extension of the potential
defence opportunities provided by Cyrenaica, British Cyprus, admirably
located close to, and between, Turkey, Syria, Palestine, and lower
Egypt, is to have an entirely new development of Royal Air Force
installations near the sea, in Famagusta district at the eastern end of the
island. As insurance against the possible failure of these two bases, for
example in the repeated event of closure of the Mediterranean, a vast
new military depot of arms and equipment is in process of creation near
Mackinnon Road, on the Kenya railway from Mombasa to Nairobi,
the location of which was chosen in relation to the partial withdrawal of
British troops from Egypt in 1947.

Just as the 'back-door' routes of Iraq and Iran were used to send
powerful succour to the Soviet forces beleaguered by the German
invaders between the Caucasus and the Volga, and just as those of Jordan
and Iraq were successfully used to build up powerful forces for the
annihilation of the enemy forces in North Africa, so, in the event of
invasion of Southwest Asia countries from the north, could the same
points of entry and lines of supply be used again in defensive warfare.
Besides the military depôt at Mackinnon Road, an East African naval
force based on the port of Mombasa is being formed; the distances from
Mombasa to Akaba and Suez, or to Basra, Khorram Shahr, and Bandar
Shahpur are significantly shorter than from Britain via the Cape. Moreover, in view of the contemplated connection of the railway line from
Mombasa to Broken Hill in Northern Rhodesia, the railway link from
Cape Town, with supplies of food and raw material along route, can
be regarded as a supplementary line of supply to that of the East African
sea route from Cape Town, quite apart from overland and air connections

that, as in World War II, may be developed from the West African ports.

On the other hand, it is significant of Soviet 'Iron Curtain' politics, that, to the north of Southwest Asia, there is only one civil air route connection between Soviet territory and this important land-bridge area, namely that between Tehran and Moscow; there are no civil air connections across the Black Sea between southern Russia and Turkey, nor any around the Caucasus from Turkey or Persia to U.S.S.R., nor from Persia to Turkestan. That is, all civil air links between Southwest Asia and Soviet territory must be effected by Soviet-operated links along this single permitted route, just as all West European air links with Soviet territory must be similarly effected via the single permitted route from Leningrad to Moscow.

PROBLEM AREAS WITHIN THE MAJOR REGION

I PALESTINE–ISRAEL

It would be true to say that ever since the inclusion of Palestine within the Roman Empire in the latter half of the first century B.C., the cessation therewith of its political independence, and the development of the Diaspora, there has existed for world Jewry the political problem of Palestine. For the Arab world on the other hand, there was no such problem until after the final disruption of the Ottoman Empire in World War I, since, until then, Palestine for the Arabs was merely part of the wider Arab lands that collectively desired to throw off the Turkish yoke.

The real beginning of the political problem of Palestine in its modern form, that is not only for Jews and Arabs, but also for the interested Great Powers, can be dated from the advance, during World War I, of the Turco-German armies on Egypt by way of Palestine in 1915, the McMahon Pledge of 24th October 1915 with the ensuing Arab revolt, and the Balfour Declaration of 2nd November 1917 which guaranteed the establishment of a Jewish National Home in Palestine. Always, or almost always, since the fall of the Jewish State in 65 B.C. some Jews have been living in Palestine; even so, in 1919 there were fewer than 60,000, and these formed only some 8% of its total population which, by contrast, was more than 80% Moslem.

The British Mandated territory of Palestine[1] was brought into being by the Treaty of Sèvres in 1920, with frontiers and conditions finally con-

[1] For a useful recent study of the development and potentialities of Palestine, see E. C. Willatts "Some Geographical Factors in the Palestine Problem," *Geographical Journal* CVIII (1947), pp. 146–79.

firmed by the Council of the League of Nations in 1922, and its areal extent and frontiers persisted without change until the withdrawal of the British occupying forces on the termination of the Mandate in May, 1948. Thereafter, military action between the Jewish forces of Palestine and Moslem forces of the five neighbouring Arab League countries, have left the territorial extents and frontiers of States still indeterminate even though the new Jewish State of Israel, partial successor to the British Mandated territory of Palestine, is now fully established. Israel was recognized *de facto* by the last remaining States, other than those of the Arab League, in January, 1949, and secured admission as a member of the United Nations in May, 1949, that is one year after the cessation of the British Mandate.

The character and extent of the political problem of Palestine in its territorial aspects are revealed clearly by the several partition plans proposed by the British authorities before the cessation of the Mandate, and later by the Bernadotte proposal under the auspices of the United Nations (see *Fig.* 11), each of which in turn was rejected by both Jews and Arabs.

Even so, the recent inflow of large numbers of Jewish Europeans and Asiatics, along with the outflow of large numbers of Moslem Arabs, have greatly altered the ethnic composition and balance of the population of the former Mandated territory. Already by 1938, before World War II, the number of Jews had more than sextupled to over 400,000, so that they formed nearly thirty per cent of the then total population of rather more than 1,415,000, of whom still some 70% were Moslems. But after World War II, already by the end of 1946 the number of Jews had increased to more than 608,000, while within the single year since the proclamation of the State of Israel a further 250,000 immigrant Jews arrived mainly from Europe. Consequently the Jewish population of Palestine is now about 1,250,000, that is about twenty times as many as at the commencement of the Mandate thirty years ago. Moreover, the Israeli Government's policy of an open door to the unlimited immigration of all Jews who wish to come is expected to result in a further annual influx of at least 200,000 persons. Indeed it is reported that Israel is planning to receive, by 1953, a further million Jewish immigrants. They will come mainly from Germany and Central or East European countries particularly Poland, but also from North Africa, south Arabia,[1] India and China. Thus it is expected that within the next four years the Jewish population of Israel will have attained at least two millions.

---

[1] 40,000 Yemeni Jews have arrived since the creation of the State of Israel, mainly by air lift, which to these primitives is the fulfilment of the prophesied return to the Promised Land "on the wings of an eagle."

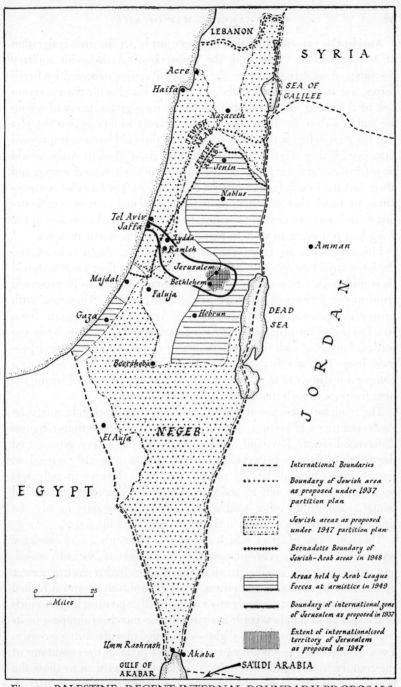

LEBANON

SYRIA

Acre

Haifa

SEA OF
GALILEE

Nazareth

JEWISH
ARAB

JEWISH
ARAB

Jenin

Nablus

Tel Aviv
Jaffa

Lydda
Ramleh

Amman

Jerusalem

Majdal

Bethlehem

Faluja

Gaza

Hebron

DEAD
SEA

J O R D A N

Beersheba

N E G E B

El Auja

E G Y P T

- - - - - - -   *International Boundaries*

+ + + + + + +   *Boundary of Jewish area*
                as proposed under 1937
                partition plan

Jewish areas as proposed
under 1947 partition plan

Bernadotte Boundary of
Jewish-Arab areas in 1948

Areas held by Arab League
Forces at armistice in 1949

Boundary of international zone
of Jerusalem as proposed in 1937

Extent of internationalised
territory of Jerusalem as
proposed in 1947

0   25
Miles

Umm Rashrash

Akaba

GULF OF
AKABAR

SA'UDI ARABIA

Fig. 11. PALESTINE: RECENT INTERNAL BOUNDARY PROPOSALS
AND CHANGES

Of the Arab League areas on this map, the Gaza strip is administratively Egypt,
while the main block in the East was annexed by Jordan in April, 1950.

Against this mass immigration of Jews must be set the mass emigration of Moslem Arabs. Following the outbreak of Arab-Jewish military hostilities, Arab refugees, from the parts of Palestine occupied by Israeli forces, are stated to number about 750,000. Faced with the enormous task of absorbing its vast numbers of Jewish immigrants, many of whom are still homeless, the Israeli Government has set its face against the plea that the Arab refugees should be re-settled in their old homes. It is argued that, even if they were permitted to return, these Moslem Arabs would now form cultural and political minorities in an environment strange and alien, and the Israelis further suggest that, with proper financial compensation by Israel, they be settled in sparsely populated parts of neighbouring Arab States, particularly the eastern side of the Jordan Valley in the Kingdom of Jordan, in western parts of Iraq, and in northern Syria.

Moreover there are at present still some 160,000 Arabs in Israel, and the latest British proposals are that roughly no more than 100,000 should be considered a safe maximum if the new Israeli State is to be preserved from undue dangers of minority irredentist activities. Therefore, with proper compensations, a further 60,000 Arabs should emigrate from Israel to one of the neighbouring Arab States, at present mainly Syria and Jordan, but later, with the development of its large-scale irrigation projects, Iraq. But, to offset this, since the 120,000 Jews in Iraq constitute a comparable danger to that State, most should migrate to Israel within the next five years. Such transfers have already commenced.

The resulting difference of population as between Israel and contiguous Arab countries will become, not only the sharply defined ethno-religious difference between Jews and Moslem Arabs, but in a very pronounced degree, the difference between on the one hand, a technically trained, in part highly educated, largely urban and largely literate (if polyglot) society from many countries and therefore with widespread interests and contacts, and, on the other hand, a largely illiterate peasantry mainly of a single ethnic group and with, in the main, only local interests.

This new State of Israel, which at best will have only a very restricted territory, is in a weak economic position. It has no coal, virtually no oil, and only relatively small potential capacity for hydro-electric power generation: its present electric power is obtained mostly from oil-fuelled generating plant. It has scarcely any raw materials, and must import much of its basic food supplies, yet it has virtually no merchant shipping of its own: also, as yet, it has only a slightly-developed manufacturing industry. Even so, the Israeli Government is determined to adapt the conditions of the country to its rapidly increasing population, rather than to allow the latter to be restricted by, and adapted to, the conditions of the country.

Before the outbreak of Israeli-Arab hostilities, the amount of land actually cultivated in the Mandated territory was nearly two million acres on which existed a rural population of 870,000, and of which area about one-fifth was in the Negeb. But the cultivated area was less than one-third of the total of the territory, and, except by irrigation, it was not generally believed that much more land could be brought under cultivation. As to irrigation, the possibilities of its extension were reviewed by the Partition Commission in 1938, which concluded that, on the most optimistic view, only an area equivalent to a further 70% of the 123,500 acres then irrigated could be added by new developments. It seems clear therefore that even with the maximum possible improvements in farming methods and land tenure, along with maximum possible increase of irrigated area, Israel can hardly hope to produce enough food for its likely population. As far as possible, however, cultivation will probably become as intensive as in the most closely cultivated parts of Holland and Belgium: within the next five years, the Government is aiming to settle on farms and in agricultural collectives partly of the *kibbutz* in type, a quarter of the total population. Production will, to an important extent, take the form of cash crops, notably the citrus fruits, grown mainly for Britain, although at present half of the 60,000 acres under orange groves in 1948 lie in a derelict state. Long-term agricultural improvements may include re-afforestation of the hilly plateau country in the east, which would gradually re-create soil there, and at the same time temper surface run-off, conserve water and modify seasonal flooding in the western plains.

Among the immigrants have come many thousands of industrialists and skilled workers who have made possible the rapid establishment of an astonishing variety of manufacturing industries. These include textile fabric mills, ready-made garment factories, diamond-cutting establishments, works for the making of optical goods and precision instruments, and factories for the production of cosmetics and pharmaceutical goods, located particularly in Tel Aviv: but almost all are on a small scale as yet. Nevertheless it is only by expanding these industries and developing others, mainly of a highly specialized kind on the Swiss model, that the new State can hope both to provide employment for many of its new arrivals and to develop the necessary amount of exports to pay for the imports of many kinds, without which it cannot even survive its present period of artificially-maintained existence, based largely on monetary gifts and loans mainly from Zionist and American Government sources. The industrial equipment necessary for the support of some two million people is still merely in the earliest stages of its creation.

At present, and probably for a long time to come, there is little hope of establishing an export trade to the neighbouring Arab States, primarily because of the boycott of Israeli goods for political reasons, but also because Israeli manufactured goods are too costly, in view of the enormous cost of living in Israel and the consequently high wages and costs of production. Hence the present trading trend is for Israel to turn away from Southwest Asia in search of markets in Europe and America. Apart from products of agriculture, mainly citrus and other sub-tropical fruits to Britain, the principal exports at present are potash from the Dead Sea, industrial diamonds, dentures, petroleum products, and soap. Imports include almost everything a modern community requires: besides food and raw materials, machinery of all kinds, building material and prefabricated houses, pipes for irrigation, motor-lorries and -tractors, fertilizers, telephone materials, and so on.

To handle these large quantities of goods, the ports of Haifa and Jaffa-Tel Aviv are to be greatly enlarged and modernized, and a new deepwater harbour is to be constructed near Tel Aviv. Further, an Israeli merchant marine is being created along with a nautical school for the training of several thousand Israeli sailors within the next few years. Schemes have been adumbrated even, for the establishment of an Israeli shipbuilding industry, in order to construct Israeli ships not only to fetch and carry food, raw materials, and manufactured goods, but also to provide 'invisible exports'.[1]

Tel Aviv, founded about 1910 on uninhabited sand dunes north of the old Arab port of Jaffa, and with a population in 1920 of only 8,000, illustrates the great recent changes: it has now over 300,000 inhabitants, and is likely to become an even larger urban manufacturing centre and port, with its own shipbuilding industry.

It can be inferred therefore that, in spite of fundamental weaknesses, Israel may well develop quickly into a powerful modern European type of State at the eastern end of the Mediterranean, which could function in relation to the less advanced neighbouring Arab States as a pioneer of both social and economic progress.

From the political point of view it is, above all, the mystical concept of the ingathering of the people of the Diaspora that unites the country and which promises to fuse its polyglot population from many countries into a Nation State. But Israel begins its independent life surrounded by the enmity of the Arab States, which are most unlikely, for a long time, to be partners in any proposed regional defence group of Southwest Asia

---

[1] Israel's navy recently made a 4,000-mile patrol in Mediterranean waters as part of its winter manœuvres.

States. Further, although far from being Communist, a declared principle of Israeli foreign policy is friendship with the U.S.S.R., therefore at present, Israel, for her part, is equally resistant to any proposal to join an alliance of Western Powers designed to defend Southwest Asia from Soviet encroachment. Moreover, Israel hopes the invaluable past Soviet support at the United Nations will be continued, and cannot forget that there are some two million Jews living within the U.S.S.R. and its sphere of influence.[1] Nevertheless, it seems unlikely at present that Israel will become an East Mediterranean foothold for Soviet domination of Southwest Asia.

Thus, as far as her political relations with other States are concerned, independence amounting almost to isolation promises to be the immediate future of Israel, with, as for the U.S.S.R., a declared policy of friendship for U.S.A., the source of so much of her indispensable financial support, both public and private, and with Britain, the Mandate scapegoat, cast largely in the role of a traditional enemy.

Finally, apart from the general political problem of Palestine as a whole, three other Palestine problems need mention. First, Jerusalem, in its Old City, site of the Temple, original cult centre of Judaism, site of the Church of the Holy Sepulchre of Christ, and site not only of the magnificent 7th century mosque of the Dome of the Rock but also of the sacred place whence the Prophet is believed by Moslems to have taken flight on his magic steed to Heaven, is of surpassing religious significance to Jewry, Christendom, and Islamdom in many countries. Moreover, consequent on the Israeli-Arab military hostilities, the New City, mixed and cosmopolitan in character, is in possession of the Israelis, while the Old City, predominantly Arab in population and character, is in that of the King of Jordan.

Permanent partition was suggested, in acceptance of the present *de facto* position, with an Israeli municipality in the New City and a Jordani municipality in the Old City, both to have wide local powers although not sovereign rights, and both to be put under the final control of a United Nations High Commissioner as international safeguard for unrestricted access to the holy places. But, on account of the mystical attraction of Jerusalem for Jews everywhere, as well as for reasons of national pride and cultural continuity, the Israelis insist on having at least the New City fully incorporated in their new State as its capital. On the other hand, the Jordanis consider control of the Old City essential for the military security of Arab Palestine. Hence, a further suggestion was to build close at hand a new Arab city, corresponding to the Jewish New

[1] In U.S.S.R. alone some two millions.

City, in which the 20,000 Arabs of the Old City could be re-housed. This would have reserved the Old City for the needs of its Christian, Muslim, and Jewish sanctuaries and their pilgrims, as also for the seat of an international body appointed by the United Nations to exercise authority over all the Holy Places. In the event, the United Nations reached a decision, in December 1949, that Jerusalem and its surrounding area shall be internationalized. But neither Britain nor the U.S.A. supported this decision; the 100,000 Jews of the New City vociferously rejected it; and the transference of Israeli Government Departments from Tel Aviv to Jerusalem was accelerated. Therefore, the problem not only remains but has become more acute: for what effective sanctions can the disunited United Nations impose against the collective and passionately opposed wills of the local inhabitants?

Therefore, Jerusalem forms a complicated international problem in itself, of which no settlement has yet been achieved.

Secondly, Akaba, Red Sea port of the Kingdom of Jordan at the head of the Gulf of Akaba, and better than the nearby port site of Umm Rashrash, is coveted by the Israelis as a port on Asiatic waters, which, among other advantages, would obviate Suez Canal dues. But equally, a port site on the south Palestine coast is coveted by the Kingdom of Jordan, as a direct outlet to Mediterranean waters. Only Israeli-Jordani reciprocity would evolve solutions for these related international problems, and as yet, no settlement of either has been achieved.

Thirdly, there is the politico-economic problem of the Haifa oil refinery. With the outbreak of Arab-Jewish military hostilities, the Arab States imposed on Israel whatever economic sanctions they could command. Included was the cutting of crude oil supplies by pipe-line from Kirkuk to the Haifa refinery. Even before the outbreak of hostilities however, more than a half of the crude oil refined at Haifa arrived by tanker from the Persian Gulf. But the Arab States' economic sanctions were effectively imposed on this source of crude oil also.

A first consequence, with the outbreak of hostilities, was the diversion to Lebanese Tripoli of a new sixteen-inch feeder pipe-line originally intended to carry annually four million tons of crude oil from Kirkuk to Haifa: this is now coming into use, to the profit of Tripoli and to the detriment of the Haifa refinery, the refinery at Tripoli having been expanded to cope with the increased flow of crude oil.

A second consequence, now that military hostilities are ended, has been the attempt to break the effect of the Arab States' sanctions by bringing crude oil in tankers even from Venezuela via the Mediterranean. But, for much of the crude oil from American sources dollars must be paid and the Haifa refinery is largely British owned. Yet the Israeli government has insisted on re-opening, both as a local source of refined oil and as a source of employment for Israelis. Moreover, both British and other European governments seek to meet their requirements of refined oil from sterling rather than dollar countries. Again, only a political settlement between Israel and the Arab States will solve this problem.

II KURDISTAN

The main part of the Kurdish homeland is in the foothills and on the lower slopes of the Taurus mountains of eastern Turkey and the Zagros mountains of north-west Iran; it forms a crescent-shaped area north-west of Mosul and southeast of Kirkuk, between Diarbekr and Kermanshah, in the upper drainage basin of the Tigris. Much of Kurdistan thus corres-ponds roughly with the ancient Kingdom of Gutium, which is mentioned in cuneiform records about 2,400 B.C., and had its capital at Arrapkha, the modern Kirkuk. In this territory, the Kurds appear to have maintained with little change through a very long period of time their racial com-position and socio-economic organization. Although in course of time they have become Sunni Moslems almost entirely, they have remained mostly Kurdish monoglots, although a few are Kurdish-Arabic bilinguals.

With an economy largely that of tent-dwelling transhuming pastoralists, they numbered in 1928 some three millions. Of these roughly a half were in Turkey, a quarter in Persia, about a sixth in Iraq, and the remainder mainly in Syria.

Their modern history can be said to begin in the early 16th century with the Ottoman victory over the Persians at Chaldiran, near Kars, where-after Ottoman and Persian Governments vied with each other in wiles to woo Kurdish political allegiance, Kurdistan being shared between them.

On the other hand with the treaty of 1639 which fixed the boundary between Turkey and Persia, began a long period of persecution of the Kurds by both Ottomans and Persians.

In consequence, towards the end of the 18th century, Turkish attempts to eliminate the last remaining vestiges of Kurdish autonomy, provoked a series of revolts which resulted in the first serious attempt by the Kurds to form a political unit larger than the tribe. During the next century, too, there was a succession of Kurdish revolts, but all were crushed, sometimes by the Persians, sometimes by the Turks, and sometimes by both at the same time. In 1880, one of their religious leaders led the Kurds in arms, this time with the expressed intention of creating a Kurdistan independent of both Turkey and Persia, but this revolt too, suffered the fate of its predecessors, as also did the later one in 1905.

During World War I, the Kurds suffered severely, firstly in that some 700,000 in the Ottoman provinces around Diarbekr were forcibly evacuated to western Anatolia, and secondly, on account of the Russian advance against the Turks in the Turko-Persian frontier zone which became a battleground. Nevertheless it is true to say that the modern political problem of Kurdistan arose essentially after World War I, when the Treaty of Sèvres in 1920 made provision for an independent Kurdish State. After the rise of Kemalist Turkey, this treaty was abrogated and that of Lausanne was concluded in 1923. As a result, Kurdistan became shared not by two States as before World War I, but among the four States of Turkey, Iraq, Persia, and Syria. There was thus even less hope than before World War I of achieving a politically independent Kurdistan.

It is not surprising, therefore, that a new series of Kurdish revolts[1] began in 1925 and characterized the inter-war period and that of World War II, and eventually led to the flight of many Kurds into the Caucasus lands of the U.S.S.R., where there are now some 80,000. Consequently the Kurdish people now dwell in the territories of five contiguous States.

Quite apart from the negation of the claims of the Kurds to political autonomy, their immemorial economy was disrupted. With the first signs of Spring, these transhuming tribes customarily left their winter pastures on the fringes of the Mesopotamian plains and drove their flocks to high valleys as far as the lands south of Lake Van. But when the political frontier between Turkey and Iraq was established in 1923, neither State would allow Kurds from the other to cross its frontiers in exercise of these immemorially-established seasonal pasturing rights. Moreover, the Turks kept large numbers of troops on the Iraqi and Syrian frontiers which hampered further these free pasturing movements, while in Persia whole Kurdish tribes were deported.

In the U.S.S.R., in contrast, the Kurds were given wide privileges, to the extent that, for a time, they constituted a separate republic. Later, although incorporated within Soviet Armenia, the Kurds retained their administrative and cultural autonomy, and Erivan has become an important Kurdish intellectual centre. Moreover the press reported early in 1949 that these Caucasus Kurds may well be used in the Soviet cold war against Persia through a campaign of Soviet-supported guerrilla warfare. This would have for the Kurds the old objective of establishing an independent Kurdistan based on territory carved out of Persia, Iraq, Syria, and Turkey, and for the U.S.S.R. the familiar objective of extending her

[1] In 1925, 1927, 1930-31, 1932, 1943, 1945.

territory peripherally outwards by the addition of a further Sovietized State. On the one hand, only Syria would stand between such a State and the East Mediterranean seaboard, and on the other, only Iraq between it and the Persian Gulf. Moreover, much of the Iraqi oilfield around Kirkuk is in traditionally Kurdish territory, which such a State of Kurdistan would, presumably, seek to incorporate.

III AZERBAIJAN

Azerbaijan, shared by Persia and the U.S.S.R., is in the focal area of Soviet, Turkish, and Persian interests, which lies mostly south of the Caucasus Mountains and entirely between the Black and Caspian Seas.

Soviet Azerbaijan, which lies east of the Soviet republics of Georgia and Armenia, spans the eastern Caucasus, and in its western part extends south to the middle course of the river Aras; in the east, it extends southwards along the Caspian lowlands beyond Lenkoran to Astara.

Persian Azerbaijan, which lies south of the river Aras, includes the inland drainage basin of the salt lake Urumiah, and is mostly high plateau country above 4000 ft, dominated by three lofty volcanic peaks, including Mount Ararat which climbs to nearly 18,000 ft.

Both Russian and Persian Azerbaijan are inhabited predominantly by Azerbaijan Turks, whose ancestors entered Iran from the plains east of the Caspian from the mid-11th century A.D. and more particularly in the mid-13th century as part of the western thrust of the Turkish peoples across northern Iran into Anatolia.   In the main they were nomadic horsemen and, although now there is much sedentary village life with dependence on cultivation by irrigation, there is also, still, much dependence on flocks of sheep and goats which make seasonal movements over dry pastures.

Besides a large proportion of the most densely populated rural parts of Iran, Persian Azerbaijan includes Tabriz, the second largest urban centre of Iran, with a population of more than 210,000. The latter is an important trading and route centre which, for a long period in the 16th century under the Safawid dynasty, was the Persian capital. It is at the convergence point, east of lake Urumiah, of the strategically important road from Erzurum in Turkey, along the valley of a right bank tributary of the Aras, with that from Mosul via Rowanduz along the valley of the Great Zab. In addition it is connected northwestwards, by broad-gauge railway, to the Soviet railway system at Julfa, whence there is connection at Tbilisi with the Batumi-Baku line.

Historically the struggle for control of the South Caucasus lands began in the latter part of the 15th century. In 1514, the Ottoman Turks invaded Azerbaijan and defeated the Safawids in the great battle of Chaldiran, which was the first of the campaigns which gradually established the northwest frontier of modern Persia. In the process, western Azerbaijan with Tabriz was held more than once by the Ottomans. But, after the treaty of Zuhab in 1639, which remained the basis of Turco-Persian frontier relations until the 19th century, though the frontier was not exactly defined, the boundary was acknowledged by both sides to be between Kars and Erivan in the Upper Aras region; farther south, the Urumiah country was considered to be part of Persia. Within this western frontier, Safawid Persia extended northwest of Tabriz to the eastern shores of the Black Sea south of the Caucasus about Batumi, and northeast of Tabriz to include the Caspian lowlands both to north and south of the Caucasus. Roughly therefore, the Caucasus mountains formed the northern limit to Persian territory.

Russian influence first created a permanent danger for Persia on her northern frontier under the imperialism of Peter the Great in the late 17th and early 18th centuries. Eventually, by treaty with Tsarist Russia in 1828, the present frontier, which surrendered to Russia all the lands south of the Caucasus mountains as far as the middle Aras, had come into being. Moreover, towards the close of the 19th century, Russian economic penetration of Persia was so intense that it seemed as if the whole of Persia would become a Russian protectorate,; after the 1907 agreement on Persia between Britain and Russia the Persians fully expected Russian military aggression in north Persia. In 1909, when civil war broke out in Persia, Russian military forces appeared in Tabriz on the pretext of maintaining order, and even afterwards for a time were maintained near Tabriz.

During World War I, in spite of Persian neutrality, Russian forces crossed the Urumiah country in their offensive against Turkey, while after the collapse of Tsarist Russia British forces entered northwest Persia to prevent a possible Turco-German invasion of Persia as part of a drive to India. In 1920, Bolshevik Russia withdrew from north Persia. But in World War II, after the invasion of the Ukraine by Germany, and the consequent threat to the Caucasus lands and Persia, the 1941 Soviet occupation of Persian Azerbaijan at the same time as the British occupation of South Persia, was inevitable.

Thereafter, north Persia was occupied by U.S.S.R. forces for several years, but with the clear undertaking in 1942 that the sovereignty and integrity of Persia would be respected.

Nevertheless, new Soviet-Persian troubles developed late in 1944 when the U.S.S.R. asked the Persian government for an oil concession in the northern occupied provinces, which was refused.

Only a short time later the Tudeh (Masses) Party was founded in 1941 by Persians imprisoned by the late Reza Shah as Communist suspects: originally liberal and progressive, but afterwards dominated by Soviet agents, it organized the 1946 separatist movement in Azerbaijan, under which Tabriz was again occupied by the Russians. The latter had large numbers of troops there, Persian government forces were vastly out-numbered and powerless, and the Soviet government virtually paralyzed all Persian government action in Azerbaijan.

The Russians repeated in Persian Azerbaijan the process favoured in other weak countries on their borders, by which a new sovietized State added to the U.S.S.R. could extend Soviet power peripherally outwards. But Anglo-American support of the Persian government, and refusal to recognize the proclaimed new government in Persian Azerbaijan as the result of a voluntary and spontaneous movement, has for the time being frustrated Soviet plans for either the annexation or control of Persian Azerbaijan. Thus, the Soviet *Drang nach Süden* via Rowanduz and the Great Zab valley towards Mosul, and perhaps later via Khaniqan and the Diyala Valley towards Baghdad and Basra for the South Persian oilfields and Persian Gulf, remains frustrated, the Persian government having felt strong enough even, early in 1949, to ban the Tudeh Party, the projected means to these Soviet ends.

IV KARS-ARDAHAN

Turkey, located almost entirely in Southwest Asia, with her entire northern boundary formed by southern shores of the Black Sea whence the only sea outlet is through the Bosporus, Sea of Marmara, and Dar-danelles, all of which have both shores formed by Turkish lands, and with both northeast and northwest land frontiers co-terminous with either Soviet or Soviet-satellite territory, forms even more than Persia a natural obstruction to Soviet *Drang nach Süden*.

In consequence, there are two major problem areas, namely that of the Straits and that of the northeast frontier.

The latter is the territory around the two towns of Kars and Ardahan, and mainly within the Turkish vilayet of Kars which, located southeast of Batumi, extends almost to Mount Ararat. It is mostly broken plateau country above 6000 ft., with many old volcanic peaks and sheets of old lava over limestone, where there is relatively little level land and where river valleys acquire very great importance as natural lines of movement:

now, a small Armenian minority apart, the major part of the inhabitants is essentially Turkish and Moslem, practising mainly a pastoral economy in exploitation of rich alpine pastures. The problem presented by this borderland is thus essentially strategic.

After forming part of an independent Christian Armenia these lands formed part of Ottoman territory during nearly four centuries, and it was only after the Ottoman defeat in the Russo-Turkish War of 1877–78 that there arose any question of change of political control. An impossible war indemnity was imposed by Russia on the Ottoman Empire, and it was through the fiction of compensation for this exorbitant sum of money that were ceded to Russia the sanjaks of Batumi, Ardahan, Kars, and Bayazid, the latter however being restored shortly after.

Thus Russia acquired these territories by conquest. Even so she held them only during the four decades until the collapse of the Tsarist régime in World War I. Under the subsequent Communist régime, by the Treaty of Brest-Litovsk, they were restored to Turkey.

It is true that for a time after World War I, they changed hands frequently, even being partly occupied by British forces, and forming part of the independent republic of Armenia as proclaimed in 1918. But, with the rise of Kemalist Turkey a final settlement was achieved in the Treaty of Kars in 1921. Because of its great development by the Russians as a Black Sea port and oil pipe-line terminus, the urban centre of Batumi, along with its surrounding country, returned to Russia, while the Kars-Ardahan country was confirmed to Turkey. Throughout the inter-war period, and for more than two decades, the question of change of political control did not arise. Its recent re-emergence is a further facet of the Soviet power-drive peripherally outwards since the close of World War II.

In March 1945, U.S.S.R. denounced the Turco-Soviet Treaty of non-aggression which had been in force since 1925. When Turkey tentatively approached the Moscow government for a renewal of this treaty, she was informed that a new non-aggression treaty could be concluded only on two conditions. One concerned the Straits, the other the northeastern frontier lands of Turkey. By the latter condition the districts of Kars and Ardahan were to be amputated from Turkey and grafted on to U.S.S.R., a condition which was unacceptable to Turkey.

The small town of Ardahan, on a headstream of the river Kura, derives considerable strategic importance from, on the one hand, its location on the motor road from Soviet Batumi to Turkish Kars, and on the other, its command of the road to Ahilkelek across the frontier in Soviet territory. But, located midway along the natural route between Tbilisi and Erzurum, the much larger town of Kars, an important stronghold for centuries, has even greater strategic importance. It lies in a deep rocky gorge on both banks of the river Kars, one of the headstreams of the Aras, and is the major fanhandle point of convergence from the northeast, of the motorable roads of the part of northeast Turkey which lies between the Black Sea and Lake Van, an area where, in general, there are vast spaces without roads. Furthermore, Kars is on the broad-gauge railway from Leninakan to Sarikamis,[1] and thus is connected without break-of-gauge to the Soviet Batumi-Baku railway system. It commands the main natural line of communication, via headstream valleys of the Aras, from the Soviet south Caucasus lands via Erzurum to the territorial core of Turkey in the Anatolian plateau, as well as headstream valleys of the Euphrates, whence the east Mediterranean shore at Iskanderun lies within easy access.

Hence this northeast Turkish borderland is as vital for the defence of Turkey as it is desirable for the expansion of U.S.S.R.

V THE TURKISH STRAITS

The Bosporus, Sea of Marmara and Dardanelles, collectively known as the Straits, form the sole water link between the Black Sea and Aegean Sea. Thus the great inland waterways of the Danube, Dnieper, Don, and (via their interconnecting ship canal) the Volga, as well as Black Sea ports such as Braïla-Galati, Odessa, Rostov, and Batumi find their only water connection with the eastern Mediterranean, and thence, via the Straits of Gibraltar or the Suez Canal, with the outer oceans.

Moreover the bounding shores of the Straits form the only isthmus land-link between Europe and Southwest Asia. Hence the concentrated traffic from widespread inland water arteries and seaports meets at the Straits inter-continental traffic by land routes. Therefrom arises the geopolitical problem of the Straits, which is as old as history at least.

Both Bosporus and Dardanelles are the drowned valleys of ancient rivers whose northeast-southwest alignment was guided by the synclines of a northeast-trending fold system. The Bosporus, some sixteen miles long and everywhere less than one mile wide, resembles a broad winding river which is dominated by steep shores and headlands of old crystalline and volcanic rocks. The Dardanelles channel, markedly different in every respect, is more than twice as long, has an average width of two-and-a-half-miles, and scenically has monotonous shores which are

---

[1] Eventually standard-gauge track is to be laid between Erzurum and Kars, so that the latter will thereafter become the point of break-of-gauge between Turkish standard-gauge lines and Soviet broad-gauge lines, whereby its strategic importance will even be increased.

formed of almost horizontal beds of chalk, marl and yellowish sandstones. Between them the Sea of Marmara, with a west-east length of one hundred and seventy-five miles attains a width of nearly fifty miles from north to south.

The Turkish Straits have had strategic importance throughout history. Already in 334 B.C. Europe and Asia came to grips there when Alexander of Macedon broke Persian power in Anatolia at the Granicus (Kocabas) on the Marmara. The early attempt by Lysimachus at unified control of the Straits by creating a 'Kingdom of the Straits', with his capital at Cardia (Bolayir) near the root of the Gallipoli peninsula and so in command of shores on both the Aegean and the Dardanelles, by the very potentiality of its strategy aroused the collective hostility of all his rivals and so perished in 281 B.C.

The Romans crossed the Straits into Western Anatolia in 189 B.C., after which the lands southeast of the Dardanelles were held against Macedon from Pergamum (Bergama) as capital. In the first century B.C. Mithridates VI of Pontus, having united politically lands along the southern shore of the Black Sea with the Uskudar (Scutari) peninsula and Bosporus shore, extended his power to the northern coastlands of the Black Sea, where he created in the Crimea a vassal kingdom, commanding furs and gold from farther north, and trade routes east to the Caspian and beyond.

In its beginning the Anatolian base of the Eastern Roman Empire was defended from Nicomedia on the Marmara. But under Constantine, New Rome was established on the opposite shore of the Bosporus in A.D. 330 at Byzantium, which thereafter, through many centuries, was to remain the major centre of political control of the Straits lands.

Early Ottoman conquests drove eastwards from the Marmaran base of Brusa (Bursa) captured in 1326, but in 1355 the Ottomans straddled the southern part of the Straits by securing a foothold in Gallipoli; thence they captured Byzantine Philippopolis and Adrianople, and made the latter their capital in 1367. Thereafter, until the fall of Constantinople in 1453, the Straits area was controlled in the southwest, by the Ottomans astride the Dardanelles, and in the northeast by the rival Byzantines, astride the Bosporus.

After the fall of Constantinople to the Ottomans, the Straits were fortified, and so either barred, or controlled to Ottoman profit, maritime trading between the rich cities of the Black Sea coastlands and the trading states of Venice and Genoa. Based on the Straits as axis, the territory under the control of the Ottoman sultans reached its farthest extension in the last quarter of the 17th century, by when nearly all of the north coast lands of the Black Sea had been conquered.

Then came the rise of Russia during the 18th century, and thereafter, continuing Russian pressure on the Ottoman Black Sea dependencies. By treaty in 1739, Russian ships were excluded from the Black Sea. On the other hand, the destruction of the Ottoman fleet in 1764 gave Russia in her turn full sea power north of the Bosporus. Furthermore, by treaty in 1774, the Ottoman government were compelled to accord Russian merchantmen the right to pass through the Bosporus and Dardanelles, a right which had been denied to all non-Turkish shipping for some three hundred years. Moreover, by 1792 Russia had recovered Azov and conquered the coastlands between the rivers Bug and Dniester.

It was in face of the rise of Russian power during the 18th century that all the Powers with Mediterranean interests thereafter supported the Ottoman Empire astride the Straits so that it might function as a buffer State in opposition to the southward advance of Russia; this was the main reason for the long survival of the Muslim and Asiatic Ottoman Empire in the Christian continent of Europe.

Between 1774 and the collapse of the Tsarist régime in 1917, it was a constant Russian aim to secure control of the Straits in order to guarantee a vital trade route, to protect Russian Black Sea naval bases, and to ensure access for the Russian fleet to the Mediterranean. In pursuit of this aim, the Russian government attempted at various times to make Turkey virtually a Russian dependency, to take possession of Istanbul, and by supporting Balkan separatist movements to undermine indirectly Ottoman control of the Straits. It was mainly through the collaboration of Britain and Austria in opposition to Russia concerning the Straits, that the Turks did not become a dependency of Russia. During the 19th century the Ottoman Empire was more than once at war with Russia, fundamentally over the Straits: in the Crimean War the Turks had the support against Russia of Britain, France, and the Kingdom of Sardinia; but in the Russo-Turkish War of 1877-8, the Turks, left to fight alone, were defeated, whereafter Russian Black Sea expansion was resumed.

Then came into being a new factor through the development of the German *Drang nach Osten* and German penetration of Turkey. Eventually this led to the expression of the problem of the Straits in the Triple Entente of Britain, France, and Russia against Germany and the Ottoman Empire. In 1914, Russia made a claim for control of the Straits, and in World War I both sides were fully aware that the geographical position of the Ottoman Empire astride the Straits made her a vital factor in the struggle: for Russia, it was a question of maintenance through the Straits of communications with her Allies; for Germany, control of the Straits through her alliance with Turkey meant the isolation of her antagonists.

The closure of the Straits in September 1914, the subsequent Turko-German fleet attack on the Russian Black Sea fleet, the imperative need of Russia for arms via the Straits, and the failure of the Allies Dardanelles campaign to force them open, all contributed powerfully to the early military defeat and general collapse of Tsarist Russia, and so to the birth of Bolshevik Russia. Yet, in their early revulsion from imperialism, when the Bolsheviks obtained power in 1917, they expressly renounced any wish to control the Straits.

By the terms of the 1918 armistice, after the Ottoman collapse, the Allies were to occupy the forts along the Dardanelles and Bosporus, and keep the Straits open. Thus, in 1919 the Straits were open to Allied navies, so that during the Anglo-Russian War the British dominated the Black Sea and so could send to the White Russian forces military supplies previously denied to Tsarist Russian forces.

In 1919 unsuccessful attempts were made to induce U.S.A. to undertake a mandate for the Straits, following which, by the Treaty of Sèvres, the Straits, open to all nations, were to be administered by an international Commission. Thus, from 1919 to 1922, until the War of Turkish Independence, the Straits and a wide zone of territory along both shores, along with some strategic islands commanding the approaches, formed a neutral zone.

During the War of Turkish Independence it was clear to Turkey that Britain was prepared to fight for the principle of freedom of the Straits, consequently in 1923 the Straits Convention was signed: a demilitarized zone along both shores of the Dardanelles and Bosporus was established, and besides freedom of passage for commercial shipping, even foreign warships were free to enter the Black Sea. But in view of the latter implied threat to Russian security, the Soviet government refused ratification.

Besides giving much assistance to Turkey during her war of Independence, Soviet Russia was the first of the Great Powers to recognize the new Kemalist State. Thereafter in consequence, for roughly a decade cordial and close friendship between Russia and Turkey, expressed in a Treaty of non-aggression in 1925, developed into a tradition. But when in 1936 the Montreux Convention on the Straits was signed by U.S.S.R., Britain, France, Turkey, and Greece, Russia's attitude revealed unmistakably a return to the traditional principle of Tsarist Russian policy that the Black Sea should be a closed Russian Sea, and fully confirmed the emergence of the modern phase of Turko-Russian antagonism.

By the Montreux Convention, Turkey was recognized as the guardian of the Straits and was even allowed to fortify them. Free passage was allowed for the merchant ships of all nations, but, during war or threat of war, no warships except those of Turkey were to traverse the Straits in either direction. During World War II Turkey exercised her Montreux powers neutrally, but this, for the second time in the 20th century, meant the effective closure of the Straits as a military supply route to Russia. But it was especially the conclusion of Turkey's secret pact of friendship with Germany in 1941, with the ensuing German attack on the Soviet Union, which was regarded by U.S.S.R. as a flagrant breach of the inter-war Soviet-Turkish tradition of friendship. It was hardly surprising there-fore that the close of World War II saw the beginning of the Soviet war of nerves against Turkey. Not only was the Turko-Soviet Treaty of non-aggression of 1925 denounced by U.S.S.R. in 1945, but claims, un-acceptable to Turkey, were formulated in respect of the Straits in the Soviet note of 8.8.46 which proposed a revision of the Montreux con-ditions of control of the Bosporus and Dardanelles.

The Soviet note embodied three effective demands. The first was that passage of the Straits should be permitted to warships of the Black Sea Powers but denied to those of others. This meant that Russian warships would have passage to the Mediterranean but that no others would have passage to the Black Sea. The second demand was that the establishment of the Straits régime should be the concern alone of Turkey and the other Black Sea Powers. This implied the exclusion of other maritime nations which had been recognized for over a century as having a right to be heard in the setting up of conditions of control for this international water-way. The third demand was that Turkey and the Soviet Union should organize jointly the means of defence of the Straits, so as to prevent their use by other Powers for purposes hostile to the Black Sea Powers. Virtually, this meant that the U.S.S.R. was to have a base or bases on the Straits, so that Turkey could only become a satellite State of her powerful northern neighbour. Moreover, thereby Greece, Syria and Palestine, as well as the Suez Canal, could be directly menaced by Soviet forces.

It is true that the Soviet note envisaged the Straits being kept open to merchant shipping of all nations, but closure to Western shipping of the Danube international waterway under post-war conditions of Soviet control is ominous augury for Western shipping through the Straits with the latter under effective control of U.S.S.R.

These demands therefore, were not only unacceptable to Turkey, which alone could not successfully resist the might of U.S.S.R., but also to the Western Powers. Thus the Soviet demands concerning the Straits have formed an important contributory cause of the marked change in Turkish policy since 1946; for example the acceptance by Turkey of economic,

military, and naval aid from Britain and U.S.A., the adherence of Turkey
to the European Recovery Programme, and the efforts to form a defensive
bloc of Mediterranean countries including Greece and Turkey, which
shall be guaranteed by the Western Powers, including U.S.A., and form
part of the defence organization of the Atlantic Community.

Both Britain and U.S.A. are in agreement with U.S.S.R. in desiring
a revision of the Montreux Convention on the Straits, but the British and
U.S.A. conception is, in some particulars, diametrically opposed to that
of U.S.S.R. The age-old problem of the Straits remains unsolved therefore, and continues to play a significant part in Great Power politics.

CONCLUSION

There remains space to allude briefly to two aspects of future development in Southwest Asia.

The first is the conception of Greater Syria. This is envisaged as a
political federation of the Arab States of the 'Fertile Crescent', namely
the Kingdom of Jordan with Arab Palestine incorporated, Iraq, and
Syria, but probably without Lebanon, in view of the fear, on the part of
its Christian population, of a Moslem majority. The Hashimites, direct
descendants of the Prophet Mohammed, and already the source of the
royal families in Amman and Baghdad, form a ready-made nucleus for the
personal loyalties of such a federation. Strategically, there is everything
to be gained by the evolution of a single political entity which would
include shores along the east Mediterranean, at the head of the Gulf of
Akaba, and at the head of the Persian Gulf. On the other hand, a factor
making for political instability in Southwest Asia would be the hostility,
on the part of Egypt, Saudi Arabia and Yemen, which would be engendered by the rise within the Arab World of such a potentially powerful rival State.[1]

The second is the economic support to be given to the Southwest
Asia States by the Western Powers. This is to strengthen them to resist
both external aggression and internal disorder, through increasing general
prosperity, and so to increase, as essential to world peace, the political
stability of this important strategic area. U.S.A., Britain, and the re-
emergent France are involved. In the general attempt to lessen the social
gulf between the small minority of rich and the large majority of very
poor and backward people, particularly in the Arab States, changes in

[1] The recently signed collective security pact between five of the seven Arab League States,
Egypt, Saudi Arabia, Yemen, Lebanon and Syria, although ostensibly against possible
aggression by Israel, also, in its present form, marks opposition to moves by Jordan and Iraq
to form a Greater Syria dominated by Baghdad and Amman.

uneconomic land tenure, improvement of agricultural method, reclamation for agriculture of lands at present waste or undercultivated, and development of industry, are to be stimulated by Western capital investment and technical help, the latter particularly by agricultural experts and engineers.

Irrigation, with flood control, is one of the more urgent problems. For example, in Iraq, it is estimated that the amount of irrigated land could be doubled, that is from roughly seven million acres to some fourteen million acres. Therefore, under long-term plans for the better exploitation of Iraqi water supplies, the Euphrates is to be controlled by turning Lake Habbaniya into a reservoir to conserve flood waters, which will be supplemented by a similar use of the Abu Dibis and Bahr el-Milh depressions west of Karbala. Under the same project the Tigris is to be controlled particularly by the construction of a dam and huge artificial lake in the Wadi Tharthar, west of Samarra, and a barrage on the Tigris itself upstream of Baghdad at Samarra, with a channel therefrom to the Wadi Tharthar reservoir. Moreover, these developments will have the additional advantage of removing from Baghdad its annual threat of inundation. Additional dams are to be constructed on the Diyala at Gibraltar, and on the Lesser Zab at Tokan. It is expected that soon vast financial loans will be made by the Western Powers to provide the necessary equipment and materials for the foregoing projects, while Iraq will both provide and pay for the necessary labour.

On completion, however, under present methods of cultivation, there will be a shortage of man-power to cultivate all the newly-available land. Hence a great extension of mechanization of agriculture, along with improved conditions of transport is envisaged, so that a remarkable transformation in the geography and economy of Iraq will be brought about. Similar, if smaller-scale developments are envisaged for other parts of Southwest Asia.

TABLE III

SOUTHWEST ASIA: AREA, POPULATION, CULTIVATED AREA AND RAILWAY MILEAGE

	Total Area (000 sq. miles)	Culti-vated area (000 sq. miles)	Irri-gated area as % of culti-vated area	Popula-tion (mil-lions)	Popula-tion per sq. ml. of total	Popula-tion per sq. ml. of culti-vated area	Railways total mileage	Railway mileage per 1,000 sq. mls. of total area
TURKEY ..	296	29·7	..	18·8	67	633	7,500	25·3
PERSIA ..	628	10·6	35%*	13·0*	21*	1,226	1,750	2·8
SYRIA ..	66	7·8	7·5%	3·0	46	385	725	11·0
LEBANON ..	3·4	..	..	1·2*	349	..	290	85·0
PALESTINE ..	10·2	3·34	3·4%	1·9	186	569	290	28·4
JORDAN† ..	34·7	1·75	5·7%	0·4	11·5	228	280	8·0
IRAQ ..	175	8·59	62·7%	4·8	27	559	966	5·5
SAUDI ARABIA ..	700	..	..	7·5*	11	..	100§	0· 14
YEMEN ..	75	..	..	3·5	..	..	..	..
SOUTHWEST ASIA ..	1988·3	..	..	54·1	27·6	..	11,901	6·0

* Estimate.
† Exclusive of the recently incorporated part of Arab Palestine.
§ Exclusive of the disused Hejaz line.

The figures above are derived from different sources. They are given with some reserve and as indicating present conditions approximately.

ADDITIONAL TABLE

SOUTHWEST ASIA: CRUDE PETROLEUM PRODUCTION
(in thousand metric tons)

Year	Egypt	Persia	Iraq	Bahrein	Saudi Arabia	Kuwait	Total	% World production
1917	118.6	894.2					1,012.8	1.6
1927	159.7	4,959.4	41.0				5,160.1	3.3
1937	150.6	9,727.2	3,978.5	971.8	9.1		14,837.2	5.8
1947	1,094.9	19,162.5	4,390.0	1,095.0	11,329.4	2,281.2	39,333.0	10.4
1948	2,500.0*	24,871.0	2,281.2*	1,368.7	18,706.2*	4,562.5	54,289.6*	11.5*
1949		26,807			23,000.0*	5,625.0	60,000.0*	
1952					31,937.5*			

* Estimate.

SELECT BOOK LIST

Antonius, G.: *The Arab Awakening*, London, 1945.

Blanchard, R.: *Asie Occidentale, Géographie Universelle*, Tome VIII, Paris, 1929.

Bonné, A.: *The Economic Development of the Middle East*, London, 1945.
State and Economics in the Middle East, London, 1948.

Boveri, M.: *Minaret and Pipe-line*, London, 1939.

Haas, W.: *Iran*, New York, 1946.

Hitti, P. K.: *The Arabs: a Short History*, London, 1948.

Hoskins, H. L.: *British Routes to India*, London, 1928.

Hourani, A.: *Minorities in the Arab World*, London, 1947. *Syria and Lebanon*, London, 1947.

Keen, B. A.: *The Agricultural Development of the Middle East*, London, 1946.

Kirk, G. E.: *A Short History of the Middle East*, London, 1948.

Kohn, H.: *Nationalism and Imperialism in the Hither East*, London, 1932.

Landshut, S.: *Jewish Communities in the Muslim Countries of the Middle East*, London, 1950.

Mikesell, R. F., and Chenery, H. B.: *Arabian Oil: America's Stake in the Middle East*, New York, 1949.

Monroe, E.: *The Mediterranean in Politics*, Oxford, 1938.

Palestine Royal Commission: Report, London, 1937.

Palestine Partition Commission: Report, London, 1938.

Parkes, J.: *A History of Palestine*, London, 1949.

Safrastian, A.: *Kurds and Kurdistan*, London, 1948.

Scott, H.: *In the High Yemen*, London, 1947.

Seton-Williams, M. V.: *Britain and the Arab States, 1920–48*, London, 1948.

Speiser, E. A.: *The United States and the Near East*, Cambridge, U.S.A., 1947.

Thornburg, M. W., Spry, G., and Soule, G.: *Turkey: An Economic Appraisal*, New York, 1949.

Twitchell, K. S.: *Saudi Arabia*, New York, 1947.

Warriner, D.: *Land and Poverty in the Middle East:* Royal Institute of International Affairs, London, 1948.

Wilson, A. Sir: *The Suez Canal*, London, 1939.

CHAPTER II

INDIA AND PAKISTAN

By O. H. K. Spate

THE INDIAN REALM AS A WHOLE

THE partition of the Indian Empire is so recent, the old concept of
'India' so familiar, the two new Dominions have still so much in common,
that it is convenient to retain the old name as a geographical expression in
general and historical contexts where no ambiguity can arise. It is unfortunate and confusing that a part of the old India should retain the name
of the whole, but it would be discourteous as well as inaccurate to use
the perhaps more logical and certainly more convenient term 'Hindustan'
for the Indian Union, and in specifically political references to the period
since August 15th 1947 'India' will mean the Union. In economic and
statistical contexts 'British India' refers to the old provincial territory,
'All-India' to the old Empire, both British and States' territory. 'States',
when initially capitalized, refers to those political units which were part
of the Empire but not British territory; these of course excluded independent Nepal and Bhután, and also States' territory held on lease and
administered provincially, such as much of Baluchistan, leased from the
Khan of Kalat, and Berar, from the Nizam of Hyderabad.

THE SETTING (*Fig.* 12)

India occupies a curiously symmetrical position in southern Asia, a
great rhomboidal landmass hanging like the keystone of the arch formed
by the Indian Ocean shores. The arch motif recurs in its own structure:
the resistance or the active pressure of the ancient peninsular block (once
part of Gondwanaland) has looped the Tertiary ranges of the north into
a sagging inner arch, in which the mountains are further recessed from the
sea than is usual in southern and eastern Asia. Between the ancient block
and the young mountains a great trough, some 1800 miles long from the
Indus delta to that of the Ganges, has been filled in with detritus from the
mountains. These three—the mountain wall, the peninsular block, and
the Indo-Gangetic plains—are the primary physical divisions of India.

The eastern and western wings of the mountain wall, wrapped around concealed projections of the peninsular block, form almost a mirror-image of each other. These border ranges are generally low (5–7000 feet, with some heights of 12–15,000) but marked by a great development of parallel scarps and ridges. The differences between the Afghan-Iranian hills and those of the Burma border are essentially dependent upon climate. The latter are rain-swept for half the year, covered with dense (often evergreen) forest, inhabited mainly by primitive animistic tribes practising shifting agriculture; the former are arid, with a more sedentary but (except in some favoured valleys) precarious agriculture, and with a good deal of semi-nomadic pastoralism and trading: in fact a typical southwest Asian against a typical southeast Asian environment. Between these wings are slung the Himalaya and Karakoram and their associated ranges, backed by the cold deserts of High Asia and forming a mountain barrier incomparably the loftiest and most massive in the world. Yet, especially south of Lhasa and where the Vale of Kashmir and the deep upper Indus gash are inset between Himalaya and Karakoram, there have passed thin trickles of trade and religion, the latter a commodity of minimal bulk and presumably of highest value. These are regions of isolated and peculiar but not negligible cultures.

The Peninsula has a deceptively simple appearance on small-scale maps; actually it contains much regional diversity. In the north the ancient worn-down Aravalli Hills thrust their gaunt ridges into the Indo-Gangetic alluvium and the arid wastes of the Thar, the last visible spur being the famous Ridge of Delhi. Here little hill-girt valleys and basins provided strongholds for the semi-feudal Rajput chivalry, last representatives of the traditions of the golden ages of Hindu culture. Across the base of the Peninsula the stresses of the Himalayan folding have produced strong east-west trends, the great wooded scarps and plateaus of the Vindhya-Kaimur Hills and the Satpura-Hazaribagh line, the faulted troughs of the Narbada and Tapti. Here too, especially in the broken jungly country of Chota Nagpur and the Orissa hinterland, is an area of refuge, this time for primitive tribes not yet included within the comprehensive embrace of Hinduism, although increasingly subject to its cultural influence. In the triangle between the Satpuras and the Western and Eastern Ghats lies the Deccan proper, a country of vast peneplains, in the northwest formed of the horizontal Deccan Lavas with their mesa-like relic hills, elsewhere broken by the fantastically craggy tors of the Archæan gneisses which form the foundation of the whole. The great rivers, almost dry for half the year, are graded nearly to their heads in the Western Ghats, save where they break through the disconnected hills lumped together as the Eastern Ghats. Most of the Deccan has a savannah aspect, but this is probably the result of human and caprine activity; the hill girdles are forested, especially the steep and wildly dissected scarp of the Western Ghats and their southern culmination in the Nilgiris.

Topographically the Indo-Gangetic plains are a vast alluvial monotony, relieved only by the floodplains (*khadar*) sunk between steep and often intricately gullied bluffs, though significant variations are also introduced by the relative depths of the water-table, particularly in the long strips of gravelly talus (*bhabar*) and marshy *terai* jungle bordering the Siwalik Hills, the low outermost vallum of the Himalayas. But essentially the broad regional differences are climatic: distance from the sea and position in relation to the Bay of Bengal branch of the wet summer monsoon are the main determinants of rainfall and so of crops, settlements, and the aspect of the countryside. Transitions are imperceptibly gradual, and contrasts extreme: from the dense evergreen tidal jungle of the Bengal delta, backed by a continuous sheet of paddy with a close stipple of unnucleated settlements, almost amphibious during the rains; through the intensively cultivated plains and strongly nucleated villages of the middle Ganges and the relatively well-watered sub-montane strip of the Punjab; to the desolate stretches of coarse grass and bush, scattered acacias, and breaks of bare sandy soil, which formed the landscape of most of the northwest before modern irrigation chequered it with the compact and geometrically rectangular fields of the canal colonies, nucleated after a new fashion in planned villages—a Roman landscape.

SOME EFFECTS OF POSITION AND BUILD (*Fig.* 13)

Within this framework, and very largely free from outside influences, has developed that extraordinarily complex and self-sufficing culture inadequately summarized, or rather symbolized, by the protean word Hinduism. Incredibly diverse as are the Indian peoples and their manners, fragmented by race, religion, and caste, there is yet an underlying unity of ways of life and of culture, a unity more readily recognizable than definable, which (except in the far western borderland) has influenced even the Muslims, most of whom after all are descendants of converts from Hinduism. Both isolation and diversity have been overstressed in the past by easy reference to mountain walls and harbourless coasts, or to multitudinous tongues and faiths, most of which as a matter of fact are mere dialects or linguistic or sectarian fossils. Yet isolation and diversity are there, and the emphasis on them has perhaps been wrongly based and twisted for tendentious inferences rather than simply exaggerated.

It is true that maritime influences have been relatively slight; but the Arabian Sea has been the scene of busy traffic since the beginnings of history; a traffic widely shared by the Indian west coast. South of the Gulf of Cambay (itself much more favourable in the days of smaller craft and before it became excessively silted) this coast is essentially one of submergence, associated with the late formation of the Western Ghats by subsidence of a landmass to the west. In the north, the Konkan, there are good harbours of ria type; in the south the lagoons and roadsteads of Malabar are protected by submarine mudbanks and backed by the broad and easy Palghat gap (1100 feet) which is, however, too near the extremity of the Peninsula to command a really wide hinterland. Ptolemy's Barygaza (Broach) and Musiris (Cranganore), Surat and Goa in the age of the Renaissance discoveries, Bombay and Cochin to-day, amply attest the continuing vitality of maritime traditions in Konkan and Malabar. The east coast is less well provided with harbours; yet thence Hindu emigrants brought civilization to Burma, Cambodia, and Champa, and in the East Indies even set up the powerful medieval sea-states of Sri Vijaya and Majapahit.[1] The central position of the Peninsula in the Indian Ocean is after all of great permanent significance, and its outlier Ceylon in the past marked the effective limits of maritime enterprise from east and west, from China and from the Græco-Roman world.

Within India we may discern two perennially important historical structure-lines. The first slants across from the Gulf of Cambay to the Delhi-Agra region. Northwest of it lies a region of cultural assimilation, accessible from western and central Asia by the all-important northwestern entrances. Here alien influences have been strongest, and it is now a part of the Islamic cultural realm, to which indeed it is linked by its arid climate and resultant ways of life. The rest of India is a region of greater isolation, and it is here that the intricacies of Hindu metaphysics, theogony, and social structure have evolved.[2] The Ganges valley has indeed been a great passageway, as shown for instance by the high degree of 'Aryanisation' in the populations of the United Provinces and Bihar, by Muslim cultural influence in Oudh, and by the Muslim outlier in Bengal. But south of this great corridor is the other great fracture-line: roughly along the Narbada and the forested uplands of Chota Nagpur lies the most persistent internal political frontier-zone of Indian history. Something of the wider arrangement is repeated within the frame of the Peninsula itself. Access across the foreland between the plains and the Deccan is easiest by

[1] Cf. pp. 185, 190 below; and for the general theme K. M. Panikkar, *India and the Indian Ocean* (1945), *passim*.
[2] Cf. S. Piggott, *Some Ancient Cities of India* (1945), pp. 1, 42.

the relatively open and fertile Malwa plateau east of the Aravallis, marked by the ancient trade route from Barygaza at the mouth of the Tapti via the old cultural and commercial centre of Ujjain to the Gangetic plain in the Muttra region; marked also by ancient holy places such as Sanchi, by the great palace-forts of Gwalior and Jhansi and by numberless hilltop holds. The old trade route was still important in the 16th and 17th centuries, when it linked Surat with the Mogul centres at Agra and Fatehpur Sikri. From this gateway in the northwest, opening southwards onto the wide and open Deccan Lava country, we again find diminishing ripples of outside influences. Thus the Muslim kingdoms of this area did not overcome the resistance of the Hindu empire of Vijayanagar, based in the southern Deccan, until 1565, and in the next century they in turn succumbed to the Mogul advance along the same lines. To the west the wild crest of the Western Ghats provided the strongholds, conveniently overlooking the cities of the plains, whence in the 17th century Sivaji extended Mahratta power over all the Deccan Lava country, terrain well suited to his wiry horsemen. Even to-day the southern boundary of the lavas remains the boundary of Marathi speech; beyond them the more ancient Dravidian cultures (perhaps affiliated with the Indus Valley civilization) come in with astonishing abruptness, though relics of Dravidian tongues remain as far away as Baluchistan to attest their one-time extension.

To sum up: the deep south remains Hindu and Dravidian; the centre and north Hindu and Aryan with important Muslim intrusions (Oudh, Bengal, Hyderabad); the northwest Islamic. Inset within these greater cultural zones are the tribal animists of the junglier hills and the semi-feudal society of the oasis strongpoints of Rajputana astride the Aravallis; and girdling the Peninsula an active littoral with close contacts with Southwest Asia, shown by the numerous finds of Roman coins in the southeast[1] and by such interesting fossil kiths (in Huntington's sense of the term) as the Parsees from Fars, the 'White Jews' of Cochin, the Nestorian Christians who were numerous in the south until brought within the Roman fold by the Portuguese.

From all this the key importance of the middle Jumna axis, of which Delhi and Agra are the poles, will be clear: on the marches between the ever-invaded northwest and the shock-absorbing Gangetic plain; in the gateway between the desert Thar and the last Aravalli spurs on the one hand, the Himalayas on the other; controlling the northern approaches to

[1] The recent discovery of warehouses of Græco-Roman pottery (including amphoræ) near Pondicherry provides important new evidence of the nature of the trade. See R. E. M. Wheeler and others: "Arikamedu; an Indo-Roman Trading Station on the East Coast of India", *Ancient India* No. 2 (July 1946), pp. 17-124.

the great Malwa passageway into the Deccan. This is one of the truly great crossways of the world; perhaps only that of Constantinople is comparable to it in sustained significance. And, until the sea-based British thrust up the Ganges from Calcutta, the other great node was around the Gulf of Cambay where our two structure-lines converge.

THE PATTERN OF BRITISH POWER

Onto this cultural division was superimposed the completely new orientation of British power. The Portuguese, influenced by their contacts with Arab traders and the needs of their struggle against them—a struggle which took them to Ormuz, Suez, and Abyssinia—had worked up the east African coast, and their major Indian bases were on the west coast: Goa, Chaul, Bassein, Damaõ, Diu. The narrowness of the immediate hinterland between the Ghats and the sea was an advantage rather than an impediment to a dominion based on fortified trade centres linked by sea-power. The Portuguese were late medievals, not early moderns like their supplanters, and something of the crusader still lingered;[1] but by virtue of this very fact their influence, persuasive and persistent as it was in some cultural aspects, was less disruptive of Asian society than that of Dutch and British, and they were themselves more intimately affected by the surrounding cultures. The Dutch used a more easterly route, sailing from the Cape nearly to Australia before turning north, and their primary interests were in the Spice Islands. But in the first half of the 17th century there was fierce rivalry between all three nations for control of the Surat node, as we have seen the terminal of the great route to the centres of Mogul power, Agra and Delhi.

The east coast was thus not pre-empted, and expansion, once the trading factories were outgrown, was much easier than in the west; the 'country powers' were weak and disunited, there was no such formidable opposition as that of the Mahrattas. Hence while Bombay came into English hands with Catharine of Braganza in 1661–68 the conquest of the adjoining island of Salsette was not completed until 1775–76, by which time expansion from Calcutta, founded in 1690, had spread far beyond Benares. The Seven Years' War virtually eliminated any danger from the French effort, spasmodically energetic and grandiose but ill-supported from home. British territorial aggrandisement really began with the acquisition in 1757–59 of certain rights over the 24 Parganas (around

---

[1] A contrast forcibly expressed by the armorial bearings and the epitaphs on Portuguese tombstones in India as compared with the more solidly bourgeois memorials of Dutch and British pioneers.

Calcutta) from the local authorities, the Mogul empire being now merely the shade of that which once was great. By 1849 the last serious country power, that of the Sikhs in the Punjab, was subjugated, and the Indian Empire, save for its annexes in Burma and Baluchistan, was substantially as it stood in 1947.

The actual distribution of British territory is too significant, in the broad, to be a mere absent-minded accident, although no other explanation will account for some of its fantastic local fragmentations and aberrations. The bases lay in the great Presidency provinces of Bengal, Madras, and Bombay, securing all the coasts with the unimportant exceptions of those of Travancore and Cochin in the south-west, one or two tiny States south of Bombay, and arid Cutch, Kathiawar, and Baluchistan (and the Oman outlier at Gwadar) in the north-west; apart of course from the Portuguese enclaves of Goa, Damaõ, and Diu, the French of Mahé, Karikal, Pondicherry, Yanaon, and Chandernagore, the total area of these amounting to under 1750 square miles. The entire alluvial crescent between the Ganges and the Indus deltas, a few enclaves apart, was British, and the three bases were linked by practically continuous bridges, with a wedge of the United Provinces reaching down to contact the Bombay-Calcutta corridor of the Central Provinces. The two great States of Mysore and Hyderabad were neatly cut off from the sea and from each other. From Kathiawar through Gujarat, Rajputana, and Central India, as far as the Orissa hinterland, stretched great but broken blocks of States' territory; but no single State in these groups exceeded 36,210 square miles or 3,050,000 inhabitants in 1941, and the political fragmentation (now largely swept away by the Union) was indescribable verbally and well-nigh unmappable: it was as if the feudal map of England in the anarchy of Stephen's reign had been frozen (cf. *Fig. 15*). In the northwest money, diplomacy, and arms, in adroit and ever-varying combinations, held a disjointed buffer-strip firmly under British control; and the key points, Peshawar and Quetta, were in British territory.[1]

Of the 1941 All-India area and population (1,581,410 square miles and 388,997,955 souls) 865,446 square miles and 295,808,722 people were in the Provinces, which had an average density of 341 to the square mile against 130 in States and Agencies: figures which need no comment.

THE FRONTIERS

Physiographically the girdle of mountains does indeed act as a wall, and its climatic importance as boxing-in air masses cannot be over-

[1] Strictly Quetta was in territory leased from the Khan of Kalat; but the tenure was good.

stressed. But from a human point of view the term 'mountain wall' is merely convenient shorthand for a complicated system of ramparts and fosses. The historical values of a given section of the barrier are determined as much by what lies beyond it as by its actual physique. The Tibetan plateaus are not attractive objectives and have themselves few resources for aggression. To the east the Assam-Burma belt of parallel ranges, 75–150 miles broad, is clothed for the most with dense humid jungle, and beyond it the Burmese dynasties enjoyed a fertile *lebensraum* of their own, with little incentive to move westwards and plenty of preoccupations in their marchlands with China and Siam. From the Indian side movement by sea to the Irrawaddy entrances was far easier, and of great importance in Burma's proto-historic period. Only in Arakan, which was not definitely attached to Burma until 1784 and has always been somewhat separatist, was there much contact in historic times, and that was merely a persistent petty warfare by land and sea. No railway (despite many proposals) and until 1944 no real road crossed the Arakan Yomas between India and Burma. Nevertheless they have been penetrated—by the remarkable Burmese general Maha Bandula in 1823–24, by British and Japanese alike in 1942–45. But between these years of crisis 'the frontier' has meant the northwest.

Here the mountain barriers narrow significantly between Turkestan and the Punjab; and in central Asia were impulses which for three millennia at least brought invader after invader across the Afghan-Punjab saddle. Whether these impulsions were primarily due to desiccation of the steppes or to distant political shifts is here irrelevant. The best-known passes, the Khyber and the Bolan, have not been so exclusively used as the traditions and preoccupations of the British period would suggest; but, except for the Arab irruption into Sind in the 8th century, which used a then more thriving Makran, the great invasions have entered by the vital gateways included in the quadrilateral Kabul-Kandahar-Jacobabad-Attock.

The Frontier hills have always been to some extent a no-man's-land: arid, almost worthless in themselves, over-populated by the toughest of tribesmen with a secular tradition of violence, their effective occupation was obviously uneconomic for more settled states. The great, if generally loosely built, empires which have straddled the saddle between the favoured Afghan basins and the Punjab naturally contented themselves, as a rule, with the control of the main strategic points and routes, supplemented by a complicated technique of punitive raiding, bribery, economic blockade, intrigue, hostage-taking, and straight assassination. In all respects except the last the British Raj merely followed traditional tactics.

Nevertheless the nature of British rule and the preoccupation with Russia, which dates back to the Franco-Russian rapprochment at Tilsit in 1807, demanded longer strategic views.

The frontier inherited from the Sikhs was the *daman*—the detrital 'skirt of the hills'—and at first the Sikh 'close border' policy prevailed; memories of the Khyber disaster of 1840–41 discouraged adventurism. The Anglo-Russian crisis of 1878 and continuous Russian expansion in central Asia, however, favoured the forward school in their demand for a 'scientific' frontier, advanced at least to the Hindu Kush and including the extremely important Kabul-Kandahar line. This was in British hands after the Second Afghan War (1878–80), but the costs and risks of its retention were obviously too great. Recourse was had to a compromise policy: direct control of the settled plains Districts of the North-West Frontier Province (separated from the Punjab in 1901), a more general supervision of the tribes in 'Agency Territories' beyond the administrative boundary on the *daman*, and preponderant or exclusive influence in Afghanistan itself. In 1893 the international boundary (the 'Durand Line') was negotiated with Afghanistan, and later demarcated south of the Safed Koh, across the Khyber between the Safed Koh and the Kabul River, and on a section east of the Kunar River.

This compromise policy was on the whole fairly successful, but clearly no complete and permanent pacification is possible unless both flanks of the broken frontier terrain are under one control, and that a very firm one. In Baluchistan this condition was fulfilled, the British-administered Districts (in part acquired by the Second Afghan War) lying along the international boundary; but in the Frontier Province the tribes had bolt-holes across the border. The whole frontier from Makran to Chitral has been called a vast depressed area. Economics alone do not, of course, account for the turbulence of the population, but they form no small part of the problem. Whether Pakistan can permanently afford subsidies for the Agencies and for economic development in the Districts is an open question, on the answer to which much depends.

The northern frontiers were for the most part indefinite, lying 'on the roof of the world' in perhaps the most desolate part of the inhabited earth. The most ardent Russophobe could hardly bring much conviction to a vision of Russian armies flooding across the Pamirs into Gilgit; nevertheless both the Tsars and the Soviets have evidenced their interest in the Pamirs; a long narrow panhandle of Afghan territory kept the Wakhan (Ab-i-Panji) valley as a buffer-strip between India and Russia, and Kashmir marches for 700 miles with Sinkiang and Tibet. There was sufficient local movement of nomads and traders to give some point to the not very deadly manœuvres for position in Sinkiang; but even in these days of aerial warfare this is not likely to be an active frontier. The boundaries between India and independent Nepal and Bhután lie for the most part in the jungly and malarial *terai*, a negative tract. There are strong trade links between Nepal and the Gangetic plains, and cultivators as well as soldiers have migrated thence; but it is only recently, with the realization of the necessity for comprehensive control of such rivers as the Kosi in their upper courses, that Indian interests across the Nepalese border have become really vital.

THE PARTITION OF INDIA (*Fig.* 14)

These frontiers and their problems have been taken over by the two new Dominions. Pakistan, beyond any comparison weaker than the old Empire, is responsible for all the Northwest Frontier in its generally accepted sense; though should India retain all Kashmir it will have a short frontier (40 miles) with Afghanistan north of Gilgit. Most of the Burma frontier falls to India, but the 125 miles or so where Eastern Pakistan and Burma adjoin includes the narrow coastal lowland, where there is traditional enmity between Chittagong Muslims and Arakanese Buddhists and where territorial demands have been advanced, not very seriously, from either side.[1]

To the old frontiers have been added the Indo-Pakistan boundaries: some 1800 miles both in the east and in the west, excluding the Pakistan-Kashmir boundary. The eastern is completely arbitrary, except where it runs along the margins between the delta alluvium and the old block of the Shillong plateau or the lateritic uplands of Tripura, and it has been drawn with an amazing disregard of communication lines.[2] In the west, most of the new boundary is already defined by the old internal boundaries between Sind, Khairpur, and Bahawalpur on the Pakistan, Cutch and Rajputana on the Indian side. So far it lies along the arid shores of the Rann of Cutch (where the precise alignment is disputed, but of negligible significance) or through the wastes of the Thar Desert; but the 180 miles of the new boundary in the Punjab, although mostly coinciding with old local boundaries, and in part with the Ravi and Sutlej, is superposed through the heart of the most developed part of the Punjab, bisecting the

[1] In 1942 these parties seem to have regarded British and Japanese as mere auxiliaries in their own local war which broke out on the collapse of civil government in Burma.

[2] For details see O. H. K. Spate, "The Partition of India and the Prospects of Pakistan", *Geographical Review*, XXXVIII (1948) pp. 5–29, and "The Partition of the Punjab and of Bengal." *Geographical Journal*, CX (1947), pp. 201–222. All boundary figures are approximations neglecting minor sinuosities.

important Upper Bari Doab Canal system and passing midway between the great cities of Lahore and Amritsar. On the north the Kashmir-Pakistan boundary (560 miles) lies mainly at the foot of the outermost Himalayan foothills, as do the India-Nepal and India-Bhután boundaries in the *terai* already noted.

Western Pakistan detached three entire provinces, Sind, Baluchistan, and North-West Frontier Province (N.-W.F.P.), with relatively or absolutely sparse populations, where the Muslim majorities were overwhelming; together with some three-fifths of the area and population of the Punjab, where the Muslims formed a majority of 57%. Eastern Pakistan comprises about two-thirds of the area and population of Bengal, where Muslims made up 55% the population of the province, plus most of Sylhet, by far the most important and densely populated District of Assam. Of the States only Bahawalpur, Khairpur, and those of Baluchistan and the N-W.F.P. have acceded to Pakistan. All other States have joined the Indian Union—Hyderabad, Junagadh, and Kashmir not without crises. At the time of writing Kashmir is partly under Indian occupation and partly under an insurgent Muslim 'Free Kashmir' government, while the remoter mountain areas probably go their own way pending a settlement. Table IV summarises the territorial position, with populations as in 1941, although in some provinces, most notably the two Punjabs, these, and the communal composition, have undergone great changes as a result of the post-partition transfers of population.

DEMOGRAPHIC AND SOCIAL FACTORS

POPULATION

The total population of the Indian sub-continent now probably exceeds 400 millions. In 1941 the average density of All-India was 246 to the square miles—about five or six times the usual estimates for the world average; the territories now within the Indian Union (excluding Kashmir) had 274 to the square mile. There was of course very great internal variation in density, from under 6 in large areas of Baluchistan, the Thar, and Kashmir, to 779 over the entire province of Bengal (77,442 square miles) and 818 in the 9155 square miles of Travancore and Cochin. In Cochin there are small areas with a rural population of over 2000 to the square mile, while Dacca Division (Eastern Pakistan) had in 1941 a density of 1077 on an area twice the size of Wales, with hardly any large towns and not inconsiderable areas of jungle.

The general geographical control of density is obvious: alluvial lowlands with either good and assured rainfall or large-scale irrigation at one extreme, while at the other areas with under 40 to the square mile are all either arid or mountainous or both. Areas of high density form a girdle, around the coast from Gujarat to Bengal and thence up the Indo-Gangetic plain to the central Punjab. Much of this area has over 450 to the square mile (Gujarat, Malabar, most of the Carnatic, the east coast deltas, the Indo-Gangetic plain as far as the Chenab), while the area with over 800 is not small: eastern Bengal, eastern United Provinces and western Bihar, Cochin and Travancore. Clearly such densities, which it must be remembered are for the most part made up of overwhelmingly rural populations, express extremely severe pressure on resources.

The increase of population between 1891 (when territorial expansion was complete and the Censuses become more reliable) and 1941 was nearly 110,000,000 or about 39%; from 1931 to 1941 it was no less than 50,878,091.[1] These figures are alarming: India is very fairly comparable with western Europe in area, population, and rate of increase over the last century or so, but the degree of industrialization falls very far short of that with which the great expansion of European population was asso-ciated. It is true that agricultural productivity has risen, but whether it has risen so fast as population is disputable, and on the most optimistic view all that can be said is that production, at least until recent years, has kept ahead of population but at a rapidly decreasing distance.

A marked feature of the growth, until 1931, has been the alternation of high decennial increases with low. This is generally taken as clear evidence of pressure on means of subsistence; so low is the standard of nutrition and health that there are no reserves of vitality to meet dearth or pestilence. The 1918 influenza epidemic cost millions of lives and the increase 1911–21 was only 2,680,091 or 0·9%. It is quite possible that the 1943 famine in Bengal (and less acute but very real famines and dearths else-where), with the specially high mortality of children and young mothers, may be reflected in a similar drop in 1941–51.

Much has been written on the influence of Indian social customs on demography. Despite disclaimers, there appears little doubt that religious sanctions place a premium on early marriage and large families. The prohibition of widow re-marriage by Hinduism would work the other way, but is of the less importance since there is a very striking deficiency of females, only 935 to 1000 males for All-India in 1941. In only two provinces (Madras and Orissa) and a few small States (including Cochin)

---

[1] Some slight doubt may attach to the actual figure, but the error is not enough to affect the argument. The relations of the increases in population and productivity are highly controversial, but the guarded statement in the text attempts a fair summary.

were there more women than men, and of the rest only Bihar, Central Provinces, Deccan States, and Hyderabad had over 950 females to 1000 males. The statistics do not admit of the calculation of net reproduction rates, and vital statistics, being very largely dependent on the sense of duty of underpaid and half-literate village officials, are grossly deficient by anything from 20 to 33%. They do however make it possible to discern some trends. Death-rates have fallen from 24–31 per thousand in 1920–27 to 22–24 in 1935–40, and during the same periods infantile mortality ranged between 175–195 and 156–164 per 1000 live births—still an appalling toll. Birth-rates oscillated between 32 and 36 per thousand from 1920 to 1940; the war years saw some remarkably sharp decreases, but these were probably due to famine and to the drain of males to war and industry, and it is too early to reach an optimistic conclusion— optimistic, for while one cannot but wish a diminution of the physical and emotional suffering occasioned by infantile and maternal mortality, some decrease of the birth-rate as well as of mortality seems essential if the Malthusian cycle of pressure on resources is ever to be broken.

URBANISM

Increasing urbanism has been a pronounced feature of this century. It is true that in 1941 no fewer than 450,902 of the 658,595 towns and villages had under 500 inhabitants, while only 4223 had over 5000; and many Indian 'towns' are such only by courtesy. But the total urban population grew between 1921 and 1941 from 20,445,823 to 27,289,823, an increase of 33·5% compared with a total population increase of 15%. More striking and (despite some inflation for communal reasons in 1941) less ambiguous is the growth of large towns; in 1931 those with over 100,000 inhabitants numbered 38 with a total population of 9,674,032, in 1941 these figures were 57 and 16,533,141, an increase of 81%. Of these seven—Calcutta, Bombay, Madras, Hyderabad (Deccan), Lahore, Ahmedabad, and Delhi, in that order—had over 500,000 each and accounted for over 6,900,000 people. Of the total population of All-India 12·8% was urban in 1941, and of the urban total 32·8% lived in cities of over 100,000.

Pakistan is less urbanised than India. There were in 1941 only 19 towns with over 50,000 inhabitants, against 133 in India (including Hyderabad and Kashmir); only one, Lahore, had over 500,000, although Karachi may now be near or beyond this figure. The total population in towns of over 50,000 was 2,672,315, under 4% of the 1941 population; the figures for India were 19,732,580 and over 6%. Despite its much higher density—

over eight times that of the western block—Eastern Pakistan was far less urbanized than Western. The figures for Eastern Pakistan are indeed almost incredibly small—only five towns of over 50,000 (total population 475,792 or 1·1%), and the largest of these, Dacca, had only 213,218 inhabitants, an extraordinarily low proportion of the population for the capital of a province of 42 million people.

COMMUNITY

The 'communities' recognized by the Indian Census and in Indian politics are primarily religious divisions, although race, language, caste, occupation, geographical localization, and broad cultural distinctions also play a part in their definition: thus the aboriginal tribes include Hindus, Christians, and even some Muslims, though the majority of them are animists. Communal distributions have been greatly altered by the vast shifts of population consequent on partition: no reliable figures for these movements are available, but a total of 10 million migrants is perhaps not exaggerated, and this mainly in the key areas between Chenab and Jumna where the two major communities were fairly balanced and where most of the Sikhs lived. Of the 92 million Muslims in All-India in 1941, some 22 million were in Western and 29 in Eastern Pakistan territories, leaving over 40 million "unredeemed". Kashmir and Hyderabad account for about 5 million, and after transfers the number of Muslims in the Indian Union may be reckoned as some 30–35 million on a 1941 basis, while Western Pakistan is now probably over 90% Muslim. Most of the nearly 6 million Sikhs are in East Punjab (India) and the associated Sikh States: this concentration, and their extreme sense of being a chosen people, may well raise serious problems for the Union. Of the 6 million Indian Christians over two-thirds are in Madras, Travancore, and Cochin; in these two States they form respectively 32 and 29% of the population. The Parsees, numbering only about 100,000 but with an altogether disproportionate share of economic initiative, are concentrated in Gujarat and western Bombay, about half of them in Bombay City. The Jains (1,449,000) have their strongholds in Rajputana and Gujarat, but they too are active commercially, as traders and financiers rather than industrialists, and their influence is strong as far afield as Calcutta. The jungly hills, especially in Assam and in a belt right across the north of the Peninsula and down the Eastern Ghats, are still largely inhabited by primitive tribesmen, numbering over 25 millions; their survival, or assimilation on tolerable terms, is not the least of the human problems facing India. Finally, within the Hindu fold there is the great cleavage between the

60 million 'Scheduled Castes' (Depressed Classes or Untouchables) and the main mass of caste Hindus.

LANGUAGE AND LITERACY

The ethnic stocks of India are numerous and much mingled, but racial differences are of very little practical significance beside those of language. Much nonsense has indeed been written about the diversity of tongues, anything from 180 to 220 distinct languages being listed. But the enormous majority of these are tribal splinters of no practical account, although exceedingly interesting to the student of linguistics; one was returned as spoken by one person.[1] There are only some 12 or 15 really important languages, and some of these are closely akin; this is hardly an alarming total for a continental area. The most important distinction is that between the Dravidian tongues of the south, of which Telugu (over 26 million speakers in 1931) and Tamil (20 million) are the chief, and the Indo-Aryan languages of the north and centre, which together are spoken by about three-quarters of the population of the sub-continent: Hindi with its various branches ranks numerically as one of the greater languages of the world, with 50 or 60 million speakers. Bi- and even tri-lingualism are widespread in all classes except the peasantry of linguistically homogeneous areas.

Yet the problem of a common language remains serious; the world has seen many examples of the use of the linguistic weapon by forces making for disunity. So far English has accounted for most serious scholarship and has been a *lingua franca* for the intelligentsia; but only 1% of the population is literate in English, though English of sorts is understood by many illiterates. The language areas are not (except for Bengali and Oriya) coterminous with provinces or states; perhaps fortunately, although a linguistic re-division of India has long been a favourite hobby of Congress.[2] The attachment of the various groups to their own scripts is a serious bar to intercourse, the more irrational in that the majority of the Indo-Aryan scripts (with the major exception of

---

[1] On which R. Palme Dutt remarks that "the philosophical conception of language as a means of communication between human beings will have to be revised in the light of Andro; Nora, with a grand total of two speakers, just scrapes through." (*India To-day* (1940), p. 264, citing *Imperial Gazetteer of India*, Vol. I (1909) pp. 390–394). In any case the number of "languages" should be reduced by about half, owing to the separation of Burma, to which country 128 of the 134 Tibeto-Burman languages listed in the 1931 Census were confined. For balanced reviews of the problem see S. N. Chib, *Languages, Universities, and Nationalism in India* (1936) and S. K. Chatterji, *Languages and the Linguistic Problem* (Oxford Pamphlets on Indian Affairs, 1943).

[2] The Commission appointed to study this problem has recommended that action be postponed indefinitely.

Urdu) stem from Sanskrit, and of the Dravidian from Pali. Romaniza-
tion would seem an impartial solution but is not very likely to be adopted.
At present English remains the main language of administration, though
vernaculars are being introduced; nationalist opinion on the whole
favours the spread of Hindi or its less elaborated variant Hindustani.
Hindi is the more literary language of the two, with a highly Sanskritized
technical vocabulary, and using the Sanskritic Nagari script; Urdu, the
court or camp language of the Moguls, is similar in construction and in
much of the basic vocabulary, but uses Persian script and draws on Persian
for its higher vocabulary. Urdu of course has been favoured by Muslims,
and preparations are being made for its use in university teaching in
Western Pakistan; in Eastern the hold of Bengali is too strong for Urdu
to be lightly substituted. The Osmania University in Hyderabad was
the only one to use an Indian language as the medium of instruction before
1947; but as the language was Urdu it could hardly be regarded as that
of the people of the State, who speak Marathi or Telugu. The Urdu-
Hindi controversy is of less importance since the creation of Pakistan;
but there is strong opposition in the Dravidian south to the introduction
of Hindi.

There is no lack of educational statistics, but a real assessment of educational progress is difficult. In 1941 the percentage of literacy (defined as
ability to read and write a postcard in any language) was 12·2% of the
whole population, against 6·9% in 1931; but of course this is very unequally distributed geographically, communally, and sexually. In 1931
15·6% of males and only 2·9% of females were literate; the total increase
1931–41 was about 75%, that for males 60% and for females 150%.
Education is on the whole badly balanced; it is impossible to serve for
long in an Indian University without feeling that the structure is top-
heavy, as if the concrete university buildings were perched on top of the
brick-built high schools and they in turn on the mere huts of village
schools. The proportion of literates who have been to a university is
higher than in the west, and while the number of university students is
certainly not beyond the needs of the country in an absolute sense, it is
too high for reasonable adjustment to current social conditions. Standards are unequal and wastage appalling, and there is a pronounced
preference for arts subjects and for legal education, leading to the creation
of a semi-trained intellectual proletariat, while good technicians are in
very short supply. The redressing of this ill-balance, for which responsibility should perhaps be shared pretty equally by British and Indian
traditions and attitudes, will be no small task. Reconstruction at the top
depends on a bold (and financially perhaps even reckless) programme of

elementary education in the countryside, an indispensable element in the indispensable agrarian revolution.

RESOURCES AND WAYS OF LIFE

CLIMATE AND AGRICULTURE

The primary resources of India are land, rain, and men; the useful elements of all three are very unequally distributed. Climate, especially rainfall, although not the fundamental, is the most significant of the trinity, since it largely conditions the use of land and the distribution and occupations of men. The climates of India are in detail varied, but they have the essential unity of the monsoonal rhythm natural in a land extending in latitude from 8° to 34°N (excluding Himalayan Kashmir), walled around by mountains on the landward side but open to great air-masses from the Indian Ocean.

Temperature, though significant in terms of human activity and comfort, is of less direct importance than rainfall, although in another sense it is primary since its alternations determine the monsoonal mechanisms: it is the super-heating of the northwestern plains which induces the steeply-graded low pressures responsible in their turn for drawing the Southeast Trades into India as the 'southwest' or rainy monsoon. On the west coast in particular, where the winds blow directly on to a narrow lowland backed by the 3000-foot scarp of the Ghats, the onset of the torrential rains in early June is abrupt and spectacular: in a few days a dreary khaki and grey countryside is clothed in every imaginable shade of green; but the rainfall decreases very rapidly beyond the crest of the Ghats. On the eastern side, where the monsoon drives up the Ganges valley from the southeast, transitions both in time and space are less abrupt. The west coast gets annually 80–100 inches or more, as do eastern Bengal, most of Assam, and a strip along the Himalayas; but in the lee of the Western Ghats the annual rainfall decreases to only 25–40 inches within 100 miles of the sea, while in the Ganges valley such low figures are not reached before western United Provinces, some 700–800 miles from the Bay of Bengal.

The rains, from June to October, bring about 85% of the total precipitation. Actual falls are of course intermittent, depending on position in relation to the main monsoon currents, local relief, and the mingling of old continental air from the northwest with older or fresher masses of monsoon air. The amount and reliability of rainfall decreases, and the breaks in the rains are longer and more numerous, with increasing distance

10

from the coasts; and in the northwest and in the western interior of the Peninsula variability is extreme and agriculture correspondingly precarious. The northwestern plains get under 20 inches, and Sind, Baluchistan, and western Rajputana under 10. In Sind and in most of the Punjab agriculture on any large scale is therefore dependent on irrigation.

Certain areas receive significant rainfall outside the normal rainy season:

(i) a sub-montane strip in the northwest, extending eastwards as far as the Jumna, receives a few inches (generally not more than two a month) in the cold weather; this originates in westerly 'Mediterranean' depressions and is of great importance for the *rabi* or winter crops of wheat and barley, in their turn largely responsible for the better diet and physique of Punjabis and so indirectly not without political significance.

(ii) Assam and Bengal receive up to 20 inches (the exact amount depending on local factors) from violent thundery depressions in May and June: the tea crop is largely dependent on these hot-weather storms.

(iii) the southeast littoral receives most of its rain from the retreating monsoon in October-December.

The prosperity of agriculture, unless safeguarded by large-scale perennial irrigation, is entirely dependent on a good monsoon. Of the total area of British India, some 512 million acres, about 90 million were reckoned as not available for cultivation, 70 as forest, 50 as fallow, 220 as sown to crops. The balance, although formerly returned as 'culturable waste', consisted very largely of broken, arid, or scrub-clad terrain practically useless except for rough grazing. Between 50 and 60 million acres were irrigated, and double or multiple cropping brought the total cultivated area to about 250 million acres. Of this about three-quarters were under foodgrains, the chief being rice with 70-75, wheat with 25-35, and millets with 40-45 million acres. All these figures are of course only approximate, and indeed the statistical machinery is so crude as to render refined calculations profitless. (See Tables VI and VII).

The special domains of rice are the wet littorals, particularly the east coast and Bengal deltas, and the Ganges valley as far as Patna: but it is of course grown in favoured or irrigated areas beyond these limits, and Western Pakistan has a useful surplus. Wheat is dominant in the Indus basin and western United Provinces, areas with under 40 inches and a marked cool season: millets are grown in all the drier and less favoured areas, especially on the plateaus of Peninsular India. Of non-plantation commercial crops cotton (12-15 million acres), jute (2-4), oilseeds (15-17), and sugar (3-5) are the most important. Cotton has two major zones: the Indus basin, producing mainly long-stapled American and Egyptian varieties, and the northwest of the Peninsula, where it is grown on the Gujarat alluvium and on the famous black cotton soils (*regur*) formed on the Deccan Lavas and very retentive of moisture. Madras is the leading province for groundnuts, followed by Bihar: the Punjab for rapeseed, Central Provinces for linseed, and Madras again for sesamum, the oil from which is of great culinary importance. Well over half the sugar comes from the United Provinces, and the great bulk of the jute from East and West Bengal. Of minor crops tobacco is widely grown, and coconuts are of great importance to life in the wetter littorals; indeed the rice-coconut combination maintains the highest population densities. The chief plantation products are tea, mainly in Assam with some around Darjeeling and in Eastern Pakistan, coffee around the Nilgiris, and rubber in Madras.

Pakistan's share of these resources is evaluated below (p. 160).

THE AGRARIAN PROBLEM

If the contradiction be permitted, it may be said that for decades India has been labouring in an agrarian crisis both chronic and acute. At least three-quarters of the population is directly dependent upon or closely connected with agriculture: the direct pressure on land is extreme, and despite the great proportion of land devoted to locally consumed food crops the mass of the people is under-nourished, an easy prey to epidemic and endemic disease, while the war years saw a recrudescence of famine not confined to Bengal.

With a rural population in British India of at least 250,000,000 and a total cultivated area—including double-cropping—of about the same number of acres, it is obvious that holdings must be small. (Cf. Table V). Small holdings are made smaller by minute fragmentation; 1/16th of an acre has been split amongst five separate cultivators; in one Deccan village in which 60% of the holdings were under 5 acres, 463 of 729 separate plots were under 1 acre, and 112 under 0·25 acre. These evils tend to increase with the growth of population; legislation fostering consolidation does exist, and in some places progress has been made, but obviously the obstacles are great. In recent decades there has been an alarming increase in the number of landless peasants, of whom there are perhaps 20 or 30 million—far more than can be absorbed by industry.

Such small holdings imply, of course, great insecurity; hence the power of the *bania* or village moneylender, who is not infrequently the local grain-broker and retail shopkeeper as well. As the peasant has little in the way of storage facilities and access to market information, he is obviously in an extremely vulnerable position even given a run of good harvests: interest rates are high, and when crop failures and festivities snch as weddings and caste celebrations are taken into account it is not surprising that a very large proportion of cultivators are permanently in debt. Something has been done by co-operative credit, which has at least provided competition to keep the *bania's* interest rates down; but the co-operative's methods are much less flexible than those of the money-lender, and when they do become flexible are liable to slide over into slackness and insolvency; and in any case co-operation directly affects only a very small fraction of the peasantry. Tenancy legislation and restriction of land alienation have done much to mitigate the helplessness of the cultivator, and in the war years high agricultural prices and a shortage of consumer goods conduced to a great reduction of debt; while progressive administrations have done much by spreading current market information. But none of these things is more than a palliative.

It is thus not surprising that methods are often primitive (though in some cases not ill adapted to the concrete problems) and that the use o fertilisers and modern implements gains ground but slowly. This is reflected in the yields per acre, which for all important crops are well below world averages. The peasant has neither capital nor (with much of his return pre-empted for debts or taxes) much incentive to improve; he cannot afford to risk even one year's crop on an experiment. Practically speaking, and except for a few favoured groups or areas, the peasant is compelled to a hand-to-mouth existence, satisfied if he can get through the year without utter disaster such as a forced sale of his draught bullocks. Indeed he may be said to have no choice but improvidence; and it is idle to blame him for the undeniable extravagance with which he marries his daughter or celebrates the birth of his son: some break in the routine he must have if he is to remain a human being.

Except in the newer alluvial areas, the *khadar* floodplains where annual inundations bring fresh silt, soils have been in general thoroughly leached by generations of tillage and exposure to seasonally concentrated rainfall. Over much of the area they seem to have reached the irreducible minimum of fertility. It is estimated that there are some 213 million head of all types of cattle, including buffaloes—nearly 30% of the world's bovine population.[1] According to R. K. Mukherjee a cattle population of 25 per 100 acres sown would be adequate; the actual numbers range from 35 (Bombay) to 102 (Bengal), and not only are these numbers in themselves excessive, but a high proportion consists of old or diseased stock, so that

[1] *Eastern Economist*, New Delhi, 3 Dec. 1948.

in some areas there are hardly enough good working cattle for tillage, while the fierce competition for scanty pasture tends to perpetuate the cycle of disease and inefficiency. But at least it would seem, at first sight, that large quantities of manure should be available. Unfortunately in many areas most of the cow-dung is used for fuel; and it is difficult to abolish this practice unless alternative supplies of fuel can be made available. Moreover there is an acute shortage of grazing ground over most of the more densely settled plains. The new government of India can hardly gainsay Hindu sentiment against cow slaughter which, with the virtual absence of eugenic breeding, keeps in being millions of half-starved, diseased, and useless cattle, often condemned to a miserable existence on wayside patches of grass and weeds. Plains forests are often more important as sources of fodder, thatch, and dye- and tan-stuffs than for timber; and over large areas trees are almost confined to village mango-groves and riverine strips of tamarisk jungle. Fuel forests are a prime necessity if cattle-dung is to be used for manure instead of fuel; but their provision is difficult in regions where the pressure on land is so great that there is little room for village-sites, which may become as congested as an industrial slum; and even if land could be found the control of illicit felling and destructive grazing would present an almost insuperable task. An extension of forest is also needed in many areas as part of a soil conservation policy. Something has already been done: the disastrous soil erosion on the Punjab Siwaliks, and the associated sandspreads below them, due to deforestation by charcoal-burners and goats, have been checked; contour-bunding and the planting of quick-growing trees, shrubs, and grasses have extended grazing and reclaimed some of the wildly-gullied badlands around such rivers as the Jumna and the Chambal; in the Punjab there are actually irrigated forests, and in Madras casuarina plantations provide fuel. The situation is not so bad in the hillier regions which, except in the arid northwest, are generally fairly well-wooded. But over most of the plains the provision of fuel, fodder, and manure still presents a joint problem of great complexity.

It is, perhaps, a realization of the difficulties attending an attempt to increase the unit-productivity of agriculture which is responsible for such projects as the 200% increase in irrigation called for by the 'Bombay Plan' for general economic development, put forward by a group of business men (among whom the driving element would seem to be the house of Tata) in 1945. Irrigation already accounted for 20–25% of the total cultivated area of British India, and for large areas in the States. The landscape of the northwest has been transformed by great perennial canals, of which the Triple Project in the Punjab ranks as one of the boldest pieces of planning in the world, while in Sind the Sukkur or Lloyd Barrage alone will soon have brought under cultivation an area nearly equal to the entire cultivated area of Egypt. A large proportion of the irrigated area is dependent on more indigenous methods—inundation canals in the *khadar* floodplains (though the more important of these were either constructed or remodelled by the British); tanks or reservoirs, either excavated or formed by earthen or masonry dams, which in the south especially are often of great antiquity and sited with an excellent topographical eye; wells worked by a variety of methods. Altogether canals accounted for 53% of the irrigated area, tanks 11%, wells 25%, the rest being supplied by a variety of primitive and temporary devices. Many schemes for extension are on foot, some, like those on the Kosi and Damodar rivers, being multi-purpose projects providing for flood control and hydro-electricity as well as irrigation.

But it is difficult to see how so large an increase as that called for by the Bombay Plan can be attained. The rivers of the Peninsula, fed only by the monsoon and practically dry for half the year, flowing for the most part in graded courses with few good barrage-sites, are obviously not so suitable as the snow-fed Himalayan streams; and here the best opportunities have already been exploited. Further schemes will call for a very high capital outlay in relation to area commanded, and while many of them will be well worth it in terms of welfare, there are limits to what can be done by Government in a country where the true function of taxation is not, for good reason, well understood. One most promising line of advance is the utilization of ground water in the thick Gangetic alluvium; in western United Provinces small power stations using artificial falls, 10 or 12 feet high, on irrigation canals supply hydro-electricity to work deep tube-wells on the higher *doabs* or interfluves beyond the reach of canal irrigation. Local agricultural industries, such as sugar cane-crushing, are also powered by this means.

Wisely directed such development may revolutionize rural life, at least locally. Along with advance on such lines an intensive development of artificial fertilizers is needed; here restriction of the export of raw oilseeds would retain useful fertilizer and cattle-feed in the country, as well as the processing profits. The present consumption of fertilizers in India is ludicrously small: pre-war it was only 0·61 lbs. per acre (against e.g. 233 in Egypt), and half of that was on the relatively very small plantation areas. This problem has been taken in hand; there is some production in Travancore, and the great state plant nearing completion at Sindri (in the Damodar valley) is planned to produce 350,000 tons of ammonium sulphate a year; the loss of the Salt Range to Pakistan may make the supply of gypsum rather more expensive, though there are deposits in Rajasthan. Great efforts are being made to bring such of the "culturable waste" as is marginal under the plough; in some provinces large-scale clearing is being done mechanically. It has been announced that at all costs food imports into India will cease by 1951. Jute acreage is being forced even into the eastern United Provinces in order to reduce the dependence of Hooghlyside on Pakistan. This will mean an increase in the competition, already severe, between food and cash crops for the available land; in Pakistan also it is doubtful whether East Bengal can be really self-sufficient in rice without some restriction of jute. There is a real dilemma for both countries here, since it is difficult to see how the financing of the great capital equipment programme, on which so much of the general advance depends, can be carried out without a large export of agricultural products; manufactures will have to meet the already re-emerging competition of Japan.

But with all this the major problem remains; an almost phenomenal increase in the standard of living of the masses is inescapably necessary if a stable and balanced economy is to be attained; and it is an open question whether this increase can be achieved without drastic limitation of births. Hitherto all increases in productivity have had as their sequel an increase of population which has largely negatived their effect. Every argument seems to point to the necessity of a restrictive demographic policy; but in the social environment of India birth control, among the masses at any rate, will remain at a discount for a long time to come.

POWER, MINERALS, INDUSTRIALIZATION

In relation to area and population the sub-continent, while not poorly endowed, is by no means so rich in industrial potentialities as enthusiastic nationalist planners tend to assume. It will simplify exposition if we note at the start that as Pakistan (excluding of course Kashmir) lies entirely in the Indo-Gangetic plain and the arid north-western hills (mainly composed of Tertiary and Cretaceous rocks), her mineral wealth is practically confined to oil, salt, chromite, and a very little inferior coal; further, she has little hydro-electric potential actually within her borders, though the inclusion of Kashmir would add much. Only in fibres does Pakistan hold a strong position. 'India' in this section thus means the Indian Union, to which the discussion is in general confined.

Most of India's mineral wealth is associated with the old rocks of the Peninsular block, and there is a very notable concentration in its north-east corner, the Bihar-Orissa-Bengal borderland being by far the most important single mineral region (cf. *Table* VIII). In marked contrast to China, India is very rich in good iron ores but poorer in coal, especially in coking coal. Of the All-India coal production, over 95% comes from the Permian Lower Gondwana rocks preserved in troughs on the Archæan surface of the Peninsula; but there are Tertiary deposits, some of good quality, in Assam, Bikaner, and the Kashmir foothills, with lignite in the Vale of Kashmir. Pakistan has poorer deposits in the Salt Range and in Baluchistan, conveniently close to Quetta. All-Indian total output fluctuates between 22 and 28 million tons a year, of which 80% come from the Damodar valley fields (especially Raniganj and Jheria) on the Bihar-Bengal border; next, but a long way after, come scattered fields in the Central Provinces and Hyderabad. Reserves in seams over four feet thick and within 2000 feet of the surface are estimated at between 5000 and 6000 million tons, of which about 1500 million are good coking coal.[1] Much of this is not readily accessible, however, and although the present rate of consumption is not high, increases are clearly called for if the ambitious industrial programmes are to be carried out; the coke position has already given rise to some anxiety. Seams are generally thick but methods wasteful, and there is great difficulty in securing adequate and stable labour from the local population, who are largely aboriginal tribes-men. As for iron, reserves are immense—at least 3600 million tons with an iron content of 60%. Most of these are on the Bihar-Orissa border, with a considerable proportion in the wild and undeveloped State of Bastar (now merged in the Central Provinces). The industry is largely localized at Jamshedpur, where the Tata family has built up one of the world's largest iron and steel works. Mysore has also important ores, and here excellent iron is smelted with charcoal.

Next in importance are manganese and mica, in both of which India is one of the largest producers and, owing to the small home consumption, the largest exporter. The Central Provinces, Madras, and Bihar are the leading manganese producers; the Hazaribagh plateau in Bihar produces 80% of the mica, and this is generally about half the world production. Gold is produced mainly from the Kolar fields in Mysore. Recently a start has been made on exploiting the great reserves of bauxite con-tained in the wide-spread laterites. The beach-sands of Travancore con-tain the richest known deposits of monazite, an important source of thorium, the significance of which needs no emphasis in an atomic age. Refractories and important chemicals are represented by chromite (Balu-chistan and Mysore), silica from Bihar quartzites, magnesite, kyanite,

---

[1] Later estimates (1946) give the reserves of coking coal at 700–750 million tons—only 65 years' consumption at present rates.

gypsum, barytes, and zircons and other abrasives. Outside the Salt Range (in Pakistan) the chief salt deposits are in the wind-impregnated saline lakes of Rajputana, but much is produced by evaporation of sea-water. Petroleum resources are limited: there is an output of 50–75 million gallons from Assam and 15–20 million gallons from Attock (Western Pakistan); further possibilities seem to be confined to Western Pakistan, where prospecting is active in Sind. Apart from oil, the chief deficiencies will be seen to be non-ferrous metals, especially tin, lead, and zinc; but these are fairly easily available from Southeast Asia, and India has sufficient resources for extensive metallurgical and chemical industries. Unfortunately, except for the Bihar concentrations, most of the minerals are far removed from adequate supplies of coal, and some of them, such as bauxite, must wait on the more extensive development of hydro-electricity.

One cannot indeed resist the impression that the word 'hydel' is used in India as a magic incantation charming away all difficulties; not indeed that great potentialities are lacking, but costs and the time-factor seem to be cheerfully ignored. Less than 1 million Kw are actually developed, but estimates of potentialities, which vary from 12 to 27 million Kw or more, obviously promise much scope for expansion. Seasonality of river régime, the very mature or even senile topography of much of the Peninsula, contorted shaly strata and liability to earthquakes on the Himalayan flanks, are all limiting factors. The most favourable areas are the Himalayan slopes and the Assam plateau, the Western Ghats and the Nilgiris; while the north of the Peninsula and even the southern Deccan have some good sites. Even in the Indo-Gangetic plain small falls on canals can be utilized, as already noted. So far the most important developments have been on the Western Ghats, powering much of Bombay's industry, and in the Nilgiris, where hydro-electricity has fostered a remarkable industrial expansion in such towns as Coimbatore, Madura, Salem, and Trichinopoly. In the north the Mandi installation, on a tributary of the upper Beas, serves both Pakistani and Indian Punjab. Pakistan itself has some, but almost certainly too little, power: around its borders sites exist in montane East Punjab, in Kashmir, and in Indian Assam; but these areas are not likely to be high on the list of Indian priorities. In India much importance is attached to the great combined schemes for flood control, irrigation, and power on the Damodar and the Kosi, which latter river is at present subject to exceptionally violent and destructive changes of course.

So far, however, heavy industry has been mainly dependent on coal. Modern industry is essentially a growth of this century, receiving a great impetus from the two wars (especially that of 1939–45), and domestic or artisan industries, including handloom weaving, are still responsible for a large proportion of village needs, despite the general decline of crafts consequent on the flood of cheap manufactures from the West after the Industrial Revolution.

Industry is strongly localized and textiles still predominate, cotton accounting for some 500–600,000 and jute for 300,000 of the 2,000,000 industrial workers of All-India at the beginning of the war. Though a true urban proletariat is growing labour difficulties are still felt; the workers often have roots in the villages and in some areas and industries there is a strong tendency to absenteeism at harvest-time; this is especially the case where, as in Bihar, mineral industries have grown up more or less isolated in the countryside. More casual absenteeism and general inefficiency, largely a result of dreadful living conditions, also add to labour costs despite low money wages. Recent figures for industrial development are given in Tables IX and X.

Geographically industry is very unevenly distributed; apart from occupations which merely follow population, such as brick-making and printing, and the scatter of agricultural processing (rice-mills, cotton ginneries and presses, sugar-refineries, oilseed presses) the following main regions may be distinguished:

(i) Hooghlyside; perhaps one-third of India's industrial development, with practically all the jute mills;
(ii) the Bombay cotton belt, with poles in Bombay and Ahmedabad, and outliers at Sholapur and Nagpur;
(iii) Chota Nagpur (Bihar) with its mineral industries, especially the remarkable iron and steel town of Jamshedpur;
(iv) the Nilgiri group in Madras and Mysore, mainly textile and agricultural industries using hydro-electricity.

The greater ports—Calcutta, Bombay, to a lesser extent Madras—have of course a good deal of miscellaneous 'metropolitan' industry. Very few inland towns, except those of southern Madras, have much industrial importance; the chief exceptions are Ahmedabad and Cawnpore, the latter the leading woollen and leather centre. Cities such as Lahore and Amritsar still have craft industries such as the manufacture of carpets, embroideries, specialized textiles, gold and silver ornaments, and small metal goods, which, although carried on in tiny units, are in aggregate not inconsiderable.

COMMUNICATIONS

The railway system of All-India was the fourth largest in the world, with over 40,000 miles of track, of which 33,904 remain in the Indian Union. In relation to population, however, the figures are less striking, only about one mile to 9,750 persons, as compared with 550 in U.S.A. and even 2000 in the U.S.S.R. with its vast areas of sparse population. Half the mileage is broad-gauge, the rest mainly metre; most of it is single track, and electrification is confined to the lines from Bombay to Poona and to Igatpuri (i.e. to the top of the Ghats) and to suburban lines around Bombay and Madras. The densest railnets are in the Ganges valley and the northern Punjab, in Gujarat, and in southern Madras; but except in the Punjab the mixture of gauges impedes through working. In the plains, especially in the Bengal delta, the need for many bridges and the lack of ballast hamper construction. On the whole the more productive parts of the sub-continent are fairly adequately served, but pressure on the system is very heavy and, although it cannot be called inefficient and has few missing links of any great importance, a good deal of minor improvement and co-ordination is called for.

The roads however are deplorably inadequate both in quantity and quality. In British India there were in 1943 95,000 miles of metalled and 200,000 miles of unmetalled roads, excluding of course town streets and roads. Of these 295,000 miles, only 43% were motorable all the year. The position in the States is generally worse. Since also the major roads often parallel the railways, it follows that a large proportion of the 655,000 or so villages have no road connections at all. In 1940 there were only about 175,000 motor vehicles of all descriptions. It is true that the war added considerably to road mileage (much of the addition however being not where it was needed economically) and to the number of vehicles, but it is clear that both the development of a more flexible distributive system and the opening up of the remoter countryside to the amenities of life are hampered by the reliance on bad dry-weather tracks and on bullock-carts, the latter often of very poor design, extremely heavy in relation to capacity. Yet of all agents tending to break down the squalid isolationism of the Indian village, the motor-bus is probably by far the most effective.

Except on the Brahmaputra and in the Bengal delta, inland water transport is now of very little importance. Coastal shipping also is relatively little developed, except on the west coast between Kathiawar and Cochin, where much of it is carried on by small sailing country craft. Minor ports have been neglected; nearly three-quarters of the total sea-borne trade of British India were shared by Bombay and Calcutta, a very large proportion in a sub-continent which has 4,000 miles of coast and in which freight charges on long hauls have been a serious impediment to industrial and commercial development. The dominance of British shipping has long been a major nationalist grievance; the largest Indian shipping company owns about 150,000 tons, and the first Indian passenger ship to England arrived there in August 1948. The war saw the start of the building of small mechanically-propelled vessels, and larger developments are under way at Vizagapatam. The Union Government is likely to give high priority to shipping interests, as well as to those of civil aviation, which is rapidly increasing in importance.

INTERNAL PROBLEMS OF THE INDIAN UNION

THE STATE STRUCTURE (*Fig.* 14).

According to the new constitution, India is a 'Sovereign Democratic Republic'; with the proclamation of the Republic in January 1950 its relationship with the Commonwealth approximates to that of Eire before it cut adrift. In structure it is a federation with residual powers vested in the Centre. The central legislature is bi-cameral, consisting of an upper Council of States and an elected House of the Peoples; the components of the Union, whether ex-British Provinces, old States, or Unions of States, will be known as States, but it is likely that habit and the convenience of the distinction will retain the old name of Province for some years, even in semi-official literature. Despite some sentimental nationalist objections, the capital will probably remain at New Delhi, which is in effect in a Federal District.

The first geographical problem confronting the Union, after the initial turmoil of partition, was simply the re-organization of its own territory. In the old Empire there were 584 States of all sorts and sizes, from countries larger in area and population than many of the states in the United Nations Organization down to petty lordships with some slight pretences to an autonomous political entity. Concretely, they ranged from Hyderabad and Kashmir, both over 80,000 square miles in area and the former with over 16,000,000 people, to such freaks as the Estates of Varnoli Nana and Nahara in Western India, which had respectively areas of 1 and 3 square miles, populations of 96 and 566, and annual revenues of £30 and £7 2s. 6d. The fragmentation of these States was extreme, Baroda for example having its 8,176 square miles split into four or five large and some 30 small pieces. (Cf. *Fig.* 15). Many were indefensible anachronisms, a princely proletariat unable to support any decent

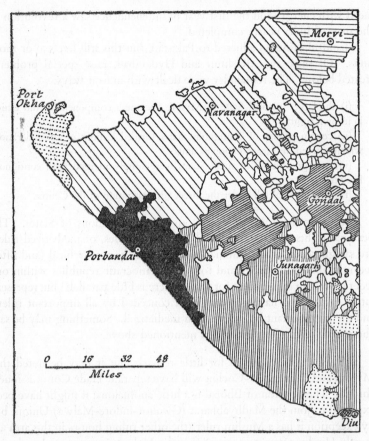

Fig. 15. TERRITORIAL FRAGMENTATION IN KATHIAWAR
The largest state shown, Navanagar, had 3791 sq. miles and population (1941)
504,006. The 106 fragments unshaded were parcelled among 40 states (E. & O.E.).
The entire area, except Portuguese Diu and the exclaves of Baroda (now Bombay;
dotted) is now part of the Union of Saurashtra.

administration, let alone social services, but often with their own legal and
fiscal arrangements and local imposts, lying across economic and communication lines. The Agencies into which they were grouped were
mere conveniences for the British Residents who exercised some supervision over them, but had no formal powers of internal interference unless
and until misgovernment reached a point at which serious disturbances
seemed imminent. There had been a few half-hearted tentatives at co-
ordination, but drastic reform was obviously long overdue. The task was

faced with energy, and the first year of independence saw a revolution of the map of India nearly completed.

A handful of States adhered to Pakistan, but this still left 550 or more units. Of these two, Kashmir and Hyderabad, raise special problems treated below. The remainder were dealt with in four ways:

(i) the large "viable" State of Mysore became a component of the Union in its own right;

(ii) certain groups of contiguous States formed Unions or sub-federations which entered the larger Union as units;

(iii) a large number of small States were simply merged with contiguous Provinces;

(iv) certain areas fell under the direct administration of the Centre.

Altogether there are now only 16 States or Unions of States. The personal rights and dignities, and the privy purses, of mediatized rulers are safeguarded. The combination of essentially monarchical (and often recently absolutist) States and formally democratic republics within one federation is an experiment for which there is little parallel;[1] but representative institutions have perforce been conceded by all important rulers, and the unimportant ones have been mediatized. Something may be said about each of the four groupings mentioned above.

(i) The larger States call for little remark, but it may be noted that Mysore and Travancore-Cochin will have separate Trade Commissioners abroad. The position of Bhopal is a little anomalous: it might have been expected to join the Madhyabharat (Gwalior-Indore-Malwa) Union; but by exception it has a Muslim ruler (the other ruling houses in this area are mostly Hindu, often stemming from the Mahratta supremacy) and, also by exception, its territory is in one compact block; as noted below, it is now under central control.

(ii) The Unions formed are Madhyabharat, Patiala and East Punjab, Rajasthan, Saurashtra, Cochin and Travancore, and Vindhya Pradesh; the antique or fancy names are probably dictated by the desire to avoid the jealousies which the use of existing names might entail, and indeed it is obvious that no small degree of tact as well as drive was needed to overcome local particularisms and friction over such matters as choice of capitals. Cochin and Travancore form an obvious unit with a distinctive geographical and cultural individuality. Madhyabharat (= 'Middle India') includes the western and more developed States of the old Central India

_____

[1] A precedent of little point may be found in the German Empire, which included the Free Cities of Hamburg, Bremen, and Lübeck as well as its kingdoms.

Agency, less Bhopal but with the important addition of Gwalior; Rajas-than includes practically all of the Rajputana States; with the accession of Jaipur, Jodhpur, Jaisalmer, and Bikaner (January 1949) Rajasthan became the largest Union, with some 130,000 square miles and 13 million people. In Patiala and East Punjab the principle of union appears to be Sikhism, and it is probably this which has brought in Patiala, which might well have insisted on its admitted viability. Saurashtra welded no less than 449 Kathiawar units (or allowing for ex- and enclaves 860 territorial fragments) into one compact block of 37,000 square miles and nearly 4,000,000 people; it has several small ports which may be expected to gain in importance with a unified hinterland. The later accession of Junagadh brings all Kathiawar, except the Baroda enclaves (now Bombay) and Portuguese Diu, under one administration (cf. *Fig.* 15). Finally Vindhya Pradesh unites the hitherto backward States in Baghelkhand and Bundelk-hand, the eastern part of the old Central India Agency.

(iii) The States merged are mainly the very petty Eastern and Chattis-garh States, which have gone to Orissa and Central Provinces respectively, save for Seraikela and Kharsawan to Bihar; and the Gujarat and Deccan States which have gone to Bombay. But two 'viable' States, Baroda and Kolhapur, have been merged with Bombay.

(iv) The list of centrally administered States is significant. Junagadh was originally so administered; it had a Muslim ruler who opted for Pakis-tan despite his State's lack of geographical contiguity and overwhelmingly Hindu population. India refused to recognize his decision and occupied the State in operations not without an *opera bouffe* aspect; subsequent plebiscites voted for India with only a handful of dissentients. This State has now acceded to Saurashtra. Except for Bhopal and Rampur—States with Hindu populations and Muslim rulers—the areas now centrally administered are all on the borders. Sikkim lies across the trade-route to Lhasa; Manipur brings Indian territory across the Assam-Burma ranges to within 10 or 15 miles of the Chindwin. Cooch Behar and Tripura border Eastern Pakistan, Cutch Western. Bilaspur and the Punjab Hill States, now known collectively as Himachal Pradesh, were mostly very small and/or thinly populated; they have some strategic significance as lying on the flank of routes into Kashmir and athwart routes into Tibet, and Mandi, one of the larger of them, contains the very important Joginder-nath (Mandi) hydro-electric installation.

There remain the difficult problems of Kashmir and Hyderabad. Kashmir (correctly 'Jammu and Kashmir') includes the mountain country of the Indus and Jhelum basins, and part of the Chenab, from the margin of the Punjab plains to the Karakoram. Most of its 82,258 square miles are thus very thinly populated; the bulk of the 4,000,000 people live in the rich Vale of Kashmir (1,500,000) or in the foothills south of the Pir Panjal range, in Jammu and Punch (about 1,750,000). Over three-quarters of the population are Muslims; only in the southeastern Districts of Jammu proper, Kathua, and Udhampur were Hindus in 1941 the majority, slight when compared with the Muslim majorities everywhere else. There is an important Buddhist minority (a local majority) in Ladakh or Little Tibet, the upper Indus valley adjoining Tibet proper. Economically Kashmir has close links with West Punjab (Pakistan): here were Kashmir's outlets, the two main roads to Rawalpindi and Sialkot, both in Pakistan. One of the main West Punjab canal headworks (Mangla on the Jhelum) is in Kashmir, and the importance of the control of the upper Indus and Jhelum, with hydro-electric as well as irrigation potentialities, is obvious. Economically Kashmir is probably all but essential to Pakistan and of relatively little use to India, and it would certainly seem that the Pakistani case was a strong one. Unfortunately the ruler, descendant of a particularly ruthless *condottiere* under the Sikh dominion, and the ruling circles were very strongly Hindu. Communal tension in Kashmir was accentuated by definite misgovernment and further inflamed by the events following the partition in the Punjab, and the situation was complicated by a long-standing feud between the Maharajah and his vassal ruler of Punch. Faced with an incipient rising the Maharajah adhered to India in October, 1947; revolt became open, but his adhesion was accepted by India subject to a vague provision for ascertaining the wishes of the people, a task impossible during the civil war which ensued. India was now committed to extensive military operations in difficult country and with poor communications through or over the foothills and mountains of Jammu and the Pir Panjal; in the initial stages (until winter atmospheric conditions set in on the mountains) much reliance had to be placed on air transport, and the campaign was a remarkable military feat.

Legalistically of course the Maharajah was within his rights in adhering to India; his position would probably have been impossible in Pakistan, and his chances of retaining the throne in independent isolation not much better. The Pakistani case was weakened by the incursions of tribesmen from the northwest frontier, faciliated either by the active complicity or the passive incapacity of local officials; a serious attempt to stop the tribesmen would however have been tantamount to civil war within Pakistan and later it appeared that Pakistani implication went further than mere tribal action. Indian action, formally correct, consorts oddly with earlier nationalist pronouncements on the position of the Princes and with the

Indian attitude to Junagadh and Hyderabad. Pakistanis allege that it is simple imperialism, and indeed economically and strategically the complete adhesion of Kashmir to India would represent the virtual encirclement of Pakistan. Perhaps the fairest solution (disregarding the claims of the Maharajah) would be a partition allotting the Hindu southeast to India; but so much feeling has been aroused that it is difficult to see any prospect of an agreed solution, unless a plebiscite were held under international control; the normal results of plebiscites under the auspices of an occupying power, if nothing else, might well excuse Pakistani suspicions of an Indian-run referendum, and indeed the promised plebiscite appeared to recede further and further into an indefinite future. At length, however, an armistice was negotiated, to commence on 1st January 1949, pending the organization of a plebiscite under U.N.O. auspices. As an alternative to partition—not likely to be acceptable to either party—the creation of an independent Kashmir under U.N.O. sanctions might be suggested, and might save face on both sides. But this also is a forlorn hope.

In Hyderabad the communal position is reversed: a Muslim ruler, descendant of a Mogul viceroy who, in subservient alliance with the East India Company, became independent of Delhi in the 18th century; and a population of which over 80% is Hindu. With 82,313 square miles and 16,338,534 people in 1941, a sound fiscal position, a well integrated rail and road system, and considerable resources both agricultural and industrial, Hyderabad is a well-found State superior to some European countries. It is however entirely surrounded by Indian territory, the nearest seaport being Masulipatam on the Madras coast, 60 miles from the Hyderabad border, though more traffic probably goes by Bombay, Madras, and Goa. The Nizam had a claim to the four Districts of Berar, assigned to the East India Company, later leased and permanently administered as part of the Central Provinces, though the Nizam's nominal sovereignty was recognized by the British Crown as recently as 1936; but the Union Government from its inception regarded these as integrally Indian. In the first year of Indian independence agreement was all but reached more than once, the principal outstanding point at issue being the validity of Union legislation within Hyderabad; but the Muslim minority includes most of the larger feudal landlords and magnates, and their pressure on the Nizam prevented ratification. Indian counterpressure at first took the form of a stringent economic blockade, but the interdigitation of Hyderabad and Indian territory facilitated numerous border clashes. On September 14th 1948 Indian troops entered Hyderabad ('to restore order'), and five days later the Nizam yielded. There is no reason to doubt that most of the Hindu majority desired the adhesion to India thus secured.

It remains to notice, for the sake of completeness, those small fragments of Portuguese and French territory which have ironically survived the greater Empire of Britain. Goa, with its valuable transit trade and fair natural resources (including salt and manganese), and with a somewhat inflated administration providing ample patronage, has more than a sentimental importance, large as that is in Portuguese eyes. How far the undeniable Luso-Indian culture which has evolved there carries any strong feeling of loyalty to the metropolis cannot well be judged; but pressure of population and of taxation impels a considerable emigration of Goanese, who as clerks, teachers, musicians, and caterers form a useful element in the population of Bombay. The other Portuguese possessions, Damaõ and Diu, are mere fossil relics, as are French Mahé, Karikal, and Yanaon. Pondicherry and Chandernagore[1] however have fairly important industries, and the mingling of French and Indian territory around Pondicherry is said to facilitate a transit trade more profitable than licit. In French India also cultural and economic ties have some weight against pan-Indian feeling. The French have handed over a number of *loges*, descendants of 18th century factories where they retained extra-territorial rights, mainly on the east coast; and in other respects they have been more forthcoming than the Portuguese, who after all have more to lose. Despite occasional tendentious hints of a desire to round off the territorial structure of India, it seems that in respect of these historical relics Indian leaders will be content to hasten slowly.

PROBLEMS OF DEVELOPMENT

The backwardness of India, economically and socially, was largely identified, in the minds of the British-created middle classes who were articulate India, with the sins of British rule. Despite the not inconsiderable achievements of the British Raj, there are certainly grounds for this view; but any judgement on it would involve the casting of a most complicated balance-sheet, in which most items on both sides are imponderable and incommensurate. It is more fruitful, and more geographical, to attempt an assessment of the actual bases for the new and independent polity.

In man-power, with a population now probably between 325 and 350 millions, India ranks with China in a class apart. The cultivable land on which these millions have to live is barely adequate in amount, even on

[1] In June 1949 Chandernagore voted for union with India by 7473 votes to 114.

the low standards prevalent, and varies in quality from the rich silt-lands of the delta areas to the poor thin soils of most of the Archæan plateau; and its utilization is in great measure dependent on an uncertain rainfall. New irrigation methods, tapping the water held at depth under the Gangetic plains, will perhaps give some relief from this dependence, and the great TVA-type schemes for the Damodar and the Kosi will mean greater security, though unfortunately not in the generally precarious belt from the East Punjab to Mysore where the uncertainties of the monsoon are most felt. Although the population is in great majority agrarian, and although food-grains account for the great bulk of agricultural production, the food-supply (even with imports on the current scale) is hardly sufficient for subsistence, and most certainly not adequate for the full maintenance of human energy: malnutrition and disease are responsible for terrible human and economic wastage. Yields for practically all crops are well below world averages, and it seems that over large areas the soil is down to the irreducible minimum of fertility. Campaigns for better farming, greater use of fertilisers, more diversified dietaries, meet great difficulties: social prejudice and educational backwardness, the problem of a fuel alternative to cowdung, the religious sanctions which increase the numbers and decrease the strength of the cattle beyond economic limits, to mention but a few. Social relationships in the countryside offer few incentives for the cultivator to improve his methods, nor has he as a rule the necessary capital. The projected abolition (on liberal terms of compensation) of the *zamindari* or landlord system in the provinces where it existed, and the growth of rural co-operation, are but the beginnings of social reforms which must be taken much further if the hold of the moneylender and the middleman is to be weakened. Although individually the peasant can rarely find the capital for improvements, much of the finance for development must come, in the form of land revenue, from the collective peasantry, whose attitude to government is that of their class the world over, that there is a deal too much of it. Education in words alone cannot overcome this suspicion; much more in the way of tangible returns for taxation must come to the countryside. The more general economic dilemma has been dealt with above (p. 141); succinctly it is food crops, or cash crops to pay for capital goods imported, many of which will be specifically needed for agricultural development. Whichever solution is adopted, it means "Planning for 400 millions", which, in the geographical and social conditions of the Indian countryside, will task severely the most able and incorrupt administration. Moreover agricultural progress will depend on at least keeping fragmentation and subdivision of holdings in check, if not on reversing their trend; and, with a population which has hitherto responded to improvements in productive potential by producing more population, this will raise in an acute form the problem of disposing of a surplus of rural inhabitants.

Emigration, discussed later, offers little relief; as for internal migration, Assam is probably the only province which has enough uncleared cultivable land to offer any serious scope for an expansion of settlement. Attention is therefore increasingly turned to industrialization. The basic resources have already been reviewed. They are on the whole adequate (except for oil) for some time to come, if in some respects inconveniently distributed; and it may be added that there is a wide variety of what may be called secondary agricultural and forest resources: oilseeds, tobacco, tan- and dye-stuffs, lac and other gums and resins, bamboo and thatching materials, tussore and other silk. In many consumption goods, in cement, and even in some heavy engineering lines Indian production already meets current demand, although of course this will increase greatly if any considerable fraction of the numerous paper Plans is carried through. The chief weakness so far is the lack of a heavy chemical industry, so essential to a well-balanced economy both in industry and agriculture; here an agreement has been reached between Tata's and Imperial Chemical Industries on terms which seem advantageous to India. Air and road transport industries are in their infancy, only assembly plants operating as yet; shipbuilding has made a small but encouraging start. The power situation is not too easy and, although hydro-electricity has great potentialities, the limitations upon its speedy development are often overlooked. Labour, by no means altogether by its own fault, is inefficient, and management often appears almost incredibly slapdash; but, even discounting the tremendous achievement of the Tatas as being a matter of individual family genius, there is no reason to believe that India will be unable to build up her industrial armies: the materials are there.

In the long run the question of markets is perhaps more serious and more fundamental than that of resources. It is true that manufactures, especially of jute and of cheap cotton goods, already bulk large in the export lists; jute manufactures far exceed in value the export of raw jute, while the raw cotton import is now much greater than that of cotton goods; and the temporary eclipse of Japan affords India an opportunity of securing eastern markets, especially in the Indian Ocean countries where she already has flourishing trade connections and active cadres of merchants. But real prosperity and the full expansion of Indian industry will depend on a healthy economic balance between city and country, and that on a vast increase in the appallingly low purchasing power of the Indian masses, who on any prospect will remain preponderantly rural.

A real solution of this problem again involves what is no less than a social, primarily an agrarian, revolution. This is clearly seen by some among the Indian directing groups, but the forces on the other side are strong. Moreover, even if industrialization should be carried to the fullest extent which can be at present envisaged, it would not of itself offer a solution of the population problem. Assuming that industrial employment were trebled in 15 years—which seems to be the current target—and allowing for the concurrent development of ancillary occupations, commerce, and administration, it is doubtful if this could do more than take up the natural increase; the problem of over-population might be no worse, but it would not be likely to be much better.

Much obviously depends on political stability. The financing of the grandiose programmes projected will be a task of extreme delicacy if inflation is to be avoided. They also call for a release of energy on a revolutionary scale; much that has hitherto gone into frustrated discontents and political girding against the British Raj may now be turned to more constructive tasks. But the malaise of Indian society has gone deep and may prove to be not easily shaken off, and there are powerful divisive and corrupting influences in times which call for the maximum of national unity and energy.

SOCIAL PROBLEMS: HINDU RAJ OR SECULAR REPUBLIC?

The most striking of the internal tensions of the old India has been to all intents removed by a heroic surgical operation. Although of course something between 30 and 35 million Muslims remain in the Indian Union, this is a bare 10% of the population, against the old 24%, and there is now not a single District in India (excluding Kashmir) where Muslims are in a majority. Hindu-Muslim tension still indeed exists, but it has been largely transferred to the sphere of external relations and the issue is in a sense simplified in consequence. The fates of other minorities— Parsees, Anglo-Indians, Indian Christians, Tribes—may be individually painful but hardly form a major issue: some form of assimilation to Indian culture and polity probably awaits them, and this is the easier in that Hindu culture is itself so multiform as to be normally tolerant of all but directly antagonistic philosophies such as Islam. Only the Sikhs, perhaps, are sufficiently numerous, concentrated, and assertive (not to say aggressive) to present a potentially serious problem of assimilation. But, despite the strong underlying cultural unity of Hinduism, its stratification socially into castes is difficult of adjustment to modern norms in economic and political organization and in social *mores*.

Caste indeed is more often roundly condemned than understood.[1] There can be little doubt that in the past it played a useful part in assuring continuity and stability to a society and a culture otherwise liable to be overwhelmed by invasion, dynastic upheaval, anarchy, and despotism. But it is now at least an open question whether Hindu traditionalism is not so ossified as to need a root and branch reformation, and the modern apologists for caste are often eloquent but not so often convincing, even to many good Hindus. Caste has now very largely, though by no means entirely, lost such occupational *raison d'être* as it had. In many respects, and particularly in the great towns, its effects are now considerably mitigated; but it is still very strong, particularly in the Dravidian south. The 'Untouchables' have indeed succeeded in general in enforcing at least nominal recognition of their rights to temple entry, common educational facilities, and the use of tanks and wells; incidentally in no other civilization has the proffer of water been a symbol of division rather than of the unity of mankind. These rights are now secured by law, but in the remote countryside at least they are probably still largely inhibited in practice by social disapproval. It is awkward enough in administration, to take a simple but common example, if a subordinate clerk is of higher caste than an executive superior; instructions may have to come by indirect crooked ways, and even then there is friction. But the real significance of the caste problem is that the solution of the other problems—agrarian, economic, educational—depends on the utmost unity of effort from the producers, who are in the main of lower castes. They cannot be expected either to grasp the necessity of this or to adopt whole-heartedly the new methods needed, without sweeping changes in their general outlook; and caste is a conservative as well as a divisive force, bound up with all the immense traditionalism of the Indian countryside. Although the holding of apparently incompatible beliefs is common enough in India (and not only there), it is difficult to change one compartment of a man's mind without affecting the others, and the efficiency of both old and new sets of beliefs is liable to be distorted if the attempt is made to introduce a new economic outlook and to retain the old social rigidity. The new India will demand new men, and that cannot be without a recasting of the old society. That is why a social as well as an agrarian revolution is needed, though the results may well be incalculable.

The Indian National Congress was rather a Popular Front than a definite party, and there are already signs of some of its components organizing themselves on new lines, with more coherent programmes

---

[1] The writer would certainly condemn caste but would not like to go on record as saying that he understood it.

based on economic groupings. The present rulers of India seem committed to the new secular state. Over against them are the dark forces
which, in the last analysis, stand for a theocratic—or Brahminocratic—
Hindu Raj. Either as a new imperialism or as the leader of the Asiatic
Renaissance, India can hardly attain her goal if internally she falls back
upon the ancient ways; and her failure would remove a vital integrating
influence from southern Asia. The outcome of the struggle between the
old and the new ideals is therefore not only of significance for the dignity
and happiness of the Indian millions; in some sort it is of vital significance
for the world.

PAKISTAN

STRUCTURE

The territorial structure of Pakistan, the largest Muslim state by
population in the world, is simpler than that of India, but unique in that
it consists of two great blocks of territory separated by nearly a thousand
miles. But of the old States it has only those of Baluchistan (Kalat,
Kharan, Las Bela) and the N-W.F.P. (Dir, Swat, Baner, Chitral, the
last under a vague Kashmir suzerainty, quietly dropped), with Bahawalpur and Khairpur from the Punjab States. Pakistan like India is a federation, with perhaps an even stronger Centre, if only because the Muslim
League has not yet to face such challenges as have been presented (for
the most part indeed ineffectually) to Congress.

The bisection of Pakistan raises serious administrative problems.
Eastern Pakistan is notoriously unmilitary; except for the short frontier
with Burma it is entirely surrounded by India, and a veritable hostage to
fortune. Western Pakistan consists effectively of an attenuated oecumene
of good (where irrigated) land, 750 miles from Karachi to Rawalpindi but
only 80 miles wide in the constricted waist south of Multan. The inheri-
tance of the Northwest Frontier is not an unmixed gain. Before 1947 the
N-W.F.P. was a Congress province, albeit with a difference; the alliance
between frontier Muslims and the predominantly Hindu Congress was
unnatural in itself, founded on common antipathy to British rule and
perhaps on geographical position—the natural tendency of a small group
to link up with its next neighbour but one. The communal massacres
which followed partition in the Punjab led to a wave of Muslim solidarity
and a hasty divorce; the agitation for self-determination for 'Pathanistan'
was a factitious substitute for the old strange mating. Short-lived as it
was, the fact remains that the people on either side of both the administrative boundary and of the Afghan frontier are essentially the same, and

Afghan solicitude for Pathan interests may yet create difficulties for Pakistan. Military and financial weakness have compelled the evacuation of strongholds in the tribal country, though subsidies to tribes are continued; inability and/or reluctance to control the tribesmen played a large part in the explosion of the Kashmir crisis. Some candid friends have indeed suggested that the relinquishment of the Pathan lands beyond the Indus might strengthen Pakistan in the long run; but, leaving aside the economic value of the rich vale of Peshawar, the proposal shows a strange lack of understanding of the dynamics of political geography. Such a confession of weakness in a young state would probably precipitate rather than avert disintegration.

The selection of Karachi as the capital of Pakistan is not without geographical interest. Over half the population is in Eastern Pakistan, but no centre there has any advantages either of economic significance or historical prestige; and all the drive of Pakistan has come from the west. Here Lahore far outranked Karachi as an Islamic, administrative, and industrial centre, but it was technically within the area of dispute with India and close to what would obviously be an exposed and might be a disturbed frontier. No other town in Western Pakistan was so convenient as Karachi, despite its peripheral position; it is well placed for contacts with the Islamic world of Southwest Asia and of great and increasing importance as an airport. A recent decision to erect a Federal District around Karachi, shifting the Sind capital to Hyderabad, has aroused heated opposition, especially among Sindhi legislators and officials: a comparison of the annual temperatures of the two places will sufficiently explain this.

THE ROOTS OF PAKISTAN

Fundamental in the Hindu-Muslim conflict in the old India was the uneven economic development, communally no less than geographically. This was determined not only by the distribution of natural resources but also (especially in its origins) by the sequence of British occupation. The regions in which the techniques and economic outlook of the west have had longest influence are non-Muslim. Even in Muslim Bengal, Calcutta, the gateway *par excellence* of westernism, lies in the Hindu west, and Hindu commercial, legal, and educational aptitudes set the pace for cultural change. Of the four great ports only the youngest and least, Karachi, is in a Muslim region, and until 1936 Sind was a mere outlying dependency of Bombay, and Karachi rather alien, not too intimately related with its hinterland; in 1941 Hindus and Parsees together outnumbered Muslims, and far outranked them in wealth and civic activity, a fact which may have contributed to the very modest degree of enthusiasm noticeable there in August 1947. Historical causes connected with the Mutiny contributed to a strong British mistrust of the Muslims. (until the rise of Hindu nationalism in the first decade of this century) and to a Muslim aversion from western education, the path to advancement in official service, trade, and industry. The awareness of economic backwardness; the sense of exploitation by a community numerically larger and economically more adroit; the recent rise of a Muslim bourgeoisie engaged in bitter competition for place and profit with its Hindu counterpart which controlled an overwhelming proportion of the country's industrial resources, was endowed with a longer tradition of commercial and industrial activity, and was very strongly entrenched in trade, industry, the professions, and administration—these are the real roots of Pakistan. There are very real cultural and ideological differences also. However factitious the arguments for the 'Two Nations', there is nothing like a young bourgeoisie for creating a sense of nationhood, and no weapons for it so effective as the cries of religion in danger and of economic exploitation. Paradoxically, its economic weakness *vis-à-vis* Hindu India is the main argument for the foundation of Pakistan. Whether it will prove a sufficient argument for its continued existence is another matter; but at least the admitted strategic weakness of Pakistan has discouraged irresponsible adventurism, while on the positive side must be put the feeling that independence has been won in a double sense, both political and economic, from both British and Indian imperialism; and a corresponding resolution to maintain this independence despite the difficulties of scarcity of capital and of trained technicians and administrators.

ECONOMIC PROBLEMS AND THE PROSPECT

To some extent both the Pakistan areas differed in economic interests from All-India, in that they were essentially primary producers (jute and cotton) with their interests in markets overseas or at least beyond their borders: the jute manufacture in Bengal was all on Hooghlyside, that is outside the Muslim part of the province, though most of the production is in the east. In both areas industrial resources and development are meagre. There the resemblance ceases: Eastern Pakistan, with one-seventh of the area, has four-sevenths of the population, a density in 1941 of 775 to the square mile against 92 in Western Pakistan, and less than half an acre of cultivated land per inhabitant against over one acre in the west. There is very little land available in the east, but in the west scope for expansion is not inconsiderable, although it will depend on costly irrigation.

Put briefly, Pakistan's shares of the resources of All-India in coal, iron, and other basic minerals (except salt) are almost negligible; it has some but not enough oil, and the possibility of more in Sind: and it has a strong position in fibres, with some 80% of the jute output, one-third (and that the better quality on one-fifth of the acreage) of the cotton, and a large proportion of the wool of All-India. In food grains it has normally good surpluses of wheat in the Punjab and of rice in Sind, while Eastern Pakistan is rather precariously self-sufficient.

These resources offer little prospect of heavy industrial development; lighter agriculturally-based industries offer surer potentialities, but the necessary power is lacking unless Pakistan secures either Kashmir or unhampered access to its power-sites. Around the Punjab hydro-electric development might produce some 1,000,000 Kw.; but, except for the Malakand site north of Peshawar (9600 Kw installed, 20,000 potential), most of the good sites appear to lie either in Kashmir or in montane Punjab, all of which is indisputably Indian; further schemes in the N.-W.F.P. are, however, being examined. Nor is the situation much better in the east, although some possibilities exist on the Karnaphuli river, at the mouth of which stands Chittagong. High hopes are entertained of developing that port to rival Calcutta, and it is well placed as an outlet for Assam. But this project as well as schemes for the rapid development of jute-mills in Eastern Pakistan (at present there are none at all) will have to meet the powerfully entrenched competition of Hooghly-side, far superior in capital and managerial resources. Yet Pakistan cannot be expected to acquiesce indefinitely in the Indian retention of the profits from a manufacture mainly dependent on Pakistan jute; there has already been friction over jute export duties. On the whole modern industry hardly exists in Pakistan and, unless the accession of Kashmir is secured, development will depend largely on access to Indian sources and is likely to be slow, the more so as Pakistan is fiscally weak. The financing of capital equipment programmes again must rely to a large extent on agricultural exports; and these may be vulnerable on the world market.

Fiscal and administrative problems in Pakistan are indeed most serious. Administratively, many of the officials and technicians in Pakistan areas were Hindus who have now emigrated, and it will take time to build up new cadres. Fiscally the Punjab was by far the strongest unit, but it has been severely strained by the dislocation of all the activities of life in the virtual civil war which followed partition; the necessity of providing for probably at least 2,000,000 surplus and destitute immigrants, demoralized by their appalling experiences, all but overwhelmed a depleted and dis-located administration. As for Eastern Pakistan, the great bulk of its taxable capacity (except to land revenue) and mobilizable capital were on Hooghlyside; and even without this amputation, Bengal was nearly always a deficit or near-deficit province.[1] Eastern Pakistan will probably need subventions from a none too wealthy centre.

That Pakistan will survive appears certain: it could not now be des-troyed short of war, and although in that event the dice would be very heavily loaded against Pakistan (owing to the negligible war potential *vis-à-vis* India, and the almost impossible strategic lay-out), India would be very unlikely to add to already too numerous internal problems that of holding down a hostile population in the granary of the sub-continent: Kashmir alone may prove a quite sufficient strain. But it would not be very surprising if Eastern Pakistan, by way of *ad hoc* regional agreements to meet local interests (so obviously bound up with those of the surrounding areas) were gradually to slip into a special position such that there would eventually be an abrupt confrontation with the issue of *de facto* Pakistan or Indian allegiance. At that point the evolution could hardly be consummated without a major crisis in the sub-continent.

Western Pakistan is fundamentally better-found than Eastern, and it has the makings of a decent if not spectacular agrarian prosperity, if only the Kashmir crisis can be settled by genuine agreement and relations of real co-operation between the two Dominions established. Otherwise the prospect is bleak indeed; at the very least a continuance of the present armed peace is likely so to strain the modest resources of the state as to produce social stagnation or even retrogression. It has been naïvely asserted—as a matter of pride—that the armed forces of Pakistan have shown the most striking development; they account for nearly 70% of budget expenditure. It seems that "nation-building" must take second place to nationalism. Survival does not necessarily mean survival on a high plane of existence.

EXTERNAL RELATIONS

In four and a half centuries the wheel has come full circle: direct Euro-pean control of the Indian Ocean coasts of mainland Asia is now confined to Aden, Goa, and Malaya[2] —the very areas which the genius of Albu-

---

[1] On Bengal finance, see R. G. Casey, *An Australian in India* (1947), p. 101.
[2] Perhaps Ceylon, despite the recent attainment of Dominion Status, should be included.

querque seized on as the keys to dominion in southern Asia, though by
historic accident Ormuz was substituted for Aden in the Portuguese
Empire. The removal of the co-ordinating power of Britain, weakened
as it was in its later phases, means new adjustments in the political and
strategic pattern, which will take time to mature. Were India united she
would seem cast for the vacated role, and even with the secession of
Pakistan she remains to-day probably the strongest independent power
in Asia.

THE ASIATIC HINTERLAND

The landward neighbours of India, except perhaps Burma, appear
at present politically quiescent. If Persia is a threat to anybody, it is
through her weakness rather than her strength; there is some maritime
trade with the Indian west coast, but except for oil it amounts to little.
Afghanistan indeed holds a watching brief in Frontier politics, and is of
more immediate significance to the Indian sub-continent, although from
a general view Persia, with its oil and its precarious position between the
two camps of the divided world, is of more importance. Afghanistan is a
country of rugged mountains and semi-desert plains, with an extreme
plateau-type climate; but where they can be irrigated the hillgirt basins are
fertile enough, and the country is famous for the variety and fine quality
of its fruits. Its 10 or 12 million people include a diversity of tribes: most
important for Pakistan, some 7 million of them are Pathans, identical in
speech and mode of life with their brethren in the N-W.F.P. But although
interference from outside has in the past produced something like a
national sentiment, there is little potentiality for aggression from Afghanistan owing to the lack of concert among the tribes and the limited technical equipment of the country. A modern administration is being built
up, and a modest beginning has been made in the exploitation of mineral
and other resources; but the rulers of Afghanistan, taught by the fate of
too-impetuous predecessors, are content to hasten slowly along the paths
of westernization.

But these countries have less significance in themselves than as buffers
between the Soviet Union and the Indian sub-continent. It is true that
Russian interest in Indian affairs is often grotesquely exaggerated—the
neurosis is of long standing, and even Lord Salisbury besought his
followers to use larger-scale maps. One may indeed hazard the opinion
that Soviet influence will grow *pari passu* with American economic
activity in India, and only so. Nevertheless both India and Pakistan will
probably wish to continue the British policy of keeping Afghanistan and

Persia as buffers; and this may be an argument for continued association with the British Commonwealth.

Further north the Kashmir struggle is not without wider implications. It is true that even in these days the possibility of the Pamirs and the Karakoram having anything but a negative strategic significance seems remote: nevertheless the buffer-strip of Afghanistan in Wakhan is less than 25 miles wide, and further west the thin trickle of trade between Kashmir and Sinkiang (via the Zoji La, Leh, and the Karakoram Pass) is of importance to the mainly Buddhist and Mongol population of Ladakh and its neighbour regions, hard hit by the decay of the road and its traffic consequent on the war. Kashmir is in some sense a part of the Northwest Frontier; on its marches in the Pamir-Karakoram 'three empires meet.' Pakistan is far the weaker of the two Dominions, yet even from the Indian point of view it might be thought well to have the whole north-west under one administration, another tier between India and the U.S.S.R. Moreover, should Kashmir pass entirely to India, unless a bold programme of social reform produced clear plebiscitary acceptance (and its fulfilment continued acquiescence), the retention of so compact a block of Muslims on the frontier might well be a source of weakness in itself, and contribute to a permanent estrangement with Pakistan ultimately disastrous to both parties.

With Tibet (unless it falls to the Chinese Communists) and with Nepal no serious problems are likely to arise; the former's policy of seclusion can only be confirmed by the present aspect of the world outside, the close economic contacts with the latter can only be strengthened by the great Kosi control and reclamation project. The northeast frontier, as we have seen, has rarely been active, and its significance of 1942–45 is likely to fall into abeyance, like its symbol the Ledo Road. But Indo-Burmese relations are better considered as part of the wider theme of India's role in the Indian Ocean.

THE INDIAN OCEAN: MARE NOSTRUM?

In the distant past India contributed very notably in civilization, and probably not inconsiderably in ethnic composition, to the peninsular and archipelagic lands of Southeast Asia. But it is a measure of the degree of truth in the traditional conception of India as a land turning away from the sea that there are so few Indians—less than 4,000,000 all told— overseas. Since the great depression of the thirties permanent emigration has been practically negligible. Nevertheless the distribution of this hand-ful (in comparison with the Indian total), of whom the great majority are in Indian Ocean lands, is extremely significant (see Table II, p. 37) above and *Fig.* 16). The Pakistan share of emigration is probably small, even in East Africa, and Pakistan's relations, so far rather rudimentary, are with Southwest Asia.

The most significant groups are five: those in Burma, Malaya, Ceylon, East Africa, and South Africa. They vary considerably in social structure and function. In Burma, where Indians are now probably well under 750,000[1], emigration until 1937 was of course merely inter-provincial. Indians had a very prominent, though naturally decreasing, share in the administration of what until that date was an Indian province: apart from British 'big business' they (and to a less extent the Chinese) controlled practically all but the pettiest forms of trade and industry: and it is hardly an exaggeration to say that so far as Burma possessed a middle class not in direct government employment, that class was Indian—whence, incidentally, much of the instability of Burmese politics.[2] At the other end of the scale Indians provided the bulk of unskilled coolie labour (at least in lower Burma), perhaps a majority of the clerical, and large numbers of seasonal agricultural labourers. These latter groups worked willingly for wages quite unacceptable to the Burmese, who had grown up in a country mercifully free from the intense pressure on resources which characterizes India; and yet these despised coolies were able to remit large aggregate sums to India. But with the depression of the 'thirties the old Burmese insouciance suffered a severe strain, and increasing economic competition led on occasion to violent clashes. As a result there was a tendency in the later inter-war years for more Indians to leave than to enter. In 1941 an immigration agreement was reached, and although this was forthwith abrogated by events it is evident that in the temper of the new Burma there will be less and less place for the two-pronged Indian penetration—of more powerful capital and of cheaper labour. Burmese proposals for land nationalization, however, have given rise to apprehension in India, as between one-quarter and one-third of the cultivated land of lower Burma was mortgaged to Indian bankers; and the post-war chaos in Burma might lead from 'good offices' to 'intervention on behalf of legitimate interests'—

> And Empire slowly broadens out
> From episode to incident . . .

In Malaya most of the Indians were originally imported as indentured

---

[1] Probably some 400,000 Indians succeeded in leaving Burma, mostly by land, during the Japanese invasion.

[2] The operative factor being the absence of a Burmese as much as the presence of an Indian middle class; the two things are of course related.

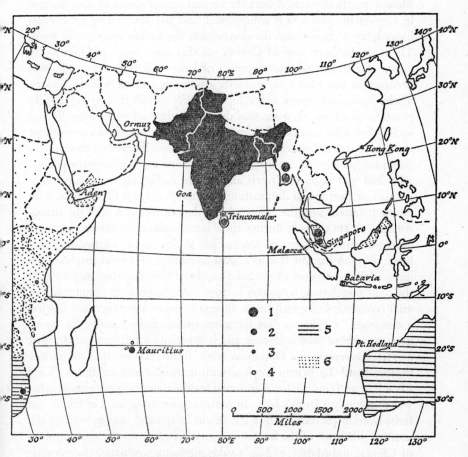

Fig. 16.   INDIA IN THE INDIAN OCEAN

1–4, Indians overseas: 1, 500,000; 2, 250,000; 3, 100,000; 4, 25,000.

5, Dominions.

6, Other British territories.

Zenithal Equidistant projection centred 10° S., 80° E.; scale and directions true from centre.

labourers on the rubber plantations, and there are also of course the ancillary middle class traders and professional men. Emigration to Malaya practically ceased with the tin and rubber slump of the 'thirties. In Ceylon the problem is complicated, and the plurality of society enhanced, by a deep-seated division within the Indian community itself. The drier northern zone of Ceylon—at that time more productive by virtue of a remarkable development of large-scale tank irrigation—was occupied in the 11th-13th centuries A.D. by organized Tamil invaders. Their descendants form a developed society of all classes, but largely peasant cultivators; they are thus sharply marked off occupationally and socially from the rootless labourers imported in recent decades to work on the rubber and tea estates. Amongst the Sinhalese themselves there is also a division (but by no means so deep) between the low-country people, who had 300 years of Dutch and of the earlier but culturally more permanent Portuguese domination, and the Kandyans of the hills, who plume themselves on the independence they maintained until the British conquest in 1815. As in Burma, there is communal friction, and again an immigration agreement was reached just in time to be nullified by hostilities. Ceylon has not Burma's great advantage of a food surplus—it is indeed largely dependent on India—and the Sinhalese are only 69% of the total population, 6,695,000 in 1946. Although both countries have vital economic links with India, Burma is rather a supplier and Ceylon a customer. Ceylon is thus far more overshadowed politically by its great neighbour than is Burma, and it is perhaps a reflection of this that Ceylon has remained a Dominion while Burma has become completely independent.[1] To Britain Ceylon, with its rubber and tea and with the naval base at Trincomalee, is still vital for the remaining interests in what was so recently a British lake. In Malaya again the spheres of China and India overlap (as they do to a less extent in Burma), and in view of the numerical balance of the Indian minority between nearly equal numbers of Chinese and Malays, and the awakening feelings of nationalism among the latter, it is clear that a situation of explosive delicacy may soon arise in this nodal peninsula where four great cultures—Western European, Islamic, Hindu, and Chinese—have met to form one of the most classic exemplars of a plural society.

In Malaya and Ceylon, as in Mauritius, Fiji, and the West Indies, the larger part of the Indian population are plantation labourers, mainly Tamils and Oriyas. The origin of the community in South Africa was similar, but the African groups on the whole are on a different footing.

[1] Only complete Indian separation from the Commonwealth in 1947 might have kept Burma as a Dominion. . . .

They find themselves in an invidious position between black masses and white rulers; a situation of great tactical difficulty, but which might be a key psycho-political position later on, if Indian social attitudes can be adjusted to grasp the opportunity. Meanwhile the function of the Indian community in East Africa is essentially that of a trading lubricant, the middlemen between large-scale European commerce and local needs; and in South Africa tension is acute and likely to remain a major difficulty in inter-Commonwealth relations for a long time to come.

All these communities, with their large and adroit trading elements in close contact with the motherland, form an important commercial asset to India: they have for example almost a monopoly of the Zanzibar clove trade. It is not surprising that in Burma and Ceylon at least there are definite apprehensions of an Indian imperialism. Such development is not perhaps inherently very unlikely, and recent events in the sub-continent itself suggest that the subjective anti-imperialist views of Indian leaders are largely irrelevant to their objective behaviour. Meanwhile however there is the need, or at least the desirability, of some form of regional co-ordination of the economy and polity of southern Asia; and with a magnificent strategical position in the Indian Ocean, with immense man-power, and with industrial resources and development and an administrative machine greatly superior to those of any other purely Asiatic state (leaving Japan aside for the time being), India is certainly well-placed to play the role of co-ordinator.

WIDER RELATIONS: INDIA AND THE ASIAN RENAISSANCE

The sphere of effective action of India, and still more of Pakistan, is as yet merely regional: the two Dominions are still of little weight in world affairs and, despite the weakening of British, Dutch, and French power, they are not even predominant in southern Asia outside their own borders. Not until there is a far greater degree of industrial development, a better agrarian economy, a far greater spread and intensity of education, and less dependence on western sources for technological equipment, can India rank as a really great power. As for Pakistan, her interests will probably remain focussed chiefly on southwest Asia, although so far her influence even on the Palestine problem, immediately affecting the Islamic world as it does, has been ineffective. This is not surprising in view of her difficulties with internal reconstruction and in Kashmir. It is at least encouraging that the very birth-week of the two Dominions saw united action over the Indonesian issue; and over a wide range of problems, such as those of Indians in East and South Africa, the interests and views of both Dominions are identical.

12

India however aspires to a wider influence. Whatever the formal relationships with the British Commonwealth may be, no-one doubts that special links between the Commonwealth and the sub-continent will continue. During the last years of British rule much importance was attached by Indian leaders to the sympathies of the United States and the U.S.S.R., and one of the first acts of the Indian Union was to appoint ambassadors to these powers. In the present condition of world economy there is obviously much scope for American economic interest in India, although its free development may be inhibited by Indian memories of an earlier economic penetration and the close ties remaining with Britain. As to the U.S.S.R., this multi-national state has an obvious interest for those concerned with building up a nation in India, although those ideological contributions to world culture which Indians like to think of as peculiarly their own are not likely to be greeted with reciprocal enthusiasm in Moscow.

There remains the leadership of southern Asia. China and Japan, despite the present troubles and disintegrated polities, are entities too large, self-conscious, and highly individualized to be easily drawn into other orbits. But Southeast Asia is in a tumult of new forces, which may it is true be abortive and destined merely to prelude disintegration and anarchy, but may also be the birth-pangs of a new Asia. India's aspiration to be its leader, and some of the opportunities and resistances likely to be met, were clearly shown in the Asian Conference held at Delhi in April 1947. But only if there is a thorough-going recasting of her social institutions and a radical reconstruction of her agrarian life is India likely to take that place in the councils of the world which she claims in virtue of her numbers, her past, and her inherent feelings of nationhood and culture.

SELECT BOOK LIST

Report of Royal Commission on Indian Agriculture, 1928.
C. C. Davies: *The Problem of the North-West Frontier, 1890–1909*, 1932
D. H. Buchanan: *The Development of Capitalist Enterprise in India*, 1934.
D. N. Wadia: *Geology of India*, 1939.
Sir W. Barton: *India's North-West Frontier*, 1939.
R. K. Mukerjee (ed.): *Economic Problems of Modern India*, 1939.
L. S. S. O'Malley (ed.): *Modern India and the West*, 1941.
Oxford Pamphlets on Indian Affairs, 1942–47.
H. G. Rawlinson: *India: A Cultural History*, 1943.
Sir R. Coupland: *Report on the Constitutional Problem in India*, 1943.
G. B. Jathar and S. J. Beri: *Indian Economics*, 1945.
K. M. Pannikkar: *India and the Indian Ocean*, 1945
A Plan for the Economic Development of India, 1945 (the "Bombay Plan")
J. Nehru: *The Discovery of India*, 1946.
T. R. Sharma: *The Location of Industries in India*, 1946.
W. C. Smith: *Modern Islam in India*, 1946.
The Indian Year Book, 1947.
N. Gangulee: *Indians in the Overseas Empire*: 1947.
N. Ahmed: *The Basis of Pakistan*, Calcutta, 1947.
V. Anstey: *The Economic Development of India*, 1948.
S. P. Chatterjee: *Bengal in Maps*, Calcutta, 1948.
P. J. Thomas: *India's Basic Industries*, Bombay, 1948.
C. C. Davies: *An Historical Atlas of the Indian Peninsula*, 1949.
R. Symonds: *The Making of Pakistan*, 1950.

TABLE IV

INDIA, PAKISTAN, AFGHANISTAN AND CEYLON

AREA AND POPULATION

	Area sq. miles	Population (thousands)	Density to sq. mile
1. THE INDIAN UNION (1941 *Census*)			
A. Old Provinces			
Ajmer-Merwara★	2,400	587	243
Andamans and Nicobars★ ..	3,143	34	11
Assam†	50,130	7,472	149
Bengal, West†§	28,033	21,195	756
Bihar‡	70,348	36,546	519
Bombay‡§	105,236	29,199	277
Central Province and Berar‡§	130,636	20,878	159
Coorg★	1,593	167	106
Delhi‖	574	918	1,599
Madras‡	127,610	49,825	394
Orissa‡§	59,869	13,766	230
Panth Piploda★	25	5	211
Punjab, East†‡§	37,410	12,697	340
United Provinces‡	111,629	55,832	500
B. Unions of States			
Madhyabharat§	47,000	7,000	149
Patiala and E. Punjab	10,099	3,424	339
Rajasthan	128,457	13,021	101
Saurashtra§	37,283	3,880	104
Travancore-Cochin	9,135	7,493	820
Vindhya Pradesh	24,598	3,569	137
C. Old States now Chief Commissioners' Provinces (responsible to centre)			
Bhopal	6,921	785	113
Bilaspur	453	156	344
Cooch Behar	1,321	641	486
Cutch	8,461	501	69
Himachal Pradesh	10,922	980	90
Manipur	8,620	512	59
Rampur	894	477	534
Sikkim	2,745	121	44
Tripura	4,049	513	126

TABLE IV—*cont.*

	Area sq. miles	Population (thousands)	Density to sq. mile
D. States adhering to Union individually			
Hyderabad	82,313	16,339	198
Mysore	29,458	7,329	249
E. States, no information on present status			
Khasi Hill Ss. (Assam) ..	3,788	214	56
Sandur (Madras)	158	16	100
TOTAL—INDIA	1,145,292	315,392	275
2. Kashmir (1941 Census) ..	82,258	4,022	49
3. PAKISTAN (1941 Census)			
A. Western Pakistan Provinces			
Baluchistan	54,456	502	9
North-West Frontier ..	14,623	3,038	213
Punjab, West†§	62,046	15,802	255
Sind	48,136	4,535	94
B. Western Pakistan States			
Bahawalpur	17,494	1,341	77
Kalat	53,995	253	5
Khairpur	6,050	306	51
Kharan	18,508	34	2
Las Bela	7,043	69	10
North-West Frontier Agencies§	24,986	2,378	95
TOTAL WESTERN PAKISTAN	306,977	28,258	92
C. Eastern Pakistan			
East Bengal	49,409	39,112	792
Sylhet (ex-Assam)	4,621	2,733	594
TOTAL EASTERN PAKISTAN	54,030	41,845	775
TOTAL PAKISTAN ..	361,007	70,103	194

NOTE.—Area and 1941 population of India, Pakistan and Kashmir on this reckoning are 1,588,557 square miles and 389,517,000 people, against 1941 Census figures of 1,581,410 and 388,997,955. In view of the culpable frequency of double-counting in official statements, this approximation may be regarded as a triumph of accuracy.

TABLE IV—*cont.*

	Area *sq. miles*	*Population* *(thousands)*	*Density to* *sq. mile*
4. FOREIGN POSSESSIONS			
Portuguese (1940 Census) ..	1,537	624	406
French** (1941 Census) ..	200	323	1,592
5 NEIGHBOURING COUNTRIES (all *estimates only*)			
Afghanistan	250,000	10,000	40
Bhután	18,000	300	17
Nepal	54,000	7,000	130
6. CEYLON (1946 *Census*)			
	25,332	6,549	263

* Chief Commissioners' Provinces.
† Adjusted for Indo-Pakistan partition but NOT for subsequent transfers of population.
‡ Adjusted for State mergers.
§ Approximate owing to discrepancies or deficiencies in official data.
‖ Ranks as Chief Commissioners' Province, in effect a Federal District; Karachi will have similar status in Pakistan.
** Includes Chandernagore (in Bengal, population 38,284) which has voted to join India. The United and Central Provinces are now styled Uttar Pradesh and Madhya Pradesh respectively.

TABLE IVa—PROVINCES GAINING BY STATES' MERGERS

	Area *sq. miles*		*Increase*	*Population* *(thousands)*		*Increase*
	1941	1949	%	1941	1949*	%
Bihar ..	69,475	70,348	—	36,340	36,546	—
Bombay ..	76,443	105,236	39	20,850	29,199	40
Central Provs. ..	98,575	130,636	33	16,814	20,878	24
E. Punjab ..	37,043	37,413	—	12,617	12,697	—
Madras ..	126,166	127,610	—	49,342	49,825	—
Orissa ..	32,198	59,869	85	8,729	13,766	58
United Provs. ..	106,247	111,629	5	55,021	55,832	—

* Population in 1941 of area included in province in 1949. *All* figures for East Punjab of course approximate.
The more important states merged are: Baroda, Kolhapur (Bombay); Bastar (C.P.); Mayurbhanj (Orissa); Benares, Tehri Garhwal (U.P.); Pudukottai (Madras).

TABLE V

POPULATION AND CULTIVATED AREA, 1941–42 (Major Provinces of British India only)

	Population (1000's) by 1941 Census	*Net area sown — All Crops	*Net area sown — Food grains	Population to sq. ml. of N.A.S. — All crops	Population to sq. ml. of N.A.S. — Food grains	*Area sown more than once
INDIA						
Assam	7,472	7,900	5,700	946	1,241	1,000
Bihar	36,340	28,100	23,500	1,286	1,551	7,200
Bombay	20,850	43,500	27,000	479	772	1,000
Central Ps.	16,804	38,600	23,000	487	731	2,600
E. Punjab	12,612	18,200	15,000	692	841	3,400
Madras	49,342	49,500	30,500	997	1,621	7,500
Orissa	8,729	9,200	8,200	949	1,065	1,000
United Ps.	55,021	56,500	48,000	974	1,146	11,500
W. Bengal	21,195	13,200	12,500	1,606	1,616	1,700
Total	228,380	266,100	193,400	858	1,171	37,100 (14% N.A.S.)
PAKISTAN						
E. Bengal†	41,845	28,700	27,900	1,458	1,500	7,200
N.-W.F.P.	3,038	3,500	3,300	868	921	700
Sind	4,535	8,300	6,500	546	698	1,100
W. Punjab‡	15,802	25,500	17,600	620	895	3,400
Total	65,220	66,000	55,300	985	1,179	12,400 (19% N.A.S.)

(N.-W.F.P., Sind and W. Punjab grouped: All crops 621; Food grains 853)

*To nearest 100 square miles. †Including area of Sylhet transferred to Pakistan. ‡The pressure in West Punjab is greater than the table indicates, as in addition to natural increase a surplus of some 2,000,000 immigrants over emigrants in the post-partition troubles must be allowed for, and in West Bengal perhaps another million.

TABLE VI

CLASSIFICATION OF AREA, 1945-46, IN INDIA AND PAKISTAN

(Old Provinces of British India only; figures in thousand acres)

	Forests	Not available for cultivation	Other uncultivated, excl. current fallows	Current Fallows	Net area Sown	Total Area
INDIA	62,491	62,413	68,556	37,937	170,808	403,044
PAKISTAN	5,335	27,930	21,159	8,906	46,277	109,607
Total	67,826	90,343	89,715	46,843	217,085	512,651

TABLE VII

ACREAGE AND PRODUCTION OF PRINCIPAL CROPS,

1945–46

INDIA   PAKISTAN

Thousand:	Provinces acres	Provinces tons	States acres	States tons	Provinces acres	Provinces tons	States acres	States tons
Rice ..	52,859	16,922	5,253	1,541	22,610	8,203	10	6
Wheat ..	17,240	4,466	7,306	1,436	9,612	2,938	819	188
Jowar★ ..	21,240	3,382	17,513	2,195	924	188	126	36
Bajra★ ..	11,601	1,627	11,396	1,054	2,223	455	164	59
Maize ..	5,506	1,758	2,279	294	964	420	25	11
Ragi★ ..	2,918	911	1,916	259	—	—	—	—
Barley ..	6,240	1,957	7	1	492	128	5	1
Gram† ..	14,036	3,024	1,148	114	2,925	621	22	5
Total Food Grains ..	131,640	34,047	46,811	6,904	39,750	12,953	1,171	306
Sugar-cane	2,997	4,160	207	388	620	876	1	1
Oil-seeds ..	16,222	3,600	6,806	1,409	1,434	240	47	10
Cotton‡ ..	6,408	1,304	4,941	815	2,884	1,217	435	194
Jute‡ ..	550	1,495	30	61	1,842	6,235	—	—
Tea ..	635	202	95	22	109	33	—	—
Coffee ..	127	16	85	10	—	—	—	—
Tobacco ..	838	285	184	46	197	92	1	1

★ Chief millets.

† A pulse of low nutritional value; probably the States' figure is seriously understated.

‡ Production figures are in thousand bales of 400 lbs.

The figures for the States are incomplete as only the more progressive ones made returns; Indian States include Hyderabad but not Kashmir.

As a corrective to Table VI, note that Pakistan has 18.7% of the food-grain areas shown, but 24.1% of the output.

Source: Tables V–VII are adapted from figures in "Estimates of Area and Yield of Principal Crops in India, 1936–46" (Ministry of Agriculture, New Delhi, 1948).

TABLE VIII

INDIA AND PAKISTAN: MINERAL PRODUCTION,

1944

Source: *Indian Minerals*, Vol. I (1947).

(Figures in tons, unless otherwise stated)

Barytes	15,299	Madras 13,567
Bauxite	12,135	All Central Provinces
Chromite	39,555	Baluchistan 20,869, rest Bihar, Eastern States, and Mysore
China Clay	89,220	Eastern States 45,380; Bihar 23,846
Coal	26,126,676*	Bihar and Bengal 21,153,768; Pakistan 264,443
Copper	326,017	All but 50 tons Bihar
Gold	188,206 oz.	All but 378 oz. Kolar fields, Mysore
Gypsum	83,706	Rajputana 44,000, Punjab 17,560, Madras 14,316
Ilmanite	100,794	Travancore
Iron	2,363,640	Eastern States 1,396,942, Bihar 940,875, Mysore 24,072
Manganese	370,980	Central Provinces 294,712
Mica	72,237 cwts.	Exported; nearly all Bihar
Petroleum	97,453,077 gall.*	Assam 82,296,025; W. Punjab 15,157,052
Salt	1,864,725	'Northern India' (Sambhar Lake in Rajputana and Salt Range in W. Punjab) 701,790; rest mainly by evaporation near Bombay, Madras, and Karachi.

* 1947 figures (Indian Union only): coal, 30 million tons; petroleum, 65 million gallons.

TABLE IX

INDIA: INDUSTRIAL DEVELOPMENT, 1939

GL	Factories Provinces	States*	Total	Employees Provinces	States	Total
Cotton	836	79	915	486,853	97,020	583,873
Hosiery	152	4	156	7,708	235	7,943
Jute	106	2	108	298,967	3,318	302,295
Silk	107	23	130	6,251	2,226	8,477
Woollen ..	13	19	32	6,807	12,625†	19,432
Other Textile ..	89	45	134	10,491	2,035	12,526
Total Textiles ..	1,303	172	1,475	817,077	117,459	934,536
Engineering and Metal Trades ..	1,001	64	1,065	148,424	5,169	153,593
Metallurgy and Foundries ..	187	29	216	55,123	6,343	61,466
Food, Drink and Tobacco ..	1,880	103	1,983	97,407	9,944	107,351
Oil Mills ..	293	40	333	16,648	3,177	19,825
Other Chemicals	295	49	344	39,297	7,614	46,911
Printing ..	655	29	684	30,942	1,179	32,121
Paper Mills, etc.	54	2	56	13,429	857	14,286
Cement, lime, pottery ..	46	16	62	13,088	7,017	20,105
Glass	74	6	80	8,934	1,231	10,165
Other Wood and Stone	345	139	484	31,268	19,868	51,136
Tanning and Leather ..	66	32	98	12,906	2,969	15,875
Gins and Presses	181	16	197	25,987	776	26,763
Miscellaneous ..	218	54	272	19,712	15,177	34,889
TOTAL	6,598	751	7,349	1,329,248	198,780	1,528,028
ALL Government Factories ..	374	127	501	132,446	38,661	171,107
Seasonal‡ ..	3,494	876	4,370	289,443	61,653	351,096
GRAND TOTAL ..	10,466	1,754	12,220	1,751,137	299,094	2,050,231

Source: Statistical Abstract for British India, No. 72 (1943).
* Including foreign possessions.
† Mainly carpet and shawl weaving establishments.
‡ Mainly tea, rice, and sugar mills, cotton ginneries and baling presses.

TABLE X

INDIA: INDUSTRIAL OUTPUT, 1938–39, 1944–45, 1947, 1948*

	1938–39	1944–45	1947	1948
Cotton Yarn, million lbs. ..	1,303	1,651	1,314	109·7
Cotton Cloth, million yds. ..	4,494†	4,726	3,816	113·7
Jute Manufactures, 1000 tons ..	1,221	1,097	no	data
Paper, 1000 cwts.	1,184	2,001	1,862	107·2
Pig-iron, 1000 tons	1,576	1,303	no	data
Steel, 1000 tons	977	1,264	893	95·6
Sulphuric Acid, 1000 cwts. ..	512	778	no	data
Cement, 1000 tons	1,512	2,044	1,441	105·2
Sugar, 1000 tons	668	1,122‡	925	108·1
Soda Ash, tons	no	data	13,623	207·0

* 1948 expressed as index number (1947=100).
† 1941–42
‡ 1943–44

The effects of the war, post-war recession, and 1948 recovery will be noted.

CHAPTER III

SOUTHEAST ASIA

By Charles A. Fisher

THE GEOGRAPHICAL AND HISTORICAL SETTING

THE PROBLEM: UNITY OR DIVERSITY

SOUTHEAST ASIA is endowed with a remarkable wealth of positional and intrinsic advantages. Of the three great focal channels whereon oceanic routes converge, Suez, Panama, and the Malacca Straits, the last alone is a natural breach, and furthermore is set in the midst of the richest and most accessible of all inter-tropical regions.

Until the Japanese occupation of 1942–45 deprived the western powers of its resources, and brought to a head a mass of common problems which still defy solution, Europeans have rarely been conscious of any inherent unity in the area comprised by the southeastern extremity of the Asiatic landmass, and the fringing festoons of islands beyond. Rather have they been impressed by the abundant diversity deriving from its articulated topography, and the juxtaposition there of contrasting cultures, for the area forms a meeting ground where ancient and modern ways of life jostle one another in far from stable equilibrium.

The more recent widespread agreement[1] in employing the term Southeast Asia to cover both the Indo-Pacific peninsula (Burma, Siam, Indo-China, and Malaya) and the Indonesian[2] and Philippine archipelagos, however, represents a departure from this typically occidental viewpoint, and a return, albeit unconscious, to the traditional Chinese and Japanese concept of the unity of the region, expressed in their respective collective names, Nan Yang and Nan Yo.

Yet while the paradox of unity and diversity permeates every aspect of the geography, physical and human, of Southeast Asia, it remains to be seen whether this changed emphasis is more than mere wishful thinking.

---

[1] e.g. The Southeast Asia Institute (of the U.S.A.) and the 'Scarborough Commission' (Interdepartmental Commission of Enquiry on Oriental, Slavonic, East European and African Studies) both accepted this definition of Southeast Asia.

[2] Throughout this chapter Indonesia is taken to cover the area of the Netherlands East Indies in 1942. Malaysia is the same area *plus* British Malaya (but not including the Philippines).

The immediate and overshadowing problem in the area today, that of meeting the rising tide of nationalism with the appropriate degree of political devolution, in turn raises the fundamental issue inherent in its political geography. With the progressive withdrawal of external control can the factors making for unity overcome the diversities, or are the latter so deeply ingrained as to make Balkanization inevitable?

If severally the territories of Southeast Asia now, at last, make good their independence, and mutually assist each other in maintaining it, the achievement may truly be termed revolutionary. For, since the beginnings of history, the greater part of this area has remained culturally, and in some degree also demographically, a colonial sphere. There are substantial geographical reasons why this should have been so.

PHYSIOGRAPHICAL FACTORS

Tectonically, no less than in human affairs, Southeast Asia is an outstanding centre of convergence, and its physiographic complexity and intricacy originate fundamentally therein. Round a core of older ranges, for the most part relics of the so-called Indo-Malayan mountain system, two major axes of Tertiary folding, the approximately latitudinal Tethys and the predominantly longitudinal western Pacific series, come here into open collision. The resultant cataclysm has given a distinctive alignment to the larger features of relief, culminating in some remarkable contortions in the eastern extremities of the archipelago.

In the Indo-Pacific peninsula, the essential trends of both the Indo-Malayan core and the Tertiary folds of the Arakan Yoma run roughly north-south. South of Cape Negrais, however, the continuity of the latter is interrupted, and when, after a brief resurgence in the Andamans, they again reappear in Sumatra, they have already begun to swing eastwards in a vast arc which continues in a WNW/ESE direction through Java and the Lesser Sundas to Wetar and the islets of the Banda Sea. Two parallel lines of these young folds traverse Indonesia, the more recent northerly one, still volcanically active, corresponding to the mountain spine of the aforementioned islands, the other giving rise to a series of lesser islands and submarine ridges.

No corresponding series of Tertiary ranges flanks the eastern side of the Indo-Pacific peninsula but, roughly a thousand miles offshore, broken portions of one of the outer Asiatic arcs form the northwest-southeast backbone of the Philippines, and extend thence into northern New Guinea. There again a marked easterly component appears in the folds as they approach the equator, and continuity once more breaks down.

In contrast to these bold but erratic lineaments, the Indo-Malayan core presents a more consistent if less imposing appearance. It begins in the north of the peninsula with a great tangle of closely constricted north-south ridges, which simultaneously fan out and lose height southwards, forming sharp divides between the principal river basins from the Irrawaddy to the Songkoi. Continuing through lower Burma and Siam, the mountains subside to little more than detached hills south of the Kra isthmus, later to reassert themselves in a more vigorous series of ridges, rising to over 7,000 ft. in north-central Malaya, before they finally peter out in Johore, and the continuity of the land ceases altogether at Singapore island, some 2° north of the equator.

To the geologist neither the Malacca nor the Sunda Straits constitutes a major interruption, for the shallow intervening seas represent but recent transgression over the continental shelf, whose real edge occurs in the vicinity of Wallace's line through the Makassar Strait. But to the geographer the break in the continuity of the landmass at Singapore is crucial for, despite the détour to the south of many hundred miles which the peninsula entails, the complete breach in the extreme western ramparts of the Pacific abundantly justifies this diversion. It is, in fact, a natural counterpart to the Panama canal on the opposite shore of the ocean.

The mineral wealth associated with this complex structure is likewise distinctive. The Indo-Malayan mountain system contains the greater part of the world's tin and tungsten. Although in the north of the peninsula remoteness and topographical difficulties detract from the commercial value of the ores, farther south, in Malaya, Bangka and Billiton, much of the tin has been redistributed in vast and readily accessible alluvial spreads.

Second in importance to tin are widespread accumulations of mineral oil, occurring in gentler undulations between the main Tertiary ridges and the older core, notably in Burma, Sumatra, and Borneo, which, although together yielding only some 3·6% of the world's output, gain enhanced significance from the virtual absence of petroleum workings elsewhere in the monsoon lands.

Apart from small scattered deposits of high grade iron ore in east Malaya, and various occurrences of workable lateritic iron and bauxite in the Philippines and the Rhio/Johore area respectively, the remaining mineral resources are as yet of little consequence, and the lack of good coal, in particular, constitutes a serious handicap.

The effect of recent geological history on the soils of Southeast Asia is equally pronounced. In many parts of Java, and in scattered portions of Sumatra, the Lesser Sundas, and Celebes, outpourings of volcanic ejectamenta, providing the acid content is not excessive, yield soils whose fertility contrasts vividly with the surrounding laterites, while on the mainland extensive patches of comparably high fertility are formed by alluvial deposits in the lower courses of the larger rivers. In no other part of the world in similar latitudes is the general sterility of the soil so widely relieved by stretches of such exceptional richness. Geomorphologically the island arc structure of Indonesia and the Philippines is strongly reminiscent of Japan, and the same 'complexity and fineness of pattern' there noted by Trewartha is characteristic of these southern islands. But the considerable difference in climate appears to favour the latter, both in its immediate effect on plant growth, and in the greater speed with which similar volcanic material has been decomposed in the equatorial regions, giving rise to a thicker soil cover and more extensive coast plains.

POSITIONAL FACTORS

From the viewpoint of human utilization, fragmentation is the keynote of the topography of Southeast Asia; on the mainland steep ridges, and in the archipelago wide stretches of sea intervene between the scattered areas which are well favoured for cultivation. Not even Europe itself can compare with Southeast Asia, peninsular as well as insular, in the high ratio of coastline to land area, and the magnitude of its rivers adds further to the ease of access by water. Paradoxically, however, penetration overland is almost impossibly difficult. Only in the northeast corner does landward ingress present no problem, and geographically the Tonkin delta and northern Annamite coasts are merely prolongations of the South China littoral, a condition reflected in both the local culture and the density of settlement.

This apart, landward entry is restricted to the great malarial and jungle-covered stretch of deeply dissected highland lying between the eastern Himalayas and Szechwan. Throughout history and pre-history this has acted as an effective filter, reducing the inflow of peoples to far lower proportions than that into either India or China from the continental interior, so that, until very recently, Southeast Asia was, in comparison to its two great neighbours, an almost empty land.

In its widest setting, the Indo-Pacific peninsula, together with the main Indonesian islands, forms a discontinuous bridge between Asia and Australasia, roughly paralleled to the east by a subsidiary and more broken line of stepping stones running through Formosa, the Philippines, and New Guinea. To this a two-fold corollary may be added. Peninsular Southeast Asia, extending almost to the equator, presents a barrier to interoceanic communication and also, in view of its internal topography, to landward movement between India and China.

At different epochs different aspects of this many-sided situation may have been most in evidence, but at all times the area has been subjected to powerful and often conflicting external influences. In order to withstand the disruptive tendencies which these entailed, and, more latterly, to profit from the rich potentialities which the geographical position afforded, a strong territorial base is indispensable. For this purpose, however, the areas with adequate agricultural resources, the larger deltas of the penin-sula and the fertile island of Java, are all excessively peripheral. The critical focus which, above all else, gives character to Southeast Asia as a whole, is the tip of the Malay peninsula, where the major breach occurs. But neither in the sterile laterites of Malaya, nor in the wide mangrove swamps of the adjacent coasts of Sumatra, does nature provide the terri-torial base for a great centralizing power.[1]

Thus, although some place in or near southern Malaya has repeatedly been the centre of gravity during both the distant and recent past, such settlements have either been extremely impermanent, or else have sur-vived as outposts of power based elsewhere. This dispersal of the richer agricultural lands round the fringes of Southeast Asia, and their con-spicuous absence near the centre, have hitherto prevented any effective integration of the region.

DIVERSIFYING AND DISRUPTING INFLUENCES IN THE PRE–EUROPEAN PERIOD

In pre-historic times the significance of Southeast Asia lay primarily in the link it afforded between the Asiatic mainland and Australasia. An almost continuous thin trickle of humanity passed through the filter of southwest China and thence into the Indo-Pacific peninsula on its way south, while subsidiary movements followed the more easterly route through the Philippines. Only a few of the diverse ethnic types concerned reached Australasia, but all have left widely scattered remnants *en route*, from which, in varying proportions, the present populations of the region are mainly compounded.

Two major waves of Pareoeans (southern Mongoloid peoples), referred to by Dutch anthropologists as Proto- and Deutero-Malays respectively, spread through the mainland and the western two-thirds of Indonesia before the Christian era and have ever since constituted the predominant strain there. Everywhere they sought out the better paddy lands, in the isolation of which they subsequently specialized out into the so-called

---

[1] It is not known with certainty what constituted the original nucleus of the kingdom of Sri Vijaya in Sumatra (see p. 185), but none of the suggestions hitherto advanced appears to invalidate this argument.

13

'sub-races' of today,[1] and in so doing successively pushed the earlier negroid and pre-Dravidian inhabitants into the hills or remoter islands, a process which, in the peninsula, has been continued until recently by further repeated invasions from the north. Hence arises the racial complexity of the contemporary indigenous population of Southeast Asia, forming a veritable ethnographic museum, and a potential breeding ground for acute minority problems.

About the dawn of the Christian era, southern Indian colonization wrought a decisive change in the space relations of Southeast Asia. The search for an alternative to the Tibetan route to China led, during the first four centuries A.D., to considerable traffic through the various channels of the archipelago, and the founding of a string of colonies in favoured localities along the adjacent routes. Thus arose Yavadvipa (Java), and Fu-nan[2] occupying the Mekong delta, probably in the first century, soon to be followed by Champa, based on a series of fertile pockets between the spurs of the Annamite Cordillera and the sea. Lesser settlements also developed along or near the shores of the Gulf of Martaban, east Sumatra, and other parts of the archipelago.

But although it is possible to sail with the wind from India to Malaya for six months during the year, and in the South China Sea the monsoonal reversal of air circulation favours navigation to and from China in alternate halves of the year, the value of the all-sea route was restricted, in the days of keel-less ships, by the absence of any regular wind to carry vessels back to India from Malaya.[3] Moreover the frequent calms which descend on the Straits placed small sailing ships at the mercy of pirates who, attracted by the lucrative trade passing through, established themselves at an early date in the protection of the fringing mangrove swamps, and remained a recurrent menace until the introduction of steam-driven patrol ships in the 19th century.

For these reasons Indian traders in general preferred during the early centuries of the Christian era not to risk the hazards of the all-sea route, but instead to make a short cut overland, most frequently, it is believed, in the vicinity of the Kra isthmus or northern Malaya. This led to the establishment of new colonies in southern Siam and intensified activity in the earlier settlements in Burma, Champa, and especially Cambodia, the last of which, by virtue of both position and agricultural resources, tended until the 13th century to overshadow most of the other Indian

---

[1] See Table XII (E). The term "sub-race" is unfortunate in this context, but seems to have gained general currency during the post-war unrest in Indonesia.

[2] Fu-nan was the Chinese name; the Indian name is not known.

[3] On this subject as a whole see E. H. G. Dobby: *The Political Geography of Malaya*, Ph.D. thesis (unpublished), University of London, 1945, Chapter IX. This thesis contains much useful information on Southeast Asia generally.

colonies of the peninsula. Access to the Menam valley via the gentle inner slope of the Nam Mun basin was much easier than movement in the reverse direction, and after the 9th century the Cambodian kingdom, centred at Angkor, succeeded in reducing one by one the various Indianized territories in what is now Siam to a state of vassalage.

Political evolution in the archipelago took a different turn. With growing navigational skill and the consequently somewhat increased immunity from piratical attacks, the all-sea route became more popular and, particularly after the closure of the overland route by disturbances in Central Asia in the 7th century, the volume of shipping increased appreciably. This in turn encouraged the original Indian colonies studded along the coasts to extend their territory, where necessary, to the opposite shores in order the more effectively to levy tolls on passing merchantmen.

The similarity of this development with that of the medieval European sea state is remarkable. Until the introduction of European political forms in recent centuries, this principle of state-building obsessed the archipelago, applying equally to the smallest units integrated round minor channels, and to the great empires which, from superior land bases, ultimately succeeded in absorbing multitudes of these petty statelets so as to control the major sea lanes traversing the region.

The first of these empires, Sri Vijaya, appears to have grown from an Indian settlement established near Palembang, and during the 5th and 6th centuries rose to a commanding position. From the 8th century onwards, under the Sailendra kings, its hegemony was slowly extended in varying degree over the greater part of the archipelago, though its focus remained the area between the Sunda and the Malacca Straits, both of which it dominated mainly from the Sumatra side. The ancient town of Tumasik or Sinhapura, situated on Singapore island, is generally believed to have been a dependency of Palembang at some stage before 1366 when Majapahit (see below) laid claim to it.

Meanwhile, to avoid the obstacle thus afforded, Indian and Chinese mariners attempted to use other routes, notably through the Straits of Makassar and the Java Sea. Ultimately this favoured the rise to preeminence in the 14th century of the rival Indianized empire of Majapahit, conceived in terms of the Java Sea, and resting on very secure agricultural foundations in central and east Java, areas which had indeed been strong enough successfully to resist all attempts by Sri Vijaya to subdue them. During the middle of the 14th century Majapahit succeeded to the greater part of the Sailendra territories, and the final flowering of culture in Java at this period represents perhaps the supreme achievement of the Hindus in Southeast Asia.

From the ethnographic standpoint the immediate effect of Indian colonization on the great mass of the Malaysian population in the archipelago, and on the closely related Mon-Khmer[1] and allied peoples of the peninsula, is the subject of acute controversy, though it appears to have been much stronger in the former case. But indirectly the broad belt of settled civilized life which they spread latitudinally across the region constituted an effective barrier to the further southward drift of peoples as yet at a more rudimentary stage of social evolution. To the Indians, therefore, may be traced the beginnings of human differentiation between mainland and archipelago which became sharpened by repeated overland migrations into the former.

Among an almost numberless succession, three such movements deserve particular consideration. The Tibeto-Burmans, who had been descending the Irrawaddy valley, probably since the later centuries B.C., began, shortly before the 11th century, to seep into the lowlands of the Dry Zone, and by 1054 were sufficiently numerous to establish the first truly Burmese dynasty at Pagan in the heart of that distinctive region.

The Annamites, farther east, originated apparently from the mixture of southern Chinese with earlier Pareoean types in the kingdom of Nan Yueh which, in the 2nd century B.C., extended from Kwangsi and Kwangtung through the Songkoi delta to the northern Annam coast. The absorption of Nan Yueh into the Chinese empire in 111 B.C. led to religious and cultural assimilation, and the arts of dyke-building and intensive rice cultivation gave the Annamites a decisive advantage over the more primitive Chams to the south. Thus, in subsequent centuries, they were able little by little to advance southwards, until at the time of the French conquest of Cochin-China Annamite settlement was already in progress there, though the difficulties of integrating the narrow and broken littoral of eastern Indo-China had meanwhile in 1673 caused the Annamite kingdom to split into the two parts later known as Tonkin and Cochin-China.

Finally, many centuries after the first trickles of Lao-Thai-Shan folk had penetrated far down the Salween and Menam valleys under constant Chinese pressure on their homeland, the overthrow of the Shan kingdom of Nan Chao, on the Yunnan-Kwangtung plateau, by Kublai Khan in 1253–54 brought about a last great dispersal. Since the plains of Burma and Indo-China were already occupied by equally or more advanced communities, the Shans moving towards these areas were largely confined to

---

[1] Mon-Khmer is strictly a linguistic term. The Mons are also known as Talaings; Khmer is the national name for Cambodia.

the plateau country, though in Burma, during the chaos following the Mongol sacking of Pagan (1287) Shan dominion was for a time widely extended over the plains.

On the opposite side of the Shan and Laos plateaus, however, the Mon-Khmer inhabitants of the Menam basin offered less resistance to the Shans, and it was there that, after prolonged internecine struggles, they created their new state, Siam. The southward expansion of the latter was marked by the occupation of a series of river valley settlements, e.g., Sukodhai, Kampeng Bhej, Nakhaun Sawan, and finally, c.1350, Ayuthia, each in turn functioning as a forward capital. By the end of the 14th century Siam, having subdued Angkor, extended far beyond its nucleus in the Menam basin, and laid claim also, not for the first or the last time, to the Tenasserim coast and the Malay peninsula. But difficulties of overland communication with these outlying regions rendered control ineffective and impermament, and in succeeding centuries Siam was repeatedly embroiled in conflict with Burma and Cambodia.

In contrast to the thalassic structure of political units in the archipelago, most of the larger mainland states were essentially riverine. The distinction between the two forms is by no means sharp. For example, in Malaya, whose small population originated chiefly in the islands, the reticulate drainage pattern was clearly reflected politically, the territories of several rajahs, each of whom dominated the *ulu* (upstream area) above his particular inland *kuala* (river mouth), together forming the larger sultanates, which corresponded roughly to the major river basins, and were controlled usually from a coastal *kuala* settlement. But the Malay sultanates were in turn linked with each other, and often with other parts of the archipelago, by maritime connexions.

The growing ethnic complexity of Southeast Asia was matched by increasing religious and cultural diversity, and already before the coming of the Europeans the region exhibited an elaborate interdigation of influences emanating from both India and China. To these a further component remained to be added. Although Arab traders had frequented the archipelago for over a thousand years, it was not until late in the 13th century, following the invasion of northern India by Turco-Afghan peoples, that Islam suddenly began to be propagated in the eastern seas by Gujarati spice merchants, a movement which, in turn, ultimately led to the decay of economic and cultural links between Southeast Asia and peninsular India. Like its Buddhist and Hindu predecessors, Islam followed the commercial routes, first to Perlak in northern Sumatra, thence to Malacca (1414), which by that time had become the principal spice market of the Indies, and Ternate (1440), the centre of the spice-producing region, and thereafter to Java and the coasts of the remaining islands.

The rise of Malacca which, although constituting the main centre for the diffusion of the Muslim faith, was none the less an extremely cosmopolitan town, frequented especially by Indian and Chinese merchants, followed speedily upon the eclipse of Sinhapura towards the end of the 14th century, and illustrates the continued attraction exercised by the coasts of southern Malaya, despite the sparseness of population in the interior. Malacca was situated at one of the narrowest parts of the Straits and at a focal point for river and coastal communication with the rest of Malaya, which for a brief period it was able politically to integrate. But far greater significance lay in the lead it began to give to the disaffected peripheral territories of Majapahit, as one by one they succumbed to the new religion, which continued to spread until checked by Spanish Roman Catholic missionaries in Luzon late in the 16th century.

Although the Buddhist states of the mainland[1] never accepted Islam, all the more advanced peoples of Malaysia, the Balinese and Sasaks alone excepted, became at least nominally Muslim. In reality, however, their religion is a unique structure, comprising on a substratum of paganism successive layers of Buddhism, Hinduism and Islam, the mythology of one faith being cloaked in the ritual of another, and crudely adapted to fit the dogmas of the third, a tendency which by no means disappears when conversion to Christianity is effected. A similar, but still more complex state of affairs prevails linguistically, the analogy extending even down to the un-European constructions of Baba English as spoken by the Straits Chinese, and the 'petjoh' Dutch of the Indo-Europeans.

UNIFYING INFLUENCES: CLIMATE AND MARITIME LINKS

Against all these diversifying tendencies, the unifying influences of climate and the sea appear relatively insignificant. Climatically, Southeast Asia is customarily divided into three major regions, approximately as follows:

(i) The equatorial monsoon belt, which extends to about 7° north and south respectively, an area with no true dry season, and experiencing little annual variation in temperature.

(ii) the tropical monsoon mainland, north of (i), characterized by a distinct seasonal rhythm, with wet and dry periods, and associated temperature changes.

(iii) the distinctive maritime variant of the tropical monsoon type found in the Philippines, with temperatures similar to those of (ii) but where the high

[1] The religion of the Annamite lands cannot strictly be termed Buddhist; like that of China, from which it is derived, it also contains Confucian and Taoist elements.

incidence of typhoons, except in Mindanao, poses peculiar problems to the cultivator.

Within these broad divisions there are numerous important variations, largely explicable in terms of relief and aspect, such as the Burmese and Siamese Dry Zones, and the similarly dry portions of East Java and the Lesser Sunda islands, which strictly speaking, lie beyond the equatorial limits. In eastern Indonesia (including East Java) the effect of relative dryness is aggravated by the widespread occurrence of limestone topography.

Yet the fact remains that all these differences are merely variations on a common theme. Everywhere the climate is monsoonal and, except at high altitudes, hot, and, although a contrast exists between the islands and mainland, no part is continental. Throughout the greater part of the region rice and bamboos grow readily and in coastal regions the coconut palm is a third characteristic element. Even the drier regions are mostly well provided with streams suitable for irrigation purposes, and the areas where neither wet nor dry rice constitutes the basis of subsistence agriculture support only a minute fraction of the total population.

More significant than the actual staple crops, however, is the fundamental contrast between shifting and permanent cultivation, the former, representing a lower stage of cultural advancement, being nowadays confined mainly to the wilder hill areas and the remoter parts of the archipelago.[1] Apart from these last, where a variety of interesting but politically unimportant cultures prevail, the overall climatic similarity has made possible a common way of life, utilizing the same essential foodstuffs and building and clothing materials. Its dependence on paddy cultivation has led to marked concentration in alluvial and coastal lowlands, where water transport and fishing figure prominently, and houses, constructed of bamboo and thatched with palm leaves, usually stand on piles in order to be above flood level. Although major differences, based on religious taboos, occur in the attitude towards animals, the buffalo and ox are everywhere used for ploughing, and poultry are likewise ubiquitous. Furthermore, despite wide variations in the forms of government, both ancient and modern, the communal village, with its council of elders or notables, is found throughout Southeast Asia. Alone among the main lowland areas, the profoundly Sinicized Annamite lands exhibit numerous and fundamental departures from these common indigenous traditions.

Clearly maritime contacts have facilitated this cultural diffusion, a process which has been aided by the coastal concentration already noted. Regional differences, like those of the Mediterranean before the Muslim conquests, appear to have been strong enough to stimulate trade between

[1] For further detail see Karl Pelzer: *Pioneer Settlement in the Asiatic Tropics*, New York, 1945.

the various shores, but not so great as to prevent the spread of a common way of life. The Chinese and Japanese names, Nan Yang and Nan Yo, both mean Southern Seas, an indirect reference surely to the unifying influence of the sea, and it is likewise suggestive that those contemporary Indian scholars, such as K. M. Panikkar, who regard Southeast Asia as being fundamentally synonymous with Further India, are likewise thinking in terms of former maritime expansion.

Sea power indeed has repeatedly proved to be the decisive factor in the political evolution of Southeast Asia. An outstanding example of this tendency occurred during the 15th century when it seemed for a time that Siam, then the greatest land power of the region, and Majapahit, the contemporary mistress of the archipelago, would come into serious conflict in the Malay peninsula, which both sought to dominate in order to control the traffic through the Straits. Precariously situated between the two rival forces, which had already brought about the downfall of Sinhapura, the port kingdom of Malacca survived only because the Chinese, reversing their traditional isolationist policy, sent large fleets into the Nan Yang between 1405 and 1430. Subsequently Malacca relied on the sea-power of the Arabs, which became dominant in this region by the end of the 15th century.

EUROPEAN INFLUENCES BEFORE THE NINETEENTH CENTURY

With the dawn of the Oceanic Age, the Bay of Bengal and the South China Sea slipped into truer perspective as mere annexes to the Indian and Pacific Oceans, and the significance of the breaks in the land bridge became still further emphasized.

In 1511 Malacca fell to the Portuguese, bent on following the spice trade to its source; thereafter their activities spread not only to the eastern archipelago but also to China and even to Japan. Their shipping routes thus coincided approximately with those of Indian mariners many centuries before, and once again this extraneous lateral movement across Southeast Asia tended to foster division.

Moreover the Portuguese in their weakness began playing off one group of natives against another, and with the arrival after 1525 of the Spaniards (who, on the basis of the Treaty of Tordesillas, laid doubtful claim to the Philippines) and then, at the end of the century, of Dutch, British and French, the commercial rivalries of Europeans were projected into native relationships, and confusion became worse confounded. Although the last two, decoyed by more brilliant prospects in India, soon withdrew almost entirely from Southeast Asia until late in the 18th century, bitter enmity prevailed between the other three, the Dutch gradually supplanting the Portuguese, while the Spaniards held their ground in the Philippines.

Since the Portuguese, like the Indians and Arabs before them, approached the area from southern India they, too, entered via the Malacca Straits and rested their power on the control thereof. Malacca town became their principal station in the Indies, functioning as a trading post, a repair centre for ships, and a base from which to defend the eastern approach to the Indian Ocean, a political pattern which in large measure was resuscitated by the British.[1]

The Dutch however, with no solid bases in India, and wishing at first to avoid the main Portuguese strongholds, sailed direct from South Africa, using first the westerlies and then the southeast trades of the Indian Ocean —the direct approach used ever since by sailing vessels of all nations— finally entering the archipelago through the Sunda Strait. Thus they established their principal settlements in Java, at Bantam (1600) and Batavia (founded 1619). The island's fertility favoured its subsequent revival as the focus of Indonesia, while Malacca remained isolated in a backwater until captured by the Dutch as a precautionary measure in 1641.

Lastly the Philippines which, before the Muslim era, had never been closely linked with the rest of Southeast Asia, became further estranged therefrom by the Spanish practice of administering them as a dependency of their American empire, thus emphasizing their Pacific rather than their Asian affinities.

In all these cases, however, the Europeans, operating as they were from distant bases, never attempted to conquer the more compact land states of the peninsula, although individual adventurers and trading companies developed extensive relations with them. Even in the archipelago the Europeans confined their activities essentially to the coastal regions else-where, except in Java. Hence, despite the practice of miscegenation adopted by all three, and their Christian missionary activity which, outside of the Philippines, proved effective only among the Eurasians, their cultural and political imprint was superficial. Until the mid-19th century these considerations applied with even greater force to the peninsular areas north of Kra. Only in Java and the Philippines was the native state system widely superseded by western administrative arrangements, leading in the former case to the pernicious practices of taxation by forced deliveries and contingencies. Elsewhere it is arguable that the indigenous way of life was more extensively undermined by the contemporary swarms of Chinese and Japanese settlers who followed the trade routes

[1] See E. H. G. Dobby, *op. cit.*, p. 150.

during the Ming dynasty (1368–1644), and the century preceding the Tokugawa seclusion of 1637, respectively.

THE POLITICAL PATTERN IMPOSED BY THE WEST

THE EVOLUTION OF THE 1942 FRONTIERS, AND PROBLEMS ARISING THEREFROM

The political pattern of Southeast Asia which prevailed at the time of the Japanese invasion bore the unmistakable stamp of 19th century Europe and was in consequence both antiquated and exotic. The gradual worldwide change of emphasis from markets to materials, or more truly from trade to production, which characterized that period entailed in Southeast Asia a corresponding political reassessment of geographical values in terms of interiors rather than coastlands. Thus, while in the opening years of the century positional advantages were at a premium, the territories possessing rich internal resources subsequently became the most highly prized.

The return of both British and French interest to Southeast Asia arose primarily from the desire to take part in the China trade, which during the 17th and 18th centuries had been virtually a Dutch preserve. British trade with China, based principally on the export thither of Indian opium and cotton, expanded swiftly in the late 18th century, a process soon to be accelerated by the Industrial Revolution. During the Napoleonic Wars the British occupation of Java (1811–16) under Raffles focused attention on the desirability of further bases in or near the Straits to ensure the access of British shipping to the South China Sea, since Penang, already acquired in 1786, was proving to be too remote for that purpose. Despite the obvious potential value of Singapore as an entrepôt for Malaysian commerce, which Raffles clearly foresaw, it was its position in relation to the China route which persuaded the British authorities to risk offending the Dutch by annexing the island in 1819.

After 1815, as also since 1945, Dutch suspicions of British motives in the area were understandable but then, as now, more urgent considerations of the European balance of power prevented open hostility between the two. Thus by the treaty of 1824 the Dutch formally exchanged Malacca for a few British posts in Sumatra, and the British agreed to establish no further settlements in any island south of Singapore. Although the last clause was ambiguous in respect of islands lying athwart that latitude, the Dutch acquiesced in the British occupation of Labuan in 1846, intended for use as a coaling station on the China route, and in subsequent further expansion in Borneo, while a supplementary treaty of

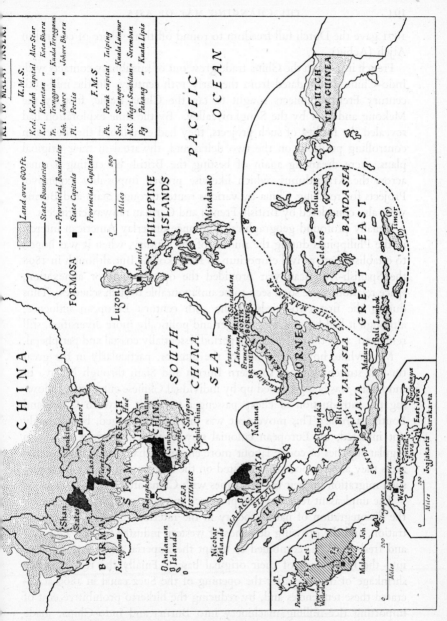

Fig. 17. SOUTHEAST ASIA: POLITICAL PATTERN, 1942

The areas shown black were territorial transfers effected by the Japanese during their occupation. All have now been retroceded.

1871 gave the Dutch full freedom to round off their sphere of control in Atjeh (Achin).

French interest in the China trade grew out of missionary contacts with Indo-China which dated from the early 17th century. In the mid-19th century French pioneers sought to tap the China traffic, first by the Mekong and later by the Songkoi valley. By the time exploration had revealed the futility of such projects, they had established themselves in controlling positions on the two deltas and, thwarted in their original plans, were dreaming again of besting the British by cutting a canal across the Kra isthmus, which likewise proved impossibly expensive. Projects for reaching China by various routes through Siam and Burma were also considered by British, French and German railway engineers.

Equally profound geographical ignorance underlay American interest in the Philippines during the middle of the century, when it was hoped to establish there a rival emporium to Hongkong. But although in 1898 the Spanish-American war provided the opportunity for annexation, space relations were soon seen to be unfavourable to such schemes. Thus during the first two-thirds of the 19th century European influence, although it had become far stronger and politically more diversified, still remained, as in the early oceanic period, essentially coastal and peripheral.

Meanwhile, however, much of the interior, particularly in the great tin belt stretching from southern Burma and Siam through Malaya to Indonesia, was being opened up by individual Chinese enterprise, following the introduction of cheap passenger transport between China and Southeast Asia. This movement was in part encouraged, but certainly not initiated, by European colonial powers which, anxious to obtain regular supplies of coolie labour more energetic than that available in the areas they already occupied, insisted on the insertion of clauses legalizing such migration in their major treaties with China after 1842.[1]

The unpleasant repercussions produced in many coastal settlements by the disintegration of native society in the interior under Chinese penetration, and the growing demands of western industry for raw materials and fresh markets, combined to tempt the imperial powers to advance into the hinterlands of their original bases. Finally the revolutionary shrinkage of distance after the opening of the Suez canal in 1869 accelerated these tendencies and, by reducing the hitherto prohibitive cost of importing rice-milling machinery into Burma and Indo-China, made possible the rapid opening up of the Irrawaddy and Mekong deltas as rice granaries.

Early in the 1870's, therefore, the European powers concerned began

[1] See Dobby, *op. cit.*, Chapter X.

swiftly to extend their control inland and, in the space of a few years, this 'forward movement' had degenerated into a scramble for what was left of Southeast Asia.

In Indonesia the initiative remained with the Dutch who, despite fears occasioned by German and Italian intrigues in Sumatra and the annexation of north-eastern New Guinea by Germany in 1885, nevertheless extended effective rule over the greater part of the territory, meanwhile reaching a boundary settlement with the Portuguese in 1893 which restricted the latter to the eastern half of Timor. Neither the replacement of Spanish by American rule in the Philippines in 1899, nor the placing of German New Guinea under Australian mandate after the First World War necessitated any further boundary changes.

With the new emphasis on interior regions, the scene of acute controversy moved from the archipelago to the mainland, where the French replaced the Dutch as the main rivals of the British. Already the two obvious *points d'appui*, the Irrawaddy and the Mekong deltas, which had attracted Indian colonists nearly two millennia before, had been secured, the former by the British after the Second Burmese War in 1852, and the latter by the French who progressively annexed the southern provinces of Cochin-China between 1862 and 1867, and in 1864 established a protectorate over such portions of Cambodia as were not under Siamese occupation.

From these beginnings, move and countermove followed in quick succession. The protection of Annam[1] and Tonkin in 1882–85 was balanced by the annexation of Upper Burma after a third war in 1885, the relevant treaties of transfer being signed with China, which in the 18th century had reasserted its claim to suzerainty over both areas. Since the successively acquired portions of Burma were thereafter constituted a province of India the Arakan mountain wall, the most sharply defined natural frontier of Southeast Asia as a whole, had only a provincial significance until 1937.

Partly on account of its relatively inconspicuous situation away from the main ocean routes, and partly because the opposing pressures of Britain and France tended there to cancel each other out, Siam continued to retain its independence. After sustaining a heavy defeat from the Burmese, culminating in the destruction of Ayuthia in 1767, Siam had experienced a great national revival. A new capital was established at Bangkok, and soon afterwards territorial expansion southwards began, leading eventually to an attack on the Malay state of Kedah in 1821. Farther south still, however, the British forward movement in Malaya

[1] i.e. what was left of the old Cochin-China, after the southern delta lands, henceforward known as Cochin-China, had been detached therefrom.

starting in 1874 successively reduced Perak, Selangor and the Negri Sembilan to the status of Protected States, and in 1888 extended the process to Pahang, over which Siam put forward tenuous claims to hegemony. In 1893 the French countered both this and a threatened Siamese advance into the Laos country (following the French reduction of Annam, Siam's traditional rival there), by establishing control over all areas east of the Mekong, thus bisecting the Laotian kingdom of Luang Prabang.

At this stage the Anglo-French convention of 1896 called a halt to territorial encroachment on Siam, which the British wished to preserve as a buffer state protecting their Indian empire on the east, analogous to Afghanistan in the west. To guard against any French revival of the Kra canal project the British insisted on making peninsular Siam a British 'sphere of influence', to be counterbalanced by a French sphere in the Nam Mun basin. But the mosaic of small Shan principalities which straddled the plateaux and gorges between the Irrawaddy valley and the Annam coast, and had continually fluctuated in allegiance between China, Siam, Burma and Annam, was too weak to function, even collectively, as a buffer. The British and French accordingly dispensed with such political insulation there, and accepted the Mekong line as the boundary, thus cutting off Siam from direct contact with China. The Chinese, however, refused to acknowledge the separation of certain Burmese Shan states from those still within their territories, and the boundary there has recently (1947) been under review.

Elsewhere, also, the new boundaries did not remain stable. In 1907 the French, after protracted haggling, reunited Battambang with the rest of their Cambodian protectorate. Thereby they aroused bitter irredentist feelings in Siam which were to flare up again during the time of French humiliation in 1940, leading to the temporary resumption, under Japanese 'good offices', of Siamese rule over the lost provinces from 1941 to 1945.

Finally, in 1909, the British, worried by German negotiations for railway construction in the strategically vital southern peninsula, prevailed upon Bangkok to abandon its claims to Kelantan, Trengganu, Kedah and Perlis, which were thereupon constituted British Protected States.

This rigid political pattern imposed by the west rested unconformably on the indigenous structure. Admittedly, since the strong hand of topography exerted constant influence throughout, it was no accident that the new Netherlands Indies corresponded closely in extent and layout to medieval Majapahit, or that the same river basins which on the mainland had been the historic state nuclei remained the cores round which new political units were integrated. But in respect of territorial organization the 19th century brought revolutionary changes. The imprecision and fluidity of traditional political forms tacitly recognized the demographic youthfulness of the region and the consequent immature adjustment so far achieved between state and terrain. Thus a British surveyor trying to demarcate the boundaries of a Malay state in 1875 could elicit no more exact information from the local potentate concerning the limits of his territory than that "if you wash your head before starting, it will not be dry before you reach the place".

The relationship between different states was likewise extremely flexible. Theoretically, the regular payment of tribute indicated vassalage, but prudence frequently dictated that it be simultaneously rendered to several powerful neighbours, each of which endeavoured to exert its control on propitious occasions, but would equally readily disclaim all responsibility for any misdemeanours that its erstwhile subordinate might commit. A confused tangle of conflicting customary obligations of this sort vaguely regulated mutual relationships between states of all sizes, from the tiny principalities of Laos or the Malaysian sultanates, to the larger units of the archipelago and peninsula, and in some cases ultimately to the Imperial Chinese court at Peking.

The Europeans, however, had no place for such ambiguity, and imposed rigid western formulæ on their territories till the latter came to resemble a series of old and mutilated paintings in cumbrous and badly fitting Victorian frames. In addition to catastrophically arresting indigenous politico-geographical evolution, the new linear boundaries, traced for the most part through completely unknown country, proved to be singularly ill-conceived in relation to both topographical and ethnographical realities.

Although, with minor exceptions, frontier questions did not trouble the Europeans in Southeast Asia, since their activities were primarily concentrated in the coastlands, the exhaustion of the more accessible mineral deposits was bound, under their régime, to lead ultimately to disputes over mining rights in the watershed regions, such as complicated the Sino-Burmese border controversy.

More serious from the point of view of the new autonomous states, which, however, will automatically inherit the above group of problems, are the minority complications associated with the modern boundaries. The most outstanding case of these occurs in the Shan country, the severely dissected tableland which, descending in steps from Yunnan, extends wide prolongations southwards at an altitude of about 3–4000 feet between Burma and Siam, and between the latter and Indo-China. On the higher slopes above this general level are found small scattered groups of hill folk in the most rudimentary stages of tribal organization, while on the plateau itself the Shans, whose reunification was prevented after their dispersal only by the difficulty of lateral communication, now form minorities of some six, one, and half a million in the adjoining areas of southwest China, eastern Burma, and northwest Indo-China (Laos) respectively.

In recent years Pibul Songgkram's Pan Thai [1] movement, emphasizing the close affinities of all these peoples with the 16 million Siamese (who alone in Southeast Asia had managed to preserve their political independence), and events during the Sino-Japanese and Pacific wars have raised the problem to the conscious level. The reorientation of Kuomintang China towards the southwest, and the associated road construction through parts of the Shan country, underlined the need for a more sympathetic Chinese policy towards the minorities in this key area. Later the Japanese, as part of more extensive changes, all pandering to Thai chauvinism, decreed in 1941 that portions of Laos, and, in 1943, that the two Burmese Shan states of Kentung and Mong Pan, should be 'returned' to Siam.

By the terms of the 1945 armistice, the 1942 boundaries were restored, and it is significant both of the disintegrating effect on Shan national sentiment of earlier partitions, and of the shortcomings of Siamese administration, that no objections to this were raised by the Shans or the Laotians, who preferred to bargain for a higher measure of self-government within the new autonomous but alien states of Burma and Indo-China. In so far as a small but uncertain percentage of the Karens further south overlap from Burma into Siam, a similar problem is raised, but the solution of this depends on Burmese rather than Siamese action.

The Malay minority in southern Siam, however, may lead to serious frontier disputes, especially if the peninsular Malays should ever become linked politically with their fellows in the archipelago. For, despite the northward advance of the Siam-Malayan frontier in 1909, there still remain some 500,000-700,000 Malays fairly compactly distributed in the Singgora and Patani districts of Siam, and the linguistic, cultural and religious divide, though complicated by the north-south grain of the country, lies well to the north of the political boundary.

Moreover, after the Siamese 'national' revolution of 1932, educational measures and religious restrictions were introduced with the intention of forcibly assimilating the Malay minority, whose position has therefore deteriorated in comparison with that of their kinsfolk in adjacent British territory. Again, in 1943, the Japanese, with cynical disregard for national

[1] The name 'Thai' means free, and extensive propagandist use was made of that fact.

feelings which they professed to respect, added fuel to the fire by 'restoring' Kelantan, Trengganu, Kedah and Perlis to Siam.

During the closing stages of the Pacific War the view was frequently
expressed in certain quarters that the British might seize the excuse thus
afforded to extend direct political control over peninsular Siam where,
before the invasion, British Malayan tin and rubber concerns had invested
considerable capital, and from which the immediate attack on Malaya was
launched. But even had such annexation been planned, which is doubtful,
the post-war political climate in Southeast Asia would have ruled it out,
and in fact the boundary has merely reverted to its former anachronistic
position.

INTERNAL PROBLEMS: PLURALISM. (See Tables XII and XIII)

The 19th century political pattern, however, was merely a superficial
expression of far more penetrating social changes which were taking place
within Southeast Asia. Indeed after 1870 a new and utterly alien way of
life, hitherto confined to a few scattered coastal localities, spread relent-
lessly throughout the region, challenging the basic concepts on which the
indigenous culture rested, and in many of the most productive regions
swamping the latter altogether.

Everywhere in Southeast Asia, apart from the Sinicized areas of
northern Indo-China, Europeans were early impressed, and too often
exasperated, by the adagio tempo of life, and the all-pervading atmosphere
of indolence and insouciance. Explanation has been sought in the enervat-
ing climate, which is doubtless a contributory factor, but a more fundamental cause was the absence of acute pressure on the land, owing to the
relatively low population density, which until late in the 19th century did
not exceed one quarter that in India or the nuclear regions of China. This
explanation is borne out by the lack of similar characteristics among the
Indians and Chinese, and the marked weakening of them in Java during
the 19th century[1] and elsewhere in Southeast Asia after the economic
crisis of the 1930's.

In contrast to the traditional indigenous ways of life, which were
almost entirely agricultural and narrowly localized, their supplanter was
essentially commercial and deracinated. But although unquestonably
European in origin, its most numerous and even most vigorous protagonists were fellow Asians from China and India who, somewhat
precociously schooled in a more competitive social environment, endeavoured to profit from the opportunities created by the introduction

[1] See pp. 208–232.
14

of a money economy into the unsophisticated pioneer lands of the south. The situation has been aptly outlined by Unger[1] as follows: "Western capital and management were available in most places but there was a lack of adaptable cheap labour to do the work, of clerical and supervisory personnel, and of traders and merchants to set up the services and provide the goods needed in remote or newly developing areas".

It was to fill these many and varied gaps which, with few exceptions, made little appeal to the indigenous population until the 1930's, that millions of southern Chinese, impelled by the paucity of opportunity at home, migrated to Southeast Asia, especially after 1870. Their motives were exclusively economic, and their present distribution reflects alike their sublime indifference to the cultural, religious, linguistic or political fragmentation of the Nan Yang, and their readiness to undertake any kind of work, including the lowest paid and most arduous. Hence arise the big concentrations of coolies in the mining areas and urban centres, in the vicinity of which also many Chinese are engaged in market gardening. In general their superior agricultural skill, compared with indigenous cultivators, has caused them to eschew subsistence farming (though an important exception occurs in West Borneo), in order to specialize in the production of more lucrative cash crops. The adaptability they display in abandoning their age-old peasant methods for others which skim profits and fertility from the soil, in keeping with the spirit of the pioneer fringe, constitutes both a source of strength to themselves, and a menace to the more conservative local populations.

But neither coolie labour nor agriculture satisfy more than a fraction indefinitely, and either they eventually return to China, as most new-comers normally intend to do, or else, having acquired the necessary capital, establish themselves as craftsmen, or petty traders, thereafter not infrequently rising to spectacular heights as entrepreneurs. Perhaps their most conspicuous success has been achieved in the great rice exporting lands of Siam and Cochin-China, where they have obtained virtually monopolistic control over the milling and marketing of the staple crop. It is variously estimated that 80–90% of the rice mills in Siam, over 80% of those in Indo-China, and 75% in the Philippines were Chinese-owned immediately before the Second World War.

Occupationally the position of Indian immigrants is similar to that of the Chinese (apart from an almost complete neglect of mining), but territorially the larger concentrations are mostly confined to the areas now or formerly under British rule. In Burma where, until 1937, they did not

---

[1] L. Unger: "The Chinese in Southeast Asia," *Geographical Review* XXXIV, No. 2, April 1944, p. 201.

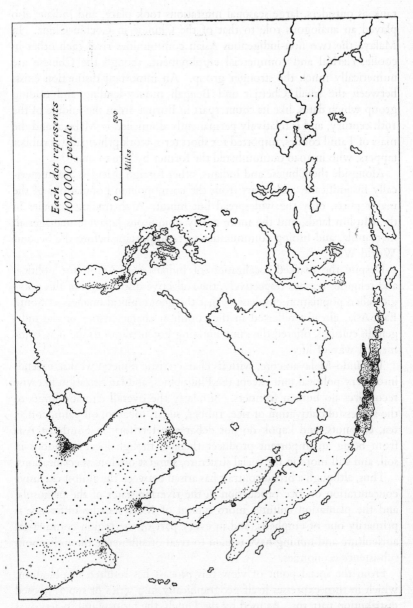

Each dot represents
100,000 people

500

Miles

0

Fig. 18. SOUTHEAST ASIA: DISTRIBUTION OF POPULATION

rank as outsiders, large seasonal migrations took place, and Indians also played an analogous role to that of the Chinese in Cochin-China. In Malaya the two non-indigenous Asian communities rival each other in coolie, clerical and commercial employment, though the Chinese are numerically much the stronger group. An important distinction exists between the small Chettiar and Bengali money-lending and trading group which dates, like its counterpart in Burma, from the middle of the 19th century, and is relatively permanently domiciled in Malaya, and the mass of Tamil coolies, imported for short term work principally as rubber tappers, who in 1940 outnumbered the former by five to one.

Alongside the Chinese and Indians, other foreign orientals are numerically insignificant, and, apart from the cosmopolitan populations of the major ports, only the widespread but minute Arab trading colonies in the Muslim lands, and the more nearly ubiquitous Japanese managerial, mercantile, and fishing communities were important before the Second World War.

Despite the marked localization of Indians and Arabs, for political and religious reasons respectively, the collective distribution of this polyglot alien population emphasizes that the geographical oneness of South East Asia, already reflected in the common characteristics of the indigenous cultures, offered the same unifying potentialities to the new commercial way of life.

The Indo-Malayan core, with its characteristic mineral wealth, extends into every political unit except the Philippines, and lateritization likewise recognizes no human frontiers. Similarly the overall climatic limits to the successful cultivation of rice, rubber, sugar, tobacco, oil palm, coffee, tea, coconuts, and kapok do not debar any territory in Southeast Asia from being an important producer thereof, though local variations in soil, and still more in the social structure, suggest obvious specializations.

Thus, although a broad contrast has arisen between the almost exclusive concentration on rice production in the riverine states of the peninsula, and the plantation cultures more typical of Malaysia, the difference is primarily one of emphasis, and in every part of the region commercial agriculture and mining have tended to rival or submerge the indigenous subsistence economies.

From the social point of view this process has resulted in pluralism, which in turn expresses itself geographically in a series of superimposed distribution patterns. As used by the Dutch, the term plural society was intended to connote a system wherein, "under an imported and an imposed régime, the two groups, native and immigrant . . . pursue their economic ends, with a minimum of contact and a maximum of social

freedom, beneath the benevolent eye of the 'white' man".[1] In fact, however, it implies that the class stratification inherent in contemporary
western society is accentuated by ethnic differences.

Such communities are therefore sociologically young, and, given time,
the division between ethnic and economic groupings should tend to
soften, and ultimately to disappear. But in Southeast Asia the sharp
contrasts of relief, and the paradox of difficult land access and easy entry
by sea, combine to perpetuate demographic immaturity. Thus, even
before the mass migrations of the 19th century introduced new elements
into the region, its society was already plural, since fusion had never
taken place between the hill peoples and the plainsmen, while the scattered alien traders and settlers remained unassimilated.

Three distinctive strands, each in itself composed of many individual
threads, are interwoven, but not compacted, in the contemporary population pattern.

The poorer lands, comprising the high mountain ranges and the rugged
plateaux of the peninsula, together with much of the interior uplands of the
main islands (apart from Java), and the greater part of the remoter islands
have been left, with few exceptions, to the more primitive peoples. Although it is difficult to disentangle cause from effect, it seems that at least
the numerical weakness, and possibly also the cultural backwardness of this
very varied group, result largely from the lack of opportunity afforded by
the terrain, and from malaria and other 'jungle fevers' so often endemic in
the uplands.

The remaining areas, the coastal and riverine lowlands, and the volcanic
plateau country of Java and much of Sumatra, on the other hand, provide
the centres of the traditional indigenous culture. Apart from the complications introduced during the 19th century, however, the varying
densities within these areas by no means corresponded to their carrying
capacity. For example, at the beginning of the imperial forward movement, the Irrawaddy and Mekong deltas supported only a fraction of their
present population, and subsequent increases there have been predominantly associated with commercialized rather than subsistance
agriculture. Again, the low densities of even the coastlands in the remoter
cul-de-sacs of the archipelago must be explained primarily in terms of
space relations.

But, in general, the outstanding feature of the distribution of the indigenous population and of the form of land utilization associated therewith,
is its coastal concentration. Only in the larger swampy areas, for obvious
reasons, does this rule break down completely, while in the deltas, where

[1] A. H. Brodrick: *Beyond the Burma Road*, London, 1944, p. 101.

maritime and river routes converge, the greatest intensities for the most part occur. Water communications, indeed, were vital in the historic scheme of things, and even today extensive areas of potentially good arable land in the interior of Siam remain virtually uninhabited because of the menace of gang robbers beyond range of police patrol boats on the rivers.

This overall distribution pattern, with its extreme emphasis on the flat lands, and its neglect of the possibilities for pastoralism elsewhere, does not differ fundamentally from that of the agrarian population in neighbouring monsoon lands, though it is somewhat accentuated by topographical articulation. But, except in northern Indo-China and Java (both of whose high densities have resulted from external causes to be considered below), the concentration of rural settlement in Southeast Asia has not advanced beyond a comparatively rudimentary stage.

The alien communities are even more sporadically dispersed throughout the region. While some of the mining centres are situated in relatively remote interiors, the majority of workings have as yet been restricted to the more accessible localities (see *Fig.* 19). Plantations, likewise, show the overriding influence of transportation costs in their localization, and the greater part of the rubber, coconut and oil palm regions of western Malaya and Johore, and the Cultuurgebied of east Sumatra, are within 60 miles of the sea. The plantations of Java and the Philippines are also, for obvious reasons, equally close to the coast.

Hence, although neither mining nor commercial agriculture is spread at all uniformly over Southeast Asia, both activities, being expressly aimed at taking wealth out of the region, have hitherto tended to concentrate near the seaboard.

Despite the great contrasts in other respects, therefore, both indigenous and alien populations exhibit a marked preference for the same restricted territories. Whereas in China, where the traditional forms of land utilization still predominate, some 85% of the population lives on one-third of the land, in Southeast Asia a comparable percentage has congregated in favoured portions of the maritime fringe[1] which collectively amount to less than one-sixth of the area. This state of affairs inevitably raises acute problems in the relationship between the two major communities involved, and the glib assumption that they can exist side by side, 'with the minimum of contact,' is rarely borne out by the facts.

The cleavage between indigenous and alien is most clearly seen in respect of urbanization. (Table XIV.) Although a rich development of

[1] i.e. within approximately 50–75 miles of the sea, or 100 miles in the case of the larger deltas. It is estimated that in Indo-China 75% of the population lives in 10% of the total area.

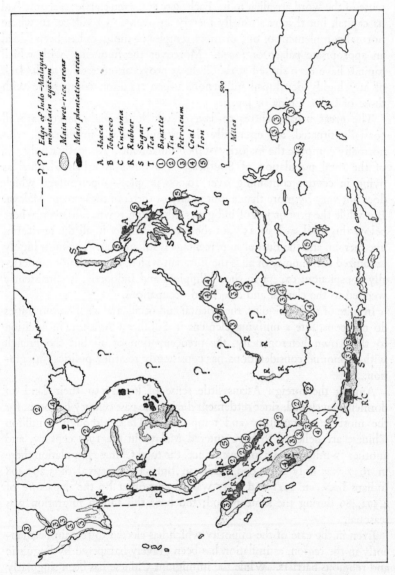

Fig. 19. SOUTHEAST ASIA: ECONOMIC RESOURCES

village life characterizes all parts of Southeast Asia, towns in the fullest sense of the word are alien to it. Each state and even statelet certainly had its capital, but that was usually merely an overgrown village, to whose normal complement of one or more temples or mosques had been added an appropriate palace or *istana*. Moreover the frequency with which capitals have been shifted at the slightest provocation testifies to the lack of any highly developed indigenous urban tradition comparable with those of India, China or Japan.

The great urban centres to-day, of which the eight largest are all coastally situated, are essentially the creation of the immigrants, who normally comprise the majority of their inhabitants. Altogether only 5% of the total population of Southeast Asia ranks as urban (defined as living in centres containing over 10,000 people)—a percentage which does not vary by more than a unit in any of the countries except Malaya. But while the proportion of indigenes inhabiting towns falls everywhere below this level, at least 25% of the foreign Asiatics in all the territories live therein, and the European percentage is still greater. The most highly urbanized community of all is the Eurasian which, although not numerically conspicuous except in the Philippines and Indonesia, is consistently wedded to the clerical and associated occupations.

In spite of their ubiquity, the oriental and occidental alien communities do not constitute a unifying element in Southeast Asia for, in addition to their own heterogeneity, the preoccupation of all but the French with economic considerations has consistently retarded political integration.

Among the foreign Asians little sense of loyalty to their land of domicile developed, since settlement during the past century has been, for the most part, transitory and temporary. Thus, although 5 million Chinese are believed to have entered Malaya in the 19th century, and another 12 million have followed since, the total Chinese population there in 1947 was only 2,615,000, while in Burma the arrival of 5,295,498 Indians between 1911 and 1927 was largely offset by the departure of 4,572,486 during the same period; much of this Indian migration was seasonal.

Even in the case of the minority which has elected to remain permanently in the region, assimilation has been gravely hampered by linguistic and religious barriers. While the immigrant Chinese has been singularly free from prejudice in these matters, and is often quite content to marry a local woman, Muslim practice for its part is ranged against such laxity. In Indo-China, Siam, Burma, and even the Philippines, however, considerable intermixture of this kind has taken place, and the offspring in general seem to be an able and respected stock. The Indians, by contrast, have rarely married outside their own community.

But all generalizations concerning either Indians or Chinese are riddled with exceptions. Major cleavages based on clan and dialect[1] among the latter tend to widen overseas with the greater range of economic opportunity, and although the barriers of caste among the former may be weakened with emigration, the linguistic divisions remain unaltered thereby. Thus in Malaya the Tamil coolie is ignored by his more prosperous fellow nationals, while the commercially progressive but politically conservative members of the Chinese Chambers of Commerce are utterly estranged from the mute masses of underpaid labour who are readily susceptible to communist propaganda.

Between these extremes is the most typical element of all, the small traders, money-lenders, and artisans, who come into closest and least harmonious contact with the indigenous population. Like the Jews in many parts of eastern Europe, these Indians and Chinese constitute an alien middle class which, lacking proper local roots, makes no contribution towards social integration. Economically also, the consequences have been unfortunate, for much of the considerable capital they amassed was lost to the area in the form of remittances to relatives at home, or savings ultimately taken out of the country, instead of being invested in productive enterprises locally.[2]

Moreover the recent growth of nationalist feeling in both China and India has spread to the oversea communities, where its effect has been particularly critical on the middle class elements, thereby aggravating an already serious problem.

CONTRASTING AIMS AND METHODS OF THE WESTERN COLONIAL POWERS

INTERNAL ECONOMIC STRUCTURE

While the stratifications within the alien oriental communities throughout Southeast Asia cut across and largely ignored political frontiers, the outstanding lines of cleavage between the several European groups tended to coincide with, and therefore to reinforce, the latter. Each of the

---

[1] "These linguistic and traditional differences of migrant Chinese have produced in Malaya a variety greater than that of the European nationalities which moved into the U.S.A."— Dobby, *op. cit.*, p. 107.

[2] In 1941 alone the Malayan Chinese remitted over £12,833,000 to China. (V. Purcell: *The Chinese in Malaya*, R.I.I.A., Oxford, 1948). But H. G. Callis (*Foreign Capital in Southeast Asia*, I.P.R., New York, 1942, p. 57) estimates that in 1937 the total Chinese business investments in Malaya amounted to some £40,000,000.

variegated and arbitrarily defined slabs of territory occupied by western powers was economically exploited in accordance with the differing ideologies and requirements of the powers concerned, and until 1930, in almost complete disregard of developments in adjacent areas.

Burma, valued originally as a market for cottons, provides a classic example of *laisser-faire* applied to the colonial field, the indigenous population being encouraged to produce whatever paid best—in this case rice—in order to spend the proceeds on British manufactures, while direct rule was introduced owing to the continued interference of native monarchs with European trade. The political connection with India and, indirectly, with Ceylon underlined the geographical arguments favouring these as markets, so that the bulk of Burmese rice and oil exports gravitated in that direction, and continued to do so even after the formal separation of Burma from India.

In Malaya, however, the free-trade sentiments of the mercantile community in the coastal settlements differed radically from the protectionist policies obtaining in the interior producing regions. But in neither area did the British attempt to exclude foreign capital, even the Japanese being permitted to invest at will in iron mines near the east coast and in Johore, and latterly in bauxite workings also in Johore.[1]

Dutch colonial practice evolved along different lines. The system of *laisser-faire* and direct rule, introduced by Raffles to Java between 1811 and 1815, continued thereafter to play into British hands, for the Dutch had few manufactures to sell. The Nederlandsche Handels Maatschappij (NHM) and the Java Bank, founded in 1825 and 1828 respectively to consolidate Dutch interests and to 'colonize Java with capital', paved the way for a return to compulsory production, under the Culture System of 1830.[2] From the profits so obtained was financed the creation of manufacturing industries and a modern merchant marine in Holland, and in 1870 the resultant new industrial and commercial class insisted on the introduction of a more liberal economic régime in the Indies.

Since by that time the possibilities of further expansion in Java were limited (the population having risen from under 5 to about 10 millions between 1815 and 1855) the effects of the new régime are most apparent in the Outer Territories, where the proportion of foreign capital—especially American and British—is much higher and the native output of cash crops, mainly tree products like rubber, coco-nuts, kapok and palm oil, exceeds the yield from plantations. Moreover the territories

[1] In fact, however, the Japanese had little capital available, and probably not more than £500,000 was invested by them in Malaya, and a similar amount in the N.E.I.
[2] Under the Culture System the native population, instead of paying taxes, had to devote part of their land to the cultivation of export crops for the government.

opened up since 1870 had before 1942 begun to overtake the original centres in economic importance, as was the case in Malaya, though in the Indies no comparable rivalry existed between production and commerce.

In contrast to the vigorous and scientifically advanced activities of the Dutch, American economic achievements in the Philippines appeared singularly ineffectual and, but for the protection of high United States tariff walls, the inefficiently produced low value export crops—copra, sugar and abacá—could never compete with those from other countries. In effect, the more handy Caribbean and South American tropics have diverted American attention from the Philippines, whose continued attraction lay primarily in their strategic position. The long-term effects of the political changes, first to Commonwealth status in 1935 and later to complete independence in 1946, can hardly be assessed as yet, though Pelzer stresses the keen sense of enthusiasm and national adventure prevailing in the Filipino colonization enterprises immediately before the Second World War (see p. 210).

French policy in Indo-China is the most difficult of all to analyze. Undoubtedly psychological overcompensation and the search for manpower obscured and perhaps overrode purely economic motives, and despite Ferry's contention that French industry needed colonial markets, economic assimilation proved a dismal failure. Particularly does this apply to Indo-China, where the ruin of many handicraft industries, which once ranked on a par with those of China, brought disproportionately little benefit to French manufacturers, and the diversion of more than half the rice and even some of the coal exports to France in defiance of geographical realities still further distorted the economy.

Siam alone remained politically independent, but its economy was unmistakably colonial. Although its rulers strove to avoid excessive reliance on any one western power for capital or advisory personnel, British interests were predominant until the 1930's.

Thus within the framework of the several political units, western commercial activities, bearing in each case the stamp of the power involved, and together fostering cut-throat competition between adjacent territories, were projecting European rivalries into Southeast Asia, and thereby accelerating the processes of disintegration. At the time of the world economic crisis of the 1930's, the law of comparative costs still operated largely unchecked, little attempt had been made to create balanced economies, and everywhere the concentration of eggs into an insufficiency of baskets aggravated the effects of the catastrophic fall in market prices of the main export commodities.

On the one hand the economic crisis induced a certain grudging co-operation among the major producers, notably of rubber and tin, taking the form of international agreements to restrict output.[1] Subsequently this process has been continued in ever-widening mergers and cartelization, precise details of which are hard to obtain, though their results are readily apparent.

In respect of consumption, the great Japanese trade offensive, following the depreciation of the yen in 1932, produced further complications, and although the cheap manufactures which thereafter flooded the markets of Southeast Asia may well have prevented serious disturbances in those days of unemployment and financial stringency, even the British and Dutch were driven to introduce protective tariffs favouring their own goods. Meanwhile long overdue attempts were made at diversifying agriculture in order to ensure at least an adequate subsistence diet and if possible also, a wider range of cash crops, though even in 1941 Malaya still supplied only one-third of its rice requirements.

Furthermore the Dutch, French, and Filipinos at last awoke to the need for more drastic measures to cope with overpopulation in Java, Tonkin and various parts of the Philippines. While the French scarcely got beyond the experimental stage, the efforts of the Filipinos in Mindanao after 1935 were both spectacular and encouraging, though in respect of numbers involved, the Dutch projects took first place. By means of the new 'systeem van kernvorming' (i.e. the creation of kernels or nuclei of settlers) under which a few pioneer families were aided to open up areas with sufficient arable land later to support whole villages, the number of Javanese agricultural colonists in the Outer Territories rose from 68,000 at the end of 1936[2] to 206,020 at the end of 1940. Of these, all but some 2500 in Celebes and 3000 in Borneo had settled in Sumatra. In addition many distressed Eurasian families were assisted to take up farming in New Guinea. Ultimately the Dutch aimed at an annual emigration to the Outer Territories of 240,000 which, if it consisted primarily of newly

[1] In 1922, during the post-war depression in rubber prices, British rubber producers in Malaya and Ceylon introduced the 'Stevenson' restriction scheme which the Dutch refused to join, ostensibly because of the difficulties it would cause to the native producers of the Outer Territories. Later, as prices rose to a peak in 1925, the Dutch (and French in Indo-China) greatly expanded their acreage under rubber, and since it was clear that the Stevenson scheme played into their hands, it was called off in 1928. In the 1930's the British producers who, owing to their world-wide interests, held a decisive position, again took the initiative. Eventually, after attempting to profit from British restriction, the Dutch, and later the French and Siamese producers, realized that their own best interests would be served by co-operation rather than by competition, and in April 1934 a comprehensive agreement was reached. In tin similar developments took place; the British Tin Producers' Association, founded in 1921, succeeded ultimately in persuading the Dutch and French to join in its restriction scheme.

[2] This is additional to the 825,000 Java-born Indonesians resident in the Outer Territories according to the 1930 census. These were mostly wage-labourers, many of whom intended ultimately to return to Java.

married couples, would go far towards stabilizing the position in Java, where the annual population increment is about 600,000.

In varying degree all these schemes for internal colonization entailed serious political consequences. Previously there had been a tendency for the more progressive Javanese, Annamites and Filipinos to seek better opportunities in the pioneer areas of their respective states, where their relatively hard-headed attitude to life, derived from the keener struggle for existence in their home lands, enabled them to play a part analogous to that of the Chinese throughout Southeast Asia. The big reinforcements which these communities received after 1930 served to exacerbate local feelings against them, and still further to pluralize society.

The Dutch also took the lead in industrialization, establishing a number of factories producing cheap consumer goods in Java. Indeed, in the decade preceding the Pacific War, the Dutch were progressively welding Indonesia into a functional economic unit, with considerable inter-insular trade in foodstuffs and a concentration of manufacturing industries in Java, which was also becoming more and more the managerial nucleus for the whole system. Similar trends were discernible in the other colonial territories and also in Siam which, however, with no European power at the helm, drifted steadily into the Japanese orbit, the Japanese share of Siamese imports rising from 8·4% in 1931 to 19·4% in 1933.

Thus in Southeast Asia the dilemma which was puzzling the rest of the world appeared in an exaggerated form. While in the field of large scale production for external markets international co-operation of a sort was increasing, in other respects the progressive abandonment of *laisser-faire*, (initiated here by anti-Japanese tariffs, and continued by the beginning of economic planning) was accentuating the significance of political frontiers.

INTERNAL POLITICAL STRUCTURE

The artificiality of the boundaries established under the stress of the imperial forward movement is shown as much in the internal diversity of the areas they unite as in the homogeneity of so many of the frontier regions which they dissect.

In Malaya the division, based fundamentally on considerations of aspect and exposure, between the relatively well-populated strip west of the Main Range and the remote and sparsely settled Pahang basin was already apparent, and the whole of British Borneo may be regarded geographically as analogous to the latter. Burma, similarly, displayed a major contrast between the Dry Zone and the potentially more productive entrance area in the delta, although as these have ever been the two poles of the Burmese polity, and are in certain respects complementary, their union is not altogether artificial. Again, the familiar description of Indo-China as "two bags of rice hanging from the two ends of a yoke" epitomizes a topographical diversity which was reinforced by cultural cleavages separating the northern from the southern nucleus. Siam, it is true, presented a relatively homogeneous pattern, but only because its more varied extremities were progressively lopped off by the encroaching British and French.

In the archipelago unifying maritime influences tended to soften the contours of contrast, yet even so the Philippines are sundered by profound religious, cultural, and economic gulfs, and Indonesia, by virtue of its position and extent, and the extreme patchiness of Dutch occupation prior to 1870, contains a mass of geographical incompatibilities.

Beyond staking out their respective spheres the westerners contributed comparatively little of a constructive nature to the political development of Southeast Asia, limiting themselves for the most part to providing the bare minimum of government necessary to enable their economic activities to proceed without interruption. For this reason the intensity of their control, although bearing but slight relation to the nominal distinction between direct and indirect rule, whose significance became purely vestigial, corresponded closely to the relative economic importance of the areas concerned.

In this respect the degree of elaboration of the railway networks (*Fig.* 20, Table XV) provides a valuable clue, and at the same time shows the extent to which the traditional territorial pattern of the individual states has been replaced by western forms.

Essentially the problem consisted in preventing serious discord between the component elements of plural society. Apart from the upland peoples of Burma, the protected principalities of Laos, and the rather more backward Great East of Netherlands India, the overlapping distributions of these precluded any satisfactory treatment along regional lines.

Within the administrative area of Burma, however, the Federated Shan States were managed by their own chiefs (sawbwas) under the supervision of a British commissioner. He in addition advised the chiefs of the feudatory Karenni states (though the latter paid customary tribute to the Burmese government), and the more primitive hill tribes of the 'excluded areas' were also under British supervision. Otherwise the administration of Burma was centralized in Rangoon which, created originally as the provincial capital on account of its water nodality, subsequently became the focus of a railway network which supplemented rather than duplicated the river routes. In 1935 The Government of India Act ruled that the

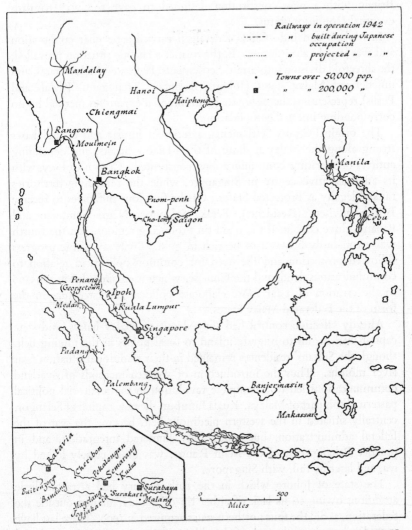

Fig. 20. SOUTHEAST ASIA: RAILWAYS AND PRINCIPAL TOWNS

thoroughly anomalous position of Burma as a province of India should come to an end, and in 1937 the country became a separate dependency of Britain with a new constitution designed to pave the way towards eventual Dominion status.

In Malaya and Indo-China federalism carried a peculiar connotation and was largely a misnomer. In the former a chaotic situation prevailed, the threefold division into Straits Settlements, Federated Malay States, and unfederated Malay states (Johore, Kelantan, Trengganu, Kedah and Perlis) representing successive stages in imperial expansion marked by no corresponding internal consolidation.

The original Straits Settlements, a series of insular and coastal bases strung along the Malayan shore of the Malacca Straits, and depending entirely on maritime communications, constituted a Crown Colony, with its administrative centre in Singapore, while the remaining territories ranked legally as Protected States. Of the first four sultanates to receive British advisers (Residents), Perak, Selangor, Negri Sembilan and Pahang, three contained the main tin producing regions, and the fourth was erroneously believed to be rich in gold. Swift economic progress followed protection and the need for common policies in relation to communications, land, and the Chinese, which it entailed, led in 1895–96 to the creation of a far more elaborate political superstructure in the form of the Federated Malay States.

Already effective control had slipped out of Malay hands, and state capitals had begun to migrate inland to focal points in the mining belt, though the Sultans' residences remained in their traditional situation near river mouths. Thus the introduction of western methods of overland communications led to a complete revolution in the territorial political pattern of this part of Malaya. Kuala Lumpur, the new capital of Selangor, centrally situated in the western piedmont belt, became the seat of the federal administration, but topography hindered integration, and in practice Pahang, east of the Main Range, was more closely linked by sea, and later by rail, with Singapore.

The state of Johore which in the 19th century had attracted little attention, owing to its lack of either tin or gold, remained outside the federation, as did the four northern states acquired in 1909. These last have accordingly preserved much of the old Malay territorial structure, based on river and coastal communications.

This anachronistic administrative fragmentation was extended further into British Borneo, where Labuan formed part of the Straits Settlements,[1]

[1] In addition the Straits Settlements also included Christmas Island and the Cocos-Keeling islands.

and Brunei constituted an unfederated state, Sarawak meanwhile remaining under the personal rule of the Brookes, and British North Borneo under the Chartered Company of that name. Both in Malaya and Borneo vested interests and local prejudices repeatedly impeded political unification. None the less geographical factors asserted themselves in the high degree of administrative centralization in Singapore which, as the obvious focus of land and sea communications, and, despite all protestations to the contrary, was the effective capital of British Malaysia. The Governor of the Straits Settlements, who was also High Commissioner for the Malay States, resided there, as did official foreign representatives, and although several government departments, whose purview extended to the whole peninsula and even in some cases to parts of Borneo, were situated in Kuala Lumpur, the major decisions emanated from Singapore.

In the contrast between the colonial status of its earliest settlement (Cochin-China)[1] and the protected nature of the rest, French Indo-China displayed a superficial similarity to Malaya. Moreover the French, likewise conscious of the need for unification had, in 1887, created a federation, the Union of Indo-China. But, unlike the Federated Malay States, this comprised both the colony and all the protectorates hitherto established; and Laos, and the concession of Kwangchowwan in south China, were incorporated after their acquisition in 1893 and 1899 respectively. (See below, p. 281).

Again, however, appearances counted for little. While the ruling houses of Cambodia, Annam and the petty Laos states were preserved, Tonkin, which theoretically enjoyed the same protected status, was subjected to a system of virtually direct rule scarcely distinguishable from that in Cochin-China. Indeed, after the turn of the century, when the capital was moved from Saigon to Hanoi, in the more densely populated north, and nearer the projected Yunnan railway, Tonkin became the main base of French power in Indo-China. However "the Governor General's annual change of residence from Hanoi to Saigon shows that this latter has not been willing to renounce entirely its claim to be the capital of Indo-China, and reflects the effects of the country's geographic structure and of the coastal location of the Annamite settlements."[2]

But this ingenious device could, of itself, do little to unite the diverse territories of north and south. Partly because elaborate networks of

[1] As a Colony, Cochin-China was represented in the French parliament by a deputy elected by the resident French citizens.

[2] Ch. Robequain: The Economic Development of French Indo-China, Oxford, 1944, p. 8. This dualism showed up after the German occupation of France when the Governor-General at Hanoi was openly pro-Vichy, while Saigon became a centre of de Gaullist sympathizers. Owing to the military situation since 1945, Saigon is at present the headquarters of French rule in Indo-China.

15

natural and artificial waterways existed in the main nodal areas, and partly as a result of the general hesitancy of French economic policy, Indo-China lagged behind the other main dependencies in Southeast Asia in respect of modern communications, and not until 1936 was the railway link completed between Hanoi and Saigon.

Cultural and religious assimilation of an ever growing proportion of the Asiatic population was the distinctive French contribution to the solution of the plural problem, but elsewhere the most characteristic approach was along communal lines.

In Malaya special government departments or other official bodies— the Chinese Secretariat and the Indian Immigration Committee— watched over the interests of these two major immigrant groups, both of which had communal representation on the councils of the Straits Settlements and the Federated Malay States, a privilege which was also extended in the largely urban Straits Settlements to the much smaller Eurasian community.

More urgent was the problem of protecting the Malays from being dispossessed of their land by immigrant moneylenders. Early experience of the Chettiars who flocked to the Straits Settlements before their separation from India in 1867, and rapidly acquired control over the best lands, led to the creation in the Federated Malay States of Malay Reservations, which include most of the land potentially suitable for rice cultivation.

In Netherlands India the process was carried further, and the Agrarian Law of 1870 forbade the permanent alienation of land to non-natives. Long leases up to 75 years, as well as short term leasing of village lands for plantation crops were thereafter regulated by legislation.

The Dutch likewise developed the most rigid and complex stratification of citizenship, designed allegedly to preserve the cultural integrity of the different groups. In addition to Dutch,[1] foreign Europeans, foreign Orientals, and natives, the Chinese acquired a special status of their own, and the Japanese and Siamese ranked legally as Europeans. As far as possible, the affairs of each ethnic community were managed by its own members, official dealings being through their own recognized heads, according to the ingrained Indies policy of 'like over like', while the Volksraad (Advisory Council), established in 1918, included 30 Indonesian, 25 Dutch, 4 Chinese and one Arab in its membership.

The confused territorial-political structure of the Indies was less significant. The division into directly and indirectly governed territories[2] can

[1] Netherlanders were defined as persons born in Dutch territory of Dutch parents. They included Eurasians, who were not classed as a separate community.

[2] About 7% of Java (Jogjakarta and Surakarta), and slightly over half of the Outer Territories were left under traditional rulers. All told there were 282 native states.

be explained historically, but these unimportant distinctions were largely obliterated by the ethnographically, historically and geographically artificial administrative units introduced after 1925.[1] (See *Fig.* 17). Although Batavia was officially the capital, government departments were shared between it, Bandung and Buitenzorg, and the whole island of Java, which since the 19th century has been administered with an elaboration unknown elsewhere in Southeast Asia, was, in a sense, metropolitan. This is readily apparent in the elaboration of its rail net, but elsewhere in the Indies, apart from a few disjointed feeder lines in Sumatra, railways are completely absent, and the outer territories are almost as much of a sea state as they were in the days of Sri Vijaya and Majapahit. Inter-island traffic was virtually a monopoly of the KPM. (Koninklijke Paketvaart Maatschappij), and was one of the greatest sources of revenue from the Indies.

Finally the national governments of Siam and the Philippines preferred in recent years to tackle the plural problem by the direct method of enforced assimilation.[2] The territorial structure of these two states has undergone relatively slight modification in modern times. Although Siam possesses a railway system comparable in extent with that of Burma, and short lines also exist in the Philippines, both areas rely very largely on their traditional methods of communications by river and sea respectively, and, despite important recent advances, still remain seriously deficient in motor roads. Their simple administrative patterns, centralized in Bangkok and Manila, the one large city (and principal port) of each, require no further comment.

EXTERNAL RELATIONS

THE IMPERIAL ASPECT

In respect of external relationships, the hitherto dependent territories of Southeast Asia (excluding Portuguese Timor, the population of which is only some 500,000) must be considered from both their respective imperial, and the local or regional points of view, a dualism which constitutes yet another facet of the problem of diversity versus unity. While the relative position of each area in the particular imperial structure con-

[1] Provinces: West, Central, and East Java. Governments: Surakarta, Jogjakarta, Sumatra, Borneo, Great East. The last included New Guinea, but under the new (1949) constitution New Guinea ranks separately (see *Fig.* 17). The term Outer Territories had no political significance as such.

[2] In Siam the teaching of the Malay language was suppressed, and in the Philippines Tagalog, the native tongue of under 25% of the population, has since 1938 become the official language. For details of anti-Chinese measures in both these countries, see Unger, *op. cit.*

cerned varies considerably, the exceptional wealth of the Asiatic tropics is such that all were of cardinal economic importance.

Most strikingly does this apply to the Dutch possessions. Although many of the once widely dispersed dependencies of Holland have long since passed into other hands, that country still retains the most valuable holdings in both the West and the East Indies, Curaçao in the former, thanks to its refining of Venezuelan oil, having an importance out of all proportion to its size. Nevertheless it took second place to the Netherlands East Indies, which in 1938 accounted for 65% of the exports of the whole Netherlands overseas empire, and contained over 99% of its population.

Indo-China occupied a less spectacular place among the more extensive and varied territories of the French colonial empire, but even so ranks second only to Algeria in the value of its exports, which in 1938 comprised 20% of the total from all the French dependencies, or approximately half that of Algerian exports. In population, however, it forms much the largest single unit, slightly exceeding the combined total of Algeria, Tunisia and Morocco, and amounting to more than half that of metropolitan France itself.

In 1939 British Malayan exports (approximately 2/3 in value those of India), aggregated 28·5% of the total from all the British possessions (excluding India and the Dominions) and were almost three times as large as those from any of the other colonies, Burma in fact coming second with 11·3%. Admittedly the greater part of Malaya's trade was of an entrepôt nature, but none the less there can be little doubt that, area for area, Malaya represented by far the most valuable portion of the British colonial empire.[1] British Borneo, by contrast, was of comparatively little economic significance.

As might reasonably be expected, the capital investments of the western powers in Southeast Asia were concentrated primarily in the territories under their respective administration, but both the British and the Americans also had important interests elsewhere as can be inferred from Table XVI. Perhaps the most outstanding feature illustrated by these figures, however, is the fact that Holland, although much the smallest of all the states concerned, nevertheless has the largest stake of any western power in Southeast Asia, even exceeding that of Great Britain.

Apart from the purely economic aspects already considered, the imperial relationships of the colonial lands of Southeast Asia were surpris-

---

[1] Malaya and Burma contained respectively 7.3% and 20% of the total population of the British colonial empire, or 1% and 3% of that of the combined British Territories of all statuses.

ingly slight. In the early oceanic age, it is true, the Portuguese, and later the Dutch, possessions had formed part of a strategically defensible line of bases extending from Europe to the Orient, and the original French settlements in Indo-China were made at a time when, from Egypt, Réunion, and the remnants of their former eastern possessions in India, and the southwest Pacific, the French hoped to play an influential and perhaps pre-eminent part in the affairs of the Indian Ocean. But already before the end of the 19th century the French possessions in Southeast Asia, like those of the Dutch and the Portuguese, had become for all practical purposes isolated outposts of the imperial domains, and their security depended inevitably on that of Burma, Malaya, and the Philippines.

These last, theoretically at least, formed integral parts respectively of the intricate defensive structures securing both the Indian and Pacific Ocean portions of the British empire, and the elaborate series of forward bases established by the United States in the latter half of the 19th century to protect its Pacific coasts and interests.[1]

REGIONAL RELATIONS

Viewed in their local context as component parts of Southeast Asia, the relative significance of these various territories assumes different proportions. Both in area and population, as indeed in their topographical layout, Burma and Siam are markedly similar, and although Indo-China is appreciably larger in both respects, all three could probably play approximately equal parts in any comprehensive regional organization that might be established. In contrast to these, however, Malaya is much more intensively developed, but has only a third of the population and a quarter the area of Siam, the smallest of its three northern neighbours, and even if British Borneo be counted in, the population discrepancy is not materially reduced.

The Netherlands Indies, on the other hand, very nearly equal the whole of peninsular Southeast Asia alike in population and area and, were the culturally, linguistically, and religiously related territories of Malaya and Borneo to be added, the Malaysian lands, far less sharply fragmented politically, economically, or ethnically than the principal mainland

[1] An interesting aspect of the inter-oceanic position of Southeast Asia became apparent with the opening of the Panama canal in 1914. While all sea traffic between London and the Far East normally uses the Suez canal, that between New York and the Orient goes partly via Suez and partly via Panama, the actual divide between the two zones in Southeast Asia running north from the Makassar Strait to Hong Kong. During the Second World War, however, from the closure of the Mediterranean until the Japanese occupation of Southeast Asia all trade between the latter and the U.S.A. used the Panama route.

states, might well exert a predominant influence in regional affairs. While the Philippines are also regarded by many Indonesian nationalists as belonging to the same realm of Indonesia Raya—Greater Indonesia—religious differences would probably prevent any close association, and the Filipinos, numerically equivalent to the Burmese or Siamese, would occupy a marginal position politically, as their country does geographically, in any regional grouping.

But, as the foregoing paragraphs almost unwittingly demonstrate, all serious discussion of inter-regional relationships of necessity anticipates the developments following the Japanese occupation. In the years prior to 1942 there had developed, apart from the limited measure of co-operation inaugurated by the world economic crisis, only superficially important links between the several territories. Economically, like the republics of South America, they "faced the world, turning their backs to one another";[1] their indigenous subsistence economies were self-contained, and in respect of commercial products the political units were competitive rather than complementary. The simple radial or even more skeletal rail networks, draining each country's wealth out through one or two large ports and, excepting the link between Siam and Malaya,[2] completely unconnected with one another, epitomise this fragmentation.

For, despite the commercial convergence on Singapore which, by virtue of its situation, its free trade heritage, and continued geographical momentum, formed the outstanding entrepôt for a large part of Southeast Asia, economic integration remained extremely rudimentary. Singapore was simply a collecting, trans-shipping, marketing and, in respect of tin, a processing centre through which much of the region's produce passed on its way to the outside world; it was not the economic capital of a great interdependent economic unit. Moreover, with the continued development of new ports and installations elsewhere, the area served by Singapore steadily contracted even though the latter's total trade did not diminish.

Only in a few essential bulky commodities, notably rice, which moved from Siam and, on a smaller scale from Burma and Indo-China, to Malaya and the Outer Territories of the Netherlands Indies, a wide range of lesser foodstuffs, and such items as petroleum, coal and cement supplied respectively by the Indies[3] and Indo-China to the rest of Southeast Asia,

[1] J. O. M. Broek: "Unity and Diversity in Southeast Asia," *Geographical Review*, Vol. XXXIV, No. 2 April 1944, p. 188.
[2] Which in any case originated in a German project designed to oust British influence from southern Siam.
[3] i.e. both the N.E.I. and British Borneo, the latter (Sarawak and Brunei) supplying petroleum for Malaya.

was there any considerable interchange for consumption within the area. Otherwise trade was oriented far overseas. In the cases of Indo-China, the Philippines, and Burma, commercial ties closely paralleled the political, but since the United States provided the greatest market for Malaysian tin and rubber, triangular trade developed there, turning Malaya into 'Britain's dollar arsenal', and enabling the Indies tail to wag the Dutch dog with characteristic trans-Atlantic vigour.

By its very nature therefore, western influence, which was largely confined to commercial exploitation by a number of rival interests, national or otherwise, continued with the passage of time to wrench ever farther apart the disjointed and artificial units which it had established for its own purposes.

In political matters also the external relationships of Southeast Asia were the concern not of the indigenous populations but of the respective imperial powers, and, except in the case of Siam, and, to a growing extent, the Philippines and Burma, were conducted entirely through western intermediaries. Particularly in respect of immigration policies was this subordination of local to imperial interests apparent as can be seen by the drastic restrictions swiftly introduced in Burma after the granting of even partial autonomy in 1937. Only in the widespread Muslim practice of making pilgrimages to the holy places of Arabia was there any really extensive contact between the indigenous peoples of Southeast Asia and outside foreign powers, and this also was carefully regulated, particularly by the Dutch who derived considerable revenues from the transit traffic and maintained consular officials in Arabia to keep a check on any pan-Islamic activities which seemed subversive.[1]

STRATEGICAL CONSIDERATIONS: THE JAPANESE THREAT

During the years following the First World War, however, one issue clearly transcended all other external problems confronting the imperial powers in Southeast Asia. Long before it became glorified with the high-sounding title of the 'Greater East Asia Co-prosperity Sphere' the Japanese plan for both continental and southward expansion was clearly taking shape, and as the difficulties in the former direction increased, the appeal of the Far Eastern tropics, with their abundance of so many commodities in which Japan was conspicuously lacking, became ever stronger.

Faithful to the doctrines of Clausewitz, the Japanese drew no sharp distinction between economic, political, or military methods of penetra-

[1] Pan-Islam has been an active force in the N.E.I. at least since 1868, when Atjeh voluntarily placed itself under the protection of Turkey which, however, did not prevent the Dutch from successfully waging the Atjeh war, 1873–1903.

tion, and the inroads made by their cheap manufactures in these areas of low purchasing power, the psychological strength of their slogan 'Asia for the Asiatics', and their skilful appreciation of the strategical possibilities afforded by the island arcs and epi-continental seas of Eastern Asia represented contrasting, but also complementary means of attaining the ultimate goal.[1]

Despite considerable apprehension on the part of the western powers, which led first to the limitation of Japanese imports already noted, no restrictions were imposed on the entry of Japanese nationals into Southeast Asia until, in view of the greatly increased numbers after 1931, the Dutch East Indies government eventually introduced a quota system in 1936. The 1937–8 figures of Japanese citizens in the Nan Yo (Table XIII) indicate graphically both the aims and means of advance which were being followed. Although they enjoyed much greater freedom and scope in Siam, the Japanese were far more interested in the wealthier Indies, and the strategic keypoints in Malaya and the Philippines. Since the last named was the most immediate objective, on grounds of propinquity, it received the greatest attention which *inter alia* included the planting of a large colony, ostensibly for the purpose of growing abacá, in the Davao province of Mindanao.

Against this elaborately planned infiltration, the imperial powers in Southeast Asia were hopelessly divided, the uncooperative attitude characteristic of their economic and political relationships extending automatically into the sphere of strategy. Ultimately the imminence and enormity of the Japanese menace produced the ABCD front in 1941, as, a decade previously, economic crisis had likewise induced co-operation. But by then French Indo-China was already in Japanese hands, and the strategic unity of Southeast Asia in consequence fatally impaired.

Since the United States had agreed at the Washington Conference, in 1921, not to enlarge its quite inadequate bases in the Philippines and Guam, no major obstacle barred the island bridge route from Japan to the Nan Yo. By the terms of reference of that conference, however, areas west of long. 110° E. were not subject to the restrictions there imposed and so, when the British decided, in view of the increased size of capital ships, to create new naval dock- and repair- yards somewhere between Malta and Sydney, Singapore, at the vital oceanic crossroads of the Orient seemed the obvious location.

The construction of the Singapore Base once again underlined the

[1] Note also the great expansion of the Japanese carrying trade between 1931 and 1936, when new and faster ships, working at low Asiatic costs, captured much of the Pacific trade from British, American and other companies. During this period the proportion of Malayan rubber exports to the U.S.A. carried in Japanese bottoms rose from almost zero to c. 33%.

dual character of this situation. To the British in India it appeared as the eastern bulwark of the Indian Ocean against attack from the Pacific, representing a revival, in modernized form, of the strategic concepts of the East India Company. But from the Australian point of view its significance lay in the barrier it interposed athwart the peninsular and island bridge extending southeastwards almost to their shores.

Implicitly this strategy admitted the fundamental geographical unity of Southeast Asia, which, it was rightly assumed, would stand or fall together. Any power moving longitudinally through the area must have the strength to advance simultaneously along both the Indo-Pacific and the Philippine routes, lest it expose an extended flank to lateral attack. But, as it was also believed, this time erroneously, that Japan lacked the forces to challenge both Britain and the United States together, the Americans, as well as the Dutch and French, were content to see the defensive potential of the region centralized in Singapore.

Strategically as commercially, therefore, Singapore became regarded as the inevitable focus of Southeast Asia. Unfortunately the similarity extended further, for the defensive structures of the several dependencies were no more deeply rooted nor more closely integrated one with another than their commercial structures. Except in the Philippines, the more advanced Asiatic peoples as a whole received[1] no proper military training, and the scattered fortified points were meaningless and indefensible apart from imported troops and equipment which, in the event, were insufficiently forthcoming. In this respect, since Malaya, in addition to its lack of industrial plant, could supply only a third of its own food requirements, Singapore was the most vulnerable of all. Thus, on 15th February, 1942, was demonstrated afresh the weakness of nodality unsupported by territorial strength. Within a few months the whole of Southeast Asia was overrun, and only the Arakan wall between India and Burma, and the combined Allied fleets in the Pacific were strong enough to stem the Japanese advance.

THE JAPANESE INTERLUDE

From 1942 to 1945 all Southeast Asia, for the first time in its history, was subjected to the political control of one imperial power. For the

---

[1] The Dutch in the N.E.I. (like the British in India) relied mainly on a few distinctive peoples from remoter areas, notably the Christian Menadonese (from N. Celebes) and the Ambonese, to form the bulk of their native army. This fact is having repercussions in contemporary politics, for these two "sub-races" fear possible reprisals from other more revolutionarily-inclined Indonesians.

purpose of bringing into being with the utmost rapidity the 'new order' avowedly based on "the concentration of predominant industrial power in Japan and the building up of Greater East Asia as a closed supply area for Japanese industry", the Greater East Asia Ministry, with its one general and three regional bureaux (for Manchuria, China, and the Nan Yo respectively) was established in November 1942. Within the framework thus provided Southeast Asia, apart from the 'friendly occupied territories' of Siam and Indo-China, was divided into five administrative provinces: Burma, the Philippines, Malaya and Sumatra, Borneo, and the rest of the East Indies. Although all except Borneo, which was a naval command, were placed under the senior military officer who had conducted the particular invasion, the original selection of Singapore as the strategic headquarters of the whole region, (as well as the capital of the Malaya-Sumatra province), indicates that the Japanese fully realized the latter's ultimate dependence on sea power.

With the exception of all the principal oil wells and refineries, and most of the larger bridges in Malaya and Burma, Allied demolitions had not been spectacular, and the great resources of the region were readily available to the occupying power. During the first year therefore, elaborate plans for their exploitation, in accordance with the original blueprint of co-prosperity, were put into operation, the Bank for the Development of the Southern Areas, with a capital of 100 million yen, being set up for that purpose under the Bank of Japan.

According to the Five Year Plan of 1942, the Philippines were to switch over from sugar to cotton production, and it was hoped to have 9·1 million acres under the new crop by 1946. Meanwhile Java was to concentrate on sugar, Indo-China on jute, and Borneo on minerals (especially oil), and timber; all areas were also to be made self-sufficient in rice. Such a drastic reorganization in the economy of the region necessitated a considerable redistribution of labour, and it has recently been estimated that several hundreds of thousands of labourers were moved overseas from Java, the obvious source of supply, to Borneo, Sumatra, Malaya, Burma and elsewhere, often with great loss of life.[1]

But these grandiose schemes were short-lived, The Japanese merchant marine, which in 1939 had been estimated at 5,600,000 tons, but was already beginning to dwindle by 1943, proved completely incapable of integrating this vast insular and peninsular empire. As early as 1942 a leading Japanese shipping expert had stated that 17 million tons of shipping were needed in order satisfactorily to utilize the economic potential of the conquered lands, and despite the absolute priority given to the

[1] See: Virginia Thompson: *Labor Problems in South-east Asia*, I.P.R., New Haven, 1947.

building of modern ships in Japan, and the manufacture of smaller wooden vessels in Hong Kong, Borneo, Celebes, and even New Guinea, it became clear by mid-1943 that the whole transportation system was rapidly breaking down.

Thereafter economic decentralization became the order of the day. Some 10,000 cotton spindles lying idle in Japan were transferred to the Philippines, nearer to the raw material sources and separated by a relatively short sea journey from Japan. Blast furnaces were to be created in Malaya, southern Borneo, and Indo-China, localization depending on the presence there of either iron or coal deposits, and various other industries, especially of the lighter varieties, were also introduced throughout the Nan Yo. Considerable developments took place in synthetic commodities, Philippine sugar being used for the manufacture of alcohol and buthanol, while Malayan and Indo-Chinese rubber were converted into petrol substitutes and textile fibres respectively.

The contemporary map of Southeast Asia bears certain notable imprints of this period, for the Japanese, in an attempt to close the gaps between the discontinuous road and rail networks of the peninsula, and thus to consolidate by land areas which they could no longer hold by sea, undertook several ambitious projects. Prominent among these were the Siam/Burma railway, finished late in 1943, and the Korea/Singapore motor road, which remained uncompleted.[1] Equally symptomatic of the changed strategy during this latter phase of the occupation, by which time control over the archipelago had become extremely weak, was the transfer of the main Japanese headquarters from Singapore to Saigon.

THE CONTEMPORARY SITUATION

In spite of the unprecedented state of political chaos and isolation which thus developed throughout Southeast Asia in 1944—45, the Japanese occupation none the less constituted an important unifying influence, for everywhere it accelerated processes of social change, already widespread although hitherto only sporadically recognized, to such an extent as to constitute a major revolution. But the so-called national awakening of these lands is not a Japanese creation, nor is it strictly to be compared with European nationalism of the last century. In reality it is a complex reaction to the whole gamut of foreign influences under whose combined impact the indigenous culture has crumbled into ruin.

In the first place, therefore, it is politically anti-western and anti-

---

[1] The attempt to link the railways of east and west Sumatra had to be abandoned.

imperialist. In the case of Netherlands India and French Indo-China the collapse of the mother countries in 1940 immediately entailed a greater measure of *de facto* independence, and although a new master speedily replaced the old one in Indo-China, the Indies enjoyed a short period of virtual autonomy, and the demand for 'Dominion status' became vocal, though this was scarcely a nationalist demand, and came rather from the Indies-Dutch. But in all the dependencies the temporary eclipse of Allied power after 1942 demonstrated that the occidentals were neither invincible nor indispensable.

Only a little less intense is the feeling against alien Asians. Although nationalist leaders have been inspired very largely by the achievements of Congress and the Kuomintang, the rapacity of so many of the Indians and Chinese in their midst has engendered deep animosity among the masses. Hence in the lands where Indian immigration has been slight, e.g. Indonesia, relations with the new Dominions may be cordial though the Chinese are penalized, while in Burma anti-Indian legislation is enacted but cultural missions are exchanged with China. In Indo-China this generalization, like many another, breaks down, and the Viet Nam movement owes much to China, especially since 1945 when, with a greater sense of geographical than of political values, the Allied Higher Command selected the latter to supply the occupation forces, north of latitude 16°.

In so far as the indigenous peasant peoples are affected by nationalism, their imagination has been fired primarily by anti-foreignism of these two kinds, for the removal of wealth overseas, and the contrast in standards of living between alien and native are not easily concealed. But the more intellectual wings of the respective movements are equally scathing in their denunciation of internal 'feudal' survivals. In spite of the variety in western forms of state and provincial government which has prevailed, all the Europeans made extensive use of native rulers in local administration. The motives behind this practice were not as uniformly hypocritical as the nationalists are apt to assert, but there is no doubt that in the bolstering up of 'feudalism' as an accompaniment to the introduction of commercialism, the Europeans frequently obtained the best of both possible worlds, and the native peasantry too often got the worst.

In short, the highest common factor in the national movement may be summed up as the determination of the bottom layer in the pyramidical structure of the plural societies which exist there no longer to occupy that position. As regards the methods to be pursued in attaining this end, however, there is no agreement. The more fanatical leaders, obsessed with the rottenness of everything extraneous, desire a return to the traditional way of life, but in so doing completely overlook both the defencelessness of their territories, whose wealth is bound to invite interference from outside, and the pressing need for aid in rehabilitation. Although Burma, which, like Siam, does not suffer from internal population pressure, and before the recent war enjoyed a considerably higher standard of living than most dependent territories, is thus better placed potentially than Indonesia, Indo-China, and the Philippines, no part of Southeast Asia can hope to survive economically without some form of contact with the capital and markets which only the West can supply. The question is therefore not whether, but in what form, such relationship should take place.

To this neither East nor West replies with unanimity. While the Americans and British, having first returned militarily were prepared subsequently to complete their political withdrawal from the vital flanking territories of the Philippines and Burma, both of which have now attained full independence, the Dutch and French have striven to incorporate Indonesia and Indo-China into the elaborate schemes of commonwealth federation that each has devised.

In view of their economic dependence on their colonial possession, the desire of the Dutch to re-establish control is understandable. Indeed it has recently been estimated that the loss of Indonesia would reduce the standard of living in Holland by some 30% to 35%.[1] Not unnaturally the greatest stronghold of republican activity is Java, the actual seat of the republican government being at Jogjakarta, the capital of the native state of that name, and Sumatra, the second most advanced island economically, contains the main subsidiary centres of opposition to the Dutch. After 1945, therefore, the latter originally concentrated on holding the dispersed and politically less active islands to the east which, despite indications of incipient centrifugality, they succeeded, at the Malino conference in July 1946, in forming into the semi-autonomous state of East Indonesia. Borneo required more careful handling, but likewise showed itself to be relatively amenable to similar overtures.

Were Dutch influence to be restricted to these areas, however, this would, in effect, still imply the loss of over 90% of their erstwhile economic assets in Indonesia, and although the potential resources of these largely undeveloped lands are by no means negligible, they do not bear comparison with those of Java and Sumatra.[2] On the other hand, the Dutch realized that a high degree of local autonomy would be a *sine qua non* of any form of rule which they might introduce anywhere in Indonesia, and, that being so, it appeared unlikely that the 75-year leases

[1] See *The Economist*, July 26, 1947: "Indonesia—The Real Issues."
[2] See J. O. M. Broek: "The Economic Development of the Outer Provinces of the Netherlands Indies," *Geographical Review*, Vol. XXX, No. 2, April 1940.

Fig. 21 (INDONESIA)   KEY

NEGARAS

1. Republik Indonesia (Republic of Indonesia)
2. Negara Indonesia Timur (East Indonesia)
3. Negara Pasundan (Pasundan or West Java)
4. Negara Djawa Timur (East Java)
5. Negara Madura (Madura)
6. Negara Sumatera Timur (East Sumatra)
7. Negara Sumatera Selatan (South Sumatra)

Negaras may be identified on the map by reference to the number. They are enclosed by a solid line.

DAERAHS OF REPUBLIK INDONESIA

a. Djawa Tengah (Central Java)
b. Bangka (Banka)
c. Belitung (Billiton)
d. Riau (Riouw Archipelago)
e. Kalimantan Barat (Special territory of West Borneo)
f. Dajak Besar (Great Dyak)
g. Daerah Bandjar (Bandjar)
h. Kalimantan Tenggara (S.E. Borneo)
i. Kalimantan Timur (East Borneo)

Daerahs may be identified on the map by reference to the letter. They are enclosed by a broken line.

NOTES—Djawa Tengah, which has no autonomous organization, is centred around Semarang.

The future political status of New Guinea is to be finally decided by further negotiations within one year.

The capital of the United States of Indonesia remains, as under Dutch rule, Batavia, but the name of this town has been changed to JAKARTA.

Foreign territories are cross shaded.

Since the transfer of sovereignty in January 1950 it has become clear that the Indonesian leaders interpret the notion of federation in a fundamentally different light from that intended by the Dutch. The negara and daerah boundaries, therefore, cannot be regarded as permanent, and the whole politico-geographical structure of the archipelago still remains in a state of fluidity.

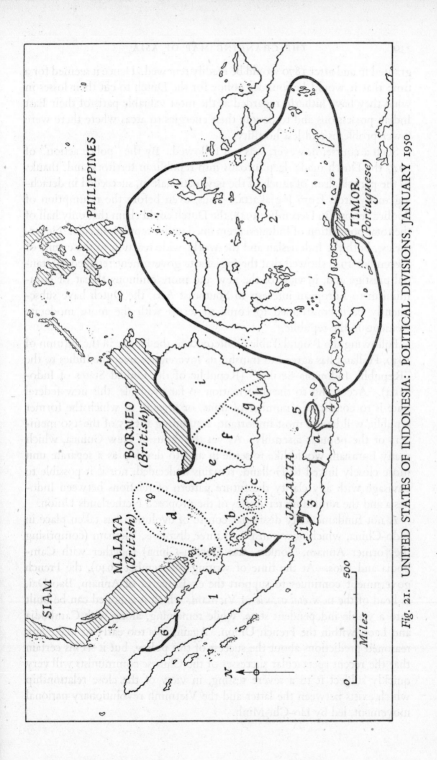

Fig. 21. UNITED STATES OF INDONESIA: POLITICAL DIVISIONS, JANUARY 1950

granted in and after 1870 would be readily renewed. Hence it seemed for a time that it would be sounder policy for the Dutch to cut their losses in what they have hitherto regarded as the most valuable parts of their East Indian possessions and to devote their energies to areas where there were fewer problems and less hostility.

Such a course, however, was not followed. By the "police action" of 1947 the Dutch made deep inroads into republican territory and, thanks to the parochialism of much of the new nationalism, succeeded in detaching many areas from Jogjakarta. Thus, even before the resumption of "police action" in December 1948, the Dutch could claim that only half of the total population of Indonesia remained under republican rule. Nevertheless, both the Indonesian and the world-wide reaction to the events of December 1948 showed that the Jogjakarta government retained substantial prestige and, in view of the new and more ominous threat of communism to European interests in Southeast Asia, the Dutch have subsequently been constrained to come to terms with the more moderate elements in the republic.

Following the Round Table Conference at the Hague in the autumn of 1949, Holland has agreed to transfer its sovereignty over the Indies to the "Republik Indonesia Serikat" (Republic of the United States of Indonesia). According to the information so far available, this new federal state is to consist of a number of units, or *negaras*, of which the former republic will be the most important, accounting for 75 of the 150 members of the popular assembly. As yet the status of New Guinea, which many Eurasians would like to settle in and to develop as a separate unit more closely linked to Holland, remains undecided, nor is it possible to envisage with any clarity the future pattern of relations between Indonesia and the remaining territories of the proposed Netherlands Union.

A not fundamentally dissimilar course of evolution has taken place in Indo-China, which now consists of three divisions, Vietnam (comprising the former Annam, Tonkin, and Cochin-China) together with Cambodia and Laos. At the time of writing (November 1949), the French government continues to support the ex-Emperor of Annam, Bao-Dai, as head of the new *état associé* of Vietnam, which it is hoped can be built into a viable independent state, while remaining, along with Cambodia and Laos, within the French Union. Again, it is too early to make any reasoned predictions about the success of this policy, but it seems certain that the recent spectacular successes of the Chinese communists will very quickly subject it to a severe testing, in view of the close relationship which exists between the latter and the Vietminh revolutionary national movement, led by Ho-Chi-Minh.

To date, however, a far from complete measure of success has attended the efforts of the national movements in Southeast Asia since 1945, and even where a former colonial power has been willing to meet their demands, as in Burma, the sequence of events hitherto suggests a tragic inability to maintain stable government and to cope with internal problems.

In these respects the contrast between Southeast Asia and the Indian sub-continent is significant, and is likely to become more acute now that developments in China may be about to expose Southeast Asia once again to powerful external pressure. Neither politically nor militarily can the weak and retarded states of Southeast Asia hope individually to resist either the remaining forces of Western colonialism or the interference of the new Communist China, should the latter prove to harbour aggressive designs on their territories.

In collaboration, however, they might succeed, as Japan did and as India now appears to be doing, in westernizing on their own terms by reversing the familiar process of divide and rule and, aided by the judicious importation of capital and technical advisers from the West, might effectively raise their standards of living far enough to counter the present threats to their continued independent existence. The most immediate step which the various national movements could make to the renewed challenges from without, therefore, would be jointly to establish some form of regional political grouping, as was frequently urged, especially in America, during the War years. In this connexion the "Manifesto of representatives of the countries of Southeast Asia" issued, significantly, at Bangkok on July 27th, 1947, indicated at least an awareness of the problem, though it contained little in the way of constructive statesmanship.

Economically speaking, there are strong arguments in favour of closer collaboration between the several territories of the region. While the continued production of agricultural staples for export would necessarily remain the means of financing the import of capital equipment, a great deal of uneconomic competition could be eliminated. This, in turn, would free more land for subsistence farming, though there is scope also for a considerable extension of inter-regional trade in rice, fish, and other foodstuffs. Meanwhile progress could be made towards industralization, by the creation of many more factories to process the export commodities and to supply more of the local demand for consumer goods.[1] Light industries of the latter type might have exceedingly good prospects in many areas, e.g., Java, where cheap electric power could be made avail-

[1] See O. H. K. Spate: "Beginnings of Industrialization in Burma," *Economic Geography*, Vol. XVII (1941), pp. 75–92.

able, if the potentially large and uniform market of Southeast Asia were not divided into a series of watertight compartments by restrictive tariff walls. Moreover, the present temporary setbacks to Japanese and Chinese manufacturing would give the infant industries of Southeast Asia valuable breathing space in which to establish themselves, though Indian competition is likely to prove intense in certain cases.

In other branches, however, the outlook is far less promising. Although small deposits of iron have been worked in both Malaya and the Philippines, the almost complete lack of coking coal in Southeast Asia severely militates against the establishment of heavy industry. Indeed the mineral resources of Southeast Asia constitute one of its gravest weaknesses, for the abundance of strategically valuable but not industrially basic minerals (tin, tungsten and oil) attracts the cupidity of outside powers, but does not provide the wherewithal to repel them. In this way the traditional defect of inadequate local resources to resist the disintegrating forces inherent in its situation is continued and even accentuated in the industrial age.

A further potential source of weakness lies in the relative sparsity of population, though this is less serious in respect of man-power shortage than in the attraction which open spaces may exert on the overpopulated and more powerful lands nearby. While the multiplicity, and frequent unreliability, of census authorities have so far obscured the dynamics of population change in Southeast Asia, it seems clear that the higher rate of increase, 2·5% per annum, compared with India (1·3%) and Japan (1·6%), is due essentially to immigration. (See Table XI). But the unparalleled growth of population in Java, from under 5 millions in 1815 to approximately 50 millions today, should be regarded as a warning of tendencies which may arise elsewhere. The Javanese birth rate, c.38/1000, is not noticeably higher than that which obtains in many other parts of Southeast Asia; the difference is essentially that Java alone has enjoyed for a much longer period than other parts of the region, approximately European conditions of sanitation and hygiene, whose introduction caused a drop in the death rate, which soon became stabilized around 20 to 23/1000.[1]

Herein is reflected the danger of rapid but only superficial westernization. Since technological advances, such as improved health services, are far easier to introduce than the psychological changes which accompanied them in the West, there is every possibility that the prolonged combination of an Asiatic birth rate and an almost European death rate, such as Java has experienced, may meanwhile counterbalance all the material

[1] But see also the comments of E. H. G. Dobby in: "Some Aspects of the Human Ecology of Southeast Asia", *Geographical Journal*, Vol. CVIII, Nos. 1–3, July–Sept. 1946, p. 44.

advantages which modernization could otherwise bring. Already several other areas, notably Siam, show a net rate of increase at least equal to that which has long prevailed in Java.

At present, it is true, only a few parts of Southeast Asia are densely populated, but the marked contrast between the extremely low standards of living in these areas, viz., Java and Tonkin (a standard which is little above that of peasant China), and the appreciably higher levels obtaining in the comparably rich deltas of Burma and Cochin-China, the lower Menam valley, or the volcanic plateaus of Sumatra, is obviously not accidental. In brief, it seems that, under present conditions, average densities of around 200 per square mile over wide areas of the better agricultural lands are not excessive, but any considerable advance beyond this figure has hitherto been accompanied by an undesirably low standard of living.

If this be so, Southeast Asia as a whole, though not necessarily each component individual territory thereof, is likely to need all its present 'empty' spaces to absorb internal increases within the next two or three generations. Collaboration between the various states concerned in the settling of these lands by Southeast Asian peasant farmers would seem to be the best way both of solving the acute problem of internal maldistribution and forestalling impending Indian, Chinese, or Japanese demands for *lebensraum* in those regions, which, if past experience is any guide, would, merely pave the way for renewed pluralization and subordination.

The urgent need for mutual collaboration, then, can hardly be gainsaid, but the chances of its being realized appear exceedingly slender. Twenty centuries of disintegration and fragmentation have produced there a degree of human diversity hardly paralleled in any other areas of comparable size or population. Linguistically, Southeast Asia contains many times the variety of Europe, and while Malay may become the *lingua franca* of Malaysia, there is no possible counterpart to this in the Indo-Pacific lands, and the next most widely known language is probably English! Again, while to the westerner the area appears unrelievedly backward, standards of living and of political advancement differ at least as much as those in our own continent, and the educated Thai or Filipino automatically assumes that any movement towards unity would mean merely a levelling down. But religion remains probably the greatest stumbling block of all, for neither the tolerance of Buddhism nor the relative laxity of Asiatic Catholicism can exert any moderating influence on the militance of resurgent Islam, emanating from Indonesia, and spurred on by the creation of Pakistan and the activities of the Arab League.

CONCLUSIONS

The paradox of unity and diversity, it has been seen, is present at all stages and in every aspect of the evolution of Southeast Asia. But at the termination of such an analysis as this, some attempt should be made to resolve that paradox. To the writer one conclusion, at least, is inescapable. In the area to-day such unity as remains no longer transcends diversity, but instead exists only in that very diversity itself. In other words, the forces of disruption have long since gained the upper hand, and the region is faced with a series of common problems, to the solution of which not only each territory, but also each of several elements within those territories, speaks with a different voice.

The apparent unity, therefore, of the contemporary national 'pan-Asian' movement is essentially negative. Since the European contribution to disintegration is the most recent and the most obvious, nationalism appears to be primarily anti-European. Yet each new state is cast in a European mould, and the old frontiers remain, despite the violence they do to the national cause. Unexpected results of this last are already becoming apparent. Everywhere the political lead has come from the most advanced indigenous element, but, owing to the artificiality of the westerners' boundaries, that is not in every case numerically supreme. Thus, in parts of Indonesia and Indo-China other peoples have come to resent the claims of the Javanese and Annamites respectively to represent the indigenous population, and the consequent 'splinter nationalities' which have recently become vocal have automatically played into the hands of the Dutch and French.

On the other hand, any attempts to reintroduce pre-European frontiers might have still more disastrous consequences, and the return to power of Pibul Songgkram, the founder of the irredentist Pan Thai movement, may increase such dangers. For, since the history of the Indo-Pacific peninsula from the 12th to the 19th century consists of an almost uninterrupted sequence of ding-dong struggles, with Burma, Siam, Cambodia and Annam as the principal protagonists, each can look back to periods when, in one direction or another, it expanded far beyond the limits of its own riverine nucleus into the territory of its neighbours. Moreover, in these matters myth tends to be more persuasive than reality, and the 'glorious past' of chauvinist politicians is usually a purely imaginary epoch into which have been telescoped all the nation's most spectacular achievements.

If rival claims of this nature develop, and are persisted in, the removal of external control will merely presage a return to the age-old conflicts, bitter memories of which are enshrined in the folk-lore of all the peoples concerned. Basically the cause of this instability is the demographic immaturity of the area in which, since geographical position has made it a zone of passage, no lasting adjustment has yet been reached between land and state. To the political geographer the parallel with the Balkans is depressingly obvious.[1] And both the historian who remembers that the Second Balkan War followed swiftly on the heels of the First, and the psychologist who recognizes the violence with which temporarily transferred hatreds may return to their original objects, will surely join the geographer in suggesting that the present phase of comparative friendliness among the peoples of Southeast Asia may be merely the prelude to a renewal of strife, should the Europeans finally withdraw from the area.

But it is not only in the peninsula that irredentism is rife; in the archipelago likewise the former conquests of Sri Vijaya and Majapahit have been recalled by the Republicans in support of their claims to Indonesia Raya. While it would be foolish to suggest that there is any foreseeable prospect of a return to the struggle between the islands and the mainland, which reached its culmination in the rivalry between Majapahit and Siam, it is none the less true that the same fundamental geographical realities are influencing the political evolution of Southeast Asia to-day. Nor is it beyond the bounds of possibility that the antithesis between land and sea power might speedily reappear in Southeast Asia if at some future date Chinese Communist forces infiltrated overland into the more vulnerable peninsular states, while the western maritime forces managed to retain control of the island fringe from Indonesia, via the Philippines, to Formosa and Japan.

As has so often been the case before, Malaya provides the meeting place of the contending and conflicting forces, both actual and potential. And once again, this time perhaps more decisively than in any previous context, its complete inadequacy to face the challenge is the crucial element in the situation. For, as the supreme focus of convergence in Southeast Asia, Malaya, with an urban population percentage five times greater than that of any of the other territories (Table XIV), and an alien population far exceeding the indigenous, is politically a median mass where opposing pressures cancel each other out and true nationalism is only in its infancy. Thus while the Indians look to the new Dominion, and the Chinese talk of Malaya as 'China's 19th province', Malay aspirations have until recently been largely confined to nebulous plans for incorporation into Indonesia Raya.

[1] Cf. M. I. Newbigin: *Geographical Aspects of Balkan Problems*, London, 1915.

Such conditions facilitate, and indeed make inevitable, the continued survival of external control in one form or another. Subsequent to their return in 1945, the British, besides striving to promote a greater degree of national cohesion by means of common citizenship, have made constructive attempts at rationalizing the chaotic political structure of Malaya. But while the new federal constitution introduced in February 1948 has at last dispensed with the tripartite political division of the peninsula,[1] Singapore, whose nodality has not diminished with the development of air communications,[2] still remains outside.

Moreover the events of 1948–49 indicate that the absence of a strong all-embracing national movement in Malaya does not guarantee internal political stability, but merely provides enhanced scope for the play of disruptive forces coming from without. Undoubtedly the course of events in Southeast Asia is being increasingly influenced by developments in the neighbouring parts of the continent, and it is there, notably in China and India, rather than in the colonial or foreign offices of the western powers that its destinies will be shaped in the not distant future.

Geographically, it is true, Singapore is still the key to Southeast Asia, and as long as that key remains in European hands, so long will the unity and the effective independence of the whole region be impaired, and its further economic evolution subjected to western pressure. But Singapore is now, more than ever before, an outpost of a kind and in a place concerning whose weakness the testimony of both history and geography is eloquent.

---

[1] Changes have also taken place in British Borneo, where the anachronisms of personal and Chartered Company rule in Sarawak and British North Borneo respectively have been removed, and the Settlement of Labuan has been incorporated in the new Colony of North Borneo.

[2] Singapore forms the meeting place for the Commonwealth air route via Karachi to Sydney, and the extension of the American trans-Pacific 'island-hopping' route passing through Hawaii and Manila. See E. G. R. Taylor Geography of an Air Age, London, 1945, and also the map p. 122 in Weigert and Stefansson: Compass of the World, London, 1945. The focality of Singapore has been further emphasized by the presence there of the British Commissioner General for Southeast Asia, whose office represents in a sense the civil continuation of the military S.E. Asia Command.

SELECT BOOK LIST

GENERAL

G. E. Harvey: *British Rule in Burma*, Faber, London, 1946.

F. B. Eldridge: *The Background of Eastern Sea Power*, Phoenix, London, 1948.

K. M. Panikkar: *The Future of South-East Asia*, George Allen and Unwin, London, 1943.

R. Emerson, L. A. Mills, and V. Thompson: *Government and Nationalism in Southeast Asia*, I.P.R., New York, 1942.

Various: *Economic Survey of the Pacific Area*, I. P.R., New York, 1942.

L. A. Mills: *British Rule in Eastern Asia*, Oxford, 1942.

Karl Pelzer: *Pioneer Settlement in the Asiatic Tropics*, A.G.S., New York, 1945.

V. Thompson: *Labor Problems in Southeast Asia*, I.P.R., New Haven, 1947.

Ch. Robequain: *Le Monde Malais:* Payot, Paris, 1946.

E. H. Jacoby: *Agrarian Unrest in Southeast Asia*, Columbia University Press, New York, 1949.

L. A. Mills and Associates: *The New World of Southeast Asia*, University of Minnesota Press, Minneapolis, 1949.

COUNTRIES

J. L. Christian: *Modern Burma*, I.P.R., University of California Press, 1942.

V. Thompson: *Thailand, the new Siam*, Macmillan, New York, 1941.

Sir J. Crosby: *Siam: the crossroads*, Hollis and Carter, London, 1945.

W. Credner: *Siam, das Land der Thai*, Engelhorns, Stuttgart, 1935.

Ch. Robequain: *The Economic Development of French Indo-China*, I.P.R., Oxford, 1944.

V. Thompson: *French Indo-China*, Macmillan, New York, 1937.

P. Gourou: *L'Indochine française*, Hanoi, 1929.

V. Purcell: *Malaya: Outline of a colony*, Nelson, London, 1946.

V. Purcell: *The Chinese in Malaya*, I.P.R. and R.I.I.A., Oxford, 1948.

B. H. M. Vlekke: *Nusantara: A History of the East Indian Archipelago*, Cambridge, Mass., 1943.

J. O. M. Broek: *The Economic Development of the Netherlands Indies*, I.P.R., 1942.

J. H. Boeke: *The Structure of Netherlands Indian Economy*, I.P.R., 1942.

J. S. Furnivall: *Netherlands India*, Cambridge, 1939.

J. S. Furnivall: *Colonial Policy and Practice*, Cambridge, 1948.

J. R. Hayden: *The Philippines*, Macmillan, New York, 1945.

SOUTHEAST ASIA

TABLE XI

AREA AND POPULATION

Country	Area (sq. mls.)	Population 1939 (thousands)	Density per sq. ml. 1926	Density per sq. ml. 1939	Increase % 1926–39
BURMA	261,610	16,600	50	63	26
SIAM	200,148	15,600	49	77	57·1
FRENCH INDO-CHINA ..	286,000	23,700	72	83	15·3
MALAYA	52,286	5,579	72	107	48·6
Straits Settlemts.	1,260	1,380		1,095	
Rest of Malaya	51,026	4,199		82	
NETHERLANDS EAST INDIES	735,268	69,435	70	94	34·3
Java and Madura	51,032	47,700	713	935	31·1
Outer Territories	684,236	21,735	22	32	45·5
BRITISH BORNEO*	81,761	951	11	12	9
PORTUGUESE TIMOR	7,330	480	56	66	17·8
PHILIPPINES ..	115,600	16,300	101	141	39·6
SOUTHEAST ASIA ..	1,740,003	148,645	64	85	32·8

* British North Borneo, Brunei, Sarawak, and Labuan.

TABLE XII

INDIGENOUS PEOPLES

(All figures in thousands)

A. BURMA—Language Groups by 1931 Census.

Burmese	9,863
Karen	1,341
Shan (Thai)	1,022
Kuki-Chin	344
Palaung-Wa	176
Kachin	154
Others	148

B. SIAM—Language Groups (estimated) 1937.

Thai	14,500	(includes various hill peoples)
Karen	60	
Malay	500–700	

C. FRENCH INDO-CHINA—Major Ethnic Groups 1936.

Province	Anna-mites	Cambo-dians	Chams & Malays	Thai	Hill Tribes	Sino-Anna-mites	Total incl. Aliens
Tonkin ..	7,759	—	—	673	214	11	8,700
Annam ..	4,934	—	23	17	665	—	5,656
C-China ..	3,979	326	8	—	52	62	4,616
Cambodia ..	191	2,597	73	20*	54	—	3,046
Laos	27	2	—	665	314	—	1,012
F.I.C.	16,890	2,925	104	1,375	1,299	73	23,030

* These are on the upland fringes of Cambodia; all lowland inhabitants of former Siamese-held territories in Cambodia counted as Cambodians.

D. BRITISH MALAYA—(i) Ethnic Groups 1931.

	Malaysians*	Aboriginals	Siamese*	Total incl. Aliens
Straits Settlements	285·3	0·1	?	1,114
Federated Malay States ..	593·7	27·8	?	1,713
Unfederated Malay States ..	1,055·9	3·9	20·9	1,426
British Malaya	1,934·9	31·8	23·6	4,253

* Not all Malays indigenous: some 9% of total are immigrants from Indonesia, who form over 30% in Johore. But nearly all Siamese in UMS born there.

TABLE XII—*cont.*

(ii) 1947 Census:

	Malays and other Malaysians	Total, including Aliens
Federation of Malaya	2,428 ..	4,908
Singapore	116 ..	941
British Malaya	2,544 ..	5,849

E. NETHERLANDS EAST INDIES

(i) Indigenous population, 1930 Census

Java and Madura..	40,891
Sumatra	7,745
Borneo	2,017
Great East:	8,485
Celebes 4,174	
Bali & Lombok .. 1,789	
Timor etc. 1,646	
Moluccas & N. Guinea 876	
Total NEI	59,138
Total NEI incl. Aliens ..	60,727

(ii) Main 'sub-races' 1945[*]

Proto-Malays	
(Batak, Dyak etc.)..	2,680
Deutero-Malays ..	56,700
of which:	
Javanese ..32,000	
Sundanese 10,000	
Madurese .. 6,000	
Balinese .. 1,200	
Others c.	10,620
Total c.	70,000

[*] Based on J. Kunst, The Peoples of the Indian Archipelago, Leiden, 1946.

F. THE PHILIPPINES

(i) Ethnic Groups 1939 (estimates)

Filipinos (excl. Eurasians)	15,000
Moros	409
Hill peoples	600
Negritos	29

(ii) Language Groups 1939

Bisayan	7,100
Tagalog[*]	4,069
Iloko	2,353
Bikol	1,289
Other Malaysian	1,195

[*] The official language: English is spoken by c. 4¼ million.

G. BRITISH BORNEO

	Coast Malays and Borneo tribes	Total incl. Aliens
British North Borneo[*] (1931)	217	270
Labuan (1939)	5·3	8·7
Sarawak[*] (1936)	350	450
Brunei (1931)	27·6	30

[*] 1947 estimates for the total populations of North Borneo and Sarawak are 331,361 and 546,361 respectively.

TABLE XIII

NON-INDIGENOUS POPULATIONS

In thousands; figure succeeding a stroke thus: 114/0.8 represents percentage of total population in given area.

Territory	Chinese (a)	(b)	Indians	Japanese	Europeans Americans &c.	Eurasians
BURMA .. 1931	114/0.8	194/1.3	1018/6.8	0.465	10	19
SIAM .. 1937	524/3.6	c.2000/13.8	?	0.522	1.8	?
F.I.C. .. 1936	c. 130/0.6	326/1.42	5.9	0.241	28	15
MALAYA*.. 1931	1200/23.5	1709/39.6	624/14.3	8	17.7	16
BR. BORNEO 1928–36	?	c.157/21	0.4	?†	0.5	?
NEI‡ .. 1930	c.500/0.8	1233/2	?	6.5	c.40	c.200
PHILIPPINES 1939	117/0.7	750/4.7	?	29	16	c.900

Chinese (a)—citizens of China; Chinese (b)—ethnic Chinese (includes (a))

* 1947 Census provisional figures show 2,615,000 Chinese of whom 730,000 are in Singapore, where they form 75.2% of the population; Indians in Malaya total 600,000.
† Included in Malaya.
‡ Java and Madura, Sumatra, and Borneo had respectively 582, 449, and 134 thousand Chinese, and 193, 27, and 6 thousand Europeans and Eurasians.

TABLE XIV

URBANIZATION

Area	Year	Towns over 200,000	No. of Towns over 50,000	Urban percentage in towns over 10,000
BURMA	1931	*Rangoon 400,415	3	5·3
SIAM	1937	Bangkok 886,000	2	c. 6
F.I.C.	1936	Cholon-Saigon 256,000	5	4·5
MALAYA ..	1931	*Singapore 445,719	4	29·5
N.E.I.:				
Java	1930	Batavia 533,015	12	8·0
		Surabaya 341,675		
		Semarang 217,796		
Outer Terr's.	1930		5	2·5
Total: N.E.I.			17	6·3
PHILIPPINES ..	1936	*Manila 355,485	2	c. 6

* Later figures: Rangoon 1941—500,800; Singapore 1947—679,659; Manila 1939—623,493.

TABLE XV

RAILWAY MILEAGE (1939)

Country	Railway Mileage	Area (thousand square miles)	Population (Millions)	Area (sq.m.) per mile of railway	Population per mile of railway
BURMA	2,060	261·6	16·6	127	8,058
SIAM	2,037	200·1	15·6	98	7,658
FRENCH INDO-CHINA	1,817	286	23·7	152	13,044
MALAYA	1,067	52·3	5·6	49	5,155
NETHERLANDS EAST INDIES	4,589	735·3	69·4	160	15,298
Java & Madura ..	3,362	51	47·7	15	11,214
Sumatra*	1,227	182	9 ·0	148	7,335
BRITISH BORNEO† ..	127	81·8	·95	643	7,803
PHILIPPINES	867	115·6	16·3	123	18,801

* Formerly there was a short length of railway in Celebes, but this was closed in 1930. No other lines exist outside Java and Sumatra.

† This line is in British North Borneo. No other parts of British Borneo have any railways.

TABLE XVI

VALUE, NATURE AND DIRECTION OF TRADE

Data for most recent year available in each case.

Country and Year		Value £ millions	Commodities, % by value	Direction, % by value
BURMA	I	18·91	Textiles 24·5; Clothing 10·6; Foodstuffs 24·3; Metal Mfrs. 9·6; Machinery 7·4; Vehicles 2·8; Chemicals 4·6; Tobacco 3·8	India 55·7; U.K. 17·3; Japan 8·1; U.S.A. 5·9; Malaya 2·6; Holland 1·4; Germany 1·2; Belgium 1·1
1939-40	E	41·16	Rice 43·9; Petroleum and derivatives 26·1; Timber 6·5; Lead 4·6; Tungsten 4·3; Tin 1·2; Cotton 1·0	India 59·0; U.K. 13·2; Ceylon 5·5; Malaya 5·5; Japan 4·0; Germany 1·3; U.S.A. ·7; Holland ·3; Belgium ·2
SIAM	I	12·96	Metal mfrs. 20·1; Textiles 17·8; Petroleum 9·1; Foodstuffs 8·2; Gunny bags 3·3; Chemicals 3·0	Malaya 25·5; Japan 14·8; U.K. 11·3; Hongkong 10·2; Germany 6·5; India 5·9; U.S.A. 4·7; N.E.I. 4·3; China 4·0
1938-9	E	18·73	Rice 42·7; Tin 15·1; Rubber 12·3; Teak 3·7; Salted fish 1·1	Malaya 56·5; U.S.A. 11·1; Hongkong 10·6; Germany 3·0; U.K. 1·4; Japan 1·2; India ·6; N.E.I. ·4; China ·1
FRENCH INDO-CHINA	I	11·68	Textiles 23·2; Metal mfrs. 14·4; Other mfrs. 10·5; Petroleum 5·4; Food 5·3; Iron and steel 4·8	France and French colonies 56·3; Hongkong 7·4; China 7·3; U.S.A. 5·0; N.E.I. 4·3; U.K. 3·2; Malaya 3·0; Japan 2·9; Siam 1·8
1938	E	17·16	Rice 35·0; Rubber 21·8; Maize 18·0; Coal 4·3; Fish 2·8; Tin 2·6; Cement ·9	France and French colonies 53·2; Malaya 9·7; Hongkong 9·6; U.S.A. 8·8; Japan 3·1; India 2·8; China 2·7; U.K. 2·1; N.E.I. 1·0

TABLE XVI—continued

Country and Year		Value £ millions	Commodities, % by value	Direction, % by value
BRITISH MALAYA	I	76·36	Rubber 18·0; Petroleum 14·3; Mfrs. 10·6; Tin Ore 9·0; Rice 8·3; Other foods 4·7; Tobacco 2·6; Copra 1·1	N.E.I. 30·9; Siam 16·8; U.K. 14·5; China 5·6; U.S.A. 2·9; India 2·9; Sarawak 2·8; Australia 2·8; F.I.C. 2·8; Japan 2·0
1939	E	90·00	Rubber 47·5; Tin 21·1; Petroleum 7·2; Copra 1·4; Rice 1·3; Other foods 2·3; Cotton mfrs. ·5; Iron ore 1·2	U.S.A. 42·9; U.K. 10·8; Japan 8·6; N.E.I. 5·5; India 3·5; Australia 2·8; Siam 1·9; Sarawak 1·5; Hongkong 1·0
NETHERLANDS EAST INDIES	I	58·92	Textiles 32·1; Metal mfrs. 28·3; Other mfrs. 6·2; Fish 2·4; Rice 2·3; Tobacco 1·9; Fertilizer 1·9; Wheat flour 1·5	Japan 25·4; Holland 19·1; U.S.A. 10·2; Germany 8·5; U.K. 8·3; Malaya 7·5; India 2·6; Australia 2·5; China 1·8
1937	E	114·12	Rubber 31·2; Petroleum 17·5; Tin 8·8; Copra 6·6; Tea 5·2; Tobacco 4·3; Coffee 2·7; Palm oil 2·7; Tapioca 1·9; Kapok 1·8	Holland 20·1; Malaya 18·8; U.S.A. 18·7; U.K. 5·3; Japan 4·4; Australia 3·1; Germany 3·0; China 1·4; India ·7
PHILIPPINES	I	27·0	Metal mfrs. 23·9; Textiles 18·5; Oils 8·0; Tobacco 5·7; Food 4·5; Paper 3·7; Chemicals 3·1	U.S.A. 68·0; Japan 6·2; Germany 3·5; U.K. 2·4; N.E.I. 2·4; China 2·2; Malaya 1·8; Australia 1·6
1939	E	26·67	Sugar 40·9; Coconut products 24·0; Abacá 9·8; Tobacco 6·0; Embroideries 4·4; Lumber 2·6	U.S.A. 76·0; Japan 6·4; U.K. 2·7; Germany ·8; China ·8; Malaya ·7; N.E.I. ·4; Australia ·3

TABLE XVII

PRODUCTION OR EXPORT OF CERTAIN COMMODITIES

P = Production.   E = Export.

All figures are % of World total.

Commodity	Burma	Siam	French Indo-China	British Malaya	British Borneo	Netherlands East Indies	Philip- pines
Tin 1939 (P)		9·6	·7	30		13·5	
Petroleum 1938 (P)	·35				·35	2·9	
Tungsten 1938 (P)	17	·6	1·5	3			
Bauxite 1938 (P)				1·5		7	
Iron 1938 (P)				1·3			·6
Rubber *1941 (E)		3	4	37	3	44	
Palm Oil 1938 (E)				11		44	
Copra 1939 (P)			·5	7	·5	30	37
Coffee 1939 (E)						5	
Cinchona 1936 (P)						90	
Rice 1938 (E)	46	28	17				

* 1941 was the first year in which the N.E.I. surpassed Malaya in rubber production.

CHAPTER IV

THE FAR EAST

By H. J. Wood

THE Far East was the last major portion of Asia to be drawn into the European (or rather Euro-American) orbit; although China and Japan were reached by the Portuguese by 1542, both countries pursued a policy of seclusion, or at least of very severe restriction of overseas contacts, which was not seriously challenged until the mid-19th century. The Japanese isolation could probably have been broken down earlier, but there was little incentive; in China there was much incentive, but from one side only, as the reply to George III's embassy showed, and the self-confidence of the Celestial Dynasty gave an impression of strength matching the great size and man-power of the Empire.

This impression was misleading: China under the later Manchus was as a giant drugged, nor has she yet recovered. The taking-up of other Asiatic options and recognition of the real weakness of China led to a virtual scramble for spheres of influence in the last decades of the 19th century; for some 20 years (c. 1890–1910) it seemed not impossible that, though the fiction of China's integrity might be preserved, in practice she would sink to colonial status; the question in debate was rather whose colony, and it may be that the number of claimants saved her. Meanwhile in Japan, with more slender but far more easily mobilized resources, a directly opposite evolution was taking place. The rise of this new power, located actually on the spot and across the approaches to central and northern China, was announced dramatically enough by her easy victory over that country in 1895, and complicated enormously the power-struggle in the Far East even before the more spectacular Russo-Japanese War of 1904–5. Clearly a completely European subjugation of China was no longer possible; and in 1898 American power had moved across the Pacific with the seizure of the Philippines from Spain. At times during the 30 years from the Chinese Revolution of 1911 to the outbreak of the Pacific War in 1941 it appeared that Japan, taking advantage of Western preoccupation in internecine wars, might complete, to her sole profit, the reduction of China to a *de facto* colony. In this long struggle—the only armed conflict between major Asian countries in modern times—the

Chinese territory of Manchuria and the small "Empire" of Korea were but pawns in the game.

The great gamble of the Pacific War failed; the Chinese national revival under the Kuomintang, which seemed full of promise in the stirring days of the great campaign into the north in 1927–28, has failed also under the weight of its own corruption at the top. China is now under Communist direction, and this in a sense represents an extension of the heartland into the monsoon littoral; over against it Japan, under American control, is now an outpost of trans-Pacific sea-power. Yet, although the old spheres of alien influence are now liquidated, and "Westernization" will follow Soviet rather than Euro-American norms, some relations of trade and finance are obviously desirable for the rehabilitation of China's war-ravaged economy, as well as in the interests of the trading powers of the West. Moreover Russian special interests in Manchuria may not, in the long run, prove altogether compatible with the interests of China as seen by her new rulers; and though Western cultural influences, as represented by the not inconsiderable Christian educational effort, may be at a discount, Soviet culture itself cannot expect to prevail unmodified by the elastic strength of Chinese traditional forces: cultures like territories have their "defence in depth".

Internationally the new régimes in China and Japan pose new and difficult problems. The building up of Japan as a base for the sea-powers is difficult to envisage (given the population pressure in that country) without industrialism; and that again (given the meagre resource-basis) without a sub-imperialism.[1] As for China's external relations, southwards there are no longer bases for British or French penetration in Burma and Indo-China, but weak states with large Chinese minorities and with social problems which may well provide favourable conditions for a penetration in the reverse direction. But here it is as well to remember that the prospect of Chinese intervention might cause a rallying of nationalist feeling in these countries where rich and poor alike feel the pressure or Chinese economic activity.[2]

---

[1] Cf. O. Lattimore, "The Inland Crossroads of China," in *Compass of the World*: "The idea that Japan could be 'revived' and with the distant support of British and American sea power made to function as the stabilizer of relations between China and Russia is fantastic. It could only be done if China were permanently held down to an approximately colonial level of industrial development. Even so, such a system would not ensure permanent peace." (p. 379).

[2] To quote Lattimore again (*loc. cit.*, p. 389): "On the southern frontier the prestige of China, as a symbol of freedom, stands higher in the eyes of the Burmese and Indo-Chinese, to whom the British and the French denied independence, than on the northern and western frontiers where the Chinese themselves encroach on the freedom and self-government of Mongols, Central Asians, and Tibetans. . . ." As far as Burma goes this statement is inaccurate: despite Sino-Burmese Cultural Committees and the like, the Chinese ranked only second to the Indians as objects of Burmese distrust—distrust easily accountable in terms of

The defeat of Japan and the Communist success in China represent to some extent a simplification of the purely political problems: the social and the geopolitical problems are complex and dynamic as ever.

CHINA AS A WHOLE

Not all the territory over which China claims sovereignty will be considered in this section. Outer Mongolia, until recently a dependency, is now recognized as an independent republic, and thus no longer forms part of Greater China. The dependencies of Chinese Turkestan (Sinkiang) and Tibet clearly lie within High Asia; this leaves for consideration the historic China of the eighteen provinces, and the former dependencies of Inner Tibet, Inner Mongolia, and Manchuria, more recently divided into provinces, and thus made part of an enlarged China Proper; Formosa must also be included.

CHINA OF THE EIGHTEEN PROVINCES

This is the 'China' of popular usage, the 'China Proper' of the nineteenth century. On the whole the frontiers are well marked. The Great Wall system in the north, designed for defence against invaders from the steppe and mainly dating from the 3rd century B.C., approximates to the northern boundaries of the provinces of Hopeh, Shansi, Shensi, and Kansu, although local deviations are important. It represents an attempt, only partially successful, to give a precise limit to an agricultural civilization in a zone of transition to pastoralism; in the east mountain terrain made defence easier, but in the west plateau steppes extending south of the Wall aided invaders.

The panhandle of Kansu, it should be noted, extends west of the Great Wall, reaching out to include an historic oasis route through desert country from the Wei ho valley towards Sinkiang. The southern boundary of Kansu, the western of Szechwan, the northern of Yunnan, all traverse the ramparts of the great plateau of High Asia, a mountain frontier zone without rival in the world in barrier function. The western limit of Yunnan is the boundary of Burma, the northern half following a high mountain divide, the southern less impenetrable, but difficult country with malarious valleys set deep between mountainous plateau sectors. The southern limits of China in Yunnan traverse country that

the "sub-imperialisms" they developed. A Communist China would have a different approach, but the situation is full of cross-currents and success in exorcising local patriotisms or chauvinisms cannot be taken for granted.

becomes easier towards the east; the southern boundary of Kwangsi follows mountain crests of moderate height. Whereas on the Tibetan borderland, and in the Yunnan-Kweichow plateau country, Chinese civilization is to-day far from completely dominant, the Indo-China boundary marked out by the French in the 19th century incorporated areas with marked Chinese cultural features. The eastern fringe of provinces, Hopeh, Shantung, Kiangsu, Chekiang, Fukien and Kwangtung, the latter province including the island of Hainan, all have coastlines that bring contact with the seas that occupy the continental shelf, and the ocean beyond. Chinese history in all but its latest phase concerns in the main continental relationships, but the invaders that have shaped so much development in modern China have come by sea. Only six of the eighteen provinces are not marginal, i.e., Honan, Hupeh, Anhwei, Kweichow, Hunan and Kiangsi.

China thus defined, predominantly rural, with cultivators reaching out towards all landward margins, presents within its borders great contrasts in relief, climate, soils and accessibility. The extent of this territory, a great compact block on the eastern margin of Asia, is impressive, quite apart from the different worlds that lie within it. Distances in China have varied meaning in terms of travelling time, not only because modes of transport vary but also because men and commodities are often in jeopardy even on frequented ways, but it is interesting to note that the space relations of Peiping (Peking), Nanking and Canton at least in terms of air travel are comparable with those of Stockholm, Prague and Rome, those of Nanking and Chungking with London and Prague. If China has a vulnerable northern frontier and a long exposed coastline she has also great space for defence in depth, with an area of nearly 1·5 million square miles, and some 1000–1500 miles in both east-west and north-south extent. We must distinguish the mountain areas of the east, the more impressive and vastly more extensive mountain and plateau zone of the west, the hill and mountain country that links most effectively in the south, and the major west-east flowing rivers. These in the main have built the lowlands that support the greater part of China's population.

The mountain areas of eastern China consist of two separate masses, one in Shantung peninsula extending west to the Tai shan and rising to between 1000 and 3000 feet, the other higher, more complex and extensive in Fukien and southern Chekiang rising on the high western edge in the Wuyi shan to 6000 feet. Both areas are fragments of a partly foundered continent.

The mountain zone of the west, through much of its extent, is bounded towards the east by a well marked edge. The Taihang shan, in places

6000 feet high, border the Shansi plateau and are traversed by the western border of Hopeh. The eastern edge of the lofty Tsinling, and Tapa shan, which rise to 8000 feet, is less well defined in western Hunan and Hupeh, but the higher plateaus of the south-west, sometimes called Yunkwei, are stepped and often present a steep edge in western Hunan and Kweichow. The Shansi plateau border marks the eastern limit of a great north-western zone of plateau, mountain ranges, and basins, with deposits of ever-fertile wind-deposited loess on lower ground, extending into Shensi and Kansu south to the Wei ho valley, which occupies a great structural trench at the northern foot of the Tsinling shan. The latter, with the Tapa shan, forms a central mountain belt in western China, a belt oriented west to east continuing the alignment of the Kun lun ranges of Tibet, and with great significance in limiting the extension of rains to the north and in protecting the Red Basin of Szechwan, lying to the south, from cold northern winds. Further south the Gorge mountains form an eastern limit to this basin, traversed by the Yangtze kiang. South of these ranges, and of the Chungking sector of the Red Basin, vast areas of plateau trenched by streams extend southwest into Yunnan and Kweichow; the western fringe of Kwangsi is also mountainous. The loftiest ranges of the west are in the Sino-Tibetan borderland, where they rise in Yunnan and Szechwan to more than 15,000 feet, to form north-south Alpine ranges.

Mountain country with an easterly trend links the Yunkwei plateaus and the eastern mountains of Fukien, in the Nanling, followed by province boundaries of Hunan and Kwangsi, Kiangsi and Kwangtung. This mountain divide, although not lofty, effectively limits to the north the subtropical zone of south China which has a long history of maritime contacts with the outside world. It acts as a divide between the drainage to the Si kiang tributaries, notably Pei and Kwei kiang, and that to the great Yangtze tributaries, the Siang and Kan kiang. The Hwai-yang ridges, to the north of the central basin zone of the Yangtze divide the Yangtze and its tributary, the Han, from the Hwai ho drainage to the north.

Three great rivers drain the greater part of China of the eighteen provinces and the most important of these is the 3000-mile long Yangtze kiang which receives several tributaries themselves ranking as major rivers. Rising in Tibet a short distance from Suifu, it loses its mountain character to form an historic link between regions: the mountain-girt Red Basin of Szechwan, the central basin region of lakes Tunting and Poyang, the lower valley, and finally the delta between Nanking and the sea. Much of the low country east of Ichang has been built by deposition; the Red Basin differs in that, apart from the alluvial Chengtu plain, its terrain is carved from soft sandstones and shales by the Kialing and Min kiang and other streams. No geographical region in China is so clearly delineated as that forming the greater part of Szechwan.

In the east the Hwai ho drainage separates Yangtze drainage from that of the Hwang ho, the Yellow river. The latter as a routeway is insignificant, but it has built of alluvium and redeposited loess a great part of the north China plain, its flood plain beginning at Kaifeng. The vagaries of its course on a bed raised above the surrounding lowland have brought recurrent tragedy to millions. Diverted from an outlet on the Gulf of Pohai as a defensive military measure in 1938 it has recently been deflected again from its war time channel (through northern Anwhei and Kiangsu to the Yellow Sea) to the Gulf of Pohai in northern Shantung. The Hwang ho, 3000 miles long, rises in Tibet and makes the striking Ordos loop to the north; the river leaves Kansu, to the northeast of Lanchow, to enter Inner Mongolia, and returns to China south of the Great Wall to provide the provincial boundary between Shensi and Shansi as far south as Tungkwan; there it turns east into a valley extension of the north China plain, continued west by the tributary Wei ho valley. Near Tungkwan also the Hwang ho receives the Fen ho from the northeast and the Lo ho from the northwest, and this concentration of waters plays a large part in creating flood havoc lower down.

In the south of China rivers with smaller catchment areas have built more limited alluvial tracts and the most notable system, that of the Si kiang, is limited in importance compared with the Yangtze and the Hwang ho drainage basins. However the Canton delta built by the Si, Pei, and Tung kiang is of great regional significance.

The climate of China is fundamentally related to its massive continental build, its position on the eastern fringe of Asia, and its range in latitude from about 20° to 40° north. Its regional features are largely influenced by the relief. The régime is, in broad terms, monsoonal and the seasonal reversal of wind direction is particularly marked in the centre and north, in which zones the tendency towards a summer maximum of precipitation, present in the south, becomes more striking. Precipitation decreases from south to north and becomes increasingly less reliable in the north and northwest. In south-eastern areas and in the lower Yangtze valley and delta region, less frequently in coastal areas further north, typhoons bring heavy falls of rain mainly from July to October. Mean annual totals of precipitation for Hong Kong, Shanghai, Peiping and Chungking are 85, 45, 25, and 43 inches respectively. Summers are hot throughout the country in all but higher mountain areas, and July and August average

temperatures generally reach 80° to 85° F. Winter conditions show
marked regional variation. In the north cold Siberian air brings continental rigour, but in the Yangtze zone winters are shorter and less cold,
and in south China mild. January averages for Hongkong, Shanghai,
Peiping and Chungking are 60°, 38°, 25°, and 49° F. respectively.

THE AGRICULTURAL BASIS

Agriculture, the main basis of the Chinese economy, shows close
relations with the physique of the country and its climate. The alluvial
lowlands are specially favoured. In the subtropical south heavy rains
cause leaching, and warmth and high humidity produce soils of low
natural value in hilly regions; in the semi-arid and drier northern plains,
concentration of alkali may be sufficient locally to limit or even preclude
cultivation. Alluvium is a term that covers a wide range of physical
textures, from clay to sand. There is much complexity especially since in
many parts of China human intervention has modified soil conditions
more than in any other considerable zone on the earth's surface. Traditional techniques are characteristic of most Chinese farming. Commercial
elements play a part (though usually small), since not all needs can be met
by a land holding; and most farmers have at least a little to spend in
village or town. The main features of this rural economy are well known,
but statistical data comparable with that available for most countries is
lacking and much estimation has entered into quantitative studies. It
seems probable that little more than 25% of the total area is cultivated,
i.e. about 0·5 acres per head of the total population.

Characteristic is the production of crops for human consumption, and
the keeping of pigs and poultry to consume waste products that have any
edible value and to provide manure. Sheep and cattle other than draught
animals play an insignificant role save in the extreme northwest. Tracts
of lowland largely alluvial in origin support a very large proportion of the
farming population. They include the north China plain extending from
the Shansi plateau edge and the eastern extremity of the Tsinling shan east
to the sea and the Shantung uplands, south from the Great Wall to the
Hwaiyang shan; the Yangtze delta, the lowlands of the central Yangtze,
and its tributaries; the coastal basins of Chekiang and Fukien; the Canton
delta, and some other valley tracts of which that of the Wei ho is the most
outstanding. The Red Basin of Szechwan constitutes a major farming
zone in which flat surfaces are produced by widespread development of
terracing, an art developed to less degree in many hill regions of China.
The typical farm throughout China is small and great intensity of land

use is generally regarded as characteristic. J. L. Buck, however, is of the opinion that "the agriculture of China is not so intensive as has been supposed, and that yields can be increased by the use of better seed, more fertilizer, and the utilization of labour now idle."[1] In rice growing regions irrigation is developed to flood rice fields; locally further north, in drier areas, to produce other crops.

The leading food crops are wet rice and wheat, grains of the millet group, including kaoliang, maize, barley, potatoes, soya beans, peanuts and a variety of vegetables of less general importance. Climatic factors confine important rice production to the Yangtze zone, stretching from Szechwan to southern Kiangsu, which has an annual crop, and to areas to the south with a year long growing season, and therefore two or even three crops a year. Wheat dominates north China and is autumn sown, save on the northern border, where spring is the growing season; as a winter crop it overlaps rice production in the north of the Yangtze zone which has nearly ten months growing season, i.e., in Szechwan, Hupeh, southern Anhwei and Kiangsu. In northern China where soils are poorer kaoliang plays an important part, and where drought is recurrent, other millets. Barley is an important crop in the central Yangtze zone while maize, with a wide distribution, is of very considerable significance in the southwest and northeast and in the zone between. Sweet potatoes, introduced from the Philippines in the late 16th century, thrive on sandy soils especially in southeast China. The valuable soya bean, and the peanut, yielding important supplies of vegetable oil, have a wide distribution, with heavy production of both in the plains of the north.

Commercial crops are limited in importance by the pressure of food crops on available land; any considerable expansion would undoubtedly have an adverse effect on rural welfare. Generally variable quality of products and persistence of old methods militate against considerable export. Silk, still of importance, especially in Kiangsu and Chekiang, is mainly reeled by hand, and greater Japanese efficiency as well as the development of rayon, etc., account for a decline in this ancient trade. The plantation tea of India and Ceylon has largely displaced the Chinese peasant product in Europe. Export in brick form by overland routes to distant markets has long been profitable. Tea is still of internal importance and is produced extensively on the hills of Kiangsu and Hunan. Tobacco is grown in many districts to meet widespread demand. The opium poppy is a tempting source of income; the product has small bulk and high value.

[1] J. L. Buck: "Agriculture and the future of China." *Annals of the American Academy of Political and Social Science*, Nov. 1930, p. 111. This issue is entirely devoted to articles on China.

In 1937 cotton of short staple types, both native and American, led commercial crops in acreage. The central and lower Yangtze regions and districts in Kiangsu, northern Chekiang, western Shantung, Hopeh, Shansi, Shensi and Hupeh were all considerable producers, and shortly before the outbreak of the Sino-Japanese war China was self-sufficient in raw cotton. Post-war output of cotton has declined, however, by two-thirds, and quality is generally poor.

China has to face grave agricultural problems, some environmental in origin, such as flood and drought, some due to historical evolution, such as irksome land tenure conditions and conservative farming technique. The incidence of shortage is made acute by poor transport, its effects tragic by pressure of population on available land. It is the flood problem that is most spectacular and that has attracted international aid at times. The Hwang ho, the 'scourge of the sons of Han', when augmented by melting snow in spring or by violent if sporadic rains in summer, provides the greatest danger; rapid run-off from its middle and upper basin has been made easy by removal of vegetation cover for fuel or by over-grazing. Other rivers of the north China plain are also liable to flood, and embankment maintenance is vital. The lakes of the central Yangtze zone to some extent regulate flow from the Siang and Kan systems, but the summer volume of the main channel is at times too great to be contained, and the lake areas, the lower Han valley, and the lower Yangtze may become inundated. Paradoxically the drought menace most afflicts the areas most liable to extensive flooding; rainfall totals fluctuate widely in north China, but effects of dry summers are greatest in the densely populated alluvial plains. Such fluctuation, characteristic of many areas on the margins of cultivation, is not new. A sequence of wet years has often in the past taken Chinese cultivators beyond the Great Wall, a sequence of dry years brought Mongol herdsmen south of the China border in search of pasture for animals and food for men. It remains to note that human intervention in the interplay of natural processes has adversely modified the landscape in many hilly districts of China. The removal of forest, the use of woodland, brush, and grass for fuel in central and northern regions especially, the cultivation of steep slopes without contour rows or terracing, the general absence of pasture, all have contributed to soil erosion, in many districts to the complete removal of top soil. The hilly regions of central and south China and the loess lands of the northwest are severely affected in some localities, moderately so over large aggregate areas.

The most vital agrarian problem is the general one of increased total production of food per head of the population; the question of improved distribution is secondary to this. J. L. Buck, a leading authority, responsible for careful sample surveys in typical regions in the years 1929–33, was of the opinion that 'no great increase' of the farmed area could be expected; ancestral graves and numerous boundaries to small fields take up valuable land, and the practice of farmland being detached in scattered fields means a loss of efficiency—but clearly reform in these matters, if possible, must also be very slow. Although the popular impression is that yields are high Buck found them variable, the range for wheat 5 to 67, for rice 22 to 169 bushels per acre; but the general concensus of opinion is that yields are good. It would seem that pressure of population on available land makes the typical small farm inevitable. The average size of a farm would seem to be between three and four acres, the average farm household to consist of about six persons. Cressey notes the striking fact that the "man equivalent required for one acre of wheat in China is 26 days compared with 1·2 days in the United States . . . for cotton the comparison is 53 and 14 days. . . ."[1] Remedies for agricultural ills clearly lie not only in flood control, drainage schemes, irrigation development and soil conservation measures, but in Buck's view in "still more intensive use of the present farm land", possibly yielding a 25% increase in total production. Improvement of seeds, measures against pests, extension of double cropping, provision of credit, development of co-operative societies, diffusion of agricultural education, all would help. Arbitrary taxation and chronic insecurity are serious matters.

Agriculture, it has been estimated, engages the attention of about three quarters of the total population of China, and full-time fishermen number approximately one million. Forest exploitation engages a smaller number, and trade and industry and miscellaneous occupations account for most of the remainder.

Salt water fishing, inshore and open sea, is a leading occupation only in many coastal localities along the southeastern coasts from south Kiangsu to Macao. Shanghai is the largest market and distributing centre; lack of refrigeration and speedy transport, and adherence to traditional methods limit the industry, and only salted or dried fish can reach interior districts. In coastal areas farming and fishing are often combined and in the interior every ingenuity is shown in utilizing fresh water fish.

It seems certain that forests with a great variety of trees once covered much of the country, with perhaps the exception of the semi-arid north-western loess regions. Removal for construction, for farming, for fuel, has denuded most areas of good timber, leaving in hilly districts bush and grass, accelerating soil erosion, and loading rivers with great burdens of silt. Considerable forest is restricted to mountain areas difficult of

[1] See G. B. Cressey: *Asia's Lands and Peoples*, 1944, p. 87.

access, mainly on the borders of Tibet and Burma, the mountain fringe of Szechwan, the Nanling and some southeastern uplands; elsewhere it exists only sporadically. The valuable bamboo is common in central and south China. The tung oil tree, often semi-cultivated, is limited to west central areas and produces oil of value for export. Commercial timber is mainly limited to types of pine, poplar and fir.

INDUSTRIAL POTENTIALITIES

The mineral wealth of China has in the past been overestimated. Cressey has summed up the position concisely—"China is bountifully supplied with coal and has major reserves of antimony and tungsten. Tin and iron are available in moderate amount, and there are small quantities of a wide variety of minerals. Copper, sulphur, petroleum, and other essentials appear very limited. China has the mineral basis for a modest industrialization, but in terms of her population she ranks well down the list of the great powers."[1]

China has virtually no hydro-electric power development (although considerable potentialities exist) and coal is therefore of the greatest significance. A clear distinction must be drawn between reserves and actual production. In 1936, excluding Manchuria, production amounted to little more than 20,000,000 metric tons in the eighteen provinces; China then imported coal from Indo-China, Japan and India. Reserves are estimated at about 240,000 million metric tons for all Chinese territory, and about 96% of this total lies within the zone under consideration. Fields occur in every province, but Shansi and Shensi easily lead, followed by Szechwan and Honan. In the grand total lignite plays a very small part; anthracite accounts for 20%, accounting for a large fraction of the reserves in Shansi and Honan. Reserves of coking coal are very limited. The better coals are largely of Permo-Carboniferous age, in the fields of Shensi, Shansi and adjacent Honan; many areas in Szechwan have but poor coal of Jurassic age. Structural factors have great influence on relative ease of mining, and in relation to actual and future exploitation, position in relation to centres of demand, and good communications with such centres, are factors of paramount importance. It is unfortunate that the effective demand is largely made by coastal and Yangtze valley industrial centres that lack nearby coal of good quality. In nearly every province small Chinese concerns have worked coal for a long time, but large pits have been sited in areas where transport exists for the despatch of coal to coastal centres, mainly in the north. Foreign initiative and

[1] *Ibid.*, p. 75.

capital have played a large part, and management has often been shared by Chinese and foreigners. In 1936 Hopeh (especially the Kaiking basin in the northwest), Shantung, Shansi and Honan accounted for about 75% of the total output, about half of which came from foreign concerns. During the recent war coal mining was stimulated in Szechwan and other western provinces in response to strategic needs.

Active seeking of petroleum deposits in recent years has done little to improve an adverse potition. Szechwan and Shensi have long had a small production; western Kansu has been the scene of some development, but cannot be regarded as a major source of supply.

Iron ore reserves have been estimated at only 300,000,000 metric tons (excluding Manchuria), leading provinces being Hopeh, Hupeh, Anwhei, Shansi and Fukien; the ores vary widely in quality, and the total reserves, in terms of any future large scale iron and steel industry, are very modest. Production in 1936 amounted to about 1,000,000 metric tons and was mainly derived from the Tayeh area in the Yangtze valley, in Hupeh; almost all the ore went to Japan and Japanese control of mines was dominant. Very little smelting took place in China, the Yangtze valley lacking suitable coking coal. War time developments in the west were of small scale and mainly located in Szechwan.

Other sources of mineral wealth in China have less relevance to possible large scale industry but some are of importance in international trade, chiefly tin, tungsten, and antimony. The Kochiu area of Yunnan accounts for a large part of the tin output, extraction being by primitive methods. Tungsten comes mainly from the Nanling in southern Kiangsi and nearby districts, antimony mainly from Hunan, in which province also manganese is mined. Gold and silver production is very small; copper in modest amounts is produced mainly at Tungchuan in north-eastern Yunnan; Hunan produces some lead and zinc. Salt, although obtained from rock deposits in Szechwan and other provinces, is largely produced from evaporation pans on the coastal fringe, especially in Kiangsu; it enters largely into internal trade and has long been a government monopoly.

Industry of miscellaneous type based on many small workshops and on peasant handicrafts has existed since remote times and persists. The old China was largely self-sufficient. It was the aged Emperor Ch'ien Lung who informed George III that "our Celestial Empire possesses all things in prolific abundance and lacks no products within its own borders. There is, therefore, no need to import the manufacture of outside barbarians in exchange for our products." The barbarians were later to force trade on China, and the Celestial Empire lost the right to regulate tariffs by the treaties of Nanking and Tientsin in 1842 and 1858 respectively. It was not until 1928 that a newly organized national government at Nanking regained the right. Moreover from 1895 foreign powers had secured the right to erect factories in the treaty ports of the east coast and the Yangtze valley, some of which slowly became industrial centres where foreign initiative, capital and management found scope, exempt from Chinese jurisdiction and the insecurity of civil war. It has been estimated that by 1937 approximately three quarters of the industrial capital of China was of foreign origin. The national government began in the years before the outbreak of the Sino-Japanese war to develop the beginnings of a national policy, influenced by the desire to diminish dependence on the foreigner and to move towards a stronger strategic situation in view of the growing Japanese threat. China has always lacked capital, organizers with initiative and experience of industrial technique of western type, and skilled and reliable factory workers. Progress has been and will be slow, and the recent war has brought disruption. Let us now examine the position in 1937, noting subsequent changes.

Manufacturing industries produced in 1937 cotton, silk, and woollen goods, glass, chemicals, cement, porcelain, etc., with the cotton industry, equipped with modern machinery, as the leading branch of industrial enterprise. Industry was located at Nanking, Hanchow, and Shanghai in the Yangtze outlet zone, higher up the Yangtze at Hankow, Hanyang and Wuchow, in northern Hopeh at Tientsin, in Shantung in the Tsingtao-Tsinan zone, and in the Canton area of Kwangtung. Shanghai, the international settlement, the leading port of the country, overwhelmingly dominated industry, as it did trade, commerce and finance. By 1937 mills owned by Chinese, Japanese and British concerns met the effective demand of the country for cotton goods, and the former consumer of large imports became an exporter to Korea, Japan, etc. Of spindles and looms about half were under Chinese, and most of the remainder under Japanese control. The historic silk industry ranked after cotton but was in a precarious condition.

The Japanese invasion meant the loss to the Chinese of the areas in which modern industry had developed, and although some equipment and personnel were successfully evacuated to the west much was destroyed or removed to Japan. Efforts were made by the National Resources Commission, which had been set up in 1932, to stimulate industry in 'Free China', notably in the Chungking area of Szechwan. This province has coal and iron resources and industrial potentiality rather than achievement in the field of modern industry. Beginnings were made in Free China that were more socially than economically valuable, and heavy industry is still lacking. The war period witnessed also a great increase of inflation; Chinese currency was modernized in 1935 but stability was not achieved, and since 1939 inflation has had increasingly serious economic consequences. An important change came in 1943 when the United Kingdom and the U.S.A., to be followed by other powers, surrendered extra-territorial rights. To-day with civil conflict persisting, with many obstacles to foreign enterprise, with generally chaotic economic conditions and fantastic inflation, it remains to be seen with what speed China will move towards an efficient utilization of her considerable resources. The auguries are not good. There is retrogression in industrial development. The output of the cotton industry, for example, now predominantly Chinese, and to a large extent under government control, has declined by about 50%, 3 million spindles existing as against 5 millions in 1937.[1] Not only is there great scarcity of foreign exchange, making the acquisition of foreign equipment almost impossible, but the transport system of the country has grave deficiencies, especially in the central and western provinces.

COMMUNICATIONS

Not only is there room for great improvement of communications in relation to the needs of internal trade, but also to make for greater administrative efficiency of provincial and national government, and to meet strategic requirements. Soon after the establishment of the national government at Nanking beginnings were made with national planning, and much progress had been made with road, and some with rail, development by 1937. War time efforts in central and western regions partially broke down their isolation.

Of the many internal waterways of China the Yangtze system, penetrating far back into the interior, is by far the most important. Ocean going vessels with a draught of 29 feet can reach Hankow, some six hundred miles from the sea, at high water, and navigation by small craft is possible into western Szechwan at Pingshan, above which the Yangtze is a torrential stream. High water occurs from June to September, and navigability and volume of traffic are then at a maximum on the whole Yangtze system. Low water imposes limitations on navigation of tributaries, and of the main stream above Ichang. There is much transhipment at the latter port since depths, gradients and rapids in the gorge section call for specially constructed small steamers with haulage at critical points; improvements have made it possible for small steamers to

[1] V. M. Bhatt: "China's Cotton Textile Industry," *Pacific Affairs*, Sept. 1947.

reach Chungking. The greater part of the Yangtze shipping is carried on
the main river itself, between Hankow and the sea. Shanghai, on the
Whangpoo near its divergence from the Yangtze, is the greatest foreign
and domestic shipping centre in all China, and it is impossible to over-
estimate its functions as a unique focus of trade, commerce, finance, and
western influence in all its forms. The shipping of Hankow is very largely
domestic.

The railway system of China developed slowly, in piecemeal fashion,
from treaty ports towards the interior, mainly financed by foreign capital,
and dependent on foreign material (Fig. 23). In 1937 the eighteen provinces possessed only about 7,000 miles of railway, mostly single track and
with a gauge of 4 feet 8½ inches. Not only is construction and maintenance of track a great problem, but also provision and maintenance of rolling stock. By 1937 the north China plain had the best system; the Peiping-
Tientsin district was the hub of an open network that linked up with
Manchuria and Inner Mongolia, with the Yangtze valley at Hankow and
Pukow (across the river from Nanking), with the ports of Tsingtao and
Tapu, and to the west with Taiyuan in the Fen ho valley and Paoti in the
Wei ho valley. Shanghai was the centre of another system, linked with
Nanking (ferry to Pukow), Hangchow and Ningpo; from Hangchow a
railway ran to Nanchang and Chuchow on the Canton-Hankow line.
The Si-kiang valley was poorly provided for; only in 1936 was the
Canton-Hankow line completed; Canton was already linked with Kow-
loon. The only railway in the south of China west of the Hankow-
Canton line was the isolated French link between Kunming and Haiphong
in Indo-China.

The recent war led to much damage to parts of the railway system of
China, but also, under pressure of strategic needs, to new developments.
Progress was made towards the linking of Hengyang on the Hankow-
Canton line with Nanning and Kweiyang, and other projects designed to
link western centres made some progress. The Japanese sponsored some
development in occupied territory, constructing for example a new line
from Peking to Jehol. The railway map of China must be treated with
reserve; in part it represents fluctuating possibilities rather than an effective
working system (Fig. 22).

Much of the traffic of China is still carried by horse, mule, donkey, or
human porter, often on tracks rather than roads, and there is still large
dependence on the cart, and in closely farmed areas even on the wheel-
barrow. By 1937 there were only some 15,000 miles of paved roads and
a further 35,000 miles of earth roads and, as in India, much of this mileage
was usable in dry weather only. The war years witnessed further road

development especially in the north-west and south-west, centred on
Lanchow and Kunming, respectively, and efforts were made to improve
links between these centres. They were linked by important roads with
the outer world on the continental frontier of China; Lanchow by the
China-Soviet highway via Kansu and Sinkiang to Russian territory,

Fig. 22. CHINA: PROVINCES AND RAILWAYS
The heavy black line is the boundary of the 18 Provinces.

Kunming by the Burma Road. The latter, opened in May 1939, runs to
Wanting on the Burma boundary, whence it continues to Lashio, terminus of the Burma railway; its construction in difficult country threaded
by the great Salween and Mekong valleys, malarious and subject to heavy
monsoon rains, was a task of great magnitude; its upkeep also raises
difficulties, and the usefulness of this back door has probably disappeared

as the natural west-east orientation along the great rivers has reasserted itself since the Japanese occupation; not to mention the post-war chaotic
conditions in Burma.

THE PROBLEM OF NUMBERS

The study of population in China is handicapped by lack of accurate
data. Computations of varied worth go back into the dim past, but their
association with such matters as taxation and military service, quite apart
from the nature of the estimating methods adopted, makes them very un-
reliable. China has never had a census in the modern sense, and marked
variations in estimates made by various agencies serve as a warning against
their use without much circumspection. It is certain that great pressure
of population on means of subsistence is a problem that first appeared
many centuries ago and that flood and drought, disease and famine, have
long taken great toll of human life. If the problem of declining numbers
arrests the attention of the student of demographic problems in many
western nations, the question of excessive numbers, it is generally agreed,
is the major problem in contemporary China, as it is in Monsoon Asia
generally. A powerful factor is the deeply rooted social ethic that makes
perpetuation of the family, and reverence for ancestors, a sacred duty.
Marriage at an early age is usual, families large. On the other hand death
rates are high and disasters attended by great mortality not infrequent; if
the birth rate is high so also is that for infant mortality, and female infanticide exists, although to an unknown extent. Moreover birth control may
have some effect on the birth rate at least of some cities. Statistics of births
and deaths exist only for recent decades for a few large cities, or so far as
collected for sample inquiries, such as those made under the direction of
J. L. Buck. The latter were made in the peaceful years 1929-31 and indicated an increasing population total for all China, with most provinces
affected and only four showing decrease. The total population of the
eighteen provinces, as estimated by the Ministry of the Interior in 1940,
approximates to four hundred million; in this respect at least China is a
great power.

The partial solution for excessive numbers in densely farmed areas in
the past has been migration to other areas within the present political
boundaries; the nucleus of Chinese civilization arose in the Wei ho
valley and expansion has gone on intermittently for some three thousand
years, despite intense attachment to ancestral land. The western provinces and the island of Hainan still witness on a limited scale Chinese
penetration. Beyond the eighteen provinces the Chinese in recent times
have made advances in Sikang, Tsinghai, Inner Mongolia, and above all

18

Manchuria; but emigration can provide no adequate solution to this immense problem. The Chinese show remarkable adaptation to varied climates and their patience and thrift make them successful in many fields, but although there has been emigration, especially from Fukien and Kwangtung, to Formosa, Indo-China, Siam, British Malaya, Burma, Netherlands East Indies, the Philippines, Hawaii and many other places, the grand total involved however computed is not large; estimates vary between 4 and 15 millions. Many nations have adopted a policy of exclusion on racial and other grounds. Besides being tenacious in their attachment to China, the Chinese are often unwelcome to economic competitors because of their capacity for hard labour for small reward. They show, in general, resistance to assimilation. Chen Han-seng has stressed "the importance of capital and its operation as a primary factor in determining the direction, the volume, and the character of emigration".[1]

It has been estimated that about one-fifth of the total population of the eighteen provinces can be classed as urban, with one-tenth in towns with more than, and one-tenth in towns with less than, 10,000 inhabitants. Precise statistics are mostly lacking, but seven cities probably have a population near or above one million. Shanghai easily leads with about four millions, and Nanking, Hankow, and Chungking, all in the Yangtze zone, are comprised within the group. Also included are Canton, Peiping and Tientsin. Soochow, Hangchow, and Tsingtao probably have populations exceeding 500,000. Tsinan, Sian, Chingyuan, Chinkiang, Wuhu, Wan, Changsha, Foochow, Wenchow, and Ningpo probably have populations exceeding 200,000. Estimates of the number of towns with total inhabitants numbering between 50,000 and 200,000 vary between 100 and 200. A large proportion of the towns of China are situated in the zones of dense rural settlement.

The outer margins of China, with the exception of south-western Kwangtung, have a very low density of population, generally less than two per square mile. The central areas of Hainan and the higher mountain areas within the country also have a very low density. On the other hand the important agricultural lowlands already enumerated have a density generally exceeding six hundred and sometimes reaching two thousand per square mile. Limited valley and former lake basin tracts in many areas of China have a high density, but averages even for *hsien* (administration districts comparable with an English county) mask these, and on the whole the generalization that density for most of upland China, mainly in the centre and south, averages between 50 and 250 is the best that can be made.

[1] I. Bowman (editor): *Limits of Land Settlement*, 1937, p. 153.

UNITY AND GROUP LOYALTIES

RACE AND CULTURE

The great extent of the eighteen provinces, and the vast total population, are often stressed as making any degree of political unity remarkable. Certainly within this great block of territory, regional differentiation rooted in geography persists, and civil war has been characteristic of recent decades. Strong unifying influences are the very large degree of uniformity of culture, with a very long and continuous historical background, and the absence of strong racial contrasts. Mongolian characteristics are dominant in a population that has absorbed invaders from beyond the Great Wall as well as many aboriginal groups within the present boundaries, because these elements too were largely of Mongolian type. The physical differences often noticed as existing broadly between the people north of the Yangtze basin and those to the south are interesting rather than profound, turning on such attributes as stature, greater in the north, and skin colour, lighter in the same zone. Within the broad zone of south China, including interior Hainan, there are to be found considerable areas in which the process of physical as well as cultural assimilation is still incomplete. It has been estimated that one-half of the population of Kweichow and two-thirds of that of Yunnan consists of unabsorbed or only partially assimilated tribes, e.g., the Lolos, Miaos, Yaos, Shans, etc., at various cultural levels. In the southeast too the physical character of the population is often very composite, e.g., in the inner mountains of Fukien.

In possessing a common written language the Chinese have an asset making for unity. It has been called the most difficult in the world however; literacy is rare. Its mastery in the past has largely been limited to the unique class of scholar officials, the mandarinate of the Empire. It has, and has had for many centuries, little relation to spoken language anywhere in China, and its function is often compared with that of Latin in the medieval west. In response to the great influx of western terms, and the need for shortening the period required for adequate education in the medium of Chinese, simpler written forms have made some progress in recent decades. Spoken Chinese is far from uniform. Forms of Mandarin speech dominate a vast area, extending south to the southern limits of the Yangtze drainage basin, and including most of Kiangsi, Hunan, and Szechwan. On the western borders of both Kansu and Szechwan there are Tibetan minorities. In the provinces of Yunnan, Kweichow, Kwangsi, Kwangtung, Fukien, and Chekiang, there is great complexity of spoken language. A multiplicity of Chinese dialects distinguishes the southeast, leading groups being the Cantonese, Fukienese, Hakka, and Wu. In the southwest, in Yunnan, Kweichow (except the northern fringe) and western Kwangsi numerous tribal groups are distinguished by linguistic diversity. These differences in speech have not given rise to separatist movements, but the value of a national *lingua franca* is clear and a strong movement to make the northern form of Mandarin the national language, has met with some success.

Loyalty to village, to family, to guild, to secret society, go deep, and national unity in the western form has made but little progress. Corruption, it is generally agreed, is rife. As to religion Latourette[1] writes "the Chinese are very eclectic. In proportion to the total population the number of simon-pure Buddhists, Confucianists, or Taoists has been and is comparatively small. The average Chinese has long been and still is an animist, a Buddhist, a Confucianist, and a Taoist with no sense of incongruity or inconsistency." Religious differences have at times created dissension and played a part in civil war, but they do not constitute an important disruptive factor in contemporary China. Chinese Muslims, originally alien groups and often differing physically from other Chinese, have adopted Chinese speech and customs to a large degree, although marriage outside the community is rare. Estimates of their total numbers vary but perhaps ten millions is a probable figure; in Kansu they form about 25% of the population and are present in considerable numbers in Yunnan and Kweichow; they have long formed groups in eastern cities, especially Canton. Christians too stand apart from the main current of Chinese religious life. Numbering some four millions in 1936 they have been responsible for a large fraction of that western influence that has led to building of schools and universities, hospitals and medical schools on modern lines.

THE CAPITALS OF CHINA

The capital cities of China have included Changan, Kaifeng, Hangchow, Peking, Nanking, and Chungking. Changan (Sian), now the provincial capital of Shensi, was the national capital for a total period of about a thousand years, before the 10th century. It was clearly well placed in the old Chinese realm of the north, in the fertile Wei ho valley, on the historic highway from the plain to the east, via Kaifeng, to the Kansu corridor and central Asia. During the recent Sino-Japanese War, when 'Free China' was restricted to the west, it was made auxiliary

[1] K. S. Latourette: *The Chinese. Their History and Culture.* 3rd edition, 1946, p. 611.

capital with Chungking, by decree in 1940, and named Siking, 'western capital'. Kaifeng was the capital of a contracted China when in the 10th century Tartars established a capital at Peking; in the 12th century when Tartars ruled in Kaifeng too, Hangchow became the capital for a while, emphasizing the southward movement of Chinese civilization. It was with the Mongol conquests of the 13th century that Cambaluc (Peking) became the capital of all China under alien rule. For a brief period under the first Ming emperor (1368) Nanking became the capital, but again in 1398 Peking was chosen. The emperor Yung Lo (1403–24) was responsible for the architectural glories that survive in contemporary Peking; capital also under the Manchus, Peking was only displaced in this function in 1927, by Nanking; in 1949 it was made the capital of Communist China. In the extreme south of China Canton has been a centre for strong political movements with separatist tendencies, but never a recognized capital for the whole country.

Peking, renamed Peiping in 1928, and Nanking, provide interesting contrasts. The former lies but a short distance south of a vital section of the ancient wall defences in the bordering mountain ranges that extend between the Mongolian plateau and the north China plain. Valley routes converge and the city is placed on the route from the north, from the inner Mongolian steppes, via Kalgan and the Nankow pass to the plain of Hopeh. Its proximity to a formerly dangerous border was an asset for defence control but made it also vulnerable; for the Manchus it was well placed, central in a domain that extended from the Amur river to the Si kiang and beyond. For control of the eighteen provinces Peiping is clearly lacking in centrality. Its only important waterway, which suffered, like the road system, from neglect under the later Manchu rulers, was the Grand Canal. This, more than a thousand miles in length, reached to Hangchow and long brought tribute of rice from the Yangtze region. The imperial courier road system reached its zenith in the 13th century under the Mongol régime, when no less than twelve highways radiated from Peking; roads provided the main link with provincial capitals. Within the rectangular walls, some sixteen miles long, grew up a Chinese and a Tartar city; within the latter is the Imperial, and again within this the Forbidden, city. The modern city, with a population of about one and a half millions, still a great cultural focus, is by Chinese standards well served by communications, partly as a result of the direct influence of the foreign legations.

Nanking had the obvious advantage of central position within the country, placed in the populous Yangtze valley, and the attraction of never having been a centre for alien rule, when it was chosen by the

Kuomintang or Nationalist party; from 1940 until the end of the recent war it was the seat of a Japanese-controlled puppet régime. Its port suburb of Hsiakwan, a few miles from the centre of the city, and the port of Pukow on the north bank of the Yangtze, provide it with river traffic facilities; the capital is on the south bank of the great waterway, only two hundred miles from Shanghai. The walls of the ancient city are almost enclosed by canals. Since 1927 its rail and road links have been greatly improved, and population has increased to about 1,000,000. Replaced by Chungking in 1938, Nanking in 1946 again became the capital of China, but only until 1949.

Although there have been important changes in the theoretical structure of central and political government in China since the overthrow of the Manchu régime in 1911, unrest and war have in fact given more scope to military dictatorship than to political reform; old ways persist. The territorial pattern of the provincial organization of China south of the Great Wall, in its broad lines, has remained unchanged since the 14th century, no doubt reflecting the generally static character of government for many centuries, but also perhaps its broad adaptation to the geographical background. Although province boundaries sometimes follow rivers, in general they follow mountain crests and traverse sparsely populated zones; the main exceptions are in the north China plain. In several instances, the provinces are sufficiently extensive and geographically defined to lend themselves to separatism when central political control has been weak, e.g., in the period of slow emergence of Kuomintang power, from its base in Canton, in the years 1912–26. Not until 1928 was a strong Nationalist Party government set up in Nanking, after a break with Soviet emissaries (influential in Kuomintang counsels from 1923 to 1927) and a series of rapid conquests. Central control of China was then in large degree re-established, but the breaking away of left-wing elements from the leadership of Chiang Kai-shek marred the achievement. Civil war continued old dissensions. By 1949 a Communist régime controlled the greater part of China.

BORDER REGIONS

I. INNER TIBET

The provinces of Sikang (Chwanpien) and Tsinghai (Chinghai or Koko Nor) were set up in 1928 as part of the policy of incorporation into the provincial system of China Proper of dependency territory on the western and northern margins of the eighteen provinces. At times the nearer Tibetan zone had been the source of threats to Chinese interests, and control dates from the 18th century. The areas concerned, distinctive in race and language, are closely related to central Asia in fundamental political geography, but Chinese interests and influences are far from negligible. The total area involved approximates to 400,000 square miles but total population has been estimated at no more than 2,000,000. Tsinghai flanks the Kansu oasis route to Sinkiang; Sikang lies between Szechwan and India, in a zone of almost complete physical separation. The western boundaries of both traverse forbidding country and Chinese authority is slight long before they are reached. The northern province, named after the Koko Nor, a lake standing 10,000 feet above sea level, includes lofty plateaus, desert basins, and the massive Nan shan. The southern has high plateaus and great north-south trending ranges, with peaks rising to 20,000 feet above sea level, separated by the spectacular valleys of the Yalung, upper Yangtze, Mekong and Salween. Climate is rigorous and only in some eastern mountain districts are forests an important potential resource. Tribal groups, pasturing yaks and goats, are dominant in more favoured areas and lamasaries are foci of trade among the Tibetans. Chinese cultivators are few since opportunity is limited to occasional alluvial cones supporting irrigated farms; trade provides a basis for a few settlements, e.g., Sining, capital of Tsinghai, west of Lanchow, and Tatsienlu, near the Szechwan border, whence a trail leads via Batang, capital of Sikang, nine thousand feet above sea level, in the upper Yangtze valley. Sikang has the Luku iron ore deposit, some oil, and coal; Tsinghai has coal reserves; both provinces at present lack industrial development but improved access may bring change in this regard.

2. INNER MONGOLIA

This constitutes another border region over which the Chinese have exerted firm control since the 17th century, and which by 1928 was divided into the provinces of Ninghsia, Suiyuan, Chahar, and Jehol. The latter province occupies a marginal position in relation to Manchuria; it was incorporated in the Manchukuo puppet state set up by Japan in 1932, but is now excluded from the Manchuria re-organized under Chinese control. Japanese interest in Inner Mongolia as a buffer zone against the U.S.S.R. was strong. The total area of the four northwestern provinces is about 400,000 square miles and the population has been estimated at about 7,000,000, more than half Chinese, Mandarin speaking, and the remainder largely Mongol.

Much of inner Mongolia consists of undulating plateau, but in the south of Chahar and the greater part of Jehol the country is mountainous; in the latter province drainage is partly to the Liao, flowing to the Manchurian plain, partly to the Gulf of Pohai. Rainfall is sufficient on the mountains of Jehol to permit the growth of forest, now largely cleared, but to the west and north, forest yields to steppe passing into true desert. The winters are severe and long, the short summer growing season of about three months in duration coincides with the period of maximum rainfall, and where the amount is sufficient and terrain permits Chinese farmers have long penetrated, often in face of the hostility of Mongolian pastoralists. Dry years lead to contraction of the farming frontier and soil erosion is often severe. Wheat, millet, barley, and kaoliang are dominant crops, but opium, although nominally illegal, is favoured in these remote areas as a high value, low bulk, cash crop. The main farming areas are south of the town of Ningsia; in southern Suiyuan along the Kalgan-Paotow railway, and further west in the irrigated Hwang ho valley; in the valleys and old lake basins of southern Chahar; and in the valleys of southern and eastern Jehol.

A strategic centre on the southern fringe of inner Mongolia is Kalgan (Wanchuan) the capital of Chahar, at the gateway to the route to Peking via the Nankow Pass, and the terminus of the motor and caravan road, some seven hundred miles in length, from Urga (Ulan Bator) in outer Mongolia. The railways from Peking, to Paotow via Kalgan, and to Mukden via Chengteh, capital of Jehol province, are important economically and strategically; the latter has branch lines to Chihfeng, and to Peikiao; the latter is an important coal mining centre. All four provinces have coal reserves but only in Jehol and Chahar is mining considerable. In the latter province iron ore is important in the Hsuanhua-Lungyen district; this was a source of supply to Japan.

MANCHURIA

POLITICAL RIVALRIES

The outstanding features of the development of Manchuria have been the political and economic rivalries of China, Russia, and until her recent defeat, Japan; and large scale 20th century pioneer settlement by Chinese farmers. In early historical times Chinese authority reached out, for defensive reasons, to southern Manchuria, in an effort to control a turbulent and sometimes menacing zone of tribal pastoral peoples. On a limited scale colonists were planted at times in the south of the Manchurian plain, and contact by sea from Shantung is by no means a recent phenomenon. China has both controlled and been controlled by the Manchus. In the mid-19th century the Chinese still claimed control of territory north of the Amur river, reaching to the Stanovoi mountains and eastwards; their influence extended to the shore of the Pacific. However their main preoccupation was with the area at present incorporated in Manchuria (*Fig.* 24).

Manchuria is essentially a great northern salient between the deserts and steppes of Mongolia on the west, and the Pacific borderlands of Russia and Korea to the east; its northern boundary following the Amur (Heilung kiang) was established by treaty with Russia in 1858, on the northeast the lower Ussuri river was made the boundary in 1860, the maritime province of Primorsk providing Russia with a Pacific margin and the port of Vladivostock. The boundary with Korea, over which China claimed suzerainty until defeated in war by Japan in 1895, follows the Tumen, flowing northeast, then a mountain zone, and then the Yalu, flowing southwest. In the west of Manchuria mountain country extends from north to south, but part of the outer Mongolian desert beyond is included within the western border in Manchuria, and in the south part of the mountain system and of the Manchurian lowland is included in Jehol. In the southwest is the narrow coastal lowland link with China of the eighteen provinces, skirting the hills of Jehol; it is reached by the Great Wall at Shanhaikwan. Manchuria is thus a distinct geographical entity. In 1903 it was divided into the provinces of Heilungkiang, Kirin, and Fengtien (Liaoning) and in 1907 incorporated in China proper, but administered in many respects as a separate political sphere and showing separatist tendencies. Strong Russian influence dates from the last decade of the 19th century; Japanese influence from 1905, in both cases largely exerted through railways (*Fig.* 23). Japanese intervention led to the setting up of the nominally independent puppet state of Manchukuo in 1932, including Jehol within its borders. Japan secured an expanding market, a source of supply for foodstuffs, coal, iron, aluminium, timber, etc., and a field for capital investment. With Japanese withdrawal the area of the old three north-eastern provinces was sub-divided into nine administrative areas, but in fact the area controlled by the central government at Nanking steadily dwindled; in the autumn of 1948 the last considerable stronghold, Mukden, fell to communist armies. Port Arthur, and port facilities at Dairen, are in Russian hands and the trunk railways of the country, by treaty made in 1946, are under joint Russian and Chinese control.

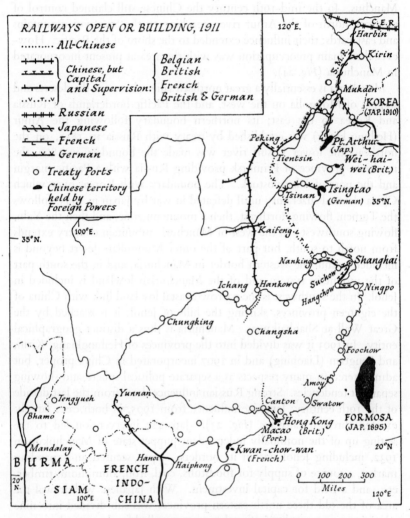

RAILWAYS OPEN OR BUILDING, 1911

.... All-Chinese

┼┼┼┼┼ Chinese, but } Belgian
┴┴┴┴┴   Capital   } British
┴┴┴┴┴   and Supervision: } French
⌄⌄⌄⌄⌄   } British & German

╫╫╫╫╫ Russian
⋉⋉⋉⋉ Japanese
⌐⌐⌐⌐ French
✕✕✕✕ German

○ Treaty Ports
● Chinese territory
   held by
   Foreign Powers

Fig. 23.   THE PENETRATION OF CHINA, 1905–11

The map represents the situation between the Russo-Japanese War and the establishment of the Chinese Republic. The extent to which the railway pattern had been sketched out under the Manchus will be noted (cf. Fig. 22).

ECONOMIC DEVELOPMENT

A brief sketch of the essential geography of Manchuria will provide a background to consideration of economic development and population questions. The area in question approximates to 400,000 square miles, and extends in latitude a distance of about 1000 miles north of 39°N.; the maximum east-west extent is some 800 miles. The undulating Manchurian plain, mountain girt and floored with alluvial deposits, constitutes the heart of the country. It is widest in the north, where it is drained by the Sungari system, tributary to the Amur, narrower in the extreme south, where the main stream is the Liao, draining to the Gulf of Liaotung. On the east hill and mountain country extends from the Liao-tung peninsula northeast to the Ussuri valley, higher ranges rising to 8000 feet. Across the north of the country extends the Little Khingan mountain system, west from the Sungari; in the northwest are the Great Khingan mountains. This variation in relief, in addition to position and size of the country, plays a part in climatic features. Everywhere however continental characteristics are dominant, winter only varying in length and severity, the hot summer in duration. Precipitation, heaviest in the eastern mountains decreases westward, from about 40 to as little as 12 inches or less, and a summer maximum is characteristic. The plains have a growing season varying from about 170 days in the extreme south to 125 or less in the north; in the west plain and mountain alike are semi-arid or arid in character. (Mukden, average January temperature 9°, July 75° F. average total precipitation 27 inches.)

Contemporary Manchuria, restored to a China in Communist control, is involved in far reaching economic adjustments. Japanese capital and initiative played the major part in industry and trade and in the relatively high development of road and rail transport. Restoration to the Chinese has coincided with currency inflation and deterioration of transport. Russian intervention in the closing stages of the recent war led to large scale appropriation of railway equipment, and industrial plant.

Although agriculture is of primary importance other resources are far from negligible. One-third of Manchuria is covered by coniferous and deciduous forests and forest industries have been developed; there is also production of coal, oil, hydro-electric power, and iron ore (*Fig.* 24). Forest has largely disappeared from the long settled areas of the southern mountains, but in the central and northern districts of the eastern uplands where river or railway gives access lumbering is important, Korean pine being a leading item. The wilderness of northern Manchuria has valuable stands of larch, birch, etc., a great potential resource in a region of hunting

and trapping. In the western mountains forests give way to steppe, still
the domain of Mongol pastoralists.

Sources of power are a great hydro-electric plant situated near Kirin,
coal, and some oil derived from shales at Fushun. Coal reserves are
modest, but in 1944 Manchukuo produced 30 million tons, exploitation

Fig. 24

MANCHURIA: COAL AND IRON DEPOSITS, AND RAILWAYS

being important to the Japanese war effort. Some was produced in all
three provinces but Liaoning easily led; important mines were at Fushun,
20 miles east of Mukden, and at Penchihu (Penki) in the eastern uplands.
Some coal suitable for coking was available, other types had to be mixed.
The Japanese utilized Manchurian iron ores, limited in supply and of low
grade, in blast furnaces set up at Anshan and Penchihu, but supplies were

not sufficient to keep the furnaces in full production.[1] In 1941 the output of pig iron amounted to 1·4, and of steel to 0.5 million tons. Iron and steel production has ceased but a reduced output of coal is produced at Fushun. Manchuria is endowed with useful supplies of lead, aluminium, asbestos and salt.

Agriculture has but recently displaced pastoralism over large areas of the Manchurian plain. It was in the late 19th century that restrictions on migration of Chinese to Manchuria were relaxed, but not until the third decade of this century did the large scale flow of peasants from Shantung, Hopeh and Honan effectively colonize the country. Permanent settlement had been preceded by seasonal migration from Shantung by sea, for the Chinese tendency to regard migration as a temporary and unwelcome necessity and to return to the ancestral home persisted. Civil war, banditry, and famine were powerful forces impelling colonists to embark on pioneer settlement; the movement reached a peak in the years 1926–28 when "the figures mounted to something like a million a year with half a million permanent settlers." Owen Lattimore has described the main features of this movement, which was checked as a result of Russian and Japanese opposition in 1929.[2] Many features of Chinese rural life have been transplanted, e.g., the attachment to pigs and poultry, but the standard of living is higher. Even so Japanese farmers were unable to compete, and only Korean rice growers, with still lower standards, penetrated into the valleys on the eastern borders. The great agricultural wealth of Manchuria lies in the plains, in the zone with a northeast-southwest axis passing through Hailun, Harbin, Changchun, Mukden, and Newchang; farther west towards Tsitsihar and Taonan semi-arid conditions have limited expansion, and in the north the pioneer fringe encounters increasingly harsh climatic conditions. Doubtless possibilities of further expansion exist. The chief crops, production of which varies in quantity with climatic fluctuations, are wheat and soya beans in the north, and kaoliang, millet and maize important additional items in the south. Until trade became disorganized the soya bean export was of world importance and in the light of present shortage its restoration is of great interest. Other crops play a part in the farming economy. In remote districts the opium poppy has yielded quick profits and stimulated development which would otherwise not have found a reward, e.g., in the lower Sungari valley. Lattimore has described how in Manchuria "opium has played the part played by gold in California, Australia, and elsewhere".

[1] See A. Rodgers: "The Manchurian Iron and Steel Industry." *Geographical Review* XXXVIII, 1948, p. 41 et. seq.
[2] See O. Lattimore: "Chinese Colonization in Manchuria." *Ibid.* XXII, 1932, p. 177 et. seq.

The Manchurian network of communications is characterized by the relatively extensive railway system, construction of which was dominated by political considerations; this system has in large part influenced the settlement pattern of the country. The rivers Liao and Sungari have only local importance. Railway construction commenced in 1896 at the instigation of Russia, the Chinese Eastern Railway (C.E.R.) giving a shorter route to Vladivostok, via Manchuli and Harbin, than the trans-Siberian, which skirts the northern frontier of Manchuria. A line from Harbin to Port Arthur was designed to further Russian influence, but with the triumph of Japan in 1905 what came to be called the South Manchurian Railway passed to Japanese control and Dairen, one of its terminals, was subsequently developed as an excellent port in the Kwantung Japanese-leased territory; it rapidly surpassed the old treaty port of Newchang (Yingkow). In the 1920's Chinese initiative led to additional construction and a new port at Hulutao, on the western shore of the Gulf of Liao-tung, was planned to give a port outlet independent of Japanese control, in defiance of treaty rights. In the north Harbin remained a focus of Russian interests until C.E.R. rights were sold to Japan in 1935. The U.S.S.R. now shares control with China of the main railways of the country, but these have deteriorated, and in places been destroyed, as a result of the recent civil war.

By 1940 Manchuria had some 6000 miles of railway, the line from Changchun to Dairen being double-tracked. Two lines provide links with China, terminating at Peking and Tientsin; two provide links with the Korean system, terminating at Najiu (Rashin) and Pusan (Fusan). In the north Harbin is linked with Blagoveshchensk (U.S.S.R.) and another line links Mutanchiang in the Kirin mountains with the Trans-Siberian, to the east.

DEMOGRAPHY

Material for study of population questions in Manchuria is very inadequate. A recent estimate of total population gives a figure of approximately 46 millions;[1] in 1929 it was estimated to be 29 millions. The pre-war Japanese and Korean elements have been largely repatriated, the former from the larger cities and the S.M.R. zone, the latter mainly from the Chientao (Kando) and Yalu basin areas. Thus the present population is almost entirely Chinese; Manchu elements, always small, have been absorbed and the Mongol tribesmen of the west are not numerous.

[1] See A. J. Grajdanzev: "Manchuria," *Pacific Affairs*, March 1946.

It has been estimated that approximately 70% of the total population is agricultural in basis. Rural population shows great variations in density. A wide zone in the north and west, often reaching a depth of two hundred miles is, with the exception of the Sungari valley which has hydro-electric and irrigation development, almost lacking in settlements. On the other hand many valleys in the eastern uplands, especially in the south, are farmed and their forests are under exploitation; the lower hills on the border of southeastern Jehol are being developed for farming. But the bulk of the population is in the central plain, in southern Heilungkiang, western Kirin and central Liaoning. The zone south of Mukden, with the hill country to the east, has been estimated to have a density of some 120 to the square mile, while further north the density decreases to less than 50 to the square mile. Owen Lattimore holds the view that " . . . aside from the political bias imparted by the regional feeling and the disruptive effect of Westernization, the new population as it grows tends to reproduce in full the situation as it is in China with the same problems of overpopulation, pauperization, economic bondage to the land and landholders, and insufficient margins of food reserve and financial security".

There are numerous urban centres in Manchuria, many of which owe their rapid growth to railway development. The old centre Mukden had in 1940 a population exceeding one million; it was the capital of the province of Liaoning. Harbin then had a population exceeding 600,000, with an important White Russian émigré community, Dairen and the capital, Changchun (Hsinking), populations exceeding 500,000. The population of the port of Antung exceeded 300,000, and those of Fushun and Anshan 200,000. Kirin, capital of the province of that name, had a population of 175,000.

FORMOSA

The island of Formosa (Taiwan) lies about one hundred miles east of the Fukien coast of China, separated from it by the Formosa Strait, in which lie the Pescadores, also recently returned to China. Formosa provided trading bases for the Portuguese, Spanish, and Dutch before, in the late 17th century, Chinese control was firmly established. However it lies to the south-east of the Ryukyu islands, on an important strategic approach to Japan, and it is not surprising that control passed to that country, after it had defeated China in 1895.

The island extends some 250 miles north-south and 100 miles east-west;

in the interior the Niitaka mountains are high and formidable. Along the east coast lowland is very restricted, but in the west alluvial plains are highly productive. With latitude ranging from about 22° to 25° N., the climate is tropical, and monsoon rains, heavy on the mountains, are adequate for agriculture on lowland tracts.

Forests, covering nearly three-quarters of the total area of 13,884 square miles, include valuable camphor, cypress and bamboo. Mineral wealth includes low grade bituminous coal, and some petroleum, both of which were of value to Japan, although production is on a modest scale. Natural gas is of local importance. The agriculture of the island, mostly developed in the western lowlands, has been almost entirely in Chinese hands; Japanese interests, when in control, gave it an orientation towards imperial needs; technique was much improved and yields increased. More than two million acres are cultivated. Crops of rice, commonly two a year, and sweet potatoes, are basic to subsistence, and pig rearing, as in China, is important. Not only a rice surplus, but sugar, bananas, tea, and jute were exported to Japan.

A good road and railway system has been developed, mainly serving the two large urban centres, Taihoku with the port of Keelung, and Tainan, with populations of about 250,000 and 100,000 respectively. The total estimated population of 5,747,000 in 1938, included 308,000 Japanese and 156,000 aborigines. The Japanese were engaged in administration, professions, trade, and industry and were resident in the towns. Of the aborigines about 95,000 were classified as 'savages', the leading tribes being the Ami, Paiwan, Taiyal, and Bunun. Rural density of the Chinese, mainly deriving from Fukien and Kwangtung, is in some localities very high, and the total population of the island doubled between 1900 and 1935. In Formosa China has recovered an asset the value of which has appreciated under Japanese rule, but the change of masters does not fully satisfy local aspirations and the imported Chinese officials have met with considerable opposition. At the end of 1949 the island was still in Kuomintang hands.

EXTERNAL RELATIONS OF CHINA

HISTORICAL OUTLINE

An outstanding characteristic of China for most of its long history has been its isolation from comparable social and political entities. It was the 'Middle Kingdom', lacking the stimulus that comes from contact and competition; those who came to trade were 'tribute-bearers' and foreigners were barbarians. External elements in Chinese culture are numerous, and in turn the Chinese have influenced other civilizations; but contacts were indirect in the main, and for a long period of time by land. China has been, and is, a continental power, despite the long established and far-reaching sea-borne trade of the southeastern ports, in Chekiang, Fukien, and Kwangtung. The effects of such trade were largely limited to immediate port hinterlands, especially that of Canton. The government at Peking was remote, complacent, contemptuous of traffic in merchandise and suspicious of the loyalty of the south-east. It was in this quarter that China, in modern times, felt the impact of the West, first in the 16th century, on a small scale; Portuguese Macao, founded as a trading post in 1557, is a reminder of this phase. In the 19th century pressure increased, and it was Great Britain, remote but with naval superiority, that led a resolute armed drive to force China to grant trade facilities. The movement became wider in scope and gains were almost always extended to others by treaty clauses. The decadent Manchu dynasty, surrounded by reactionary vested interests, controlled a social and political structure that was corrupt, stereotyped, and unadapted to change. China was impotent against the technique of western intrusion and in the last decade of the century plumbed the depths of humiliation at the hands of Great Britain, France, Germany, Russia, and Japan, the latter newly powerful, her reaction to a similar stimulus having taken a fundamentally different course. The Celestial Empire was reduced to semi-colonial status. The mechanism of foreign intervention and control included the treaty port system, restriction of the right to impose tariffs, foreign participation in coast and river traffic, extra-territorial rights, autonomous concessions and settlements, railway zones, spheres of influence, leased territories (*Fig.* 23). The impact of the Occident, felt in its full strength on the eastern seaboard and accessible inland centres, brought fundamental changes in political, economic and cultural life. Slowly the buttresses of foreign privilege have been, in large part, removed; less because conditions that were held to justify them have changed than because after a long period of turmoil following the revolution of 1911–12, a national government emerged at Nanking in 1928 that found favour with western powers. The process of change was hastened by the Sino-Japanese war, virtually though not formally continuous from 1931.

THE JAPANESE PHASE

Manchuria was the setting for that phase of Japanese expansion that was to culminate in the 'China incident' which began in July 1937, became a declared war, and merged with the second world war in December 1941.

19

Japan had gained concessions as part of her 'Twenty-one Demands' in 1915. Tension arose over railway developments in the 1920's. Japanese economic, military, and naval strength was such that in 1931 the disapproval of the U.S.A. and Great Britain was at last ignored. A successful campaign in Manchuria followed, and ended in 1933 with the four northeastern provinces incorporated in the puppet state of Manchukuo, set up in 1932. Japan proceeded further to exploit the weakness of China and the contemporary international situation, determined to create an economic bloc that would provide vital coal and iron, fields for investment, and markets. An attempt to set up an autonomous régime to include much of eastern inner Mongolia and northeast China failed and Japan in 1937 resolved to extend her conquests.

Only the major features of the prolonged war in China can be noted here. Fundamental was the fact that in the first year of conflict Japan had already secured control of southeastern inner Mongolia, the north China plain, and a continuous eastern Yangtze area, including Shanghai, Hangchow, and Nanking. In the next year occupation was extended into the central Yangtze region and blockade of the eastern coast was made virtually complete. The main railways and roads, the great food producing areas, and large towns with industrial development, remained in Japanese hands throughout the war. In 1944, the invaders' grip on communications was further extended to the links between Hankow and Canton, and between Hengyang, on that route, and the Indo-China border—part of a Japanese controlled land route that extended from Manchuria to Singapore. The lines of Chinese strategy became clear early in the war, when not only was the capital moved to Chungking, but a large migration of Chinese of all classes took place and some equipment at least was also moved west. Unoccupied China provided a great extent of territory, in large part difficult of access to the Japanese, with a natural nucleus in the rich Red Basin of Szechwan. State control of many aspects of economic development followed, and rail and road projects were launched, both to link the northwest and southwest with Szechwan centres, and to improve vital land routes with the outside world, since air transport could not alone suffice. The China-Soviet highway in the north-west (which ran from Lanchow to the Turksib railway), and the Burma road, opened in May 1939, became of great importance. Early in the war the Kuomintang-Communist feud was in abeyance. However in 1940 the rift widened once more and this factor along with steadily increasing inflation seriously impeded the Chinese effort. With an accession of allies late in 1941 paradoxically the position worsened; by the spring of 1942 Hong Kong, Malaya, and Burma had been added to the Japanese controlled territories of Indo-China and Siam, and aid to China was greatly reduced. By 1944 assistance was again considerable, but it was primarily the success of Anglo-American naval and air power in the Pacific war that led to the collapse of Japan in the following year and obviated the need for large scale campaigns in China.

AFTER THE WAR

China emerged from the war with recognition as a 'great power' and regained control of Formosa, the Pescadores, and Manchuria—although the U.S.S.R., a belligerent only in the last few days of the war, secured valuable privileges in the latter country. The U.S.A. and Great Britain had given a lead in the surrender of privileges. France in 1945 surrendered the leased territory of Kwangchowwan, seized in 1898 as a base for influence in south China, and used as a naval station. Great Britain however retains a foothold off the coast of south China as a base for her interests.

The hilly island of Hong Kong lies at the eastern entrance of the Chu kiang (Pearl river), only some forty miles from Portuguese Macao, at the western entrance; the latter is a free port based on a peninsula, with control extending to the islands of Taipa and Colowan. Macao has a poor harbour and has long since lost its commercial importance; it functions mainly as a fishing centre and as a resort. Hong Kong is of much later foundation, with a free port which, although it has suffered from some decline of traffic, is still of international importance. The island was ceded in 1841 after war with China, and was then frequented only by pirates and fishermen. Situated some 90 miles south-west of Canton, and 32 square miles in extent, it provided a secure base for trade, with excellent deep water harbour facilities, and was to develop as an *entrepôt* centre of the first rank, handling food, raw materials, coal, oil, manufactures, etc. It also became a naval and military base. The city and port of Victoria faced a Chinese controlled mainland a mile or so away, until Kowloon, now an extension of its harbour, and linked by rail with Canton, was ceded after war, in 1860. Leasing of the 'New Territory' in 1898, for 99 years, extended British control on the mainland and over nearby bays, strengthening the strategic position of the Crown colony, which now covered 391 square miles. The 1931 census showed a total population of nearly 850,000 with only some 28,000 non-Chinese, but the number of inhabitants, almost entirely of Cantonese origin, fluctuates widely according to conditions on the mainland. Trade is largely with China but many nations participate.

Foreign trade is an important aspect of the external relations of China, although it was but little developed even in pre-war years and in the post-war period is highly restricted. Great Britain long controlled a large proportion, but after 1932 the U.S.A. emerged as the leading power, with about 23% by value of the total in 1936—followed by Japan with 16% Great Britain and Germany each with 11½%, and Hong Kong 8%. In the same year the share of the U.S.S.R. was but 0·3%. The dominant position of the U.S.A. in China's external trade extended also to cultural influences. During the war and post-war years this lead has been greatly enhanced by the great scale of her economic and military aid and the collapse of Japan; but it has suffered eclipse with the triumph of Communism in contemporary China. Relations between the leading world maritime power, at present occupying Japan, and the U.S.S.R. are clearly important to China.

KOREA

Korea, 'Chosen' of the Japanese, 'Choson' of the Koreans, as a result of its strategic position has figured largely in Far Eastern power relationships in recent decades. A peninsula, with a broad mainland base, it approaches to within a hundred miles of Japan; only the Chosen and Tsushima Straits, respectively north and south of the Tsushima islands, separate the south-east of Korea from the Japanese island of Kyushu. Numerous small island groups fringe the intricate western and southern coasts, which are rich in natural harbours; the islands of Kturyo and Cheju (Saisyu or Quelpart) are further detached from the mainland. The mountainous east coast of the country, poor in harbours, borders the Sea of Japan; the west coast, subject to a considerable tidal range, borders the Yellow Sea. The northern land boundary, separating Korea from a salient of Soviet territory and a much larger extent of Manchurian, trends from northeast to southwest. It follows the Tuman (Toman) river, the lofty Paitoushan, rising to 9000 feet, and the Amnok (Yalu or Oryoku) river. The area of Korea exceeds 85,000 square miles, and the maximum north-south and east-west distances are about 450 and 170 miles respectively.

The terrain is predominantly mountainous, and in detail the relief is intricate. The outstanding facts are the close approach of mountains to the east coast, and the lower relief in the west and south. The more important river basins are those sections of the Tuman and Anmok systems within the northern boundary; the basins of the Taedong (Daido), Han (Kan), and Kum (Kin) in the west; and the Naktong (Rakuto) in

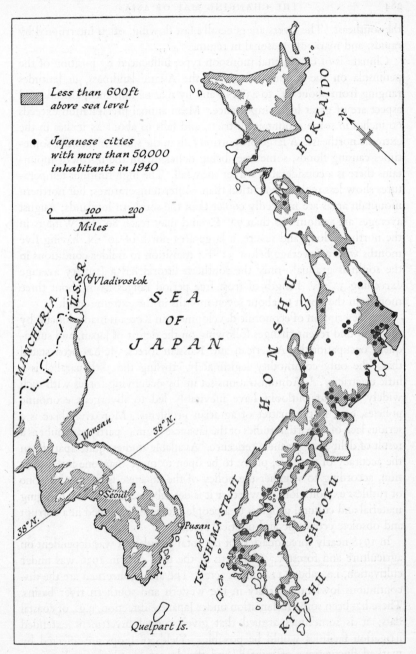

Less than 600ft
above sea level

Japanese cities
with more than 50,000
inhabitants in 1940

0   100   200
        Miles

MANCHURIA

U.S.S.R.

Vladivostok

SEA

OF

JAPAN

Wonsan

38° N.

Seoul

38° N.

Pusan

TSUSHIMA STRAIT

Quelpart Is.

HOKKAIDO

HONSHU

SHIKOKU

KYUSHU

Fig. 25. JAPAN AND KOREA: LOWLANDS AND CITIES

the southeast. The rivers are generally fast flowing, often interrupted by
rapids, and markedly seasonal in régime.

Climate is of continental monsoon type, influenced by position of the
peninsula on the eastern margin of the Asiatic landmass, in latitudes
ranging from about 34° to 43° N., and by marine influence; altitude and
aspect are of great local importance. Mean annual precipitation exceeds
60 inches in some mountain districts, and falls to about 25 inches in the
extreme northeast. A large proportion falls in the summer months, sometimes causing floods, sometimes being deficient. In the northern mountains there is a considerable winter snowfall. The high summer temperatures show less regional variation than winter temperatures, but northern
mountain areas are markedly cooler than the southern lowlands; August
averages are seldom less than 72° F. and may reach 80° F. Winters in
the north are long and severe, a large area north of 40° N. having five
months with an average below 32° F.; transition to milder conditions in
the south is gradual—only the southern littoral has a January average
exceeding 32° F. Length of frost free period ranges from about three
months in the north to about seven months in the extreme south.

Any description of economic development in Korea is made difficult by
the profound recent changes following on the defeat of Japan, and subsequent occupation by American and Russian forces. It has been stated
that "the only commodity legitimately crossing the 38th parallel is a
little electricity".[1] Administrations set up by occupying forces with such
widely different outlooks have inevitably led to divergent economic
policies, e.g., in the matter of agrarian problems. Moreover there is a
serious lack of impartial studies of the Japanese régime, partly no doubt as a
result of deliberate Japanese reticence. Available studies, quite apart from
the accuracy of statistics, prove to be open to more than one interpreta-
tion, according to whether the policy of the Japanese is indicted as one
of ruthless exploitation, or whether it is described as beneficent, bringing
material and cultural progress to a people previously gripped in a corrupt
and obsolete economic and political system.

In 1938 nearly three-quarters of the total population was dependent on
agriculture and forestry. One-fifth of the total area in 1936 was under
cultivation, i.e., about 11 million acres. The areas concerned are the discontinuous lowlands, mainly in the western and southern river basins.
There has been some reclamation under Japanese direction, e.g., of coastal
flats; it is sometimes argued that given capital investment extended
irrigation facilities would be possible. Yields of crops are affected by
marked fluctuations of rainfall, and the degree to which fertilizers are

[1] Y. Kim: "Korea in Crisis," *Eastern World*, December 1947.

used. The use of machinery is uncommon and rural poverty is characteristic. Controversy centres on how far the Japanese policy of fostering
exports, notably of rice and cotton, and promoting capitalistic farming,
aggravated the situation, or at least ignored the need for an increase of
food supplies for domestic consumption. Fundamental is the fact that the
available agricultural land of Korea carries too dense a population for
maximum *per capita* output; tenancy is dominant, and there is an acute
agrarian problem. The average land holding was 3·6 acres in 1938, but
many holdings were much smaller.

Crop production is the main agricultural activity, cattle and pigs playing
a lesser role; despite Japanese efforts the number of sheep has remained
extremely small. In 1938 crops accounted for 93% of the estimated gross
value of agricultural production in Korea.[1] Rice leads, many varieties
being grown, according to climatic conditions; the irrigated paddy fields
of the south produce the heaviest yields but are exacting in needing
abundant water and level terrain; about half the total rice acreage was
irrigated in 1936. Barley and millet are also important food crops, and
beans (especially soya), wheat, oats, maize, Irish and sweet potatoes, all
figure in the farm economy of various districts. Barley is often grown as a
winter crop in the south. To judge by statistics, the production of two
crops a year would seem to be characteristic of about one-third of the
total cultivated area. In some hill districts the ancient practice of 'fire-field'
farming persists, clearings in wooded country being cropped with millet,
oats, or potatoes, and then left to revert to waste; thus a migratory form
of land exploitation is operative. The leading commercial crop of Korea
under the Japanese régime was cotton, grown mainly in the south, and
of both native and American types. Japanese interests also stimulated
sericulture, important in the southeast of the country.

Approximately one-third of Korea is statistically classified as forested,
but good lumber, mainly larch, is limited to the north. Large areas consist of woodland and scrub, yielding only wood for miscellaneous uses.
Preservation and extension of forest cover is clearly important as a check
to soil erosion, as well as a sound basis for exploitation; the Japanese were
responsible for some afforestation.

In pre-war years fisheries were rapidly developed and exports to Japan
were large. Fishing is mainly inshore, and much of the catch is dried,
salted, or canned. In 1939 about half a million persons were engaged
in an industry that yielded food, fertilizer, and oil, providing some for
export.

The Japanese paid a good deal of attention to mineral wealth. It has

[1] Data from A. J. Grajdanzev: *Modern Korea*, New York, 1944.

been estimated that about 6 million tons of coal were produced in 1943, more than double the output of 2·3 million tons in 1936. Reserves are estimated at a figure that would make the latter output possible for several hundred years; soft coal and anthracite are the types produced. The chief producing areas are in the P'yongyang (Heijo) region and further north near the Russian border. Beginnings have been made with the production of oil from soft coal, since the country lacks petroleum resources. Iron ore deposits in Korea are of low grade; in 1936 about 250,000 tons were produced. Musan (Mosan), near the Manchurian frontier, produced low grade magnetite ore; other centres of ore production included the Kyomipo (Kenjiho) and Kaisen districts. Gold production, from widely distributed placers and lodes, was encouraged by the Japanese régime, output in 1937 amounting to 20 tons. War needs led to production of aluminium and magnesium.

Coal plays a part in providing power for industry, but hydro-electric sources were developed by Japanese corporations, and there is scope for further construction of dams and reservoirs, the latter being essential to overcome the effects of markedly seasonal river régime. Important power stations are at Chosinko and Fusenko; some power is used for manufacture of nitrogen fertilizer.

Industrial developments in 1938 (in order of value, chemicals, food, textiles, and metals) employed some 231,000 people, part-time household industry still being important in the textile and lumber groups. In textiles cotton led, followed by silk, the main centres being Pusan (Fusan) and Keijo (Seoul). There were several large scale silk filatures. Iron and steel industry was on a small scale. In 1936 the output of pig iron was 155,000 tons (smelted with Japanese coke), of steel 87,000 tons. Kenjiho is an older centre, newer plants being located at Chemulpo (Jinsen), Musan (Mosan), and Ch'ongjin (Seishin).

In 1940 Korea possessed some 3500 miles of railways, only feeder lines being in private ownership, and a road system which included about 7500 miles of first and second class highways. Waterways play a minor role. Strategic as well as economic considerations played a large part in these developments. The port of Pusan (Fusan) was linked by rail with Keijo (Seoul), and this city with Antung, served by Manchurian railways. Keijo was linked also with Wonsan (Genzan) and Najiu (Rashin), the latter a rapidly developed new port, in the northeast, with railway connections to a hinterland that includes much of Manchuria.

The total population recorded in the 1940 census was 24,326,000; at that time there were approximately also one million Koreans in Manchuria, mainly rice cultivators, one million in Japan, mainly industrial labourers, two hundred thousand in Russian Asiatic territory, and a smaller number in China. Pressure of population on means of subsistence produced not only extreme poverty in the country but a stimulus to emigration. Estimated population at the time of annexation by Japan in 1910, was 13·25 millions. The average annual birthrate per thousand, for each of the years in the period 1929–38 was 32·4, the death rate 19·9. Average density of population for the country as a whole in 1940 was 285 persons per square mile, but there are great regional variations. The zone north of 40° N., and the eastern zone, throughout, has a low density, while lowlands in the west and south carry large populations. In 1940 about 12% of the total population was concentrated in the fifty towns which had a population exceeding 15,000; the fraction is small, but represents an increase on earlier figures. The largest city, Keijo (Seoul) with a total of 935,464 in 1940, was the administrative capital under the Japanese régime, as well as the main focus of industry, trade, and commerce. P'yongyang (Heijo) followed with 285,965 inhabitants, then Pusan (Fusan), the chief port, with 249,734. Three other towns had a population exceeding 100,000 namely Ch'ongjin (Seishin) with 197,918, Taegu (Taikyu) with 178,923 and Chemulpo (Jinsen) with 171,165. Eight towns had a population between 50,000 and 100,000.

The population of Korea in 1940 included 650,000 Japanese, almost entirely dwelling in towns and engaged in administration, commerce, and industrial organization. Recently almost all Japanese have been repatriated; on the other hand about 200,000 Koreans have been expelled from Manchuria.

The Koreans, forming a distinct physical type, are united by a traditional culture, that has borrowed much from China and given much to Japan, and by a common language. Japanese was the official language for thirty-five years after the annexation in 1910, and statistics for 1939 show that 14% of the population understood that language. In that year Japanese students outnumbered Korean at the one university of the country, that at Keijo (Seoul); a large proportion of the Korean population was illiterate. Organized religion has but a weak hold; ancestor worship, animist beliefs, Confucian and Buddhist elements are all present, also Christianity, providing an important channel of western influence. Christian missions claim half a million converts. The problem of creating an independent democratic state, as envisaged in the Cairo declaration of 1943, is formidable and remains to be solved. No experience in self government was given by the Japanese régime, even in the thirteen provinces, and the Korean administration that preceded it was archaic, corrupted, and faction ridden. The divergent policies of the two occupying powers are a grave impediment to the development of a unified Korea.

In the external relations of Korea both China and Japan have long played a part; it was only in the late 19th century that Russian interest became strong. Japanese interest in the peninsula is easily explained in terms of its geographical position. In the grip of a hostile power Korea might well have been a menace; in the control of Japan it offered a substantial footing on the mainland of Asia. The Koreans had followed a policy of exclusion for some three hundred years, before the Japanese forced its abandonment in 1876. Defeat of China in 1895, of Russia in 1905, preceded the declaration of a Japanese protectorate in the latter year; annexation followed in 1910. China had claimed some sort of suzerainty since 1627. Under the highly centralized control of an autocratic Japanese Governor General, Korean economy was orientated towards Japan, with the aid of tariffs and subsidies. Korea supplied rice, beans, fish, cotton, iron ore, coal, etc., and imported Japanese manufactures. With the defeat of Japan the Koreans changed their masters; Soviet troops occupied the area north of the parallel of 38° N., American troops the zone to the south of this completely arbitrary line of division. In the Cairo declaration of November 1943 the independence of Korea 'in due course' was guaranteed by U.S.A., the U.S.S.R., the U.K., and China. The powers were to exercise trusteeship for five years after Soviet-American agreement on plans for the setting up of a democratic government had been reached. However the post-war world has no agreed conception of democracy and such an agreement has not been reached; Korea is the meeting place of rival ideologies and great power contention. In August 1948 an American sponsored Republic claiming legal authority over the whole country was proclaimed in Seoul; earlier in the north. Few boundaries have more explosive possibilities than the 38th parallel.

THE JAPANESE PROBLEM

As a result of her recent defeat Japan has lost control of the Kuriles, and the island of Sakhalin (Karafuto) south of 50° N. to the U.S.S.R.; control of Formosa to China. The fate of the Ryukyu (Loo-choo) islands remains to be decided. The islands of Japan proper, Hokkaido (Yezo), Honshu (Hondo), Kyushu, and Shikoku, the nucleus of a short-lived empire, form the subject of this section; the total area is little more than 146,000 square miles, but the population exceeds 78 millions, and its destiny is a major problem in the post-war world.

THE GEOGRAPHICAL BACKGROUND

The insular character of Japan, and the position of the islands relative to the Asiatic mainland, are fundamental geographical factors. No part of the country is remote from the sea and few districts are more than fifty miles distant. The long and intricate coastline provides good natural harbours, generally backed by upland however; the densely populated lowlands are provided with harbours largely man-made. The island-studded Inland Sea is a particularly striking feature; following the structural trends of southern Honshu its alignment is nearly east-west, for about 250 miles, from Osaka Bay to the Straits of Shimonoseki. The latter provide an entry from the Sea of Japan and Tsushima Strait; the two entries from the Pacific Ocean, the Kii channel and Bungo Strait, pass the eastern and western ends respectively of the island of Shikoku.

The Japanese islands are dominated by mountainous or hilly country showing numerous evidences of complex folding and faulting. The Japanese Alps, with peaks exceeding 10,000 feet in altitude, at a meeting place of structure zones in central Honshu, form the highest and most extensive mountain mass. More than a quarter of the land surface of the country consists of outcrops of volcanic rocks, of lava and ash, and volcanoes, some active, are numerous; earthquake shocks, occasionally of disastrous proportions, are characteristic of this unstable Pacific margin zone. There is a mosaic of regions each with a complicated relief pattern. Numerous short fast-flowing streams, liable to flood, have played a large part in the evolution of landscape elements from rock outcrops that are diverse even in small areas. Such streams have built the greater part of the separate lowlands, some in the interior, but mostly coastal, that are vital to the life of the country. The largest of these, the Kwanto plain, is but some 5000 square miles in extent. Typically in the coastal plains, the mountain edge is flanked by old alluvial deposits (diluvium), coarse gravels and sands arranged in terrace form and dissected by stream action as a result of uplift. Then follows the continuous plain of recent alluvium, sloping gently seawards, across which the shallow sluggish river flows on a raised floor of its own making; finally on the seaward margin sand dunes or sandy beach ridges, tree covered, terminate the lowland. Rather less than one-fifth of the total surface of the country is composed of such tracts.

The climate of Japan is far from uniform throughout. The islands, lying approximately between the parallels of 31° and 45° 30′ N., thus have a latitudinal range of about a thousand miles, and local relief has important effects, both on temperatures, and mean annual precipitation; the latter ranges from 40 to 120 inches. Position off the east coast of Asia accounts for winter cold, somewhat ameliorated by the influence of the Japan and China Seas. Cold Siberian air, brought by the northwest winter monsoon, gives severe winters to the northern areas, with precipitation on the western mountain slopes, much in the form of snow. It is in this season that depressions are most numerous. January average temperature falls in northern Hokkaido to about 15° F., and rises to the south, to about 43° F. in southern Kyushu. In summer there is a strong tendency for a southeastern monsoon to dominate, and Japan is influenced by warm maritime Pacific air moving towards Siberia. This is the season of heaviest precipitation, and there is high humidity and temperature except in eastern coastal districts, north of about 35° N., which are influenced by the cool Okhotsk current. The average August temperature in southern Japan is about 80° F.; it falls to 70° F. in the northwest, and to 65° F. in the northeast. The south-east coasts of Japan, as far north as about 40° N., in late summer and early autumn, are occasionally traversed by violent tropical cyclones, typhoons, which bring torrential rain and may cause flood havoc.

THE JAPANESE ECONOMIC ACHIEVEMENT

In describing the economic resources of Japan it would seem to be desirable to outline the developments in pre-war years, despite the fact that defeat has shattered the economic structure. The physical foundations at least have a permanent character. Exploitation of forests, fisheries and, agricultural land will presumably follow established lines, and it is the industrial and commercial future that is conjectural.

Rather more than half the area of Japan has been classified as forest land for statistical purposes, and it dominates much upland country, yielding timber, fuel, charcoal, pulp, etc. Altitude zones, as well as latitude, play an important part in the distribution of forest types. There has been systematic planting, mainly of conifers, and there is scope for further afforestation; not only national needs for timber, but the protective function of forests in checking soil erosion, have been keenly appreciated. Although coniferous forest occupies only about one-quarter of the total forest area, it yields a very large proportion of the cut of commercial timber. Central and eastern Hokkaido are the leading areas dominated by pure stands of conifers, with fir outstanding, but exploitation is also active in accessible areas of central and northern Honshu, where mixed forests occur; here pine, fir, etc., are mingled with maple, birch, and other deciduous trees. In southern Japan dense broadleaf evergreen forest includes several varieties of oak. Before the war Japan supplied about three-quarters of her needs in lumber products.

The fisheries of the country make a large contribution to food supplies, fish being popular in the national diet and second to rice in importance; *per capita* consumption of fish is the highest in the world. The meeting of cold and warm currents in Japanese and nearby waters favours abundant supplies, and with the main centres of dense population never far removed from the coast, distribution of the catch is relatively easy. Coastal fishing, mainly in shallow but also in the deep waters of the Pacific, leads in importance. Although the industry is partly modernized, many small sailing craft are still used, fishing often supplementing farming. A great variety of fish is caught; although the herring and mackerel fisheries of Hokkaido are important, it is the sardine catch that leads both in volume and value, for the country as a whole. The fisheries produce not only food in large quantities, but much oil, meal, and fertilizer. Deep sea fishing, which accounted for one-quarter of the total value of fishery products in Japan proper in 1938, was mainly organized by large concerns. It was partly conducted from home ports, and partly from factory ships operating in more distant waters, e.g., seeking salmon in Alaskan waters, whales in the Antarctic. Canneries handle sardines, salmon, and tuna in large quantities, and in past years export has been important.

The main features of Japanese agriculture are closely related to the possibilities of the physical environment, traditional technique, and high density of population; its primary concern is with subsistence crops and self-sufficiency was all but obtained in pre-war years. In 1939 approximately 16% of the total area was under cultivation, and some five and a half million families were wholly or partly engaged. The average holding was little more than two and a half acres. In the north, and in upland areas, where land produced less than in the favoured south, holdings tended to be somewhat larger. The present century has seen less than 5% increase in the area under cultivation and considerable expansion of urban areas; there would seem to be little scope for further reclamation, even in the upland areas. The important farming regions are the numerous small alluvial lowlands, more especially the recent alluvial tracts, with good soils. About half the total area of recent alluvium, and about a quarter of the total area of older alluvium, are under cultivation. Broadly these are the areas that can yield enough susbsistence, with intensive manuring, to cultivators using hand implements on small farms, usually made up of scattered plots. A small fraction of the upland area, where slope is not excessive, is used also, often terraced. The practice of migratory fire-field farming is carried on in some uplands, fields cleared by burning yielding crops for a year or two before reverting to waste.

The favoured crop of the Japanese farmer is irrigated rice, and in 1937 rice occupied more than half the cultivated area. The total yield fluctuates with climatic conditions but has steadily increased. Paddy fields are ubiquitous in most lowland tracts as far north as Honshu, and some occur in the southwest of Hokkaido. Length of growing season plays a large part in influencing agricultural possibilities and returns. It is influenced by distance from the sea as well as by latitude. The northeast of Hokkaido has a season of some four months, while the southern coastal areas of Kyushu have a season of eight months. Very limited areas in the extreme southeast of Japan produce two crops of rice in one year; south of about the parallel of 38° N. in addition to summer rice a winter crop of barley, or wheat, or beans, etc., is commonly produced from paddy fields that can be drained. The upland unirrigated fields of Japan are also frequently double-cropped in the south; they produce wheat and barley, Japan being self-sufficient in the former cereal in pre-war years, as a result of organized effort. In 1939 the total acreage under wheat and barley combined was more than half that under rice. Oats, grown for animal feed, have local importance in Hokkaido. Other crops include millet, maize, beans, potatoes, fruit, and a variety of vegetables, the latter produced especially near the large cities. There is however a striking reliance on cereals in the national diet, and little inclination towards consumption of meat or dairy produce. In any case several factors, notably the absence of good pasture, militate against animal husbandry. Cattle, together with horses, only augment human labour on farms where they are kept; poultry are a popular supplementary source of food.

The well-being of the Japanese farmer, generally heavily in debt, is closely linked to the price of rice, and also that of silk. Approximately one family in three raised silk-worms in 1939, and the mulberry is cultivated, mainly in upland country, as far north as about 39° N., with intensive producing districts mainly located in central Honshu. Generally the selling of silk cocoons is a side line. Despite government interest in sericulture standards there was in pre-war years decline in output, and competition of other fibres adversely affects the outlet for silk. Before the war some 50% of the silk produced was exported, mainly to the U.S.A. Other important commercial crops in Japan are tobacco, the production of which is widely distributed even as far north as northern Honshu, and tea, produced in numerous small gardens as far north as 37° N., and in normal years exported in quantity to the U.S.A., where green tea is favoured. Flax, hemp, and rape play a minor role in the rural economy.

Industrial development in pre-war Japan rested upon limited mineral resources, vigorously developed for expanding requirements after a programme of aggrandisement was embarked upon in the 1930s. The

position in relation to coal, gold, and copper was regarded as fairly satisfactory, but petroleum, iron ore, lead, zinc, manganese, tin, and aluminium were markedly deficient in supply; doubtless this played a part
in expansionist plans.

The coal resources of Japan are modest. Reserves have been variously
computed, but seem to indicate supplies sufficient for from one to two
hundred years, at the low pre-war rates of exploitation. Coal production
in 1937 reached a total of only 45 million metric tons, showing a marked
increase over earlier years, and meeting about 90% of domestic needs.
Often mined from thin and faulted seams, the quality was mainly low
grade bituminous or sub-bituminous, with small contributions of anthracite and lignite. About two thirds of the total production came from
fields in north and northwest Kyushu, where coastal position favours
exploitation and the Chikuho field leads. More recently developed fields
in west central Hokkaido accounted for about one-fifth of the output,
the Ishikari field being a leading producer. Only small fields exist in
Honshu, with the Joban area leading.

Japan is poor in petroleum resources and the 1936 production of about
one million barrels left some nine-tenths of requirements to be imported,
largely from the U.S.A., the Dutch East Indies and Borneo. Increasing
amounts were refined at centres in Japan. The leading domestic oilfields
are in western Honshu, i.e., those of Akita and Niigata; a very small
output came from Hokkaido. Nationalization of the petroleum industry
in 1934 showed realization of its importance, and a policy of increasing
storage was adopted, to make 'stock-piling' possible. Further the production of petroleum from coal was stimulated, and commenced on a commercial scale in 1939.

Japan is poorly provided also with iron ore resources, a very serious
weakness. The output of 1936, of some 600,000 metric tons was nearly
double that of 1933, but only represented one-eighth of consumption
needs, in that year of heavy imports. The chief producing areas were the
Kamaishi (magnetite ore) and the Sennin (micaceous iron) areas of northeastern Honshu, and the Kutchan (limonite) district of Hokkaido.

The modern Japanese economic structure, the roots of which go back
to the revolution of 1868, had reached a peak of development when the
Pacific war broke out. Growth for a long time had been slow, but
periods of marked impetus coincided with opportunities presented by the
world war of 1914–18 and the preparations for the second. After 1931
notable features were increasing variety of industrial development, greater
emphasis on heavy industry, and especially after 1937, an increasing proportion of producer goods. A measure of national control was used to

foster industry and direct its expansion; tariffs and subsidies helped to shape development. To some extent old forms of economic organization persisted, as in the silk industry, with many small factories, but there was large-scale introduction of features made dominant in the Occident by the industrial revolution. An important feature of the Japanese economy was the concentration of control in the hands of a small group of families, the Zaibatsu, with resulting ease of manipulation for political ends. Prevalent poverty made for a large supply of cheap docile labour, Japan's greatest industrial asset; the necessity of looking to external markets was urgent. Limitations of natural resources made imports vital; available power was largely augmented by hydro-electric developments, especially in the mountainous areas of central Honshu.

The Japanese industrial belt, a zone of cities, large and small, extends from the Tokyo area to the Nagasaki district and has about three-quarters of the factory population; heavy concentrations are in the Tokyo-Yokohama, Osaka-Kyoto-Kobe, northern Kyushu (Straits of Shimo-noseki), and Nagoya areas; the latter is mainly a centre of light industry. In this zone were the major centres of the cotton, heavy iron and steel, shipbuilding, metal, machinery, enegineering, chemical, and other industries. Only silk reeling and weaving were notably important outside this urban zone, and within it only the northern Kyushu area lacked large scale textile industry, its coalfield being notably associated with iron and steel production.

The Japanese textile industry, although relatively declining, still played an important role in 1939; it then employed about one-third of the factory employees in the country, as against one-half in 1927, and raw silk and cotton cloth were important exports. Silk reeling centres were widely distributed in silk producing districts, workshops for weaving, mainly for the domestic market, were located in many towns. Cotton spinning and weaving were closely limited to the manufacturing belt, carried on in large and small factories respectively, and dependent on imported raw cotton. Rayon industry, centred in large factories, using both home and imported supplies of pulp, developed rapidly in the pre-war years.

From 1930 on the iron and steel industry, dependent largely on imported ore (from China, British Malaya, etc.), imported pig iron from Manchuria and Korea, and scrap from the U.S.A., as well as imported coking coal from China and Indo-China, was expanded at an increasing rate, especially in the Osaka-Kobe area, and in the Muroran district of Hokkaido, as well as in the older Kyushu coalfield area. Japanese production of pig iron in the years 1930, 1937, and 1943 was respectively 1·2, 2·3, and 3·8 million metric tons, and that of steel, in the same years,

2:3, 5·8, and 7·8 million metric tons. Even so the nation was short of steel in the war years, and plants were not running to full capacity owing to lack of materials. During the war supplies of chrome, tungsten, manganese, and nickel were partly met from home sources, including stock piles, and partly by supplies from Korea and China. With the expansion of the iron and steel industry went a great increase in the output of machinery, mainly in the Tokyo and Osaka-Kobe areas, and of chemical industry products, from various centres in the industrial belt. Important shipbuilding industries were located in Yokohama, Kobe, Osaka, and Nagasaki.

Japan is well served in the matter of transport facilities, railways and coastwise shipping playing a dominant part. The road system is poorly developed and mainly serves local needs; the national roads are suited to heavy traffic but reached a total mileage of only 5400 in 1939. Motor transport is rare outside the larger cities. The modern railway pattern largely reflects the old post road system that centred on Tokyo, which was influenced by the physique of the country and distribution of population. The main railways, of narrow gauge type, are state owned; in 1939 there were 10·5 miles of railway per 100 square miles of area, or about one mile to every 4,500 inhabitants. The greater part of the system is single-tracked, the main double-track line being that which links the large urban centres of the manufacturing zone, from Tokyo to Shimonoseki; thence a tunnel leads to the railways of Kyushu. In 1938 about 40% of Japan's tonnage of tramp vessels was engaged in coastwise trade, the high proportion of coastal population and the often rugged terrain of the interior favouring this mode of transport.

DEMOGRAPHIC PROBLEMS

It has been estimated that an almost static population total of about 30 millions was characteristic of Japan for a long period before 1868, when the so-called Era of Enlightenment began. Subsequently the rate of increase was remarkable as estimates prior to 1920 and the census figures for that and for later years show. In 1920, 1930, and 1940 the census totals were 55·96, 64·45, and 73·11 millions respectively, i.e., the annual increase approximated to one million. A declining crude death rate and a crude birth rate of from 30 to 35 per 1000 of population were characteristic of the present century down to about 1935 when, doubtless owing to an increase of restrictive practices, signs of a decrease in the latter appeared. The recent war led to some separation of the sexes and to casualties, and the demographic position was further complicated when,

20

after the defeat of Japan, 4.5 million troops and civilians were repatriated. Allied headquarters in Tokio gave a total population figure of 78,627,000 for October 1st, 1947, as the result of a nearly complete census.[1] This total includes a large proportion of younger people and it is estimated that the total population will increase by 6·5 millions in the next five years.

Internal migration, apart from movement to urban centres on a large scale, has largely confined itself to increased settlement in Hokkaido (Yezo), since 1868 part of Japan proper. In 1870 the Japanese population of this island was about 60,000, mainly concerned with fishing; in 1940 the figure was 3·3 millions, and in addition to fishing, farming had assumed importance, as well as exploitation of lumber, coal, etc.

Emigration from Japan has never taken place on a large scale, and in pre-war years the total of Japanese domiciled outside Japan proper was rather less than two million; of the total, about half were resident in foreign countries. It seems that tropical and sub-tropical climatic conditions attract, and northern climates repel, Japanese settlers.[2] Koreans and Chinese are effective rural competitors, and before their recent expulsion from Korea, Manchuria, and Formosa, the Japanese there were largely town dwellers. Capital invested outside Japan has always tended to be in the field of industry and trade, and this has no doubt had influence on the character of the small scale emigration that has taken place. In the past the Japanese emigrated in some strength to the Hawaii Islands, to Brazil, and to the U.S.A., but exclusion or restriction has become the rule. Reasons include race prejudice, objection to the tenacious allegiance to the home land shown by Japanese nationals, and to their competitive frugality and industry.

The average density of population per square mile in Japan, in 1940, was about 500. Per square mile of cultivated land the density was some 3000; in terms of agricultural population to cultivated land about 1250, a remarkably high figure. The total numbers engaged in agriculture have shown singularly little change in recent decades; the proportion of the entire population so engaged in 1940 was approximately 40%. The distribution of rural population largely reflects intensity of agricultural development, the alluvial lowlands showing high densities, especially south of about 37° N., where climatic conditions are most favourable. The urban population has shown remarkable increase in recent times. Dwellers in towns with more than 10,000 inhabitants, in 1920, numbered 18 millions, in 1940, more than 36 millions. Growth of industrial towns

---

[1] The *Times*, May 10th, 1948.
[2] K. J. Pelzer: "Japanese Migration and Colonization," in *Limits of Land Settlement*, 1937.

with war industries was especially rapid after 1930. In general urban centres, largely located on coastal plains and especially numerous in southern Japan, have old nuclei with a history extending back for many centuries; feudal castles, markets, road centres, ports, shrines, have all played a nuclear role in the development of towns. Exceptional in being of recent origin are some ports, such as Yokohama and Kobe, and towns in recently colonized Hokkaido. Very striking is the concentration of cities in what has become the great manufacturing zone. In western and northern Kyushu are Fukuoka (1940 population 0·32 million), Yawata (0·26), and Nagasaki (0·25). On the shores of the Inland Sea the Settsu plain has no less than 14 cities, including Kyoto (1·09), Kobe (0·97), and Osaka (3·25). On the lowland behind Ise Bay there are 13 cities including Nagoya (1·33). Finally the Kwanto plain is the setting for 28 cities including Tokyo (6·78), Yokohama (0·97), and Kawasaki (0·3). It will be noticed that six of these cities have a population of nearly, or more than, one million. Tokyo, Osaka, Nagoya, Kyoto, Yokohama, and Kobe are metropolitan centres, the two latter, with Osaka, are the three great ports for foreign trade. Between the group of six outstandingly large towns and the next in order of number of inhabitants, Hiroshima (0·34) there is a wide gap; this city, on the shores of the Inland Sea, was one of a group of twelve, which in 1940, had totals between 200,000 and 400,000; some twenty-eight cities had totals between 100,000 and 200,000; fifty-six had between 50,000 and 100,000 and seventy-eight, between 25,000 and 50,000.

THE CONTEMPORARY PROBLEM

Defeat in war brought abrupt cessation to many of the industrial and trading activities of the Japanese. The crux of the contemporary problem is evident from our brief survey of the national economy as it existed in pre-war years. It is the provision of a workable economy in the post-war world for a large population, which must to a very considerable extent be dependent upon foreign trade and urban industry. Many countries checked both any influx of Japanese people and any importation of Japanese goods in pre-war years and Japan has lost the control of those pre-war sources of raw material, and markets, which she had gained by a policy of territorial expansion. The avowed policy of the American occupation authority is to seek to make Japan selfsufficient by 1952–53, if possible, and to make Japan "the workshop of the Far East". It is hoped to obviate the necessity for large American supplies, of food, fertilizer, seeds, and petroleum, by restoring the 1930–34 level of Japanese industry;

in fact the American plan is to permit further expansion, so long as war industries are not revived.[1] Early in 1948 coal production had reached nearly three million tons a month.

The Japanese nation shows a high degree of unity, aided by a long tradition of existence as a separate entity. It is not divided by important differences of ethnic type, of religion or language. Short in stature, yellow skinned, with straight black hair, the Japanese are of dominantly Mongol stock, the outcome of mingling of elements from the mainland of Asia, i.e., from the north, and of other elements from the south; the source of a Polynesian strain is disputed, but not its strong influence on the Japanese physical type and on cultural characteristics. A component element in the physical make up of the nation is the Ainu, the contribution of the aboriginal inhabitants of the Japanese islands. The Ainu people are strongly contrasted with the Japanese, but only a mere remnant remains, some 16,000 in Hokkaido, and small groups in mountain areas elsewhere. The process of annihilation and absorption lasted for many centuries. Many features of Japanese civilization are of Chinese origin; the spoken Japanese language is difficult in itself and difficult to classify. The written language is quite distinct and was borrowed from the Chinese. Illiteracy is rare and the educational system highly developed. It has been argued that the earlier cultural borrowing of the Japanese made easy the adoption of many features of Occidental life after the revolution of 1868, features which, save in the largest cities, form but a veneer on an ancient oriental civilization. A strong military tradition, and habits of diligent and self-sacrificing obedience survive from the long feudal period in Japanese history. Until her defeat Japan was ruled by a small group, closely knit, of army leaders, industrialists, and bureaucrats, with the Emperor, revered as of divine descent, crowning the edifice. Not the least task of the occupation authorities pledged to lead Japan in the ways of western democracy, has been that of undermining belief in the divinity of the Mikado.

The 46 prefectures into which Japan is divided for administration have little significance since there is a high degree of centralization in government, and the capital has dominant influence. The older capital cities were in the west, notably at Kyoto for many centuries. Yedo, since the 1868 revolution known as Tokyo, commenced its rise as a great administrative, commercial, and industrial centre, with its selection as a focus by the feudal rulers of the country in the late 16th century. The choice was deliberate; the new centre was originally a fishing village on the shores of Yedo Bay, in the east, away from the influence of the court. A castle

[1] Report of the *Times* correspondent in Tokyo, March 26, 1948.

was erected on a strong defensive site, bordered by swamps, overlooking
the flood plain of the Sumida river; the mountain approaches to the
Kwanto plain could be defended. A road system was developed that
made possible a grip on all the provincial districts by the usurper Shoguns,
and Yedo grew apace, with a population by 1800 of one million or more.
The castle site, when the Emperor's power was restored, was used for his
palace; it is central in the modern city. The destructive fire and earthquake of 1923 provided an opportunity for planned development. The
port of Tokyo, with an artificially deepened approach channel, some
twenty feet in depth, was in 1941 combined for administrative purposes
with the port of Yokohama, some twenty miles distant, and the joint
port named Keihin.

It was in 1853 that an American squadron, under the command of
Commodore Perry, arrived at Uraga Bay, and effected the opening of
Japanese ports to trade, thus ending a long period of almost complete
self-imposed isolation. In the years that followed it became clear that the
pressure exerted by the western powers could not be resisted, and the dis-
credited feudal régime was overthrown; Japan embarked, in marked contrast to China, on her rise to the status of a great power. Armed forces
were built up on western models, the army after the German, the navy
after the British pattern; a merchant navy was also developed. The Anglo-
Japanese Treaty of Alliance of 1902 only lapsed in 1921 and was of great
value to Japan in a critical phase of her history. Japanese acquisitions on
the Asiatic mainland have already been noted, in relation to Korea, annexed outright in 1910, Manchuria, dubbed Manchukuo in 1932, and
China, invaded in 1937. Islands were steadily acquired as a basis for
naval power in the western Pacific; Kuriles in 1875, Bonins in 1876,
Ryukyus in 1878, Pescadores and Formosa in 1895, southern Sakhalin in
1905, and, as the outcome of participation in the 1914–18 war against
Germany, the Marianne, Caroline and Marshall groups. In the 1930s it
became clear that Japanese plans for a "Greater Sphere of Co-prosperity
in Eastern Asia" were developing on a grandiose scale. Over-confident
of her military, naval, and air strength Japan challenged the United States
by a shattering attack on Pearl Harbour in December 1941. For some
time successes followed in rapid sequence, and Japanese forces controlled
not only Asian territory extending in a continuous zone from Korea to
Burma, but also the East Indies, including the Philippines, in the period
1942–45. However heavy shipping losses doomed this tropical empire to
eclipse, and a series of disasters culminating in the devastation wrought
in the homeland by the atom bomb, brought about the surrender, in

August 1945, of all Japanese forces. G. C. Allen has written, in conclusion to his study of her economic history:

"Japan might well have been expected to render great services to mankind. She was the first and only Asiatic nation to show a great practical capacity in spheres in which Western nations had led the way. By her geographical and her cultural affinities, she was well-fitted to introduce applied science and industrialism to the peoples of Asia and to supply the organizing ability and the advanced technique which those peoples needed so that the burden of their grinding poverty might be lifted. She had already made available to them new kinds of consumption goods at prices which they could afford, and she might have played a leading part in raising further their standard of life. She possessed a resilient economy lacking the rigidities that had appeared in the western world. An immense field of industrial expansion lay before her; but she turned aside from it to pursue other ends."[1]

The ends she now pursues are dictated by her conquerors.

---

[1] G. C. Allen: *A Short Economic History of Modern Japan*, 1867–1937. 1946, pp. 159, 160.

SELECT READING LIST

G. B. Cressey: *China's Geographic Foundations*, 1934.

A. J. Grajdanzev: *Formosa Today* (I.P.R.), 1942.

A. J. Grajdanzev: *Modern Korea* (I.P.R.), 1944.

G. F. Hudson: *The Far East in World Politics*, 2nd ed., 1939.

G. F. Hudson and M. Rajchman: *An Atlas of Far Eastern Politics*, 1940.

E. H. King: *Farmers of Forty Centuries*, 1926.

K. S. Latourette: *The Chinese. Their History and Culture*, 3rd ed., 1946.

O. Lattimore: *Manchuria: Cradle of Conflict*, 1932.

H. K. Lee: *Land Utilization and Rural Economy in Korea* (I.P.R.), 1936.

Sir John T. Pratt: *The Expansion of Europe into the Far East*, 1947.

P. M. Roxby: "The Expansion of China". (*Scottish Geographical Magazine*, 1930).

P. M. Roxby: "China as an Entity". (*Geography*, 1934).

G. B. Sansom: *Japan, A Short Cultural History*, 1946.

G. H. Smith and D. Good: *Japan, A Geographical View*, N.Y., 1943.

R. H. Tawney: *Land and Labour in China*, 2nd ed., 1931.

G. T. Trewartha: *Japan. A Physical, Cultural and Regional Geography*, 1945.

FAR EAST

TABLE XVIII

AREA AND POPULATION *

	Area in sq. miles	Population in '000	Density per sq. ml.	Density per sq. ml. cultivated land
CHINA				
18 provinces ..	1,405,764	400,000	285	
Inner Tibet	434,178	2,869	7	
Inner Mongolia ..	422,236	7,027	17	
Manchuria	407,100	36,903	91	
Formosa	13,890	6,084	434	
CHINA. TOTAL ..	2,683,168	452,883	170	1,480†
KOREA	85,246	24,236‡	284	1,410
JAPAN PROPER ..	147,492	73,114‖	496	3,078§

* Date mainly from *Statesman's Year Book*, 1943; for China estimates for various dates.
† From Cressey, *China's Geographic Foundations*, Table XXXVI.
‡ 1940 census.
‖ 1940, when approximately 50% of the total was urban; total in 1947 78.6 million.
§ From Trewartha, *Japan*, Table 69.

TABLE XIX

PRODUCTION OF COAL, PETROLEUM, IRON AND STEEL *

('000 metric tons 1943).

	Coal	Petroleum	Iron ore	Pig iron	Steel
CHINA					
Manchuria ..	30,000	60†	5,300	1,726	830
Formosa	1,744‡	6‡	—	—	—
Other areas ..	22,250‡	—	1,750‡	156‖	—
KOREA	6,000	—	629	217‡	87‡
JAPAN PROPER ..	41,803‡	341‡	2,770	3,813	7,821

* Data from M. Erselcuk: Iron and Steel Industry in Japan. *Econ. Geography*, April 1947;
A. Rodgers: Manchurian Iron and Steel Industry, *Geographical Review*, Vol. XXXVIII (1948);
Jan. 1948; *Statistical Year Book of the League of Nations*, 1940–41, Geneva 1941.
† Oil from shale 1935.   ‡ 1936.   ‖ 1934.

TABLE XX

JAPAN

AGRICULTURAL PRODUCTION, 1935; % of total crop area.*

Rice	40·8
Barley	10·0
Wheat	8·5
Other cereals	5·2
Beans	7·6
Tubers and Roots†	7·6
Mulberry	7·5
Green manure crops	6·4
Industrial crops‡	3·6
Vegetables	2·8
	100·0

Note.—The Census of October 1947 showed 16·8 million persons employed in agriculture and forestry.

* Based on statistics in *Statistical Abstract of Ministry of Agriculture and Forestry* 1935–6, Japan 1936.
† Irish and sweet potatoes, etc.
‡ Tobacco, sugar, rapeseed, etc.

TABLE XXI

JAPAN

NON-AGRICULTURAL EMPLOYMENT, average monthly, August 1947–July 1948— number in each occupation expressed as percentage of total.*

Manufacturing	36·2
Commerce	17·3
Transport and communications	9·3
Government and other services	9·1
Construction	7·6
Professional services	7·0
Mining	3·4
Fishing	3·3
Other	6·8
	100·0†

* Statistics from *Japanese Economic Statistics*, Bulletin No. 29, Research and Programs Division, General Headquarters, Supreme Command for Allied Powers, Japan, 1949.
† Average total number in employment, approximately 18 millions, of which males numbered 13 millions and females 5 millions.

CHAPTER V

SOVIET ASIA

By W. Gordon East

WHAT has been called the 'invulnerable hugeness' of Russia pays no regard to the conventional limits, many and various, which geographers have assigned since the days of ancient Greece to Europe and Asia north of the Caucasus mountains.[1] 'Asiatic Russia', or 'Soviet Asia' as it is now more appropriately known, is thus an arbitrary truncation of the Soviet Union which, although detached here for study, is politically significant only in relation to the whole U.S.S.R. There are no precise limits defining Soviet Asia on its European side. Modern geographers have usually selected a line along the eastern foot of the Ural mountains and another along the Manych depression of north Caucasus to delimit Europe and Asia, so that Soviet Asia is not one continuous land area. At the end of the 19th century the Volga above Stalingrad was a significant divide between the well settled country to the west and the vast scantily peopled lands to the east, although even then astride the southern Urals population was denser than in the areas to the north, south, and east. Now that the Ural industrial region has developed on both flanks of the southern Urals, the transition from Europe to Asia is increasingly blurred. Further, the boundaries of the constituent states and administrative areas of the U.S.S.R. in no sense recognize a clear continental divide. The dominant republic within the federated Soviet Union, the Russian Soviet Federative Socialist Republic (R.S.F.S.R.) strides from the Baltic, White, Azov, Black, and Caspian seas to the Arctic and the Pacific, and the summit levels of the Urals do not delimit any of its administrative sub-divisions. The crest line of the high Caucasus range, which oddly enough has never been selected by geographers as a boundary between Europe and Asia, is in fact politically significant, for it defines the northern limit of the Soviet Socialist Republics of Georgia and Armenia, and the southern limit of a medley of administrative territories within R.S.F.S.R.

---

[1] Humboldt, writing a century ago, recalled that Herodotus considered northern Scythian Asia (Siberia) part of Sarmatic Europe—this stretched westwards to the Don and Azov Sea —and even part of Europe. *Cosmos*, 7th ed. (1849), II, 137.

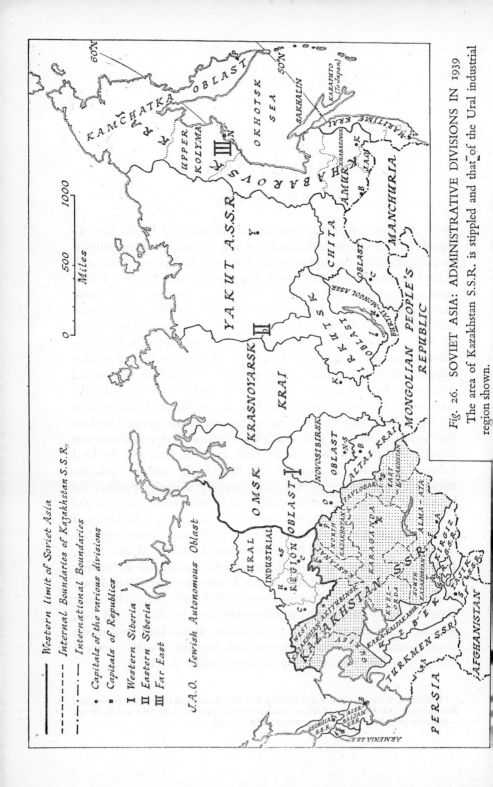

Fig. 26. SOVIET ASIA: ADMINISTRATIVE DIVISIONS IN 1939

The area of Kazakhstan S.S.R. is stippled and that of the Ural industrial region shown.

Map legend:

————	Western limit of Soviet Asia
– – – –	Internal Boundaries of Kazakhstan S.S.R.
–·–·–·–	International Boundaries
•	Capitals of the various divisions
■	Capitals of Republics
I	Western Siberia
II	Eastern Siberia
III	Far East
J.A.O.	Jewish Autonomous Oblast

Scale: 0 — 500 — 1000 Miles

Labels on map: 60 N, KAMCHATKA OBLAST, UPPER KOLYMA, OKHOTSK SEA, SAKHALIN, KARAFUTO (to Japan), MARITIME KRAI, KHABAROVSK, III, KHABAROVSK, AMUR OBLAST, B, K, MANCHURIA, YAKUT A.S.S.R., Y, CHITA OBLAST, C, II, KRASNOYARSK KRAI, IRKUTSK OBLAST, K, BURIAT-MONGOL A.S.S.R., MONGOLIAN PEOPLE'S REPUBLIC, OMSK OBLAST, O, NOVOSIBIRSK OBLAST, N, ALTAI KRAI, B, URAL INDUSTRIAL REGION OBLAST, S, C, C, KAZAKHSTAN S.S.R., WEST KAZAKHSTAN, AKTYUBINSK, NORTH KAZAKHSTAN, PAVLODAR, KARAGANDA, EAST KAZAKHSTAN, SOUTH KAZAKHSTAN, KYZL-ORDA, ALMA-ATA, KIRGIZ S.S.R., KARA-KALPAK A.S.S.R., UZBEK S.S.R., TADJIK S.S.R., TURKMEN S.S.R., AFGHANISTAN, PERSIA, GEORGIA S.S.R., AZERBAIJAN S.S.R., ARMENIA S.S.R.

THE GEOGRAPHICAL SETTING

EXTENSION AND LOCATIONAL FACTORS

Soviet Asia east of the Urals comprises the vast continuous yet strikingly contrasted regions of Siberia and Turkestan, yet to the Soviet citizen these terms grow increasingly less familiar. He would think rather in terms of the Urals, the East, the Arctic, Transbaikalia, the Far East, Kazakhstan, the four Central Asian, and the three Trans (or South) Caucasian republics. Alike in sheer extent and in geographical position, Soviet Asia east of the Urals is comparable only with, as it exceeds in area, the combined territories of Canada, Alaska, Newfoundland, Labrador, and Greenland, its counterpart in the western hemisphere. It stretches west-east for some 4000 and north-south for nearly 3000 miles It flanks the Arctic Ocean for 3000 miles, extends to the north Pacific, abuts in the south on the mountain chains of Central Asia, and in the extreme south-east on the cool, temperate lands of Manchuria. Atlas maps centred on western Europe tend to obscure the proximity of Soviet Asia to North America: only the Bering Strait, fifty-five miles wide and frozen over in winter, divides Siberia from Alaska, which Russia sold—cheaply as it proved—to the United States in 1867. Arctic and sub-Arctic U.S.S.R.. lie on the most direct air routes between North America and monsoon Asia. South Caucasus —the southern limit of which lies as far south as the latitude of New York, Lisbon and Peking—projects towards the isthmian route across Persia to the Indian Ocean. The U.S.S.R.'s Asiatic territories impinge on the frontiers of Turkey, Persia, Afghanistan, and China, as well as on some dependent territories, formerly parts of China, notably Sinkiang and Outer Mongolia. The Soviet-Japanese boundary (along lat. 50° N.) bisecting the island of Sakhalin has disappeared with the cession to the U.S.S.R. in 1945 of its southern part (Karafuto so-called). In area Soviet Asia totals no less than 6·3 million square miles (16·4 million sq. km.): three-quarters of the Soviet Union, nearly two-fifths of the area of Asia, and one-eighth of the land surface of the earth. For statistical purposes (see Tables) certain administrative limits to Siberia in the west and to Caucasia have been used. The western limit of Omsk *oblast* (as in 1939) is taken as the western limit of Siberia, whilst Soviet Asia in the Caucasus region is taken to mean the three republics of South Caucasus[1] (*Fig.* 26). The major constituents of Soviet Asia then appear in area as follows:

[1] This western limit to Siberia seems fitting, since the *oblasti* of Sverdlovsk and Chelyabinsk to the west of it extend across the Urals and form the major elements of the Ural industrial region. If parts of these *oblasti* were included in the concept 'Siberia', clearly the figures for

			Thousand sq. miles
Siberia	..	.. ..	4,730
Kazakhstan		.. ..	1,056
Central Asia	..	.. ..	478
South Caucasus		.. ..	71

6,335

GEOGRAPHICAL PHYSIQUE: SIBERIA AND THE FAR EAST

Siberia, a geographical and not an administrative entity, means the 'northern' land. It includes island groups in the Arctic Ocean which project it northwards beyond lat. 80° N., while in the Far East the peninsula of Kamchatka, the Kurile islands and Sakhalin girdling the Okhotsk Sea, carry it eastwards towards the Pacific Ocean. In the south-west, the Kazakhstan hills and Tarbagatai mountains, lying within the steppe zone, divide Siberia from the Turanian Basin, whilst elsewhere in the south it impinges on the outer ramparts of Central Asian mountain systems and ends in the east along the Amur river or its tributary the Ussuri. Despite the broadly uniform climatic régime and vegetation zones which characterize it, Siberia provides physical contrasts between its western and eastern parts. The Ural mountains descend somewhat abruptly to the West Siberian Basin which is an old sea floor covered by fluvio-glacial deposits; it lies lower than European Russia and its less diversified surface slopes gently towards the Arctic coast. The great Ob Irtish, and Tobol rivers flow sluggishly northwards in steeply-sided valleys and, since the surface is so gently graded, drainage is incomplete, mosses absorb the water, spread and convert great areas into impassable marsh, while peat bogs form from fallen trees. Tundra vegetation in the far north, giving way southwards to tundra forest and marsh forest, is succeeded southwards of the Polar circle by the *taiga*, or coniferous forest zone which, with its included marshes, covers much the greater part of the basin. In the latitude of Tobolsk and Tomsk extends the belt of mixed and deciduous forests which is absent farther east in Siberia. Southwards of latitude 55° this gives place to the feather grass and pasture steppe. These two zones, now widely if discontinuously cultivated, define the optimum zone of western Siberia for rural and urban settlement, for which the Trans-Siberian railway provides the essential means of transport and access. To the south-east, where the steppe is prolonged, although

its area, population and resources would be appreciably greater. It is difficult to reconcile terms like Siberia with present Soviet administrative patterns, and this term may well be regarded as obsolescent.

the *taiga* re-appears on the higher ground, lie the rich agricultural
plateau of Altai and the Kuznetsk basin (Kuzbas), the coal seams of which
condition the chief industrial base of Western Siberia. In contrast to
these more favoured and relatively developed areas of Western Siberia,
the regions of coniferous forest and tundra are scantily settled and inaccessible, save for the summer navigation of the Ob and Irtish rivers and for
maritime intercourse via the elongated Gulf of Ob.

The swiftly flowing Yenisei river, nearly 2400 miles in length and
wholly contained within Soviet territory, lies inside the West Siberian
depression but marks its eastern limit and the approach to the uplands of
Eastern Siberia. This stretches beyond the Yenisei to the Lena-Aldan
valleys: level lowland is now relatively restricted and pre-Cambrian rokcs
(some of the most ancient rocks of the earth's surface) are exposed in
worn-down mountain ranges but mainly in plateau masses. The Yenisei
receives its major affluents from Eastern Siberia, notably the two Tunguska rivers and the Angara, which, carrying more water than the Yenisei
itself (having received the overflow from lake Baikal), descends in a series
of rapids which afford great opportunities for hydro-electricity under-
takings. The Lena is the greatest, as it is the most picturesque, river of
Eastern Siberia. In its change of course above and below Yakutsk it
broadly reflects the trend lines of neighbouring mountains, and flows
between steeply-rising banks of red sandstones, grey granites and slates,
clothed with silver firs and even deciduous trees. The vegetation zones
of Western Siberia are continued but with significant modifications. The
tundra zone lies mainly north of latitude 70° and broadens only where
the Taimyr peninsula projects northwards. Almost the whole of Eastern
Siberia, which is drier and in winter colder than the western basin, even
as far south as the mountain slopes of Transbaikal, is the domain of the
silent and gloomy *taiga* where the spruce, silver fir, and cedar of Western
Siberia give precedence to the pine, and above all, to the larch, which can
tolerate the frozen subsoil and has the most northerly extension. Although
the mixed forest belt does not continue eastwards of Krasnoyarsk, the
taiga includes a substantial proportion of deciduous trees, including the
birch. Nor is the grass steppe represented: it ends in the Kuludinsk area,
east of the upper Irtish. But in Transbaikalia, where 'permafrost' is
reduced or absent, wooded steppe characterizes a number of high-level
basins which extend towards the international frontier. These include the
Minusinsk basin astride the upper Yenisei and, east of the deep structural
trench occupied by lake Baikal, the Ulan Ude and Chita basins: they are
geographically important. They provide grain bases and have thus
fostered rural and urban settlement, and through them passes the Trans-

Siberian trunk railway. In contrast to these pockets of settlement in the south, Eastern Siberia is an almost vacant land, more so than the Far East at comparable high latitudes. Even so, many small settlements have grown up in the goldfields along the Lena and Aldan and on the Lena and Tunguska coalfields; it has also Arctic stations, the new seaport of Igarka, with its lumber mills, over 400 miles up the Yenisei and, situated in latitude 62° N. by the middle Lena river, the pioneer town and airport of Yakutsk. Eastern Siberia, too, is much less inaccessible owing to encumbering marsh. The Yenisei and Lena provide summer waterways far inland, although many of the rivers are too ill-graded for navigation; roads are not wholly lacking and airways now follow the major valleys.

The Soviet Far East, which is enclosed between the Lena-Aldan, the Arctic, the Pacific and the Amur-Ussuri, is rightly conceived as distinct from Siberia, since landforms, climate, vegetation and orientation introduce differentiating factors. The region is mountainous, notably towards the Pacific coast, although the many ranges—Stanovoi, Sikhote Alin, etc.—rarely ascend above 7000 feet. The summer Pacific monsoon and the winter continental monsoon, which are effective coastally as far north as Kamchatka, reduce both winter and summer temperatures. In the south, with the summer rains, the rivers, chief of which is the Amur, rise in flood. The rains continue into August and are followed by hurricanes: harvesting faces many difficulties, and the *taiga* prevails, except in parts of Kamchatka, the lower Amur basin and that of the Ussuri which, especially the last named, have temperate dense monsoon forests, rich in their varieties of trees, mainly coniferous but including some summer-leaf species. The Arctic coast, well embayed, receives many rivers with their loads of fallen trees, and has some small maritime stations. The Pacific coast, which is even longer, stretches as far south as Vladivostock (latitude 43° N.) but the winter freeze, the dense fogs, gales, and the mountainous unsettled hinterland make it as yet of little use for shipping which finds access in the south at a few points, notably Vladivostok, Nikolaevsk, and Petropavlovsk in Kamchatka. Northeast Siberia, although so close to North America, is little passable except by air and by sledge. In the south, the Soviet Far East lies contiguous to Manchuria and Korea and close to the Japanese islands. Vladivostok, situated on the periphery of the Sea of Japan, can be reached from the Pacific only through straits which are either wholly or in part controlled from Japanese territory; this is especially true of the more southerly Tsugura strait which has to be used in winter. As in Siberia, population is largely confined to small areas in the south, where the Trans-Siberian provides transport and lowlands bordering the Amur and the Ussuri make agricul-

ture possible but not flourishing, for the climate grows marginal. Goldfields (notably in the Kolyma valley), lumber camps, fishing, and Arctic
stations draw small isolated groups farther north. It may well reflect the
severities of life in the Far East that it has the highest proportion of town-
dwellers in the Soviet Union.

GEOGRAPHICAL PHYSIQUE: SOUTHERN REGIONS

The most important physical element in the human geography of
Soviet Central Asia is the mountain zone which occurs on, within, and
beyond the southern border of the Turanian basin. Soviet Central Asia
there abuts on the Kopet Dagh, the northern mountain rim of the
Iranian plateau, and on the eastern ranges of the Hindu Kush; farther east
it encloses the lofty Pamir and part of the Tien Shan with its many subsidiary ranges trending generally westwards, and lastly the north-western
end of the Altai system. This mountainous world, by reason of its interior
continental position, its latitude (between 35° and 55° N.), its physical
history and its remarkably high levels with peaks rising to over 20,000 ft.,
constitutes a very distinctive physical environment, the complexities of
which can be only hinted at here. Some of these mountains, notably the
Kopet Dagh and Tien Shan systems, are in origin young and broadly
contemporary with the Alps and the Caucasus; the Pamir, in contrast, of
which the western part is truly mountainous and the eastern part plateau,
represents, like the Altai mountains, ancient folds peneplaned and later
uplifted—a crust block or *massif*. The variety of climates at different
altitudes is reflected in a wide range of vegetation zones. Low precipitation is the outstanding feature: the Kopet Dagh, the highest parts of
which lie in Persia beyond the Soviet border, presents steppe and desert
characteristics, sends virtually no streams down to the Turkmen plain,
and does not raise its summits high enough to produce snow-caps. The
higher ranges to the east have only a moderate precipitation, but they
carry glaciers and snow fields below the limit of perpetual snow and are
thus the source of lakes and rivers which provide, especially with the melting of the snow in summer, the fertilizing streams for the parched plains
and enclosed basins of Turkestan. In short, these mountains in at least
three ways provide opportunities for settlement and exploitation. Their
varied topographic zones allow 'Alpine' high level pasture in summer,
fruit growing and the cultivation of cereals in their valleys up to very high
levels—10,000–14,000 ft., and mineral exploitation, notably in the desert
plateau of Pamir, which has been called a miniature Tibet. Secondly, they
make possible irrigated agriculture (and thus the concentration of popula-

21

tion) along piedmont zones, in enclosed basins (notably those of Ferghana and Vakhsh), on lake-sides and in river valleys in the otherwise desert plain. Thirdly, they provide an effective insulation between U.S.S.R., Persia, India and Sinkiang (Chinese Turkestan), although at the same time they afford a few practicable lines of movement, e.g., from Andijan in Ferghana to Kashgar in Sinkiang.

Physical geography thus defines broadly the location of areas in Kazakhstan and Soviet Central Asia where settlement based on agriculture has been able to establish itself. There is first the broad hilly zone of northern and eastern Kazakhstan which lies astride but mainly to the south of latitude 50°. There the dry semi-steppe, with chestnut or brown soils, less rich in humus than the black earths of the West Siberian steppe, has seen the advent of villages and collective farms with their fields of spring-sown wheat. To the south, with increasing aridity, desert steppe prevails, with numerous salt pans and salt meadows of juicy thick-leaved plants or low-growing wormwoods dispersed over the bare and largely lifeless surface. In the true desert, still further south, which extends from the eastern shore of the Caspian beyond lake Aral to lake Balkhash, only the oases, such as those of Bokhara and Merv, and the valleys of the rivers, notably the Amu Darya (Oxus) and Syr Darya (Jaxartes) provide sites for permanent settlement and the essential water for crops. Again along the southern margin of the Turanian basin, where water and shelter from violent mountain winds are found, a ribbon of irrigated fields extends; there, too, along the piedmont, big cities—Ashkhabad, Tashkent, and Alma Ata—villages, and the routes which bind them, vitalize the desert's edge. But the area of cultivated and settled land is very small, dwarfed by the vast extent of deserts of clay, of stone and above all, of moving sand dunes where little grows for long. Only the sturdy saxaul tree, apart from some scattered vegetation of leafless stalks, finds conditions fit for life in such expanses as Kara Kum and Kizil Kum: useless for shade, it offers valuable hard wood for fuel.[1] Yet the desert is not without potentialities: the grey soils which extend widely are rich in carbonate of lime, and grandiose plans, for example the diversion of the Amu Darya from the Aral lake to the Caspian, may overcome in some areas the negation of drought.

The availability of mineral, fuel and power resources, too, lies behind recent and continuing changes in the population map. In the Central Asian republics water power from mountain-fed streams, as well as small

---

[1] See D. N. Kachkarov and E. P. Korovine, *La Vie dans les Déserts*, Paris, 1942. On the general aspects of the vegetation of Soviet Asia, see L. Berg, *Les Régions Naturelles de l'U.R.S.S.*, Paris, 1941.

coal, oil, and iron resources, allow some industrial development. In Kazakhstan the mineral and coal endowment, associated with Hercynian *massifs*, is generous: coal, copper, chrome, lead, zinc, and iron are all now being exploited—almost wholly a Soviet achievement. In addition oil is derived from the Emba salt dome region north of the Caspian.

To Soviet Asia beyond the Urals must be added Caucasia. Although its economic and political orientation is largely towards European Russia, its Asiatic character is underlined by its proximity (via the Caspian Sea) to Soviet Central Asia and by its position *vis-à-vis* its neighbours of Southwest Asia—Persia and Turkey. The Caucasus mountains, 'Alpine' in structure, extend for some 900 miles N.W.-S.E. across the isthmus between the Black and Caspian seas. The lofty central range, wild and majestic in its scenery and with pyramidal peaks higher than Mont Blanc (15,780 ft.), carry glaciers and snow fields, and are forested below the level of the summer Alpine pastures. As in Central Asia the mountains give rise to great rivers, useful for irrigation and hydro-electric power—the Terek and Kura draining to the Caspian, and the Kuban and Rion to the Black Sea. Low ranges extend parallel to the main chain or obliquely to it; the Suramski range, striking off southwestwards from the main chain, links the mountains with the high Armenian plateau. The Caucasus mountains present a truly formidable obstacle to transverse passage: this is easiest along the maritime plain below the eastern spurs (used by the railway from Baku to Rostov), less easy from Batumi along the Black Sea littoral, and intermediately practicable by two motor roads—the Georgian and Osetian military highways—which, spiral fashion, wind their arduous way up respectively to the Krestovy and Mamisson passes. To the north the descent is steep to the arid Nogai steppe and to the moderately watered Kuban steppe; more gradual to the Stavropol plateau. Southwards of the mountains extends the tectonic depression occupied by the Rion and Kura valleys—but lowlands are limited and discontinuous. The Mugan steppe, south of Baku, is the largest but is arid, and there, as in the Nogai steppe, Caucasia is an extension of Turkestan; that of the Rion basin, smaller in area, receives heavy cyclonic rains. The climatic contrast between the western and eastern sides of Caucasia is striking: in coastal Georgia subtropical conditions obtain—high rainfall, frost-free winters and hot summers (cf. Batumi: January and July average temperatures 43° F. and 73·4° F. and 93 inches of rain); in Azerbaijan, on the eastern side, cold winters, hotter summers and scanty precipitation (cf. the corresponding figures for Baku: 38·1° F. and 77·4° F. and 9·5 inches).

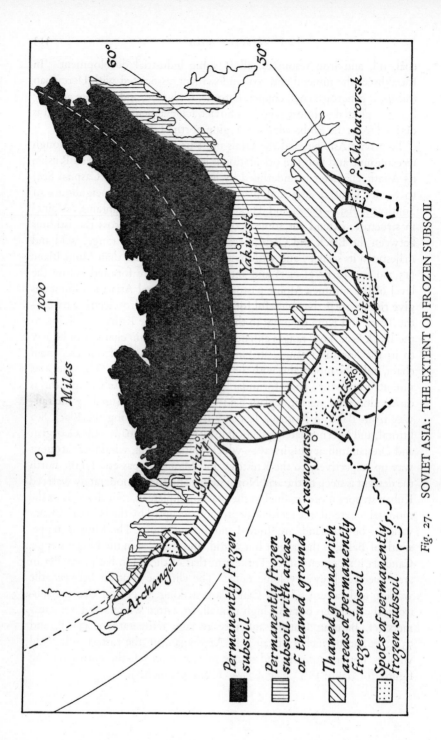

Fig. 27. SOVIET ASIA: THE EXTENT OF FROZEN SUBSOIL

Permanently frozen
subsoil

Permanently frozen
subsoil with areas
of thawed ground

Thawed ground with
areas of permanently
frozen subsoil

Spots of permanently
frozen subsoil

CLIMATE AS A LIMITING FACTOR TO DEVELOPMENT

The well-marked continental régime of the climate dominates the physical setting of Siberian life and regulates the rhythm of its activities in field and forest; it interferes less imperatively with work in factory and mine, but clearly affects more or less rigorously the various means of communication and transport. There are of course climatic contrasts within Siberia, for example the higher summer temperatures of Eastern Siberia compared with those in similar latitudes in Western Siberia where, however, Atlantic cyclones penetrate, if weakly, to bring more rain and less severe winter cold. But the climate generally is characterized by low precipitation (partly as snow), by short but hot summers with rain, and by winters hard and long. A few figures for selected stations broadly illustrate the conditions. July temperatures are as follows. Tomsk 66° F., Irkutsk 65·1° F., Yakutsk 66·5° F., Verkhoyansk 59·7° F., Vladivostok 65·5° F. January temperatures for the same stations are: — 3°, — 5·4°, — 46°, — 59°, and 4·8°. Precipitation, as high as 20 inches a year in the Altai plateau, falls to only 8–12 inches over the greater part of the West Siberian basin; is 14·5 inches at Irkutsk, 4 at Verkhoyansk, and 14·7 at Vladivostok. The winters of Eastern Siberia are much colder but not longer than those of the Western basin: their rigours, however, are not unbearable because the air is dry and largely windless, and the skies clear and sunny. The snowfall is not very heavy and least in Transbaikalia and the Maritime region. Over nearly all of Siberia east of the Yenisei and the larger part of the Far East, but only in the northeast of Western Siberia, 'permafrost' obtains: the subsoil is either everywhere or sporadically frozen all the year.[1] (Fig. 27). This is partly the result of the lack of a deep snow cover and causes trees to root laterally in the shallow top soil which thaws only during summer. The Arctic ports are accessible for little more than two months and even then their use calls for considerable organization; but Vladivostok, with the aid of ice-breakers, is now an all-the-year port. The snow cover is not without considerable value: while it lasts, it offers snow roads everywhere by sledge, but there is not always enough snow for sledging in Transbaikalia and Maritime krai; although in spring rivers flood violently in Siberia, the melted snow usefully waters the ground before the sowing. Air navigation, so well adapted to the great empty spaces, encounters special difficulties in the Arctic, with its long season—three-quarters of the year—without daylight and its winter blizzards. Fogs and gales, too, occur at all seasons in the

[1] The southern limit of permanently frozen subsoil coincides with the average annual isotherm of—2°C.

Bering Strait and in the sea of Okhotsk in summer; in addition, there are the problems of airfield construction above a permanently frozen subsoil.[1]

Siberia accounts for three-quarters of Soviet Asia beyond the Urals, the remaining quarter coinciding broadly with the Turkestan of Tsarist administrative geography. The dead heart of this region is Turkestan proper, now more often called either the Aral-Caspian depression or Turanian basin, which extends westwards to the shore of the Caspian and north of it westwards beyond the Ural river through the broad low gap south of the Urals. The northern two-thirds of Turkestan in the larger sense, which stands much higher than both the West Siberian and Turanian basins respectively to north and south, is geographically transitional. Only part of its drainage is internal, since the upper Irtish and the Ilim drain seawards, whereas in the Turanian basin all the rivers drain either to interior lakes—notably to Aral and Balkhash—or dry up in the desert. The higher elevation secures a rainfall which though low (10–12 inches a year) is higher than that to the south (4–10 inches); and for this reason on the higher ground the steppe presses south with semi-steppe or semi-desert elsewhere, in contrast to the sheer desert (with as little as 4 inches a year) which obtains widely within the Turanian basin proper. Soviet geographers mark the distinction by not including Kazakhstan S.S.R., which covers the northern region, in Central Asia which consists of the four republics located farther south. In recent geological times the Turanian basin was a great sea, connecting via the Strait of Dzungaria with that in the Tarim basin of Chinese or Eastern Turkestan. The enclosed waters of the Caspian, Aral, and lake Balkhash are relics of this sea, and its low floor owes its relief features largely to the effects of erosion and deposition by wind. As in Siberia, a continental climatic régime holds mastery. Despite its latitude, for Soviet Central Asia extends south to less than 40° N., it suffers by its remoteness from the Atlantic, its separation from the Indian Ocean by the mountain ramparts of Central Asia, and its exposure to cold winds in winter from its open northern flank. The winters are very cold for the latitude, for example at Kazalinsk, in the latitude of Crimea, they are as cold as at Murmansk which lies 24° farther north. Winters without freezing are restricted to only a few areas, for example the Ferghana and Vakhsh basins, Ashkhabad, and Termez. Summer heat is intense (July shade temperatures average 80° F.) and produces drought, for precipitation is everywhere scanty.

---

[1] If water mains are laid in frozen subsoil, steam pipes are laid alongside. Highway engineers make use of permanently frozen ground, but have to protect it from summer heat by special ballasting 'to prevent the cold from escaping'. C. A. Middleton-Smith, "Engineering Developments in Asiatic Russia", *The Engineer*, Aug. 31—Nov. 23, 1945.

THE HISTORICAL BACKGROUND

THE WINNING OF SIBERIA

Each of the major parts of Soviet Asia had its own distinctive history, although in different ways and at different times each fell under the sway of an expansionist Russia, the nuclear area of which was the principality of Muscovy founded in the later middle ages. Siberia has become essentially a field of Russian colonization: its varied semi-nomadic population, always scanty, has steadily dwindled before the advance of Russian pioneers. As early as 1499 an army from Novgorod advanced across the north Urals to the mouth of the Ob river and moved upstream to the Tobolsk region. Although this expedition effected the submission of the Ostiaks and Voguls, the Tatars, established to the south in the wooded steppe, were not overcome until nearly a century later, when their defeat near Tobolsk by the Cossacks sent out by Count Stroganov opened up to Russia the route into Siberia. The penetration of Siberia by hunters, trappers, and merchants seeking furs (especially sables) had already begun in the mid-16th century, by which time Russian power was being consolidated up to the Volga—Kazan was captured in 1552—the White Sea and the Caspian. This enterprise was state-sponsored, for furs (to which were added mammoth tusks) were a very valuable source of revenue and the chief item in Russia's foreign trade.[1] The priest and the monk went forward with the trapper and the soldier, their routes through the virtually trackless forests being marked out by the rivers, navigable over great distances and separated by relatively short 'voloks' or portages.[2] The Kama and the Pechora were navigated in the advance towards the Urals en route in turn for the Ob and its tributary the Irtish in Western Siberia. Between the years 1580 and 1618 the Russians reached and set up posts on the Ob river at Obdorsk and Berezov, on the Irtish at Tobolsk and Tara, and even beyond the upper Ob at Tomsk and Kuznetsk. From Tomsk they continued eastwards to the Yenisei and Angara rivers whence they penetrated first northwards down the Yenisei and then east again up its tributary the lower Tunguska. The result of this intrusion was the establishment of a post at Yakutsk in 1630, from which within twenty years pioneers had reached the lower Amur, the Pacific coast at Okhotsk and Anadyrsk and Nizhne Kolymsk in extreme northeast Siberia. With superior weapons—firearms—and political organization, the Russians

---

[1] R. H. Fisher, *The Russian Fur Trade*, 1550–1700, University of California, 1943.
[2] R. J. Kerner, *Russia's Urge to the Sea*, University of California, 1942.

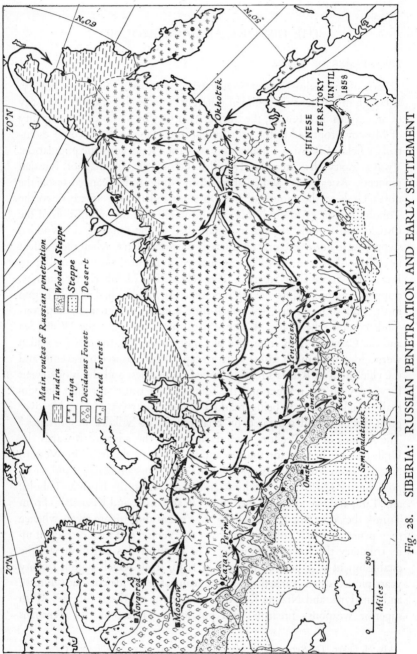

Fig. 28. SIBERIA: RUSSIAN PENETRATION AND EARLY SETTLEMENT

had little difficulty in overcoming the largely nomadic and ill-organized local tribes. Russian settlements, called 'ostrogs' and girt around by strong timbered stockades, were set up at riverside points well chosen for the control of river and portage routes, of the local tribes, and of the collection and shipment of furs, which were exacted as tribute by the Russian masters. Private enterprise was responsible for the advance beyond the Irtish, but the State took charge of territory won. The Siberian settlements made by the Russians in this early phase—before 1700 and mostly before 1650—were nearly all within the *taiga* and mostly towards its southern border (*Fig.* 28). This preference is doubtless explained by their governing interest in the fur-producing forests, doubtless too by the need to avoid the dangers of the steppe lands with their mobile horsemen. Few of the oldest settlements, but notably Krasnoyarsk and Irkutsk—the latter destined to become the gateway to Eastern Siberia—rank among the chief cities of Siberia today, which are found farther south in the wooded and grass steppes. The settlements made at Omsk in the wooded steppe in 1716 and at Semipalatinsk in the grass steppe in 1718 mark the initial stage of their southerly penetration and the beginning of the second phase in Russia's conquest of Siberia during which colonization by Russian peasants was undertaken. The necessity of shipping grain from Russia for the Russian settlers in Siberia was a handicap in the early stage of the conquest.

As in the comparable opening-up of North America in the 19th century, the intruders persisted until they had reached and secured the Pacific shore. The approach to Transbaikalia and the lower Amur, first made from the Lena valley, was later supplemented by an approach from Irkutsk. It is perhaps not always remembered that the Russians reached the Pacific as early as c. 1645, before they had reached the Baltic, and long before they reached the Black and Azov seas. In the lower Amur basin it was hoped to develop an adequate grain base, the lack of which for two centuries made somewhat precarious Russia's hold on the Pacific coastlands. And although they reached the lower Amur valley early, they were unable to hold this sector of the Far East. It formed part of China and was settled by Chinese peasants. The Russians were not strong enough to conquer land held by a sedentary organized population. Indeed Russia had to withdraw by a treaty made in 1689, and it was not until treaties were signed with China in 1858 and 1860 that it secured a legal title to its territorial gains and trading activities in what is now called the Soviet Far East.

EXPANSION TO THE SOUTH

By its more recent conquest of South Caucasus and of Central Asia, Russia embarked upon enterprises of economic exploitation rather than of colonization. In South Caucasus, which after a half century's effort, it conquered between 1859 and 1864, Russia intruded into regions of ancient settlement and civilization on the borderlands of Persia and the Ottoman Empire. With this accession of territory Russia acquired the rich Baku oilfield, which Peter the Great had temporarily annexed from Persia in 1723,[1] an area well adapted to sub-tropical crops, and command of a route, later utilized, acrosss the Caspian Sea into Turkestan.

The Russian advance into Central Asia began in the 1860's. In the north the Russians already held lands bordering Western Siberia which formed part of the steppe habitat of the Kazakh nomads whom they wrongly called Kirgiz. In one sense their advance marked the mastery by the West of the nomad steppes of Central Asia; in another the attempt to secure in its oasis cities control of new markets for Russian manufactures. Already for centuries caravans had plied a small though lucrative trade between Orenburg (now Chkalov), south of the Urals, and the oases of Khiva, Bokhara and Samarkand, whose civilized history can be traced back beyond the Arab conquest (8th century A.D.) and even beyond that of Alexander the Great in the 4th century B.C. Indeed Pumpelly's excavations at Anau, which lies in the extreme southwest of Turkestan near the Caspian shore, showed that grain cultivation and pottery-making began earlier than the domestication of animals on which was to depend the economy of the mounted nomad.[2] The peoples of Central Asia are mainly Turkic-speaking, although there are Mongol elements and the Tajiks are Iranian. In contrast to the vast and scantily occupied areas given over to nomad pastoralists, the small watered areas which supported agriculture and sedentary life were relatively populous and formed politically the bases of Moslem khanates. Russian military expeditions were launched against them first from lake Aral and later from the Caspian coastland: hazardous and protracted ventures, chiefly owing to the acute transport problem of moving supplies, including water, over great areas of steppe and desert. Once begun, the military operations got largely out of control of the Russian government at St. Petersburg and

[1] Peter the Great was already interested in the oil wells which were being exploited in a rudimentary way by the Persian state and Baku was also an important centre for Russian trade. "Go to Baku as quickly as possible" wrote the tsar to the commander of the expedition to Baku in 1722, "and take this city with the help of God because it is the key to our affairs": cited by D. Shakhmazarov, "Oil of the U.S.S.R." in *La Revista Italiana del Petrolio*, No. 130, Feb., 1944.

[2] See T. Peisker, "The Asiatic Background", *Cambridge Medieval History*, Vol. I, Ch. XII.

local commanders were able to extend their conquests freely. Already in the 1860's the cities of Chimkent, Turkestan, Tashkent, and Samarkand fell into Russian hands, to be followed by Krasnovodsk (on the Caspian coast) in 1869, Khiva in 1873, and Merv in 1884.

The consolidation of the Russian conquests involved railway construction. The strategic Trans-Caspian railway was completed by 1888 from Krasnovodsk, via Ashkhabad to Merv and Samarkand, while a branch line from Merv to the Afghan frontier at Kushka was opened in 1898. The Orenburg-Tashkent (Central Asia) line, which had also economic value, was not completed until 1906. The effect of these conquests and railways, by uniting Russia politically with Central Asia and South Caucasus was to establish new frontiers fraught with international interest with Persia, Afghanistan, India, and China in Sinkiang. Russia became much more significantly an Asiatic state: and already in the 1870's, long before Russian railways penetrated Central Asia, grave fears for the safety of India were entertained in Britain.[1]

Into the Central Asian region Russians came at first only in small numbers as officials, soldiers, traders, and experts, settling in separately built quarters of the old towns, and they have never become relatively numerous.

ECONOMIC DEVELOPMENT

THE NATURE OF THE SOVIET EFFORT

This century, and more markedly the last twenty years of the Soviet period, has witnessed such remarkable economic progress in Soviet Asia that geographical accounts of it written as recently as the 1920's appear outmoded and misleading. During the inter-war years 1919-39, by the loss of western territories which accounted for 20% of the industrial potential of Tsarist Russia, the Soviet Union was in effect pushed eastwards, and plans for the better development of its Asiatic territories consistently engaged the attentions of Soviet leaders. Lenin himself was struck by the remarkably uneven concentration of economic resources in a few regions of European Russia, despite the rich natural bases, alike for agricultural and industrial production, afforded in Asia. For the Tsars Asiatic Russia beyond the Urals was a vast colonial dependency, remote and backward, convenient *inter alia* as a place to which Grand Dukes (as colonial governors) as well as political prisoners, criminals and exiles (as

[1] B. H. Sumner, *Russia and the Balkans*, 1870-80 (1937), pp. 35-56.

workers) might be sent and usefully and harmlessly employed.   But already under the Tsars the provision of a skeletal railway system made colonization and industrial development really practicable; by 1913 Baku was producing 7 million tons of oil and the Urals, the metallurgical industries of which began under Peter the Great, produced pig iron and coal.

Soviet policy in the East was clearly defined and rigorously applied in the course of successive five-year plans, the first of which started in 1928. Nothing less than an economic revolution has been effected by the application to Soviet Asia under the direction of Moscow of capital, science, technology, and leadership.   Strategical considerations lent urgency to the task.   The Soviet leaders sought to develop the resources of the Far East the better to counter persistent Japanese pressure.   They sought, too, to strengthen European Russia by adding to it the economic potential of its Asiatic territories.   The aim was to create food and industrial bases, well distributed in relation to natural resources and to consumers, so that productive forces would be better distributed, backward regions and peoples developed, and unnecessarily long rail hauls curtailed. To attain this aim the man-power of the native peoples was necessary: although illiterate and in part nomadic, they have been trained to work in factory, mine, and collective farm.   The plans gave emphasis in turn to different parts of the Asiatic territory, and above all to the Urals.   The Trans-Siberian line was duplicated under the first five-year plans; the Kuzbas industrial base was created under the second (1933-37)—to cite two instances.   Under the third five-year plan (1938-42), the provision of capital and the rate of capital construction were greater in the Urals and eastern regions than elsewhere in the Union.   Moreover, in view of likely war with Germany, factories were built ready later to receive masses of heavy industrial equipment from areas threatened by the German advance.   In the Urals and East armament factories were set up, safe from likely attack.   And the five-year plan for the period 1946-50, while primarily one of rehabilitation and restoration in the war-devastated areas of European Russia, envisages no slackening of economic progress in Soviet Asia.

INDUSTRIAL RESOURCES

As our brief review of the physical background of Soviet Asia hinted, the natural resources for modern industry and agriculture are available there in variety and scale, although their exploitation, largely because of climate and accessibility, raises difficulties, even for Soviet planners armed with optimism and self-confidence. Geological prospecting goes on apace and has a long way still to go; whilst agronomic stations study the problems of plant adaptation to regional environments and the improvement of agricultural technique. In minerals and metals Soviet Asia stands very high for reserves whilst production, rapidly growing and accelerated under the stress of the Russo-German war of 1941–45, is mounting. If the Ural region is included, Soviet Asia contains twice the industrial reserves of coal of European Russia: Kuzbas and Karaganda, in Western Siberia and in Kazakhstan respectively, are now big producers of coal (including coking coal); the first yields over 40 million and the second over 10 million tons a year.[1] In all Soviet Asia is producing 70–80 million tons of coal and is planned to produce 90 million tons in 1950. About three-quarters of Soviet proven oil reserves are located in Caucasia and more than this proportion of its production is derived from Caucasian wells, mostly from Baku: in all Soviet Asia produced about 24 million tons in 1940. There are a number of small oilfields in different parts of Soviet Asia—at Emba[2] (north of the Caspian sea in Kazakhstan), in the Ferghana valley (Uzbekistan), and in the Far East in Sakhalin and near Petropavlovsk in Kamchatka. Oil is imported into the Urals, Siberia, and Central Asia by pipeline (for example, Emba oil is piped from Guriev to Orsk), by tank waggons (e.g., Baku oil by the Trans-Caspian railway from Krasnovodsk), and by sea to the Far East. In contrast, Soviet Asia fuels the Ural smelters and steel-making plant, by railing coal (mainly coking) from Kuzbas and Karaganda, for although the Urals produce over 20 million tons of coal a year, there is not enough of the requisite grades. Return wagons bring back to Kuzbas and Karaganda iron ore from the Urals, for as yet ironstone deposits there are not sufficiently developed. The Ural-Kuznetsk combine is one of the most striking Soviet industrial achievements: this involves long hauls of some 1200 miles, but has facilitated a large-scale development of the iron and steel industry.[3] The 1942 plan to produce over 9 million tons of steel in the Urals and East (cf. Japan's pre-war output of 7 million tons) has now been exceeded: the Urals produce the giant's share; Kuzbas, at Stalinsk, produces over

[1] See Miss D. K. Roberts, "The Soviet Coal Industry," unpublished thesis for the M.Sc. (Econ.) degree of the University of London, 1947.

[2] The Emba oilfield, prospected and developed since 1930, consists of a great number of small oil-bearing beds, in contrast to that at Baku where oil is concentrated in numerous horizons one above the other over a few square miles. The name 'Second Baku' applied to the Emba field was dropped as inappropriate and attached to the immense region between the Urals and the middle Volga.

[3] Had the potentialities of the Karaganda Coal Measures been better known, a Urals-Karaganda combine would have effected some economy in transport. Under the current fourth five-year plan local ore supplies from the Shoria highlands (Kuzbas) are to lessen shipments from the Urals.

2 million tons; whilst other areas, though relatively small producers—Karaganda, Tashkent, Baku, Petrovo-Zabaikal (in Buryat-Mongol A.S.S.R.) and Komsomolsk in the Far East—will expand their capacity. At the present time a heavy industrial base is being created in Kazakhstan at Karaganda. The situation of Kuzbas and Karaganda, remote from the frontiers of the U.S.S.R., is noteworthy.

The resources of uranium in Soviet Asia, as geological prospecting in the 1930's showed, are clearly considerable—and the economic potentialities of atomic energy in this vast region, though difficult to assess, would appear very great. The main deposits occur in a zone extending 300 miles east of Samarkand to the north of the Alai mountains. The principal mines, some of which yield ores as rich as 65–80% uranium, lie within Kirgiz S.S.R. at the eastern extremity of this zone, not far from Osh and its new motor road. Valuable ferro-alloys, such as vanadium and wolfram, are to be got from ores usually found in association with uranium, while thorium, a substitute for uranium, is obtained in the eastern Pamir.[1]

To the fuel and mineral resources already noted must be added the range of precious and non-ferrous metals. The Urals and Eastern Siberia provide the whole of Soviet gold and platinum output: this has been vigorously developed, and the U.S.S.R. is second world producer of gold. In the Urals above all, but elsewhere, notably in Kazakhstan, virtually the whole range of non-ferrous metals are under exploitation—copper, lead, zinc, chrome, nickel (at Norilsk in the Arctic peninsula of Taimyr), aluminium (in Kuzbas), quicksilver (Central Asia), manganese (Georgia, Kuzbas and Kazakhstan), ferro-alloys (Transbaikalia, Kazakhstan, and North and South Caucasus). Add to the output of metals, the availability of other industrial minerals—asbestos (Urals), mica and graphite (Eastern Siberia), abrasives and common salt and, in the mountainous regions of Central Asia, South Caucasus and in the Far East, developed and potential supplies of hydro-electricity, and it is easy to see that the Soviet policy of creating a series of distributed industrial bases can, under rigorous planning, be achieved. It is noteworthy that U.S.S.R.'s domestic supplies of tin, which were seriously deficient, are increasing substantially: to the few thousand tons extracted from the ores of the Chita region of Transbaikalia, must now be added much greater supplies from those of northeastern Siberia unless Soviet reports are grossly exaggerated.[2] The great

[1] "Soviet Uranium Resources," The Economist, Nov. 26th, 1949. This summary draws some of its information from The Great Soviet Encyclopaedia, vol. 56, pp. 245–247, published in 1936.

[2] See Major C. J. Webster, "The Development of Industry, Agriculture and Transport in the Soviet Arctic and Sub-Arctic north of Lat. 60°," unpublished M.A. thesis of the University of London, 1948.

wealth of the forests, limited mainly by transport deficiencies, provides another industrial asset in Siberia, Caucasia and Central Asia. Agriculture, too, offers some valuable industrial raw materials—especially the cotton and raw silk of Central Asia.

AGRICULTURE, POSSIBILITIES AND PROBLEMS

New forms of agrarian organization—the *Kolkhoz* (collective farm) and the *Sovkhoz* (state farm), the mechanization of agriculture made possible by the provision of All-Union motor tractor stations, the appilcation of science to agriculture (seed selection, pest control, the use of mineral fertilizers, etc.), construction works for irrigation—all these planned measures have been instrumental in the development of agriculture in the Asiatic territories. The local difficulties to be overcome are many: the short growing season, irregular, marginal or even inadequate precipitation, the long winter freeze, transport deficiencies and, in some regions, native populations which traditionally followed the nomadic way of life and despised sedentary agriculture. Remarkable success has been registered during the Soviet period in expanding the area under grain and that under irrigated crops, chiefly cotton. Nor, although Nature sets somewhat rigid limits to this expansion, has the whole area of cultivable land yet been brought under the plough.

In the whole of Asiatic Russia beyond the Urals 13·6 million hectares were cultivated in 1911; by 1938 the cultivated area was 26·1 million hectares and subsequent increases, especially during the Russo-German war, must have raised this figure well above 30 million. Yields too are much higher. The outstanding areas for grain production are Western Siberia and Kazakhstan. Effort has concentrated there on the steppe which is in part covered by 'black earth' soils rich in carbonate of lime. These areas have at least the necessary minimum of trunk railways and feeder lines—the Trans-Siberian from Novosibirsk and Omsk, the Turk-Sib linking the Trans-Siberian with Central Asia and the Barnaul-Akmolinsk line, while their level, broad, open surfaces, recalling the North American prairie, invite the tractor and the combine-harvester. Snow melt and spring and summer rains are usually just about enough for the crops, which are very largely spring-sown; wheat predominates, with some oats, millet, barley, and flax. The increase of the area under cultivation has been considerable:

TABLE XXII

WESTERN SIBERIA AND KAZAKHSTAN

CULTIVATED AREA (MILLION HECTARES)

	(1928)	(1938)		(1950 plan)
Western Siberia	7·76	10·30		..
of which:				
Omsk oblast	..	1·99	3·14	..
Novosibirsk oblast ..		2·35	3·23	..
Altai krai ..	..	3·43	3·90	..
Kazakhstan S.S.R. ..	4·25	6·11		7·286
Totals ..	12·01	16·41		

Western Siberia and Kazakhstan have become in fact supply regions for the industrialized urban regions of Central and Northern Russia; they supplement, too, the local production of Central Asia, Eastern Siberia and the Far East. Russians claim that they have created in Western Siberia and Kazakhstan a new Ukraine. The claim is not unreasonable. In 1937 they produced about two-thirds as much grain as the Ukraine, whose grain area was shrinking. This was 17·8 million hectares in 1938, as against about 13·5 million in Western Siberia and Kazakhstan, but the Ukraine's yield is relatively high since the greater part of the cereals are winter-sown. Kazakhstan, too, stands out as the largest cattle-rearing base of the U.S.S.R., much use still being made of its abundant seasonal pasture. North Caucasus, too, just outside Soviet Asia as defined above (p. 307) produces much surplus grain, sunflower oil and meat.

Central Asia, in contrast, is normally deficient in grain, for the reasons that it specializes on technical crops the cultivation of which is made possible by irrigation and that much of its grain area is unirrigated. Irrigation, of the gravity flow type, had already been started there in Tsarist times, and has been extended steadily during the last twenty years. The irrigated area, some 3·5 million hectares in 1937, is now some 6 million hectares and further increases are planned: it adjoins the chief rivers (Syr Darya, Amu Darya), covers parts of the floors of the basins of Ferghana and Vakhsh, and sporadically edges the plain below the mountains. Cotton is the chief product (of which Uzbekistan produces most), but rice, citrus fruits, tobacco, wheat, fodder and sugar beet enter into the rotations. For the most part the cotton is railed to Central Russia, although large textile factories, such as those at Tashkent and Barnaul, have been built and others are being completed at Kuzbas, Ferghana, and Stalinabad. The needs of the cotton fields for nitrate fertilizer (an alternative use for which is high explosive) explains the great nitrate plant, near Tashkent, which derives its power supplies from the neighbouring hydro-electric plant on the Chirchik river. The grain deficiency of Central Asia is overcome by shipments from Western Siberia by the Turk-Sib railway which also brings timber and takes back ginned cotton, fruit, and wine. The rest of Soviet Asia, for various reasons—the high proportion of town-dwellers, the extent of mountainous land, climatic difficulties and specialization on technical crops, is deficient in grain. South Caucasus, which, in Georgia, enjoys an abundant rainfall, provides maize, tea, wine, cotton, citrus fruits, silk, and imports grain by sea from either North Caucasus or Ukraine. Eastern Siberia,[1] although it produced in 1938 four times as much grain as in 1913, cannot wholly meet its own needs; but animal husbandry, cattle and horse-rearing especially, is more important there. The Soviet Far East, despite the fact that its agriculture enjoyed the highest degree of mechanization in the U.S.S.R., actually registered only a small increase in grain area from 608,000 hectares in 1913 to 662,000 in 1938 when it was necessary to import—from North America and Western Siberia—60% of its total grain requirements. Shortage of labour, which is attracted to urban industries and to the more congenial city life, as well as deficiencies in the climate, are the main causes of this backwardness in agriculture, for which remedies are now being sought. In contrast to the shortage of breadstuffs, there is an abundance of fish. The summer fishery, organized from Vladivostok, Nikolaevsk, Sakhalin and Kamchatka, yields a rich harvest—some 400,000 tons a year—and has given rise to a large-scale canning industry. The rearing of animals, chiefly cattle and horses, is less important than in Eastern Siberia.

The economy of Soviet Asia has been conceived and developed as an integral part of that of the Soviet Union as a whole, but enough has been said to show that it is expanding and will continue to expand and that, in accordance with Soviet plans, its several major regions should achieve an increasing degree of self-sufficiency in foodstuffs, fuel and power, and in the products of heavy and consumer industries. In contrast with many other regions of Asia, this region escaped war damage; not only that but its economy was stimulated under war conditions. It has not yet reached the limit of its agricultural development, despite the considerable expansion—some 12 million hectares—recorded for the Urals and eastern regions between 1938 and 1944. Indeed the Soviet expert Laptiev gave official estimates in 1940 for a potential increase in the arable area beyond the Urals of some 30 million hectares—half in Kazakhstan and nearly half

[1] I. D. Laptiev, *Distribution of the Socialized Grain Industry* (in Russian) 1940, pp. 159–163.
22

in Siberia. Coal, oil, and minerals set no narrow limits to industrial expansion, although oil, so necessary for mechanized agriculture, aviation, and industry, has in part to be imported. Other deficiencies—manganese, cement, tin, and aluminium[1]—are being overcome. Natural rubber is deficient, despite the attempts to produce it from kok sagiz and other plants; but at least one of the synthetic factories is located in Asia—at Erivan in Armenia S.S.R., where ample supplies of hydro-electric power are available. The major limits to the economic stature of Soviet Asia, as also of its political stature, are found, not so much in its natural resources as in its climate (drought and cold) and also in its relative command of man power and means of transportation.

DEMOGRAPHIC CONSIDERATIONS

PIONEER DYNAMISM

The population of Soviet Asia is remarkable not only for its paucity in relation to area and for its uneven distribution, but also for its rapid rate of increase (see Tables XXVI and XXVII). The population which totalled 41 millions in 1939 now exceeds 50 millions, for there was a considerable inflow of workers and their families from European Russia during the 1941–45 war and natural increase has doubtless continued to operate.[2] Thus a population numerically comparable with that of the British Isles occupies an area fifty times as large. *Fig.* 29 shows broadly the distribution of urban settlement and the areas which are in varying degrees settled. It shows also that the chief concentration of towns occurs in the contiguous zones of Kuzbas and Altai Territory in Western Siberia. The average figures of population density (see Table XXVII) of course obscure the fact that vast areas are virtually empty. Actually *Fig.* 29 gives an exaggerated impression of the distribution of population for, apart from scattered mining settlements, Arctic stations, etc., this is largely confined to towns and villages within the cultivated area which amounted in 1938 to only 110,500 square miles—merely 1·7% of the total area. One can conceive, therefore, of the bulk of the population of Soviet Asia as being concentrated within an area about as large as the British Isles in elongated zones

---

[1] The chief refinery is in the Urals at Kamensk, and another has been built in Kuzbas. Plans exist for building refineries in Soviet Asia where hydro-electricity can be made available.

[2] F. Lorimer has estimated that some 10 million people were evacuated from the areas occupied by the German army in 1941. The greater part was re-settled in the Volga and Ural regions. Few were sent to the Far East, but the number moved to Western and Central Siberia, Kazakhstan and Central Asia must have totalled a few millions. These transferences were made in accordance with plans for agricultural and industrial development under the third five-year-plan (1938–42). See his *The Population of the Soviet Union* (1946).

and discontinuous oases, surrounded by much greater expanses of *taiga* and desert where only outliers of scanty population sporadically occur. But, whereas the average density of population per square mile for Soviet Asia in 1939 was only 6·5 persons (a figure similar to that for High Asia), the average density per square mile of cultivated land was 363 persons. That is to say, the population of Soviet Asia as a whole falls short of its food supplies. The above figure—363—may be compared with those for Canada (115) and Australia (260), each of which in stage of development and in physical environment is in some degree analogous with Soviet Asia. It contrasts sharply with figures for the monsoon lands (see above p. 302).

But although the population of Soviet Asia is relatively small, it nevertheless shows that remarkable rate of growth characteristic of pioneer lands. The following figures show how the population of Soviet Asia has grown in this century, most markedly in Siberia:

TABLE XXIII

SOVIET ASIA: POPULATION IN 1897, 1926 and 1939, in millions.

	1897	1926	1939
Siberia	5·76	11·35	16·58
Kazakhstan	2·47	6·07	6·15
Central Asia	5·88	7·59	10·48
Soviet Asia (east of Urals) ..	14·11	25·01	33·21
South Caucasus*	4·05	5·86	8·03
SOVIET ASIA	18·16	30·87	41·24

* The figure for 1897 is adjusted to apply to the comparable Soviet area.

An important cause of this increase was the immigration of Russians (Great Russians, White Russians and Ukrainians) from beyond the Volga. It is estimated that over the period 1901–1914 about 6·5 million Russian migrants settled in Asiatic Russia, and of this total about two-thirds moved in during the years 1891–1901 when railway construction gave new mobility and opportunities. The Trans-Siberian, in particular, by opening up the steppe zone to agricultural settlement, stimulated the movement. Only about one-sixth of the total number of migrants 1801–1914 is accounted for by political prisoners and exiles, the great bulk being free peasants.[1] Indeed the inflow of population was due to popula-

---

[1] Serfdom had no place in Siberia: hence the political alertness of the Russian settlers (Sibiriaks) and their movement for political autonomy which failed with the victory of the Bolshevik forces in 1920.

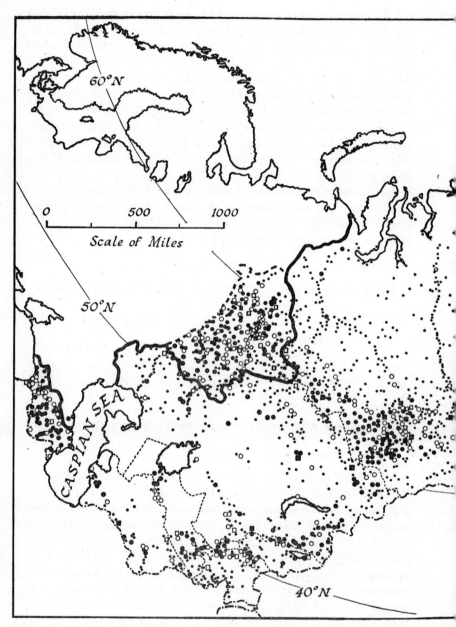

Fig. 29. SOVIET ASIA: DISTRIBUTION

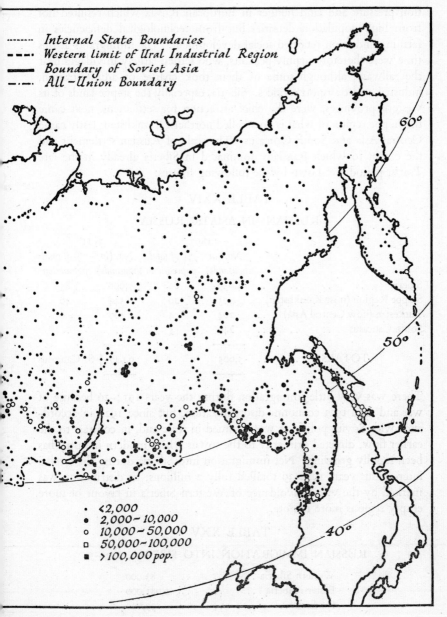

Internal State Boundaries
Western limit of Ural Industrial Region
Boundary of Soviet Asia
All-Union Boundary

- <2,000
- 2,000 ~ 10,000
- 10,000 ~ 50,000
- 50,000 ~ 100,000
- >100,000 pop.

60°

50°

40°

OF POPULATION CENTRES

tion pressure and land hunger in European Russia which resulted not from high population densities but from technological deficiencies in farming and from retarded social development. The immigrants at this time were therefore mainly peasants, who settled largely in villages near the railways, although some of them took charge of administration, industry, and transport services. Siberia, especially the steppe lands of its western provinces, were the chief attraction for settlement, next came the steppe region of what is now called northern Kazakhstan; lastly came Central Asia and South Caucasus. The scale of Russian settlement and the extent to which Russians dominated in Siberia already in the late Tsarist period are shown by the following figures:

TABLE XXIV

RUSSIANS IN ASIATIC RUSSIA

	1897		1911	
	No. (in thousands)	% of total population	No. (in thousands)	% of total population
Siberia	4,659	80	7,996	85
Steppe Region (now Kazakhstan)	493	20	1,544	40
Turkestan (now Central Asia) ..	204	4	407	6
South Caucasus	249	5	..	..
TOTALS	5,605		9,947 +S. Caucasus	

There was very little immigration during the years 1914–26 because of war and until 1921 economic disorganization, but since 1926 in accordance with Soviet policy, it was resumed in scale and, in contrast to the earlier flow, directed primarily to the towns where modern industry has been rapidly growing. Net immigration into Siberia during the twelve inter-census years 1926–39 totalled fully 2 millions; its distribution was marked by the virtual avoidance of Western Siberia in favour of more empty regions more remote.

TABLE XXV

RUSSIAN IMMIGRATION INTO SIBERIA, 1926–39

Western Siberia	83,000
Eastern Siberia	1,081,000
Far East	899,000
TOTAL ..	2,063,000

Western Siberia has the highest density—9.8 persons per square mile: this compares with 1·9 in Eastern Siberia and 2·1 in the Far East (see Table XXVII). Similarly about 1.5 million immigrants contributed to the growth of population in Central Asia during the same period. In contrast to Central Asia, Kazakhstan showed a virtually stationary population over the period 1926–39, whilst the Kazakh ethnic group, as recorded, sharply declined (see Table XXIX). This is probably in large measure the result of excess deaths among this formerly nomadic people when disorganization and livestock depletion occurred with the introduction of collective farming during the years 1928–34; but there was also some emigration across the frontier into Sinkiang. South Caucasus, the most densely settled part of Soviet Asia (113 per square mile), also showed its own demographic peculiarities. It has not attracted immigrants in large numbers and its rapid increase of population is attributed mainly to the high fertility rate of its peoples. Thus in South Caucasus and Central Asia the indigenous populations remain predominant; in contrast Russians dominate Siberia, except in Yakuk A.S.S.R. and the remote north generally, forming 90–95% of its population; whilst in Kazakhstan S.S.R. they are now approaching one half the total population.

URBANIZATION

Side by side with the inflow of people from outside, an internal movement from the country to the town has also stimulated a remarkable growth of towns in Soviet Asia. Collective farming, coupled with mechanization, has served to economize labour in the country notwithstanding increases in the cultivated area. Rural population increased during the period 1926–39 only in South Caucasus and Central Asia, decreased in Kazakhstan where the growth of towns was phenomenal, and remained stationary in Siberia. The proportion of the population classified as urban is shown in Table XXVI for the various regions: for Siberia as a whole the figure was 33%; compare those for South Caucasus 32%, and for Kazakhstan and Central Asia, 28% and 23% respectively. In Siberia it was lowest in the West (29%), rose to 35% in Eastern Siberia, and to 48% in the Far East. There are now probably about forty towns in Soviet Asia beyond the Urals with populations of over 50,000, including eight containing 200,000 or more people (Table XXVIII). Tashkent, the largest, continued to grow rapidly during the Russo-German war (1941–1945) as a centre for refugee population and evacuated industrial plant: it may now number some 750,000. Next in scale is Novosibirsk, followed by Omsk, Irkutsk, Alma Ata, and Vladivostok. Some of the industrial towns are mushroom growths of the inter-census period, notably Stalinsk (in Kuzbas), Karaganda and Balkhash (Kazakhstan), and Komsomolsk, Blagoveshchensk and Magadan in the Far East, but many are old cities revitalized by new industries. The growth of cities is evidenced in all the major regions of Siberia but most strikingly in the Far East, formerly noted for its extractive industries only—timber, furs, gold, and fish. Yakutsk reached the 50,000 mark soon after the 1939 census; the gold-mining 'towns' of the Aldan river region together have a population of over 50,000; Port Igarka in the Arctic has a permanent population of more than 30,000; whilst the new industrial town of Magadan on the Pacific coast, with its deep sheltered harbour of Nagaevo, both of which serve the Kolyma gold industry, is believed to have already a permanent population of 50,000 greatly swollen during the summer season. Komsomolsk ('City of Youth'), founded on the lower Amur in 1932 by 4000 members of the Communist Youth Organization, grew to 71,000 in seven years; it is on the Baikal-Amur railway, has a river port, big ship-building yards and the 'Amurstal' iron and steel works, the heavy industrial base of the Far East. Stalinabad, capital of Tajik S.S.R., grew in numbers 15 times between 1926 and 1939, largely as a result of its railway link with the Central Asia system. The old cities of South Caucasus expanded at more sober rates: Baku with well over 800,000 inhabitants, remains the largest city of Soviet Asia. And Tbilisi (Tiflis), with 519,000 inhabitants in 1939, exceeded the biggest Siberian city Novosibirsk, which had 406,000 and now doubtless exceeds half a million.

Enough has been given to indicate the currents of change which are drastically altering the demographic scene in Soviet Asia. This now commands a large and growing industrial population, which includes native peoples once engaged in either agriculture or nomadic husbandry. The great bulk of the population aged nine years or over can now either read or write (Table XXVI) and, whilst native languages persist, Russian is clearly destined to provide the *lingua franca*. An addition to the man-power of Soviet Asia are the unfree labour gangs, for which reliable figures are not available, and which, under the control of the political police of the All-Union M.V.D. (Ministry of Internal Affairs), are used in various ways—in the mines, forests, in railway construction and in remote and desolate regions to which it is difficult, even with inducements, to attract enough free labour.

TRANSPORTATION

RAILWAY POLICY

Soviet Asia depends primarily on railways for the integration of its political and economic life (*Fig.* 30). Built in stages as Russia conquered and consolidated its authority, and virtually doubled in length during the Soviet period, the railways were designed mainly for political and strategical purposes. Inevitably they fostered colonization and economic development, and in recent decades economic needs clearly account for many of the new lines, such as the Turk-Sib, Barnaul-Kartali and those from the Karaganda coalfield. There is strictly speaking no real network of railways in Soviet Asia, only trunk lines with a small number of feeder lines, which serve rather to bind Moscow to the Asiatic regions and to the ports of the Pacific and Caspian than to interrelate closely Soviet Asia itself. Indeed proportionately to its area Soviet Asia appears poorly served by railways—it has rather less than 3 miles of track per 1000 square miles.[1] But the great importance of these railways should not be underestimated. Built 5 ft. in gauge, reasonably well maintained and capable of carrying train loads very heavy by British standards, they are united with the railway network of European Russia, the main base of Soviet population, economy, and power. Further, since railways are as yet little developed north of latitude 56° N., those available are concentrated within the southern settled areas, serve all the important towns and make many approaches to the international frontiers. More than that, lines on the same broad gauge are prolonged outside the U.S.S.R. into neighbouring territory—to Tabriz in north Persia, to Ulan Bator (Urga) in Outer Mongolia, and into Manchuria.

The Trans-Siberian railway should be regarded as an efficient continental railroad,[2] comparable in its functions with those of Canada and the United States. For the U.S.S.R. it is an arterial way, which unites European Russia, the Urals and Siberia; it gives access to the Pacific ports of Port Arthur, Dairen, Vladivostok and Soviet Harbour; it is also, as Stanford's map described it in 1907, if now only for Soviet citizens, 'The Great Land Route to China and Korea'. From the Urals the main line runs from Chelyabinsk, while another, from Sverdlovsk, where lines

[1] The length of track in Soviet Asia has increased considerably since 1913 when it was equivalent to 0.6 km. per 1000 sq. km. (1.54 miles per 1000 sq. miles), the figure given by *Les Chemins de Fer en U.R.S.S.*, Presses Universitaires de France, 1946, p. 10. A rough estimate of present mileage reaches a figure of 16,400, divided as follows: Siberia 8000 miles, Kazakhstan 4000 miles, Central Asia 3000 miles and South Caucasus 1400 miles.

[2] The automatic block system is installed and S.O. tender-condenser locomotives are used to eliminate the cost of heating of low temperature feed-water in winter.

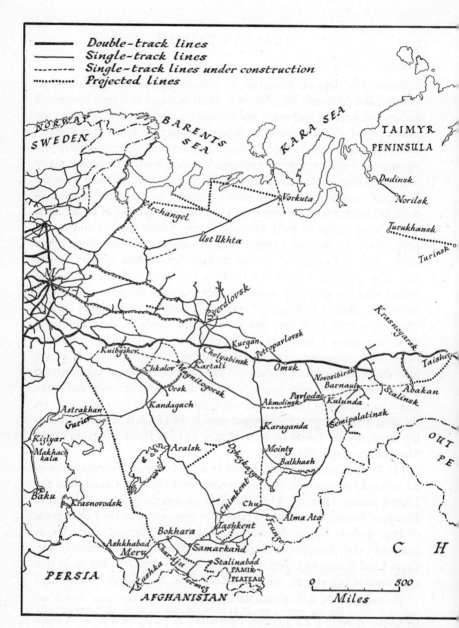

Fig. 30. SOVIET ASIA

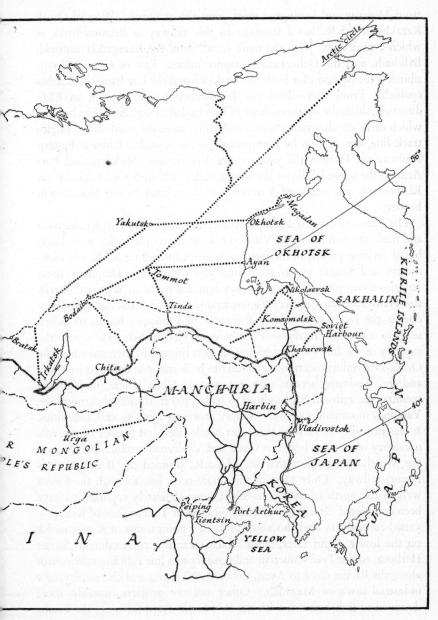

RAILWAY PATTERN

from Moscow and Leningrad meet, joins this at Omsk. West of Omsk Kazakhstan S.S.R. has a frontage to this railway at Petropavlovsk at which a feeder line joins the main trunk from the Karaganda coalfield, Balkhash, and the Dzhezkazgan copper mines. East of Omsk, Novosibirsk is the junction for both the Turk-Sib and the line from the Kuzbas coalfield. From Novosibirsk the Trans-Siberian continues in an ESE. direction, skirts the southern shore of lake Baikal *en route* for Chita beyond which there are alternative routes to Vladivostok: the more direct single-track line, the first to be constructed, is the so-called Chinese Eastern Railway via Harbin, the junction for Vladivostok, Mukden, and Port Arthur; the second follows the Amur valley within Soviet territory via Khabarovsk and sends off a number of short lines to the Manchurian border.

The Trans-Siberian is double-tracked from Chelyabinsk to Khabarovsk and triple-tracked thence to Vladivostok. It is provided with well distributed fuelling points, numerous repair shops for rolling stock, and locomotive and wagon works (at Stalinsk and Ulan Ude). Despite its great length—some 5000 miles—and heavy regional traffic in Western Siberia, the Trans-Siberian can carry a considerable through traffic, as was shown during the recent war by the shipment to European Russia of Allied supplies unloaded throughout the year at Vladivostok. However, the capacity of the line for through transport is limited by two stretches: the Omsk-Novosibirsk section which carries bulk traffic in coal and iron ore, and the 'Molotov' section east and west of Chita where, in highland country, the railroad has to climb to over 3300 ft. to tunnel through the Yablonoi mountains and water supply in winter raises special difficulties. It was probably in view of this latter bottle-neck and further of the vulnerability of the line between Chita and Vladivostok which lies close to the Manchurian border, that the U.S.S.R. planned the BAM (Baikal-Amur) railway. Only parts of this single-track line through the forests well to the north of the Trans-Siberian are definitely reported to have been completed. It leaves the Trans-Siberian at Taishet (east of Krasno—yarsk) *en route* via Bodaibo and Tynda to a point south of Komsomolsk on the lower Amur river, from which there is a connection to Soviet Harbour, to the Trans-Siberian and possibly to a line running northwards along the Pacific coast to Ayan, Okhotsk, Nagaevo and the nearby new industrial town of Magadan. Other railway projects, notably those designed to link Yakutsk with the BAM, the Trans-Siberian, the Pacific coast and the extreme northeast of Siberia, have as yet scarcely started for, even if abundant forced labour is available, these require great lengths of track and face very considerable physical difficulties. The line from the

Trans-Siberian near Never, which is projected to Yakutsk, has been built only so far as Tynda, through which the BAM will pass.

The BAM in Eastern Siberia—duplicating the Trans-Siberian railway— is to be continued through Western Siberia and Kazakhstan by the Southern Siberian trunk line, *south* of the Trans-Siberian, connecting Taishet, Abakan, Stalinsk (the ferrous metallurgical centre of Kuzbas), Barnaul, Kulunda, Pavlodar, across the Kuludinsk steppe to Akmolinsk, Kartali, and Magnitogorsk, whence the line continues across the Urals to Kuibyshev on the Volga. The sections Akmolinsk-Magnitogorsk and Kulunda-Pavlodar, the former built during the Russo-German war, are already in use; the rest, except for the Abakan-Taishet section, is to be constructed under the 1946–50 plan. The South Siberian trunk line will serve *inter alia* in carrying westwards coal from Karaganda to Magnitogorsk and the Volga, and grain from Kazakhstan and the Altai Territory of Western Siberia. Through Kazakhstan also passes the Central Asia line from Uralsk to the State capitals of Tashkent, Frunze and Alma Ata, a north-south line from Petropavlovsk on the Trans-Siberian via Karaganda to Mointy and lake Balkhash, and the Turkestan-Siberian line via Semipalatinsk. The only other trunk line in Soviet Central Asia, single-tracked like the others, is the Transcaspian line from the Caspian port of Krasnovodsk which runs to Ashkhabad, the Turkmen capital, thence via Merv and Bokhara to Stalinabad, Samarkand and Tashkent. It is a difficult line to operate, since part of its capacity has to be used in carrying the fuel and even water essential to its working but lacking along its route. From Merv and Bokhara lines leave the Transcaspian for Kushka and Termez, stations on the Afghan frontier. The recent development of the Kazakh port of Guriev near the mouth of the Ural river on the north Caspian should be noted: it is equipped for handling oil and piping it inland (to Orsk) and has railway connection to the Central Asia line at Kandagach. The Soviet press reported recently that a railway is being built 400 miles long across the Kara Kum desert: this may well be the line, known to be projected, along the Amu Darya valley on its western side between Chardjou and Kungrad. None of the railways of Soviet Central Asia and Western Siberia continues beyond the international frontier: mountains forbid such extension almost everywhere. Finally in South Caucasus railways are few: the main trunk line from Baku via Tbilisi (Tiflis) to Batumi—is partly electrified, notably in the sections which lead to the Suram Pass; the coastal line from Baku via Makhach Kala *en route* for Rostov with a connection via Kizlyar to, but not across the Volga, near Astrakhan; and the line which follows the Arax valley, hard by the international boundary, to Erivan and beyond, from which lines continue (on the same gauge) to Tabriz in northern Persia and to beyond Kars in northern Turkey.

To the skeletal railway system of Soviet Asia, the extension of which is in progress,[1] must be added the facilities now provided by highways, airways, and navigation by river, lake, and sea. In contrast with North America, motor transport does not bulk large, but metalled highways, closely following the railways, are available throughout the length of Siberia, with many military roads leading off to the border in Eastern Siberia and the Far East. These highways are not always all-weather roads; some are little passable when the ground thaws, while river floods, such as those of the Amur in summer, may suspend traffic. Roads, too, often provide the only surface means of transport in areas such as Yakutsk, remote from railways, and in the mountainous country of Caucasia and Central Asia, where, for example, a 600-mile motor road passes from the railhead at Osh across the Pamir to Khorog. They serve, too, in agricultural areas as feeders to the railways. Further, during the long winter when snow covers the ground, snow ways are widely available for sledge traffic and mobility contrasts strikingly with the standstill imposed by the spring thaw.

WATERWAYS AND AIRWAYS

The great rivers of Siberia, coastwise navigation of Pacific and Arctic seas, together with navigation of the Caspian, lake Aral and the Amu and Syr Darya rivers of Central Asia play an increasing role in this vast country inadequately served by land transport. A fleet of cargo steamers and motor vessels in the Caspian Sea carrying mainly oil, fish, and cotton, serves the railhead ports of Krasnovodsk and Guriev and relates Soviet Central Asia to the Caucasus regions, to the Volga cities and to north Persian ports. The Aral lake, like the Caspian little affected by winter freezing, carries several hundred thousand tons of freight between Aralsk station on the Central Asia line and towns along the banks of the Amu Darya river which is navigated as far upstream as Termez on the Afghan border. Relatively little use has yet been made of the Syr Darya, which should become increasingly useful to the Ferghana basin. The Ob and Irtish rivers carry the heaviest freight of the Siberian rivers: sea-going vessels can reach Novi Port and river craft Ishim and Omsk. Port Igarka, situated far inland on the Yenisei, is a seaport for the export of timber,

---

[1] The current five-year plan envisages an addition of over 1500 miles of new lines in the Urals and Siberia and of over 400 miles in Central Asia. The Trans-Siberian in Western Siberia and the Akmolinsk-Kartali line are to be electrified.

whilst this river gives navigation upstream for large barges as far as
Krasnoyarsk on the Trans-Siberian railway to which is carried *inter alia*
nickel matte from Norilsk (latitude 69° N.) via Dudinsk on the Yenisei,
destined for the refineries in the Urals. The Lena waterway carries
ocean-going vessels 1000 miles upstream to Yakutsk, whence roads now,
and in time railways will, give access to various parts of Eastern Siberia
and the Far East. It is navigable too, for river craft and rafts for an even
greater distance above Yakutsk, indeed up to Ust Kut, through which
the BAM railway will pass to Olekminsk, whence a road continues to
Irkutsk. The open season of the Siberian rivers is reduced to about three
months, but lasts longer upstream; as much as six or six and a half months
in their upper courses. Among the rivers of the Far East the Amur is
outstanding since it is navigable for about half the year for 1800 miles,
whilst regular steamer services connect its seaport of Nikolaevsk with
Komsomolsk, Khabarovsk and Blagoveshchensk. In northeast Siberia the
Kolyma river, noted for its thriving goldfield, is navigable up to Verkhne
Kolymsk, whence there are roads to Yakutsk and the Pacific coast.

The Northern (or Roundabout) Sea Route, which affords a slender
link via Arctic seas between Soviet Pacific ports and Archangel and Murmansk (a distance of 7000 statute miles), has become practicable only
since 1932 when the ice-breaker *Sibiryakov* made the first continuous
passage in one season from end to end of the route. The use of the route
for Soviet through traffic is limited to the open period in the Arctic seas,
which lasts two months east of Cape Chelyuskin, two to two and a half
months in the Kara sea, and three and a half months in Barents sea. The
months of August and September in fact alone permit through navigation. Apart from the varying intensity and distribution of ice, fogs in
summer, especially off southern Kamchatka, in the Bering Strait and in
the Kara Sea, present an additional difficulty. Even this limited use of the
route has been made practicable only by the provision along it of
numerous radio-meteorological stations, ports of call, coaling stations,
seaplanes to act as scouts and ice-breakers to pilot the convoys through
the most difficult sections. The Northern Sea Route Administration,
known briefly as G.S.U.M.P., which was set up by the All-Union
authorities in 1932 and has been heavily capitalized, is responsible for
organizing the route. It is now available for regular shipping services as
well as for purely scientific expeditions: there are many small ports,
notably Tiksi Bay on the Lena estuary, and coal from Arctic mines is
provided along the route. Traffic is largely cabotage, i.e. concerned
with supplying Arctic stations, but goods can also be shipped inland by
river, especially by the Lena, down which much timber will be increas-

ingly carried for export from Tiksi Bay. Soviet interest in the Northern
Sea Route clearly springs from many considerations: the desire to exploit
the mineral and timber resources of northern Siberia but, above all,
strategical requirements. Certainly the opening up of the Northern Sea
Route permits new currents of trade, although small in scale, with Europe
and North America; it permits, again on no large scale and at substantial
cost, some through shipments between Vladivostok and Archangel
(7000 miles)—at most one voyage in each direction per season; it permits,
too, the unobserved interchange of small naval vessels and ice-breakers
between Atlantic and Pacific bases.

Finally, much has been done during the last twenty years to establish
air routes in Soviet Asia which, because of its great area and scattered
settlement, clearly offers a great field for development. Regular air lines
link the chief cities of Siberia and Central Asia with Moscow, carrying
passengers, mail, and freight. Air lines follow the Yenisei and Lena rivers
and keep Arctic stations in touch with the rest of the Union. In the Far
East, airways, owing to their directness, have a great advantage over sea
navigation; the Soviet shore line there extends for 7000 miles, but the
distance by air between north and south is only about 2500 miles. The
aeroplane is useful for the carriage of valuable freight of light weight, for
example, gold from Bodaibo, Aldan, and Magadan, important centres of
the East Siberian gold industry. Ground facilities are available for the
use of various air routes from Alaska to the U.S.S.R., the shortest of
which is 1900 miles from Nome to Yakutsk. Air navigation in Eastern
Siberia, the Far East and neighbouring seas encounters formidable
weather but this, together with the difficulty of building aerodromes and
installations on a permanently frozen sub-soil, are being resolutely met.
For defence purposes, too, ground provision for aircraft is available,
especially in the lower Amur valley and in the region around Vladivostok.

POLITICAL AND ADMINISTRATIVE ORGANIZATION

THE ADMINISTRATIVE DIVISION

In its territorial as in other aspects the political and administrative
organization of Soviet Asia marks a complete break with that of Asiatic
Russia in late Tsarist times. Already then it had become clear that the
traditional territorial structure based on the military and fiscal needs of
Moscow were inadequate in relation to changing economic and demographic conditions. Siberia then comprised nine provinces, most of which
were enormous in scale; Central Asia eleven, and South Caucasus six (*Fig.*

31). The Soviet Union, a federal and not a unitary state like Tsarist Russia, grew by the association with the R.S.F.S.R. (Russian Soviet Federative Socialist Republic) of a number of similarly constituted republics. The R.S.F.S.R., the territory of which extends from the Baltic and Black Sea to the Arctic and Pacific, includes the whole of Siberia and the Far East; the rest of Soviet Asia contributes eight republics to the Union which (since 1940) includes sixteen: these eight are Kazakhstan S.S.R., the four Central Asian and the three Caucasian republics.

The principles on which the U.S.S.R. reorganized the Asiatic territories in the 1930's were, first that of nationality and second, that of administrative efficiency.[1] Four grades of nationality groupings were recognized, and accordingly four forms of politico-administrative territory set up. At the highest level stood the constituent or union republics (S.S.R.—soviet socialist republic) of major nationalities fit to manage their own affairs and enjoying the legal right of secession from the Soviet Union. Next came groups not then sufficiently advanced for this status, which were organized as autonomous soviet socialist republics (A.S.S.R.) and enjoyed a lesser degree of autonomy. The last two categories were the autonomous oblasts (A.O.) and the *okrugs*: the former fell within the orbit of the adminstrative sub-divisions of union republics, as did formerly also the A.S.S.R.; the *okrugs*, now obsolescent, were formed of smaller groups of relatively primitive peoples who had very limited, and mainly cultural, privileges. The second principle adopted by the Soviet leaders was that of administrative convenience. This principle was subordinated to that of nationality: that is, administrative efficiency had to accept the union republic state patterns. Similarly schemes devised by planning commissions, notably GOELRO and GOSPLAN, for economic regions as the basis for administration, had to give place to the two principles stated above which, in operation, have had two effects on internal administrative boundaries. On the one hand, the limits of the union republics, since they are broadly coincident with those of nationality, have remained stable; on the other, the limits of administrative regions, notably those of *oblasti*, since they aimed to achieve optimum areas for efficiency during times of major economic change, have been remarkably dynamic.

Table XXVI lists the republics of Soviet Asia, together with figures for their areas and population, and the major administrative units of Siberia as they existed in 1939. Fig. 26 shows the general outline and location of these republics and administrative areas as in 1939.

[1] See J. A. Morrison: "The Evolution of the Territorial-Administrative System of the U.S.S.R." *American Review of the Soviet Union*, I, 3 (1938).

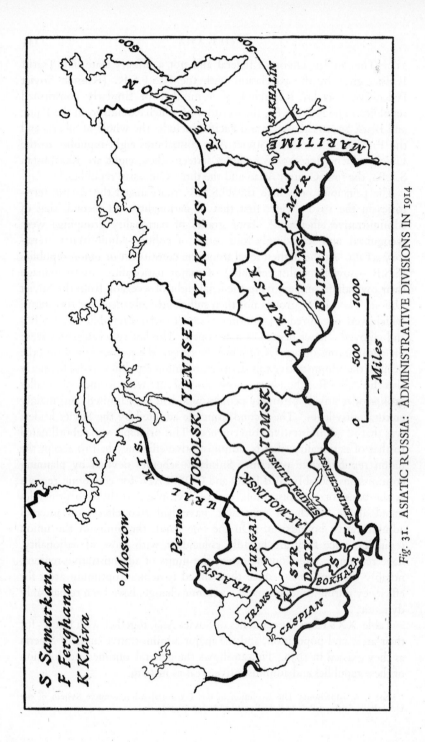

Fig. 31. ASIATIC RUSSIA: ADMINISTRATIVE DIVISIONS IN 1914

All the eight republics lie peripherally in relation to the Soviet Union as a whole and parts of their boundaries coincide with international limits of the U.S.S.R. They vary greatly in area from the giant Kazakhstan, which is larger than the Arabian peninsula, to the relatively small Caucasian republic of Armenia, comparable in size with Belgium. In population there is less disparity but no uniformity. Kazakhstan and Uzbekistan are the most populous, but neither contains a population as numerous as that of either the London or the Moscow region. Each republic, *krai* and *oblast* has its own limited powers and machinery of government and its elected soviets or councils, but the central government of the Union at Moscow, itself controlled by the Politbureau of the All-Union Communist Party, has control of finance, internal boundaries, foreign trade and foreign affairs, whilst it defines and controls the main lines of domestic activity. There is no reason to believe that this system has not worked satisfactorily: certainly during the Russo-German war of 1941–45 Moscow received the loyal co-operation of the Asiatic republics. The point to be re-emphasized here is that, notably in foreign affairs but also in major internal matters, the Asiatic republics do not possess independence of action.

The constituent republics are divided for administrative purposes into *kraia* and *oblasti*.[1] The terms do not translate easily into English: the nearest equivalents are 'territory' and 'region' respectively. As already noted, the *oblasti* inject a dynamic element into the administrative geography. The Tobolsk and Tomsk provinces of the 1914 map of Siberia (*Fig.* 31) gave place in the Soviet map to the *oblasti* of Omsk and Novosibirsk and the *krai* of Altai (capital Barnaul), thus reflecting changes in urban values. The pattern was further modified by changes during the late war. The southeastern part of Novosibirsk was detached in 1943 to form the new *oblast* of Kemerovo, whilst from adjacent parts of Omsk and Chelyabinsk *oblasti*, in the same year, the new *oblast* of Kurgan was set up. These two instances illustrate both the reason for such innovations and how they are effected. The reason in both cases was local growth of industry and population: Kurgan, situated nearly two hundred miles east of Chelyabinsk on the Trans-Siberian railway and an outpost of the Ural industrial region, was doubtless increasing its stature rapidly under the stimulus of immigrant workers and plant from the areas of Russia threatened by the German advance. Kemerovo, also an industrial city with great coke-oven batteries, was selected as the centre for a new *oblast* broadly coincident with the Kuzbas coalfield which was undergoing

[1] *Krai* and *oblast* are pronounced respectively 'cry' and 'or-blast'. The word *krai* which occurs in 'Ukraine' has the sense of 'borderland'.

rapid exploitation. In the latter case the change was made by sub-division of a single *oblast*; in the former, by the detachment of parts of two neighbouring *oblasti*. In the same way the changes in the administrative divisions of Kazakhstan S.S.R. between 1926 and 1939 mirror the rapidity of the controlled development there of both agriculture and industry. Eight *oblasti* are shown in the *Great Soviet Atlas*, published in 1937: there were eleven in 1939 which make a pattern quite different from that of 1926: the new *oblasti* of Guriev, flanking the northeastern shore of the Caspian, and of Karaganda, with its coalfield and iron works, are significant novelties. Nor has this administrative map stabilized, for in 1948 there were as many as 16 *oblasti* in Kazakhstan S.S.R.[1]

In Eastern Siberia and the Far East, the least populous regions of Soviet Asia, the administrative map has changed less drastically than in Western Siberia. Irkutsk remains as an *oblast*, and Krasnoyarsk *krai* replaces the Yenisei province. East of lake Baikal, the old Transbaikal province now consists of the Buryat-Mongol A.S.S.R. and Chita *oblast*, whilst the old Yakutsk province re-appears as Yakut A.S.S.R., its limits now withdrawn farther from the Pacific. The old Maritime province, now enlarged, still conceived by Russians as the core of their Far East, is comprised of Primorski (or Maritime) *krai* in the south, and the vast Khabarovsk *krai*. The latter now contains the Amur and lower Amur *oblasti*, those of Kamchatka and Sakhalin (the Kurile islands therein included), and the Jewish autonomous *oblast*, organized in 1936, of which Birobijan is the centre.[2] In the far north of Siberia but not of European Russia, as far south as latitude 62° N., the administration and economy, as well as navigation problems, were entrusted to the Northern Sea Route Administration.

SIBERIA AND THE EIGHT REPUBLICS

Space is not available here to sketch even in outline the geographical backgrounds of the individual states and major administrative regions of Soviet Asia. It must suffice to supplement what has already been given in the text and Tables by a few summary references to each.

Two Siberias may be distinguished. The one, roughly south of latitude 58° N., is a land of Russian colonization—'a human peninsula of European Russia'—and includes nearly all the principal populated areas; the other, much the greater in area, in the remote north, although scantily settled,

---

[1] Needless to say these continual administrative changes make statistical comparisons a laborious task.

[2] The population of the Jewish autonomous oblast reached 108,419 in 1939, of which only a quarter were Jews. The population in 1928 was 34,000, 78% of which were Russians.

contains numerous indigenous peoples with only 'islands' and only minority groups of Russians, as notably in Yakut A.S.S.R. Russian Siberia, together with the Far East, provides many things for the U.S.S.R.: in Western Siberia a 'Middle West' with surplus wheat and meat; the riches of its forests and its minerals and metals, especially coal, gold, platinum, lead, tin, and wolfram; and a Pacific seaboard and colonial space in the east. In the more remote Siberia dwells the bulk of the native population, now reduced in the whole of Siberia to less than one million, some engaged in semi-nomadic hunting, fishing and reindeer breeding within the expanses of the *taiga* and tundra zones. Politically of little account, their survival is of interest primarily to the anthropologist. Many belong to the Finno-Ugrian language family, notably the Samoyeds, the Ostiaks, the Voguls[1] and the Zyrians; with the exception of the last named, who are settled in the Tobolsk region, they live a nomadic life. The Tunguz are another relatively important group—perhaps 75,000 strong—scattered in the forests and tundra zones east of the Ob; whilst the Yakuts, numbering some 200,000, occupy the vast basin of the Lena. But Soviet activity and organization are not lacking in 'native' Siberia. A special administrative body 'Dalstroi' was started under the ægis of M.V.D. in 1931–32 to develop northeastern Siberia, in particular its wealth in gold (and to a lesser extent tin) with the aid of forced labour camps. It was claimed[2] recently that over 10,000 new names—of mining centres, fishing villages, state farms, etc.—have been marked on the map of the Kolyma region in recent years; that there are 65 large gold fields in the region and hundreds of miles of all-year roads. G.S.U.M.P. now appears to confine its activities solely to the northern sea route where, too, new Arctic stations, linked by air routes, have been established. The polymetallic combine at Norilsk (Taimyr peninsula) produces nickel and other ores. Indeed it seems that even 'native' Siberia is not able to resist the process of Russian settlement.

Kazakhstan S.S.R. stands geographically between Siberia and Soviet Central Asia. The Kazakhs, a Turki-speaking people with Mongolian elements, were organized tribally and nomadic in culture. Their mode of life has been radically transformed as mines are sunk, factories set up, railways built, and irrigation canals cut, and land assigned to collective farms for cultivation and to state farms for animal husbandry. Kazakh-

---

[1] It is now suggested that the Samoyeds, Ostiaks and Voguls entered northern Siberia from northeast Europe, not from the Altai region: K. Donner, *La Sibérie* (1946), Ch. I. Siberia presents complex ethnic and linguistic problems still far from solved.

[2] See "Stalin's Eldorado," by Boris Nikolaevsky, *Fortune*, August, 1947, and H. A. Wallace, *Soviet Asia Mission*, N.Y. (1946).

stan is rapidly becoming, although less emphatically than Siberia, a settlement region for Russians. Even when allowance is made for the extent of desert and semi-desert, it nevertheless remains a land of great opportunity which has already made remarkable economic progress. There are already some 5000 miles of railway, and already in 1937 railway freight was nearly twenty times that of 1913. Briefly, Kazakhstan is a storehouse of food, chiefly wheat, although now sugar beet too is being grown, and also of the requirements of modern industry: coal and oil, iron, copper, chrome, lead, and ferro-alloys. Positionally, it commands the approach to Sinkiang, and its physical character makes it an excellent retired training-ground for the Red army and air force. Its capital Alma Ata (formerly Verny), situated in lattitude 44° N. on a piedmont site in the extreme southeast of the republic on the Turk-Sib railway, is *inter alia* a centre for the Soviet film industry and headquarters of the Central Asia Military District.

Among the Central Asian states, where the native Turkic peoples are in the ascendancy and are increasing in numbers, Uzbek S.S.R. is the most important. The Uzbeks, long sedentary and noted for their handicrafts, are Sunni Moslems and owed their culture to Persian influences. The Uzbek republic has four *oblasti* grouped around towns, whose names, unusually for the Soviet Union, have been left unchanged and recall a rich history of contact between China, the Mohammedan world and Europe—Tashkent, Ferghana, Bokhara, and Samarkand. The inclusion within Uzbek of the Kara-Kalpak A.S.S.R. is geographically logical in extending the republic down the Amu Darya valley to lake Aral. Uzbek has wide areas of irrigated land under cotton and rice and produces raw silk; it is exploiting its mountain streams so as to provide power for industry; its modest oil, coal, and iron resources, too, are in process of development. The war in Europe doubtless stimulated industrial development there: it was reported, for example, that the large agricultural machinery works at Rostov was dismantled and set up again in Tashkent.

Tajik S.S.R. is an area of mountains and valleys which was detached from Uzbek S.S.R. in 1929. Like the Uzbeks, the Tajiks are Persian in culture and Sunni Moslems. Russians numbered less than 1% of the population in 1926, and Tajiks continue to grow in numbers. To the life of the shepherd moving his flocks seasonally between mountains and valley is added irrigated cultivation, whilst the Pamir, now crossed by motor roads, is exploited for rare minerals. The capital of Tajik is Stalinabad, formerly Diushambe; Termez is a trading place and ferry on the

Amu Darya, which here, within a frontier of contact, defines the boundary between U.S.S.R. and Afghanistan.

Kirgiz S.S.R. and Turkmen S.S.R., the one largely mountainous, the other mainly desert with a fertile piedmont and oases, have the smallest populations of the Central Asian states. Like the others, they contain growing indigenous nationalities whose traditional economy is now modified and stimulated by Soviet policy—typified by the collective farm, irrigation works, factory construction and the search for oil and metals. Kirgiz also is becoming a fuel base of Central Asia, now that its coal resources are being exploited. It engages All-Union interest because of its wealth of scarce metals (including uranium), the production of which is being expanded under the 1946–50 plan. Russians have settled rather more in these two states than elsewhere in Central Asia, and now constitute about one-fifth of the population of Kirgiz. Although this state abuts on Sinkiang, there is no practicable route across the mountain barrier. No railways penetrate from Turkmen into Persia, but there are four roads, one of which—that between Ashkhabad and Meshed—is metalled.

The three Caucasian republics, which, despite their large areas of mountain, high volcanic plateau and steppe, are the most densely populated parts of Soviet Asia, differ remarkably among themselves and were notorious for their antagonisms, e.g., that of Georgians and Armenians, which have abated somewhat since their incorporation into the Soviet Union. The Azerbaijans are a Turki-speaking people of Persian culture who came via Persia from Central Asia to an environment physically comparable; in religion they are Shiite Moslems. In contrast, the Georgians and the Armenians are classified as 'Caucasian' or 'Japhetic' and are Christians, although they belong respectively to the Greek Orthodox and Armeno-Gregorian churches. The human geography is in detail complex, for there are many pockets of distinct culture groups: amongst these, three of the chief are organized as autonomous soviet socialist republics within Georgia and two others similarly in Azerbaijan S.S.R.

THE 'NATIONALITIES PROBLEM'

It may well be asked to what extent the Soviet Union is possibly weakened politically by the large number and variety of ethnic groups and nationalities which it comprises. In the Union as a whole there are more than 60 fairly large nations and in all some 180, whilst 149 languages can be distinguished. Similarly, the peoples of the Union represent

sharply different levels of material culture. The problem of the nationalities so-called engaged the close attention of Soviet leaders, notably of
Stalin, and a fresh approach has been made to it.[1] In Tsarist times 'Russifi-
cation' was the policy towards the non-Great Russian subjects of the
Empire: this involved the imposition of the Russian language, Church,
and culture. Little too, was then done to develop the economy of the
colonial lands, except where developments, such as the Baku oilfield and
cotton-growing in Central Asia, served Great Russian interests. Race
prejudice has no place in the Soviet scheme; great importance is attached
to cultural autonomy (including the use of native languages), and also to
the provision, so far as is possible, of equal opportunities for men *and*
women of all nationalities. The Constitution of 1936 actually recognizes
the right of the nations to secede from the Union —but clearly the application of this right in a particular case would not be tolerated. The constituent republics of the Union have equal representation, as have the
autonomous republics (A.S.S.R.), in the Council of Nationalities which
is one of the two co-equal chambers of the Supreme Soviet of the
U.S.S.R. Industrial projects, capitalized by the whole Union, are undertaken everywhere, and native Asiatic peoples man the factories and farms
(as also the Union's armed forces) and are encouraged to develop a Soviet
patriotism and cherish the Marxist-Leninist creed. It may fairly be
claimed that much has been done during the Soviet period to reduce
sharply old animosities between different nationalities, to raise the
educational and cultural levels of the more backward peoples, and to
enlist the co-operation of multi-national groups in a Soviet community,
the official aspirations of which are not national but international in
scope. There is no ground for believing therefore that, fortified by the
political police of the M.V.D. and by the power of the press and radio,
and guided and controlled by the Communist Party (which includes
members from the Asiatic peoples), the Soviet Union derives anything
but strength from the constituent and autonomous republics and smaller
groups of Soviet Asia.

EXTERNAL RELATIONSHIPS

Soviet Asia, of its own, plays no independent part in external trade[2]
and foreign affairs; it is merely one of the theatres for All-Union activity

[1] For a short balanced discussion of this large question the reader is referred to Sir John
Maynard, *The Russian Peasant and other Studies*, 1942, Ch. XIX.
[2] U.S.S.R.'s trade with Asiatic countries, excluding Japan, but including Turkey, amounted
to 16% of its imports and 15% exports in 1937.

directed from Moscow. Our subject of discussion thus resolves itself into a geographical review of those Soviet external relationships which are related to its Asiatic territory. Here our starting point must be the geographical position and frontiers of Soviet Asia, its neighbours and near-neighbours, whilst we must look back and forward a little since the Asiatic matrix in which it is set is politically molten and re-shaping. Further, it is fitting here to re-examine briefly the geopolitical ideas associated with the so-called 'Heartland' of the Old World, since this region is so largely coincident with Soviet Asia.

Soviet Asia makes direct touch with three of the major compartments of Asia—Southwest Asia, High (Central) Asia and the Far East, while in Tajik S.S.R. it closely approaches a fourth—the Indian sub-continent. Its boundaries extend some 8000 miles, about four times the length of those of Soviet Europe. The importance of the former to the U.S.S.R. is, however, inversely proportional to their length. Since European U.S.S.R., including the Ural region, contains (in round figures) 75% of the population and economic potential of the Union, its European frontiers in a populous and politically unstable Europe must always remain the more vital, as they have always proved in modern times the more vulnerable. In contrast, the boundaries of Soviet Asia, despite their great length, appear relatively stable and secure. The major reasons for this spring from the geographical nature of the frontier regions in which they lie. Many of these are frontiers of separation: they coincide with country so constituted physically and so considerable in extent that it repels rather than invites close settlement. The extent to which this generalization is justified will become apparent in a discussion of Soviet frontiers with Southwest Asia, High Asia and the Far East.

SOUTHWEST ASIA

Soviet interest in Southwest Asia arises naturally from the location of the boundaries of the Caucasian republics. These cut across the physical units—the high Armenian plateau, which is shared with Turkey, and the Iranian plateau, which is shared with Persia. Similarly the Black Sea coasts are shared largely by U.S.S.R. and Turkey, while the Caspian shores lie wholly in U.S.S.R. and Persia. The main patterns of the ethnic map, no less than those of the physical map, are at variance with the political patterns: Armenians live equally in Turkey and in Armenia S.S.R., whilst the Azerbaijan province of northern Persia is contiguous with Azerbaijan S.S.R. From Tbilisi, capital of Georgia S.S.R., the main railway focus of South Caucasus and the headquarters of the Trans-Caucasian Army District, a railway runs to Leninakan near the Soviet-

Turkish frontier and thence continues, with a change of gauge, across Turkey to Kars, Erzurum and Ankara and Mersin, and thus to the Mediterranean. Soviet access to the Mediterranean via the Turkish Straits is still controlled in peace and war by the provisions of the Convention of Montreux of 1936, which the U.S.S.R. has been seeking to revise. Across northern Turkey, 250–300 miles from the Soviet frontier, lies Iraq, but there is no continuous railway directly linking Turkish and Iraq territory. As recently as 1940 the U.S.S.R. opened the circuitous strategical railway linking Baku and Tbilisi via Julfa which follows the Arax valley hard by the international boundary; and from Julfa a line, on the same gauge, penetrates a hundred miles to Tabriz in Persian Azerbaijan. Although the political independence of Persia is formally maintained, it has been long recognized that southern and northern Persia are spheres of British and Soviet interest respectively.

Soviet interest here is two-fold. First, the U.S.S.R. wishes to acquire the right to exploit the somewhat problematical oil resources of northern Persia and, more generally no doubt, it cannot fail to be interested in southern Persia, which is not only rich in productive oil resources, but controls in the Persian Gulf an oceanic entry to the railway and roads leading to the Caspian and thus to the Soviet Union.[1] Secondly, the U.S.S.R.'s interest in the Middle East is concerned with its ultimate need of oil (its own resources being far from inexhaustible)[2] and with defence considerations: the states and airfields of Southwest Asia lie uncomfortably near its main oilfield at Baku. Geopolitically, the situation is simple in in outline. For U.S.S.R., Southwest Asia forms an outer defence zone, comprised of weak states under 'Western' influence, and easily accessible to the sea and air power commanded by the Western powers. The fact that Turkey is one of the 'Marshall Aid states' and that the United States was interested in oil concessions in southern Persia illustrate this point. The fact that Russia once held the now Turkish areas of Kars and Ardahan provides a possible pretext for irredentist claims.

The remaining long stretch of Soviet frontier with Persia and its continuation with Afghanistan is relatively stable, for desert and semi-desert conditions and mountains extend widely, defying logistics and reducing trade contacts. Historically, it is true, there was no frontier here; on the contrary, at confined points there were movements of conquerors and traders. Alexander the Great moved through north Persia and across Afghanistan *en route* for the Oxus (Amu Darya) and Samarkand—by a

[1] See above, pp. 105–109.
[2] U.S.S.R.'s oil resources, at present rates of consumption, may not be enough for much more than 30 years, but, since geological prospecting is still at an early stage, their scale is not yet certain.

devious route via Kandahar, Kabul and Balkh. The Persian Empire before him and the Arab Caliphate long after him extended north to the Aral Sea; the Mohammedan world to this day continues across these political frontiers deep into Soviet Asia. The Roman silk route, too, passed across northern Persia to Samarkand and Ferghana—but all these routes made entry into Central Asia via Balkh crossing the Oxus near Termez, thus emphasizing the limited possibilities of movement. Under present conditions the paucity of railways emphasizes the difficulty of access. A Persian single-track line reaches the Caspian seaport of Bandar Shar, and another is being prolonged to Meshed; the Soviet Transcaspian line, also single and difficult to operate under desert conditions, approaches the boundary; but in Afghanistan railways are still lacking. The preservation of an independent Afghanistan as a buffer state is of obvious defensive value both to the U.S.S.R. and the Indian dominions. For offensive operations use of the road through Afghanistan from Tajik S.S.R. to Pakistan presents very considerable difficulties, notably those of mountain gradients and passes and, for the U.S.S.R., campaigning in Afghanistan would be rendered difficult by its remoteness from its major supply bases. A salient of Afghan territory in Wakhan, around the Ab-i-Panji headwaters of the Amu Darya, lies between the lofty Pamir and the Hindu Kush and effectively denies access between the U.S.S.R. and Pakistan where their boundaries lie only twenty-five miles apart.

HIGH ASIA

From 72° E. longitude to the Pacific coast Soviet territory abuts on lands which were traditionally parts of China and are settled almost wholly by peoples neither Russian nor Chinese. The coincidence of the frontier with high mountains in the west (notably the Tien Shan), the vast desert expanses (Taklamakan and Gobi) save in Manchuria, and the limited development of the better lands, serve to make these separative frontiers, penetrated by relatively few routes. With the development of Russian railways, Sinkiang, Outer Mongolia and Tannu-Tuva became spheres of Soviet politico-economic penetration. Soviet prestige stands high amongst the bordering peoples who note how Soviet rule has brought relative prosperity and new opportunity to the peoples of Soviet Asia. A mountain road runs from the Ferghana Basin to Kashgar, whilst motorable roads, leading from railheads on the Turk-Sib at Alma Ata and Ayaguz (Sergiopol) to Tihwa (Urumchi) in Sinkiang and thence to Lanchow (*Fig.* 33), provide the main overland trade routes between the U.S.S.R. and China. These routes were of some value in carrying Soviet arms to China in 1937 and during the 1941–45 war for the transport of supplies, especially Chinese tungsten and tung oil. Sinkiang, outside the effective limits of Chinese authority, clearly provides an outer shield to Soviet Central Asia and Kazakhstan and a field for economic exploitation. Farther east, on the southern side of the Sayan mountains, Tannu-Tuva, which contains the headwaters of the Yenisei and has livestock, gold, and reputedly other mineral resources, has been exclusively a Soviet sphere since 1921, and in recent years has slipped quietly into the Soviet Union as an autonomous oblast of the R.S.F.S.R. Southwards and eastwards of Tannu-Tuva and contiguous with Irkutsk oblast and Transbaikalia, stretches Outer Mongolia, peopled by Mongols as is the adjacent Buryat-Mongol A.S.S.R. Outer Mongolia is also a Soviet sphere, which formerly balanced as it were Japanese-controlled Inner Mongolia. The building of railways and the provision of air routes (see below p. 374) are binding the Mongolian People's Republic, with its pastoral wealth and mineral resources, tightly to the U.S.S.R. A Soviet-Mongolian treaty of defensive alliance was signed in 1936, which involved local military operations against the Japanese in 1939. Outer Mongolia is strategically important to the U.S.S.R.: defensively, it covers the direct approach from the Far East to Eastern Siberia and thus protects the vital and vulnerable Trans-Siberian railroad (*Fig.* 33). Its offensive value is shown by the four-pronged drive towards Kalgan and north China made by Soviet and Mongolian motorized forces in July, 1945, when the Soviet Union, having renounced neutrality, was at war with Japan. The position of Irkutsk at one end of this route and as the gateway between eastern and western Siberia suggests why it was chosen as the headquarters of the Siberian Army District.

THE FAR EAST

It is in the Far East especially, where the U.S.S.R. has a great length of open frontier with Manchuria and for a few miles direct contact with Korea, that the frontiers of Soviet Asia have raised the most serious defence problems. The rise of an imperialistic Japan and, with the construction of the Trans-Siberian railway, the interests of Russia in its Chinese Eastern Railway and in the ports of Port Arthur and Dairen brought inevitable conflict. The U.S.S.R., seeking to limit its commitments, sold its rights in the C.E.R. in 1931, but fortified its frontier by stationing armies suitably trained and equipped in military districts grouped around Vladivostock, Khabarovsk, and Chita.[1] Such precautions were clearly necessary in view of Japanese expansionist policy and of the long rail hauls involved in moving men and material from European

[1] John Scott, *Duel for Europe*, Boston (1942), p. 210.

Russia. There were numerous military incidents on the Manchurian border in the early 1930's, in which the Russians on the whole had the better of the encounters.

Now that the Japanese Empire has been destroyed and Communist forces dominate China, the Soviet position in the Far East has become correspondingly strong. By the secret agreement made at Yalta in 1945,[1] which provided for its entry into the war against Japan after Germany had been defeated, the U.S.S.R. was assured substantial territorial and other gains: the return of southern Sakhalin (which has coal mines) and of the Kurile islands which extend from southern Kamchatka to Hokkaido; maintenance of the *status quo* in Outer Mongolia; restoration of the lease, formerly held from China by Russia, of Port Arthur as a naval base; internationalization of the commercial port of Dairen where U.S.S.R.'s pre-eminent interests were to be safeguarded; and, subject to the retention by China of full sovereignty in Manchuria, the operation by a joint Soviet-Chinese company of the Chinese Eastern Railway and those of South Manchuria where again U.S.S.R.'s pre-eminent interests were to be safeguarded. The Soviet Union clearly made a good bargain with the United States and the United Kingdom. Recognition of its privileged position in Manchuria is clearly the greatest gain, for this productive pioneer land has much to offer—grain, edible oil and iron ore, which are insufficiently available in the Soviet Far East, not to mention industrial equipment, much of which was carried off by the Russians. By the acquisition of the Kurile islands, the Sea of Okhotsk has become a Soviet lake, whilst in Outer Mongolia the Mongolian People's Republic has become a nominally independent state and, less nominally, an exclusively Soviet preserve. For the rest, the U.S.S.R. remained until 1948 in military occupation of northern Korea and takes a share in the Allied occupation of Japan.

THE ARCTIC

The Pacific and even the Arctic coasts of the U.S.S.R., like its land frontiers, are zones of intercourse and strategical interest. Foreign trade via the Pacific is virtually concentrated at Vladivostok, now an all-the-year port and naval base. As political conditions stabilize in Manchuria, Port Arthur will provide a naval base situated (in direct lines) only 600 miles from Nanking and 700 miles from Nagasaki. Use of Dairen will economize rail haulage of goods to and from Chita and westward regions. The Soviet Arctic ports, with as yet small capacity for handling goods, notably Ambarchik (Kolyma), Tiksi Bay (Lena) and Port Dickson

[1] Published as a White Paper Cmd. 6735, H.M.S.O., 1946.

(Yenisei), have short-season usefulness for external trade, especially in timber. Doubtless strategical reasons *inter alia* lie behind the remarkable Soviet effort to establish ports in north Pacific and Arctic waters and communications with the vast interior. Thus Soviet Harbour, Komsomolsk, Nikolaevsk, and Nagaevo, the first two having facilities for clearance of goods by railways, are all recent creations. The strategical consideration, it would seem, was the need to develop transport links with Russia and the outer world, should Vladivostok and the Trans-Siberian railway be denied to them in war.

The collapse of imperial Japan and the civil war in China, in whose affairs the U.S.S.R. can always intervene on behalf of the Communist forces, have altered the geopolitical setting. The apparent incompatibility of the U.S.S.R. and the U.S.A. in international affairs and the consolidation by the latter of its strategical position in the Pacific and the Far East, draw attention to the proximity of Soviet and American territory (Alaska and Aleutian islands) in the north Pacific. The Kurile islands[1] which, together with the American Aleutian islands, form part of a short direct chain across the north Pacific, have less strategical value than their geographical position might suggest. Both sea and air navigation encounter great difficulties: in winter and spring pack ice precludes access by sea and gales occur, whilst in summer, fog, worse than in the Aleutians which lie much farther north, is encountered on ten to twenty days a month. Soviet pilots demonstrated as early as 1937 the practicability of trans-Polar flights; the Northern Sea Route, for what it is worth, now provides an exclusively Soviet waterway; roads, rivers, aerodromes and the sledge make possible limited transportation inland; Yakutsk bids fair to become a focus of road, river, air and (eventually) rail routes in the far north of Eastern Siberia, whilst Nagaevo, which is situated 1000 miles north of Vladivostok in latitude 60° N. and longitude 150° E., is a summer-season port and naval base.

Canada and the United States share with the U.S.S.R. the possession of Arctic territories, and all three clearly envisage the possibility of an extension of war to Arctic settings. The technique and logistics of such warfare, in which it would seem only small numbers could be engaged, and limited objectives sought, raise novel problems for the general staff: to whom modern (hot) desert warfare has become familiar. The importance of the Arctic theatre to the Soviet Union should not be exaggerated, north of latitude 55° N. in the rugged and mountainous lands east of the Yenisei, the natural riches in timber, coal, minerals, and water power which are as yet but little developed, U.S.S.R. has little of immediate

---

[1] Administratively these are included in the Sakhalin *oblast* of Maritime *krai*.

value to lose except gold and platinum, nickel, tin and the fishery of the
Sea of Okhotsk.

SOVIET ASIA AND THE 'HEARTLAND'

As long ago as 1904, when he was struck by the contrast between the
Boer war waged by Britain at the end of a 6000-mile sea route and the
war waged by Russia at a comparable distance by land against Japan, Sir
Halford Mackinder discussed his concept of the 'pivot area' in History,
later to be developed in terms of the 'Heartland'.[1] His basic ideas, derived
from a reading of history and geography in association and expressed as
geographical realities behind international politics and war, have, so far,
stood well the test of time and were re-iterated in 1943.[2] Mackinder made
clear the dichotomy in a global world of continental and oceanic power—
a dichotomy that was never more evident than now when U.S.S.R. and
the Western powers fail to agree on common action in Berlin, Germany,
Korea and elsewhere. Mackinder's concept of the 'Heartland' as the
citadel of continental power, a concept carefully explored by geopoliti-
cians in Nazi Germany and in Japan, has also clear validity, at least in
relation to defensive warfare. The daring generalization (or is it a prediction?) to which Mackinder's study led, with its ominous ring and
uncanny relevance to the present world political situation, has a much
more questionable validity. In 1919 he wrote:[3]

> *Who rules East Europe commands the Heartland:*
> *Who rules the Heartland commands the World-Island:*
> *Who rules the World-Island commands the world.*

Soviet Asia forms the great bulk of the 'Heartland', which is at once
both more and less. More because it extends westwards to the Volga
and southwards to include the mountain-desert zone beyond the Soviet
frontiers, less because it excludes the mountainous lands east of the Lena
where penetration from the sea is possible (*Fig.* 32). Indeed the 'Heartland' is not easily fixed geographically: it has more than one geographical
content. Mackinder defined it variously as the territory of Arctic and
continental (or interior) drainage of Euro-Asia, and as the territories to
which, under modern conditions, access from the sea could be denied.
It is clear that the Arctic Ocean in the north and the mountains and

[1] "The Geographical Pivot of History", *Geographical Journal*, XXIII (1904); *Democratic Ideals and Reality*, 1919, Pelican edition, 1944.
[2] "The Round World and the Winning of the Peace", in *Compass of the World*, edited by H. W. Weigert and V. Stefansson, N.D.
[3] *Democratic Ideals and Reality*, Pelican edition, p. 113.

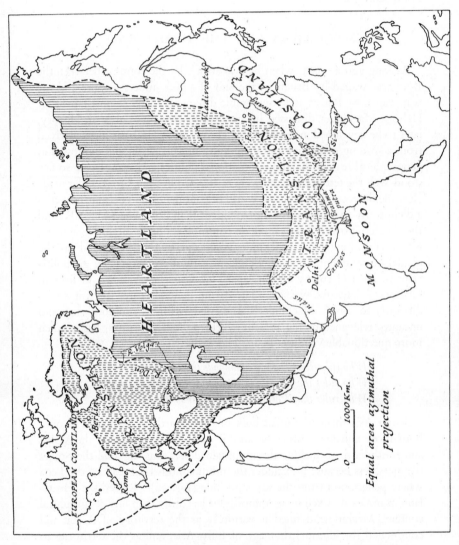

Fig. 32. THE HEARTLAND OF THE OLD WORLD ISLAND
(after Mackinder)

deserts in the south provide strong natural shields to the 'Heartland', which also permits defence in depth and the means of strategic retreat— the more so now that its population is growing fast, its communications are being developed and its food, armament and other industrial resources increased. The southern borderland of the 'Heartland', too, bids fair to fall increasingly under Soviet rather than Chinese control and contains considerable possibilities of development in population, food supplies and nodality for air routes. The development of air power has certainly strengthened not weakened the 'Heartland' for offensive if not for defensive action and does so increasingly as the range of aircraft extends. A mere 1000-mile range from points within the boundaries of Soviet Asia includes Alexandria, Cairo and Suez; Ankara, Istanbul and the Turkish Straits; the Iraq oilfield, Tripoli and Haifa; the Persian Gulf and oilfields; Karachi and Delhi; Korea, Japan and Alaska; Nanking, Shanghai and (from Outer Mongolia) Chungking.[1] The Heartland's defensive strength and its relative inaccessibility to an oceanic invader, are clear enough: the virtual impossibility of conquering Russia, because of its grand scale, its ever mounting man-power and virtual self-sufficiency in supplies, has been a continual theme of German strategical thinking for a long time, but the value of the space factor in war must depend also on the factors of political organization, economic potential and morale, more difficult to assess. It is true, too, as Mackinder believed, that, now that its former enemies on both western and eastern flanks have been overthrown, the U.S.S.R. emerges from the 1939–45 war as 'the greatest land power of the globe'. It would appear to follow, according to Mackinder's ideas, that since in large measure it already 'rules East Europe' the U.S.S.R. 'commands' the World-Island of Euro-Asia and Africa. But, as the lawyers might say, even if Mackinder is right, to accept this prophecy as valid would be to stultify efforts towards a sane international organization of the world. In any case, our whole conception of mobility and accessibility, considerations to which Mackinder attached prime importance, have changed and are changing fast; not less rapidly the technique and weapons of modern war are changing. The territory of the U.S.S.R., at least on its western flank, exposes vital areas and places vulnerable to sea and air assault from the outer margin of the natural fortress of the 'Heartland'. Consideration of the 'Heartland' concept in relation to Soviet Asia and geopolitical realities of the present time, while it underlines the great strength of the U.S.S.R. in defensive warfare, justifies no certain prediction about the future mastery of the world.

[1] From Soviet territory in Europe within the same range lie all the capitals of Europe except Dublin, Lisbon and Madrid.

24

SELECT READING LIST

Among introductory geographies of the Soviet Union may be noted: N. Mikhaylov's lively *Soviet Geography* (1937), *The Geography of the U.S.S.R.* by C. Jorré, translated by D. Laborde, 1950, and S. S. Balzak, V. F. Vasyutin and Ya. G. Firgin, *Economic Geography of the U.S.S.R.*, translated, New York, 1949. In addition may be noted L. Berg, *Les Régions Naturelles de l'U.R.S.S.*, Paris, 1941, and P. Georges, *U.R.S.S.*, *Haute Asie-Iran*, Paris, 1947. G. B. Cressey's *Basis of Soviet Strength*, N.Y., 1945 and the relevant chapters of the following works may be consulted: I. Bowman, *Limits of Land Settlement*, N.Y., 1937, Ch. IV; I. Bowman (ed.), *The Pioneer Fringe*, N.Y., 1931, Ch. XII; W. L. G. Joerg. (ed.), *Pioneer Settlement*, N.Y., 1932.

For historical background, see works by R. J. Kerner, *e.g. Russia's Urge to the Sea*, Univ. of California, 1942 and B. H. Sumner, *Survey of Russian History*, 1944.

On particular aspects of the U.S.S.R. as a whole or of Soviet Asia in particular, the following works are useful:

F. Lorimer: *The Population of the Soviet Union*, League of Nations, Geneva, 1946 (an excellent statistical and well mapped study).

Sir John Maynard: *The Russian Peasant and Other Studies*, 1942.

V. Conolly: *Soviet Economic Policy in the Far East*, 1933; *Soviet Trade from the Pacific to the Levant*, 1935; *Soviet Asia*, Oxford Pamphlet, 1942.

M. Edelman: *How Russia Prepared: U.S.S.R. beyond the Urals*, Penguin Books, 1942.

J. D. Littlepage and D. Bess: *In Search of Soviet Gold*, 1939.

T. A. Taracouzio: *Soviets in the Arctic*, N.Y., 1938.

H. R. Smolka: *Forty Thousand against the Arctic*, 1937.

E. Rackman and B. Yuedensky: *The Economic Dividend of the Soviet Far East*, Institute of Pacific Affairs, N.Y., 1926.

M. H. Dobb: *U.S.S.R.: Her Life and Her People*, 1943.

U.S.S.R. Speaks for Itself (small illustrated volumes on agriculture, industry, transport, etc.,) Lawrence and Wishart, 1941.

R. A. Davies and A. J. Steiger: *Soviet Asia*, 1943.

E. S. Bates: *Soviet Asia*, 1942.

H. W. Weigert and V. Stefansson: *Compass of the World*, 1945.

C. Steber: *L'Asie Centrale et le Kazakhstan*, Paris, 1939.

D. J. Dallin: *Soviet Russia and the Far East*, New Haven, 1948.

Amongst article literature in periodicals may be noted the valuable articles by C. A. Middleton-Smith on "Engineering Developments in Asiatic Russia," in *The Engineer*, Aug. 31, 1945–Nov. 23, 1945; K. Mason, "Notes on the Northern Sea Route," *Geographical Journal*, XCVI (1940); "The Roads of Soviet Asia," *Geographical Review*, XXIII (1943); C. D. Harris, "The Cities of the Soviet Union," *Geographical Review*, XXXV (1945); "New Railroads in the U.S.S.R.," *American Review of the Soviet Union*, March, 1947.

Mention should be made of the invaluable *Great Soviet Atlas*, vols. I and II, Moscow, 1937. In English only small atlases are available, e.g. G. Goodall (ed.), Soviet Russia in Maps, Philip & Son, 1942.

TABLE XXVI

SOVIET ASIA: AREA, POPULATION, URBANIZATION AND LITERACY

Administrative and Geographical Units	Area (000 sq. miles)	Population (millions) Jan. 1939	% Urban as at 1939	% able to read or write 1926 Aged 10 years or over	1939 Aged 9 years or over
1. SIBERIA*					
Omsk oblast	556·20	2·367	21		
Novosibirsk oblast†	236·85	4·023	41		
Altai krai	112·60	2·520	16		
Total Western Siberia	905·65	8·910	29		
Krasnoyarsk krai	827·70	1·940	28		
Irkutsk oblast	347·35	1·287	44		
Buryat Mongol A.S.S.R.	127·95	0·542	30		
Chita oblast..	278·00	1·159	44		
Yakut A.R.S.S.	1170·25	0·401	20		
Total Eastern Siberia	2751·25	5·329	35		
Khabarovsk krai	993·05	1·431	45		
Maritime krai	79·50	0·907	51		
Total Far East ..	1072·55	2·338	48		
TOTAL SIBERIA ..	4729·45	16·577	33	51·1‡	81·2‡
2. KAZAKHSTAN S.S.R. ..	1055·85	6·146	28	22·8	76·3
3. CENTRAL ASIA					
Uzbek S.S.R.	158·50	6·282	23	10·6	67·8
Turkmen S.S.R.	187·15	1·254	33	12·5	67·2
Kirgiz S.S.R.	77·85	1·459	19	15·1	70·0
Tajik S.S.R.	54·95	1·485	17	3·7	71·7
TOTAL: CENTRAL ASIA	478·45	10·480	23		
4. SOUTH CAUCASUS					
Georgia S.S.R.	26·75	3·542	30	47·5	80·3
Armenia S.S.R.	11·55	1·282	29	34·5	73·8
Azerbaijan S.S.R.	33·00	3·210	36	25·2	73·3
TOTAL: SOUTH CAUCASUS	71·30	8·034	32		
5. TOTAL: SOVIET ASIA	6335·05	41·237	30		

* 'Siberia' in this appendix excludes the Asiatic parts of administrative areas, such as the Sverdlovsk and Chelyabinsk oblasti, which lie astride the Ural mountains.

† The Kuzbas area within this oblast was detached as a new oblast—the Kemerovo oblast—in 1943.

‡ These percentages refer to the R.S.F.S.R. of which Siberia is part.

TABLE XXVII

POPULATION DENSITIES AND CULTIVATED AREA

(i) In major geographical regions:

Regions	Population (millions)	Area (ooo sq. m.)	Cultivated area (sq. m.)	Population per sq. mile	Density per sq. mile of cultivated land
Siberia	16·6	4,730	57,600	3·5	289
Western Siberia ..	8·9	906	39,800	9·8	224
Eastern Siberia ..	5·3	2,751	14,300	1·9	370
Far East	2·3	1,073	3,500	2·1	657
Central Asia ..	10·5	478	19,600	22·0	536
Kazakhstan	6·1	1,056	23,600	5·8	259
South Caucasus ..	8·0	71	9,800	112·7	816
SOVIET ASIA ..	41·2	6,335	110,600	6·5	363

(ii) In republics:

Republics	Population (millions)	Area (ooo sq. miles)	Cultivated area (sq. miles)	Population per sq. mile	Density per sq. mile of cultivated land
Uzbek S.S.R. ..	6·28	158·5	10,900	40	576
Tajik S.S.R. ..	1·49	55·0	3,100	27	481
Kirgiz S.S.R. ..	1·46	77·9	4,000	19	365
Turkmen S.S.R. ..	1·25	187·1	1,600	6·7	781
Kazakhstan S.S.R.	6·15	1056·0	23,600	5·8	259
Georgia S.S.R. ..	3·54	26·8	3,800	122	903
Azerbaijan S.S.R.	3·21	33·0	4,300	97	747
Armenia S.S.R. ..	1·28	11·6	1,700	110	753

In the table above figures for cultivated area are for the year 1938; total area and population figures are given as at the last census of January, 1939.

TABLE XXVIII

PRINCIPAL TOWNS OF SOVIET ASIA

1. SIBERIA

WESTERN SIBERIA* Administ. Status			Population (millions) 1926 (Dec.)	1939 (Jan.)
Novosibirsk	oblast capital	.. ..	120,128	405,589
Omsk	oblast capital	.. ..	161,684	280,716
Stalinsk			3,894	169,538
Barnaul	capital of Altai krai	..	73,858	148,129
Tomsk			92,274	141,215
Kemerovo	oblast capital	.. ..	21,726	132,978
Prokopyevsk			10,717	107,227
Leninsk-Kuznetski			19,645	81,890
Anzhero Sudzhensk			30,199	71,079
Kurgan	oblast capital	.. ..	27,996	53,224

EASTERN SIBERIA				
Irkutsk	oblast capital	.. ..	108,129	243,380
Krasnoyarsk	krai capital	.. ..	72,261	189,999
Ulan Ude	capital of Buryat-Mongol A.S.S.R.	.. ..	29,918	129,417
Chita	oblast capital	.. ..	61,526	102,555
Cheremkhovo			14,485	65,907
Yakutsk†	capital of Yakut A.S.S.R.	..		50,000 (1940)

FAR EAST				
Vladivostok	capital of Maritime krai		107,980	206,432
Khabarovsk	krai capital	.. ..	52,045	199,364
Komsomolsk†			..	70,746
Voroshilov	capital of Ussuri oblast		36,344	70,628
Blagoveshchensk†			..	58,761
Magadan†			..	50,000 (1947)

2. KAZAKHSTAN S.S.R.

Alma Ata	republic capital	..	45,395	230,528
Karaganda†	oblast capital	.. ..	..	165,937
Semipalatinsk	oblast capital	.. ..	56,871	109,779
Petropavlovsk	oblast capital	.. ..	47,361	91,678
Chimkent			21,018	74,185
Uralsk	oblast capital	.. ..	36,352	66,201

TABLE XXVIII—*cont.*

3. CENTRAL ASIA	*Administ. Status*			*Population (millions)* 1926 (*Dec.*)	1939 (*Jan.*)
Tashkent	Uzbek capital	..	..	323,613	585,005
Samarkand	oblast capital	..	..	105,206	134,346
Ashkhabad	Turkmen capital		..	51,593	126,580
Frunze	Kirgiz capital	..	..	36,610	92,659
Kokand				69,324	84,665
Andijan	oblast capital	..	..	73,465	83,691
Stalinabad	Tajik capital	..	..	5,607	82,540
Namangan	oblast capital	..	..	73,640	77,351
Chardju	oblast capital	..	..	13,950	54,739
Bokhara	oblast capital	..	..	46,778	50,382

4. SOUTH CAUCASUS

Baku	Azerbaijan capital		..	453,333	809,347
Tbilisi	Georgian capital		..	294,044	519,175
Erivan	Armenian capital		..	64,613	200,031
Kirovabad				57,393	98,743
Kutaisi				48,196	81,479
Batumi				48,474	70,807
Leninakan				42,313	67,707

Note. ⋆ Ural cities on the eastern side of the mountains are not listed above. (These include Sverdlovsk 140,300 (1926) and 425,544 (1939); Chelyabinsk 59,307 (1926) and 273,127 (1939), and Magnitogorsk, a new urban growth, 145,870 in 1939.

† Towns for which no population figure is given for 1926 are 'mushroom' towns of the inter-census period, 1926–39.

TABLE XXIX

PRINCIPAL NATIONALITY GROUPS OF SOVIET ASIA

1. CENTRAL ASIA AND KAZAKHSTAN

			1926	1939
Uzbeks	..	..	3,954,701	4,844,021
Kazakhs	..	..	3,968,289	3,098,764
Tajiks	..	..	980,509	1,228,964
Kirgiz	..	..	762,736	884,306
Turkomen	..	..	763,940	811,769
Karakalpaks	..	..	146,317	185,775

2. SOUTH CAUCASUS

Azerbaijanians	..		1,707,000	2,274,805
Georgians	..	..	1,821,000	2,248,566
Armenians	..	..	1,568,000	2,151,884

CHAPTER VI

HIGH ASIA

By R. R. Rawson

THE GENERAL SETTING

THE plateaus of High Asia occupy an area of about 2,500,000 square miles and extend from the Pamirs to the mountains which overlook the densely populated basin of Szechwan and the agricultural lands of northern China: they are bounded on the south by the Himalaya and on the north by parts of several mountain ranges including the Tien Shan, Tarbagatai, Altai, and Sayan. In the south between the Himalaya and Kunlun ranges is the highest plateau of all, that of Tibet, with a mean altitude of nearly 16,000 ft. North of Tibet extend plains at varying altitudes: the Tarim basin between 2000 and 6000 ft; that of Dzungaria at 1000 ft; the smaller Turfan basin which sinks below sea level, and further to the northeast, between 3000 ft and 5000 ft, the plains of Mongolia and the Gobi desert. While some areas on the outer edges of the plateaus drain to the river systems of India, China, and the U.S.S.R., most of the rivers in the interior flow towards the centres of drainage basins which have no outlet to the sea. The high altitudes and rarefied atmosphere are associated with great daily and annual ranges of temperature and strong winds. Mean temperatures are below 32° F. for six months of the year over much of Mongolia and Tibet, and for two to three months in the Tarim basin. The July mean temperature is about 70° F. on the plains of Sinkiang and reaches 90° F. in the Turfan depression. Rainfall occurs mainly in summer and is very slight everywhere except on the higher mountain slopes along the northern border of the area and in a few localities in the south and east. The summer monsoon from the Bay of Bengal penetrates in places to the north of the eastern Himalaya and gives a moderate rainfall sufficient for agriculture to the southeast corner of the Tibetan plateau. The average annual rainfall on the southern edge of the Mongolian plateau is about 14 inches but annual amounts vary greatly with the strength of the southerly monsoon.

Mosses and short grasses make up the vegetation over most of the Tibetan plateau; parts of it are completely barren, and forests grow only

Fig. 33.

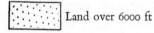 Land over 6000 ft

Areas of desert and dry scrub in Sinkiang and Mongolia (after Grenard)

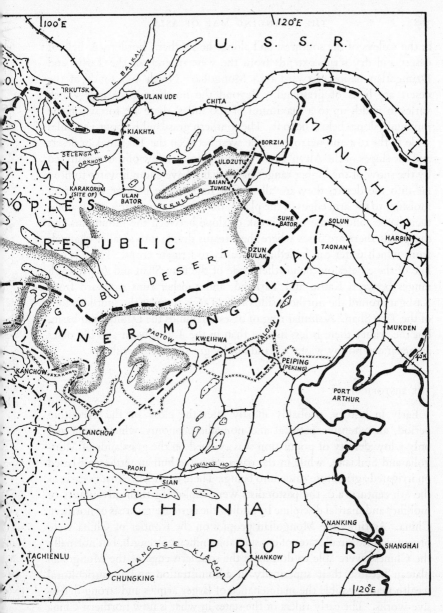

xxxxxxxxxxxxxxxx   Main alignment of the Great Wall

----------   Railways reported to have been built in the Mongolian People's Republic

—·—·—·—·   Kalimpong-Lhasa trade route

in the valleys of the southeast and along the southern border. A belt of desert and dry scrub extends from the western ends of the Tarim and Dzungarian basins eastward into Mongolia. North and south of the desert are belts of grassland. Beyond the northern grassland, which varies in width up to a maximum of 500 miles, there are forests on the mountain slopes below 9000 ft. The southern grassland is about 150 miles wide in the east and narrows to the west between the Taklamakan desert and the slopes of the Altyn Tagh. Although only a few of the streams fed by the snow of the higher ranges of Sinkiang have enough water to flow far into the desert, they are all of first importance because they bring moisture to the arid edges of the plains; trees and rich pastures grow along their banks, and at the main break of slope between the mountains and the plains there are oases where the streams divide into smaller channels from which water can be led away easily to irrigate crops. There is one line of these oases on the northern side of the Nan Shan and Altyn Tagh ranges between Kansu and Yarkand, and another runs eastward from Kashgar around the northern side of the Tarim basin at the southern foot of the Tien Shan. A similar ring of oases surrounds the Dzungarian basin, but the aridity there is less intense than in the Tarim basin and the oases are separated not by wastes of sand but by grassland and scrub.

THE HISTORIC PAST

Early in history, probably shortly after the close of the Neolithic period, an extensive pastoral and nomadic economy which supported only a low density of population was evolved on the grasslands of Mongolia and Sinkiang, while in the oases intensive human settlement based on irrigated agriculture came into being. There is evidence that as early as the 8th century B.C. the pastoralists were exploiting their advantages of mobility and martial discipline by raiding the agricultural areas of northern China. At times the Mongolian peoples on the frontier of China were organized into small states of considerable military strength, but normally the Chinese were able to dominate the southern edge of the Mongolian plateau because their superiority in administration and in agricultural wealth made possible the maintenance of larger armies and strong defensive works. The early rulers of the states in what is now northern China built a series of massive stone and earthen walls along their northern borders, and about 220 B.C. parts of these separate defences were strengthened and extended by the emperor Shi Huang Ti to form the Great Wall which became the northern boundary of China under the Han dynasty (202 B.C. to A.D. 226). The Great Wall, with its smaller

subsidiary defences running parallel to it and at varying distances up to
100 miles north and south from the main alignment, marked the frontier
between agricultural and pastoral economies; to the south the land was
largely settled by Chinese cultivators and was suitable for intensive agriculture on the traditional pattern of northern China, while to the north
lay the steppe of the Mongolian nomads, too dry for intensive cultivation
and suitable at best for extensive farming of a type unfamiliar to the
Chinese. The Great Wall, in common with all systems of static defence,
had the disadvantage that it could be easily breached since it could not be
manned continuously and kept in repair. Moreover it could be out-
flanked at its western end by invaders from the north. Therefore the
Chinese emperors sought to strengthen their northern border by occupying the eastern oases which became useful strategic bases on the flank of
the steppe. Under the Han dynasty the oases acquired additional
importance for they determined the caravan routes which carried the
growing trade between China and the west, and at that period Chinese
power reached beyond the Pamirs to the shores of the Caspian Sea. In
the 7th and 8th centuries Chinese interest in the caravan routes declined
for it had become more convenient to maintain contact with Europe and
northwest India by sea, and the small states located around the western
groups of oases united under Muslim invaders against the local Chinese
forces. The Chinese retreated and in 751 they retained their hold only
on the eastern oases in what is now the province of Kansu.

In the 10th, 11th, and 12th centuries a number of strong tribal associations emerged among the pastoral peoples of High Asia, and those in the
southeast invaded northwest China and devastated great areas of agricultural land. Ruins of towns and irrigation works dating from that time
can be seen to-day on the desert's edge in Kansu. These developments
resulted in the military supremacy of the Mongol tribes of the Mongolian
grasslands, under the leadership of Genghiz Khan. The Mongols established a vast empire which included all High Asia except parts of the
Tibetan plateau and reached westward to the Mediterranean; by 1280
they had occupied all China and were conquering parts of Annam and
Burma. Centralized administration of so large an area with poor communications was impracticable, and the empire began to disintegrate even
before it had reached its maximum extent. The Mongols concerned
themselves mainly with military activities and left the administration of
the conquered lands to adventurers from western countries and from
India and China. When Kublai Khan, grandson of Genghiz Khan, became ruler of the empire in 1263 the capital was moved from Karakorum
in the northern grassland of Mongolia to Peking, and Kublai Khan's

successor ruled only the eastern part of the empire for he, a Buddhist, was regarded as an infidel by the western Mongols who had been converted to Islam towards the end of the 13th century. By the 14th century the Mongol power was no longer sufficient to suppress the Chinese, and in 1368 the last Mongol ruler was driven from Peking by Chinese armies led by the founders of the Ming Dynasty. Over two hundred years elapsed before China recovered sufficiently to contemplate imperial expansion into High Asia. In the 17th, 18th, and 19th centuries, after the military power of the eastern Mongols had been undermined by the spread of Lamaist Buddhism from Tibet, Chinese suzerainty was gradually extended by the Manchu rulers to include all the steppe and desert to the border of Siberia, all the desert and oases as far as the Pamirs, and also, for the first time, the whole of the Tibetan plateau.

POLITICAL DIVISIONS

To-day there are five main political divisions in High Asia: Inner Mongolia, the Mongolian People's Republic, Inner Tibet, Tibet and Sinkiang. These vast territories form a sparsely populated and economically undeveloped frontier zone over 2000 miles long from the borders of Manchuria and India and varying in depth from 700 miles to 1500 miles between China, the U.S.S.R. and the new states of India and Pakistan; they contain reserves of coal, iron, copper, and petroleum, and an asset which will probably be of more permanent value than any fuel or ore deposit, a vast area of unoccupied land which could be made suitable for agriculture and stock raising by modern systems of irrigation and water supply. 'The dead heart of Asia' has been an apt description for the area. How long it will remain so will depend on the growth of population and on the progress of industrialization in the neighbouring provinces of China and the U.S.S.R. to a level which will make essential the fuller exploitation of these mineral and agricultural resources. Since the revolution of 1911, Chinese connections with all except Inner Mongolia and Inner Tibet have weakened, and the U.S.S.R. has now become the dominant power. Tibet and the Mongolian People's Republic have become virtually independent states, the latter closely associated economically and politically with the U.S.S.R. Sinkiang remains politically a province of China under strong Soviet influence.

The political boundaries shown in modern atlases were drawn by cartographers of western countries and are sometimes misleading. Centralized administration is only feebly developed in High Asia; the influence of governments decreases rapidly with increasing distance from such capitals as Ulan Bator and Lhasa, and many frontier areas are controlled by local chieftains who recognize no central authority. Very little of High Asia has been accurately surveyed, and detailed topographic maps exist only for a few small areas on the borders of India and along some of the more important trade routes. In these circumstances it is hard to fix boundaries, especially where, as in the steppes and desert of Sinkiang and the Mongolian People's Republic, there are no convenient surface features like rivers and mountain ranges. Even where there are suitable topographic features, their selection as political boundaries might not conform to local usage. For example, on the Survey of India topographic maps[1] the boundaries between Bhután, Sikkim and Tibet are shown to follow the crests of the Himalayan ranges, while the line recognized by the local inhabitants of the three states is the junction of the pine forests and bamboo forests which roughly coincides with the 11,500 ft. contour.

INNER MONGOLIA AND THE MONGOLIAN PEOPLE'S REPUBLIC

The word Mongolia has no exact political meaning; it is applied in a general way to the territory extending northward from the Great Wall to the southern border of Siberia. Within that area are two relatively habitable zones, a southerly one of grassland and a northerly one of grassland and some forest, separated by an expanse of desert and arid steppe. Though all three zones were dominated by the Chinese in the latter part of the Manchu period, special importance was attached to the strategic value of the southern belt of grassland adjacent to the Great Wall, and a two-fold political division into Inner Mongolia and Outer Mongolia came into being. Inner Mongolia, where Chinese control was direct and accompanied by Chinese colonization, included the southern belt of grassland and the fringe of the desert, while Outer Mongolia, in which Chinese control was weaker and exercised through tribal authorities, and where economic ties with Russia were strong, contained the greater part of the desert and all the northern grassland and forest. After the revolution which ended the Manchu dynasty in 1911, Inner Mongolia was formed into the new Chinese provinces of Chahar, Suiyuan and Ninghsia. In Outer Mongolia Chinese power declined rapidly, and in 1921 a series of revolts culminated, with Soviet help, in the establishment of the Mongolian People's Republic. Later, Soviet influence in Mongolian affairs grew with the probability of conflict with Japan as Japanese

[1] Survey of India ¼-inch series, sheets 78A (1937) and 78E (1934).

forces spread through neighbouring territory in Manchuria and parts of Inner Mongolia. After the population of the new republic had voted in favour of closer co-operation with the U.S.S.R. in 1945 China officially renounced all claims to sovereignty in Outer Mongolia.

For tactical reasons the Great Wall was built not on the edge of the Mongolian plateau, but along some hill crests to the south, and so the three provinces of Inner Mongolia each have two main physical divisions, an area of high grassland over 4000 ft. in altitude and a lower region of more varied topography. On the plateau rainfall is uncertain and the growing season too short for many crops of the northern plains of China to ripen, and although some agriculture is practised in favourable parts the area is occupied almost exclusively by nomadic herders. Sheep, cattle, and horses are raised, and hides, wool, and livestock are exported to China. On the lower ground in the south, where the rainfall is slightly higher in places, there are better opportunities for agriculture and it is there that Chinese farmers have settled on cultivable land among the pastures of the Mongolian tribes. The width of this lower zone is about 40 miles in the easternmost province of Chahar, increasing to 250 miles in the central province of Suiyuan and narrowing again to a few miles in the westernmost province of Ninghsia. In Suiyuan and Ninghsia most of the lower ground is desert. The main Chinese settlements are in the eastern, moister half of Inner Mongolia: in the plain around Kweihwa, along the Peking-Paotow railway, in the area immediately north of Kalgan and along the left bank of the Hwang ho where there are small irrigation works. The crops are oats, barley, wheat, rape, linseed, beans, potatoes, and soft fruits, but only with irrigation can they be raised by the intensive farming methods of the northern plain of China; away from the irrigable areas extensive mixed farming is practised, and this latter system provides the cultivators with only a precarious subsistence. Much agricultural land was abandoned during the Japanese occupation between 1937 and 1945. More recently, both the agricultural and pastoral economies have suffered in the fighting between Chinese Communist forces and the Kuomintang armies. Hostilities were largely concentrated around the strategically valuable city of Kalgan and the railway to Paotow, in the areas of greatest agricultural development.

In 1936 the population of Inner Mongolia was about 4,850,000 and its average density 15 persons to the square mile. In 1932 it was estimated that about 70% of the population were farmers. There is little prospect of expansion of the farming areas. With large capital expenditure more efficient irrigation works could be made in the Hwang ho valley. In areas away from that river, settlement is hindered by uncertain rainfall and also by the lack of reliable sources of surface water on which agricultural populations are more dependent than nomadic pastoralists. It has been estimated that with full development of river and underground water resources Inner Mongolia might support a maximum population of about 7,000,000.[1] There are large reserves of iron ore and some coal, but these minerals are worked only on a small scale.

In 1945, an autonomous administration was established at Wangyeh-miao, about 200 miles west of Harbin, while an Inner Mongolian provisional government was set up at Kalgan. The former body had the support of the pastoralists in Jehol and Manchuria, numbering about 2,000,000 in all, and the latter was intended to serve the interests of the 1,250,000 or so pastoralists in the eastern half of Inner Mongolia. Both authorities had the support of the North China Communist régime. In 1947, after the Communists had been driven from Chahar and Suiyuan by the Chinese Nationalist forces during the campaign of 1946, these two political movements were combined to form the Mongolian Autonomous Government with headquarters at Wangyehmiao. About 250,000 pastoralists in central and western Inner Mongolia remained loyal to the central government of China. The headquarters of this group was near Paotow. Their aim was Mongol autonomy, and dominion status for Inner Mongolia. It is reported that the Chinese central government, traditionally fearful of a large and well-organized state dominated by Mongol elements on its northern border, was prepared only to grant autonomy to pastoralist peoples within the framework of the existing provincial administrations. This attitude, and the failure of the Chinese to supply modern arms for use against communist raiders from the north were obviously shortsighted. The younger elements in this western group were already beginning to consider their political future in terms of co-operation with the Mongolian People's Republic[2] before the downfall of the Nationalist régime in China.

The most populous part of the Mongolian People's Republic is in the north, and it is separated from China by the Gobi desert. The results of this physical separation were intensified in the years 1937 to 1945 by the Japanese occupation of most of Inner Mongolia; movement of people and goods by camel, cart and motor transport across the desert from Ulan Bator to Paotow and Kalgan declined in importance and the Mongolian People's Republic became increasingly caught up in the economic slip-

---

[1] G. B. Cressey: "Chinese colonization in Mongolia : a general survey." (in *Pioneer Settlement*, American Geographical Society Special Publications No. 14, 1932).
[2] *Among the Mongols*: special article, *The Times*, 13th August, 1948.

stream of the U.S.S.R. In 1944 the population was estimated at 2,078,000 and its average density 3 persons to the square mile. Pastoralism is the main occupation but the old nomadic form is undergoing a slow change. Scientific ways of breeding cattle, horses, and sheep are being introduced. Drilling of new wells is enabling greater use to be made of grazing land far from surface water and there is an increasing cultivation of hay for winter feeding. With a rainfall almost everywhere below 20 inches and winter temperatures almost Siberian there is little scope for agriculture; small amounts of barley, millets, oats, hay, and vegetables are grown, especially in the Orkhon and Selenga valleys where irrigation schemes are reported to be under consideration. An agricultural research station has been established. Surplus wool, hides, and furs are exported to the U.S.S.R. At Ulan Bator, the capital, a group of factories for preparing wool and for making leather and felt footwear has been in operation under Russian supervision since 1934. There were reported to be 3492 industrial workers in the country in 1935, 90% of them Mongolians. Surveys were undertaken by Soviet geologists during the years 1930 to 1935. Coal is known to exist in three areas and there are deposits of iron, copper, lead, gold, and silver. In 1934 the mines at Naraikha which are connected by light railway to Ulan Bator, 19 miles to the north-west, produced about 6000 tons of coal. The coal reserves in the Baian Tuman district on the Kerulen river, about 70 miles from the border of Manchuria, are probably larger than those of Naraikha; no production figures are available but it is significant that between 1939 and 1945, according to one report, a railway was built from the Siberian system of the U.S.S.R. at Borzia to Baian Tuman with branches to Uldzutu, Dzun Bulak, and Suhe Bator.[1] There are no published reports of the third area of coal reserves in the Altai mountains.

Apart from the southerly route to China, the main lines of communications all lead to Soviet territory: Ulan Bator is connected by road through the Siberian border town Kyakhta to Ulan Ude on the Trans-Siberian railway, and there is some water-borne traffic on the Orkhon and Selenga rivers. The Ulan Ude-Kyakhta railway was extended to Ulan Bator in or about 1940. An airline, too, operates between Ulan Bator and Ulan Ude. Internal communication is maintained largely by ox cart, and to a small extent by horse and camel transport. Motor transport is not greatly used owing to difficulties of fuel supply. It is likely that construction of military roads progressed rapidly between 1939 and 1945.

[1] New Railroads in the U.S.S.R.: a report on an interview with the Minister of Railroads of the U.S.S.R.: translated from OGONEK, No. 29, July 1946 and published in *The American Review of the Soviet Union*, March 1947.

INNER TIBET AND TIBET

In the Tibetan plateau, as in Mongolia, a political division into inner and outer territories relative to China Proper can be traced from the later part of the Manchu period.[1] Inner Tibet, which occupies the eastern half of the plateau, includes the headwaters of the Hwang Ho and of the Yangtze, Mekong and Salween rivers.[2] In the south, where the rainfall is moderate and forests grow at altitudes up to 12,000 ft., and where some of the valley floors lie below 5000 ft., Chinese farmers have settled and raise crops similar to those of Mongolia and northwest China. To the north aridity increases, forests give way to grassland, there are fewer Chinese settlers and farming decreases in importance; in the Koko Nor district and in the Tsaidam depression, both of which include large areas of poor grassland, the inhabitants live entirely by their herds of cattle, sheep and camels. The northern half of this inner territory, though useless for agriculture, was important strategically for it lies on the southern flank of the routes through the oases of Kansu to Sinkiang. After the establishment of the Chinese republic, Inner Tibet was divided into two provinces, a southern one, Sikang, which includes most of the cultivable land, and a northern one, Chinghai, which is an area of pastoral economy. Most of the plateau surface is above 12,000 ft. in altitude and the natural vegetation is inferior to that of Mongolia as animal fodder. Much of Chinghai is uninhabited, and the average density of population is only about 6 persons to the square mile, compared with 10 persons to the square mile in Sikang. Inner Tibet is largely unexplored and no mineral surveys have been made. A few small towns like Tachienlu, Chamdo, and Batang, located on trade routes to the interior of the plateau, serve as caravan staging posts and as markets for the exchange of local pastoral and agricultural products.

Tibet, the outer territory occupying the western part of the plateau, is the homeland of Lamaist Buddhism, the dominant religion not only of the whole of the Tibetan plateau but also of Mongolia: political control of the country was therefore important to the Manchu rulers of China. Both the Kuomintang and Communist governments of China claim

[1] O. Lattimore, *Inner Asian Frontiers of China*, 1940. Ch. VII.

[2] The boundary between Inner Tibet and Tibet shown on Figure 33 is based on tentative agreements made by representatives of the British, Chinese and Tibetan governments at the Simla Conference in 1914, and in the absence of a more valid treaty is the one generally accepted internationally. The agreements reached at Simla were not confirmed by the Chinese central government. China claimed that the boundary should be fixed about 100 miles west of the line on Figure 33, while, according to some European and Tibetan authorities, it should lie about 300 miles to the east of the position indicated so that Tibet would include much territory now regarded as part of Chinghai and Sikang.

25

suzerainty over Tibet but the country has been practically independent since the Chinese political representative and his military escort were expelled from Lhasa by Tibetan forces in 1912. Independence has not brought economic progress comparable with that of the Mongolian People's Republic. The Cretaceous and Jurassic sediments which cover much of the plateau show no sign of important mineral wealth. Beneath them however lie older formations with ores of gold, silver, copper, lead, and iron; some of these deposits have been worked on a small scale but their exact extent and nature await detailed geological study. There are two main physical divisions. The more extensive is the largely unexplored plateau of northern and central Tibet, the Chang Tang, which occupies over three-quarters of the total area. The plains of this region have a mean attitude of about 16,000 ft and there are several east-west mountain ranges with peaks over 20,000 ft. No crops can be raised, and the sparse nomadic population live by the products of domesticated yak and sheep, supplemented by barley which is imported from the south. The remaining quarter of the area contains a variety of topography including plateaus at altitudes of about 15,000 ft, the valley of the Tsangpo river which falls from 17,000 ft in the west to 6000 ft in the east, and the broken country along the southern border where the deep gorges of the Himalaya drain southward to India. This southern and southeastern area contains most of the population; there, on the high plateaus grazing is better than on the Chang Tang and supports a greater density of livestock, while in the valleys below 12,000 ft there are permanent villages and small farms growing barley, potatoes, beans, and vegetables, with wheat and soft fruits in sheltered areas below 10,000 ft. Irrigation is practised in the Tsangpo valley. In this southern area the density of population might average 15 persons to the square mile and it decreases northward over the Chang Tang. Lhasa, the capital, is the largest town and lies on a marshy plain beside a tributary of the Tsangpo at an altitude of 11,800 ft and 300 miles from the border of India. The buildings are mostly of stone, flat-roofed, two-storeyed, and they sprawl over a roughly circular area about a mile across. There is no drainage system. Household refuse is thrown into the streets. Some of the public buildings are connected by telephone. Electricity for lighting is supplied from a small hydro-electric power plant in the neighbouring hills. A mile to the west of the town two hills rise steeply about 700 ft. from the plain. On the larger of these is the Potala, a group of high fortress-like buildings which contains the residence of the Dalai Lama who is the primate of Lamaist Buddhism and head of the central government. The permanent population of the town is about 20,000; in addition there are usually several thousand pilgrims attending religious festivals, and also traders from China, Mongolia and other parts of Tibet. The only other towns are Shigatse and Gyantse.

'Feudal' conditions prevail throughout the country. The best land is owned by the monasteries and the few aristocratic families. The priesthood, numbering about 300,000, live mostly on the proceeds of large monastic estates and are a severe economic burden on the country. In 1936 the population was estimated at 3,700,000. The high mortality rate, the alleged celibacy of the priesthood, and the polyandrous society of the poorer people in this harsh environment are powerful factors which, acting over long periods, would probably result in a low and static population.

Throughout history Tibet has been isolated by the high barren ranges of the Kunlun in the north, by the Pamirs in the west, and by the Himalayan ranges and the dense jungles of their lower southerly slopes in the south. No easy ways lead outward to countries of more advanced economy, and even along the few difficult routes to Bengal, Kashmir, and China there has been insufficient trade to cause much movement of people and ideas. The plateau itself is almost as formidable an obstacle now as it was in the past. The main land routes of High Asia avoid it, and so do modern air routes because the surface is so high that even if landing grounds were provided civil aircraft could not take off from them.[1] In the future, improvements in aircraft design and particularly in jet propulsion and rocket-assisted take-off will surely make it practicable for civil aircraft to operate with economic loads from airfields and lakes at altitudes of 16,000 ft. The plains and lakes of the plateau will then acquire new geographical values. Meanwhile Tibet remains the last great physical barrier in Asia. This natural isolation has been reinforced by the attitude of the Tibetan government which is opposed to economic and social progress on western patterns: only rarely are Europeans permitted to enter the country, and this policy has long had the active support of the authorities in Delhi in the regulation of movement over the mountain passes which lead to Tibet from India. The small foreign trade is almost wholly with India and China. Tibetan wool, hides, and borax from the lake shores of the Chang Tang are exchanged for brick tea, cotton, and manufactured wares. The Indian trade flourishes at the expense of the

---

[1] Civil airfields are usually built at low altitudes. At high altitudes longer runways and reduced payloads are necessary on account of rarefied air. There is an altitude limit above which the atmospheric pressure is too low even for unloaded aircraft to take off, however long the runway. This limit varies with local conditions and depends on several factors including engine power and aircraft design, but for the civil aircraft of to-day it is about 10,000 ft.

Chinese owing to political unrest and danger from bandits on the Chinese border. There are no roads and practically no wheeled vehicles; goods are carried by porters, mules, and yaks, and in the northeast also by camels. Parts of the middle Tsangpo are navigable, and coracles and rafts are used on a 400-mile stretch of the river. The main trade routes from China and India converge on Lhasa: at best they are narrow stony tracks, and even the most important of them, the Kalimpong-Lhasa route which carries over half the trade between India and Tibet, would be hard to discern in parts if it were not for the poles of the telegraph line which follows it. This latter route and its eastward continuation from Lhasa were used for sending small quantities of war materials by pack mule to China after the capture of the Burma Road by the Japanese in 1942: it was ultimately abandoned for that purpose in favour of 'The Hump', the air route from Assam over the mountains of northern Burma and Yunnan to Kunming and Chungking.

For the last seventy years the security of the northern border of India has been the chief motive of British interest in Tibet. In the early years of the present century, British and Russian explorations proved that there is no route across the western part of the plateau suitable for the construction of roads which could be used by either power for the invasion of territories of the other. There could therefore be no important military threat to India from the direction of Tibet. Yet it was possible that so long as Russian and Chinese prestige were high in Lhasa, there might be unrest among the people of southern Tibet which would necessitate for Britain the enormous expense of maintaining garrisons along the whole of the 1800-mile Indo-Tibetan border. After several unsuccessful attempts to persuade the Chinese and Tibetan governments to agree to closer relations between Britain and Tibet, a military mission was sent from Bengal in 1903 under the command of Colonel (later Sir Francis) Younghusband. The original intention was merely to occupy some small forts a few miles inside Tibet in the hope that the Tibetans would feel that here was a strong power with whom they should come to terms. Far from achieving this end, the mission encountered sharp resistance. More troops were sent from Bengal and the mission became a full military expedition which ultimately fought its way to Lhasa in 1904.[1] The Dalai Lama fled to Mongolia, but a treaty was made with the

[1] The expedition entered Tibet by the track now known as the Kalimpong-Lhasa trade route which crosses the main ranges of the Himalaya by two passes, the Jelep La (14,250 ft) and the Tang La (15,220 ft). These passes are difficult to cross in bad weather, and are often blocked with snow for long periods. Though the numbers of Indian troops involved were small and the Tibetans poorly armed, the physical difficulties of soldiering at 15,000 ft. and of supplying a force with ammunition and most of its food by mule transport over two Himalayan passes make this expedition an outstanding military achievement.

Tibetans which provided for better trading facilities between India and Tibet and for Britain to be the dominating foreign influence in the country. Trading posts accessible to merchants from India were to be established at Gartok in western Tibet and at Gyantse and Yatung, and the Tibetans agreed that no foreign power be permitted to intervene in the affairs of the country or to build roads or open mines without British consent.

In the southeast of Tibet several valleys are suitable for Chinese methods of agriculture. British concern with the prospect of dense Chinese settlement so near the border of India was one of the main reasons for the Simla Conference of 1914. At that conference Britain recognized Chinese suzerainty over Tibet, and secured agreement that no Chinese settlement should be permitted in that country and that British trade agents and small military forces should be stationed in Tibet at Gyantse and Yatung on the Kalimpong-Lhasa route to encourage and protect the trade with India. It remains to be seen whether the new régime in China will acquiesce in this virtual inclusion of Tibet within the Indian orbit.

SINKIANG

In Sinkiang there has been no division into inner and outer political zones. The most arid part is in the south and southeast, and strong Chinese rule both there and in the oases and grasslands to the north and west was essential for the control of the several routes to the west. The most important route, the 'North Road', leads from Kansu through the oases of Hami and Barkul to Tihwa (Urumchi), the capital of Sinkiang,[1] and then westward to Russian territory through the border town of Chugu-chak (T'a Ch'eng). North of Hami a second route branches from the 'North Road' and runs westward through the Turfan oases and the oases of Kuchu and Aksu along the northern edge of the Taklamakan desert to Kashgar where it is joined by a continuation of the 'South Road' which connects the southern oases of Yarkand, Khotan, and Cherchen with Kansu. From Kashgar and Khotan other tracks lead to the U.S.S.R., Afghanistan, and Kashmir.

The population of Sinkiang has been estimated at about 4,055,000. About 77% are Muslim farmers of the oases; they belong to a variety of tribes referred to collectively as Turki, a linguistic term, and also by the

[1] Tihwa's population is given as 69,275 by The Times, 23rd September, 1948.

word Uighur which was the name of one of the Turki tribes in medieval times. Some of the oases like Kashgar, Khotan, Yarkand, Hami, and Turfan are large enough to support urban populations including merchants and craftsmen in addition to agricultural workers.[1] On the grasslands there are a few nomadic tribes, mainly Muslim but some Buddhist. Of these, the Kazakhs, Muslim pastoralists of Turkic speech, make up 10% of the total population, and the Kirgiz and Mongol pastoralists nearly 3%. There are also small groups of White Russians, Tartars, Uzbeks, and Manchus. The Chinese, about 8·4% of the population, are mainly town dwellers, though a turbulent minority among them, the Tungans or Muslim Chinese, have important agricultural holdings especially in the southern oases.

The Muslims of Sinkiang have always opposed Chinese rule. In Manchu times there were several revolts. An armed rising lasting from 1930 to 1934 ended only when the Chinese with Soviet help defeated the Muslim rebels and gave assurances of more liberal provincial government. Another rising in 1937 coincided with the Japanese invasion of northern China. The U.S.S.R. reacted by strengthening its hold on the affairs of Sinkiang; British-Indian traders were expelled, and Soviet troops were stationed as far east as Hami, only 150 miles from the border of Kansu. In 1942 when the U.S.S.R. was being hard pressed at Stalingrad, the Chungking government did much to restore Chinese authority. Soviet troops and political advisors were withdrawn in 1943 and Soviet trade agencies were closed. The present phase of Soviet activity in the province began in 1944 with the revolt of the three northern districts of Ili (Sui-ting), Chuguchak, and Altai (A Shan). These districts, where the population is 53% Kazakh and 23% Turki, proclaimed themselves a republic centred on the town of Ili. The immediate cause of the rising was possibly the Chinese attempt to settle refugee farmers from Hunan in Sinkiang, but its deeper roots, like those of earlier risings, are to be found in the oppressive and often corrupt Chinese provincial government. Soviet authorities, after supplying arms to the rebels, arranged a settlement between the Ili régime and the provincial government at Tihwa which provided for a large measure of local autonomy. The settlement has not been effective. Early in 1947 there were Muslim revolts in Tihwa and Turfan, and since August of that year the border between the three northern districts and the remainder of the province has been closed. The British consulate-general at Kashgar, maintained

[1] Kashgar oasis, area 2,650 sq. km., estimated urban population 35,000. Yarkand oasis, area 2,100 sq. km., estimated urban population 60,000. Khotan oasis, area 1600 sq. km., estimated urban population 26,000.—F. Grenard, *Haute Asie, Géographie Universelle*, Tome VIII, 1929, pp. 319–21.

partly to protect the interests of British-Indian traders but mainly to counter Tzarist and, later, Soviet influence in Sinkiang has recently become the joint responsibility of India and Pakistan, while the British consulate at Tihwa has been created a consulate-general. The greatest single factor in the way of political stability is the extremely low standard of education of the non-Chinese element of the population. In the whole province there are only 15 'middle schools', while of the 200 students at the one college of higher education only 50 are reported to be Turkis.[1]

Wool, leather, and livestock from the northern oases and grasslands where agriculture is combined with stock-raising, and small quantities of silk and American varieties of cotton form the greatest proportion by value of the exports of the province. Since the completion of the Turk-Sib railway in 1930, the flow of trade has been mainly to the Soviet railheads such as Alma Ata which are only about 600 miles from Tihwa. The nearest Chinese railhead to Tihwa is Paoki, about 1500 miles distant. Since 1930, partly as a result of the need for military communications within the province but mainly owing to the importance of the Sinkiang routes for the supply of war materials from the U.S.S.R. to China, several of the old caravan tracks of the north including the whole of the 'North Road' from Kansu to the Turksib railway have been made into roads fit for heavy motor transport. The effect of this has been to bring more of northern Sinkiang into easy communication with the U.S.S.R. In the south, where pack-animals and carts are still the only means of transport, a small amount of trade is carried on with India, China, and Afghanistan, but only China is accessible by wheeled vehicles. The passes over the Pamirs and Karakoram are exceedingly difficult and are suitable only for porters and mules. An airline of the Sino-Soviet Aviation Corporation, almost wholly under Soviet control, has been operating since 1939 between Chungking and Alma Ata with stops at Hami, Tihwa, and Ili.

A series of five-year plans of reconstruction and development was begun under Soviet guidance in 1937. Progress has been mainly in agriculture and stock-raising, and it is estimated that by the extension and repair of irrigation works the area of cultivable land had been increased by 150,000 acres by 1942. Full use of water resources would enable Sinkiang to support a much larger agricultural and pastoral population than it has at present. Deposits of coal, copper, and iron along the lower slopes of the Tien Shan and in the Chuguchak neighbourhood are worked in small quantities for local requirements. Over twenty small petroleum fields have been reported, and some of them are worked by primitive

---

[1] *Struggle for Power in Central Asia.* Special articles, *The Times*, 22nd and 23rd September, 1948.

methods to produce kerosene and motor spirit for local markets. While no adequate geological surveys have been undertaken, the mineral resources are reported to be sufficient for the requirements of heavy industry should a need arise for such a development in the future.

SELECT READING LIST

Sir Charles Bell: *Tibet, Past and Present*, 1924; *Portrait of the Dalai Lama*, 1946.

M. Cable and F. French: *The Gobi Desert*, 1942.

C. P. Fitzgerald: *China. A Short Cultural History*, 1935.

F. Grenard: *Haute Asie: Géographie Universelle, Tome VIII*, 1929.

A. Guibaut: *Tibetan Venture (Second Guibaut-Liotard Expedition)*. Trans. by Lord Sudley, 1947.

O. Lattimore: *Inner Asian Frontiers of China*, 1940 (American Geographical Society Research Series No. 21).

Y. Misshima and Y. Goto: *A Japanese View of Outer Mongolia*, 1939.
(Translated from the Japanese by A. J. Grajdanzev, and published by the International Secretariat, Institute of Pacific Relations, New York, 1942).

M. R. Norins: *Gateway to Asia: Sinkiang*, 1944.

Articles by O. Lattimore and G. B. Cressey in *Pioneer Settlement*. American Geographical Society Special Publication No. 14 (1932).

O. Lattimore: *Pivot of Asia*, N.Y., 1950.

TABLE XXX

AREA AND POPULATION OF HIGH ASIA

Territory	Area (sq. miles)	Estimated population (to nearest 1000) and date of estimate	Density per sq. mile
Inner Mongolia	326,285	4,842,000	14·8
of which:			
Chahar	107,677	2,036,000 (1936)	18·9
Suiyuan	112,493	2,084,000 (1936)	18·5
Ninghsia	106,115	722,000 (1944)	6·8
Mongolian People's			
Republic	625,783	2,078,000 (1944)	3·3
Chinghai	269,117	1,513,000 (1940)	5·6
Sikang	172,863	1,756,000 (1940)	10·2
Tibet	469,294	3,722,000 (1936)	7·9
Sinkiang	705,769	4,055,000 (1948)	5·7
Total for High Asia ..	2,569,111	17,966,000	7

Sources: Population estimate for Mongolia from *Population Index*, January 1948, and for Sinkiang from *The Times*, 22 September, 1948. Other figures from *The Chinese Yearbook* 1944–1945.

EPILOGUE

THE UNITY OF ASIA?

Asia ...
Who cost her mother Tellus keener pangs,
Though feminine, than any of her sons:
More thought than woe was in her dusky face,
For she was prophesying of her glory;
And in her wide imagination stood
Palm-shaded temples, and high rival fanes,
By Oxus or in Ganges' sacred isles.

KEATS, *Hyperion*

PROBLEMS OF UNITY AND DIVERSITY

THE several chapters of this book have presented the main geographical factors relevant to the political life, internal and external, of the countries of Asia, considered in those major groupings which seem most conformable to the natural and the human environment. Two tasks, foreshadowed in the introductory survey, remain: to attempt an evaluation of the politico-geographical entity of Asia, if indeed we find upon examination that we can conceive it as a whole; and to place the continent in the wider setting of the world to-day, a world in which there seems less and less refuge for regional, let alone continental, isolation, a world of which the locational geography is being revolutionized by air transport.

ASIA, OR ASIATIC ASIA?

In what sense, other than the mere verbal definition of a continent, can we speak of Asia as one? Is there, in its geography and its polity, any peculiar quality of which we can say confidently 'this is essentially Asian'? Is the recurrent phrase 'Unity in Diversity' anything but a faded cliché, an expedient to beg questions and to evade thought?

These questions admit of large conjecture, and voices, both occidental and oriental, are divided. "Asia is one. The Himalayas divide, only to accentuate, two mighty civilizations. ... But not even the snowy barriers can interrupt that broad expanse of love for the Ultimate and Universal, which is the common thought-inheritance of every Asiatic race." "Asia

385

is one, and from now on must be regarded as one; there are connecting links between the new revolutionary states which give a grave unity to the whole." On the other side we can also cite observers from the East and from the West. "There are two Asias: Asiatic Asia, and the Asia which seems to merge so imperceptibly into Europe. . . ." "Asia is not interlocked, intertwined, as Europe is; though it is interlocked *with* Europe . . . Asia is a long distance round. It is too big to be a unit. It is three continents in one." Finally two geographers may speak. "Few common denominators unite Asia except location." "Geography has ordained that the great sub-continents surrounding the central mountain core look not towards but away from each other."[1]

Three continents in one; and on varying criteria one might find varying triads. Our introductory survey distinguished at least three macro-regions: Asiatic or Monsoon Asia; the Eurasia of the northern lowlands; the great central divide; and these (perhaps recklessly broad) divisions do at any rate keep some validity when checked with more than one criterion. Structure, climate, vegetation, demographic characteristics, broad ways of life at least show a reasonable measure of correlation with these great realms. Allowance must of course be made for the blurring of the divide in Southwest Asia, and regard be had to Codrington's protest against the cursory simplification of central Asia as undifferentiated 'steppe', 'desert', and 'mountain', and its identification with Nomad Man, a treatment neglectful alike of 'the rich variety of the actual terrain' and the symbiosis of the desert and the sown.[2] Physically then Asia is at best a trinity, each member of which is itself intricately complex. Since the days of Arius and Athanasius, however, the right evaluation of a triune relationship has been notoriously difficult, and so our discovery of a trinity which seems to hold with fair consistency is not really of very much use in our search for unity.

The title of Datta's book, however, suggests an alternative if more limited approach: subtracting Soviet Asia as Eurasiatic, and neglecting High Asia as essentially negative (both proceedings being more bold than legitimate), is there any unity in the Asiatic Asia which is left? Mentally,

---

[1] These quotations, in the order given, are from: Kakuzo Okakura, cited in C. A. Fisher's article (below); R. Payne, *The Revolt of Asia* (1948), p. 9; S. K. Datta, *Asiatic Asia* (1932), p. 9; J. Gunther, *Inside Asia* (1939), p. 626; G. B. Cressey, *Asia's Lands and Peoples* (1944), p. 12; C. A. Fisher, "The Concept of Asian Unity", *Asian Horizon*, Vol. I, No. 3 (1948), p. 11. Cf. E. S. Kirby, "The Disunity of Asia", *ibid.*, Vol. I, No. 4 (1948), pp. 3–7.

[2] K. de B. Codrington, "A Geographical Introduction to the History of Central Asia," *Geographical Journal* CIV (1944), reference at p. 28. It should not, perhaps, be necessary to emphasize the fact that a 'pure' nomad society is mere illusion—without some agricultural links it is difficult to see how pastoral nomadism could either arise or be maintained. The three ways of life of the central divide—pastoral nomadism, urban trading, settled agriculture—are interlocked in many ways; see Codrington, *loc. cit.*, for good examples and analyses.

probably, most of us do in fact automatically visualize Asia as this part of Asia rather than as the whole; but this vague impressionism is a very unsure guide. It is clear enough that few areas in similar latitudes are more different than are Arabia and Malabar, and few expressions of the human spirit more alien each from each than Islam and Hinduism. Yet, as we saw in our opening survey, the transitions from the arid lands of Southwest Asia to the hot and humid deltas of southern China are but gradual, often almost imperceptible; and since most human beings, fortunately, do not hold their personal philosophies with the rigid distinctiveness of dogmatic theologians and their text-books, there has even been a not inconsiderable amount of give-and-take between Islam and Hinduism. Akbar the Emperor and Kabir the weaver were both eclectics:

O Servant, where dost thou seek Me? Lo, I am beside thee.
I am neither in temple nor in mosque: I am neither in Kaaba nor in Kailas.
Kabir says: O Sadhu, God is the breath of all breath.

And for very much of this Asiatic Asia, there is much in common in the physical environment, in the daily and the secular manner of life in the paddy-carpeted deltas, the open niggardly fields of the uplands, the shifting patches of hill-top cultivation in the wild jungle. Most of Asia south and east of the central core is, after all, the realm of the monsoon, and the half of mankind which it contains lives—and dies—in much the same manner, however much the technical details of religious thought, social structure, and folk culture may differ.

This is true enough, and yet in the concrete language of the world today it means little or nothing. At best it adds up to a confused mosaic in which the individual pieces are ill-assorted in size, shape, and material. In every chapter dealing with the lands from the Red Sea to the Sea of Japan the dominant note has been diversity, and it is only secondarily that we have been able to discern, in the actual expression of the environment and in man's use of it, some few similarities on which to base the question-begging paradox 'Unity in Diversity'.

THE CLAIMS OF RELIGION: PHANTASY AND FACT

The same must be said of the high claims made on the basis of religion. A case can be made out (it is usually grotesquely exaggerated,' as in the quotation from Okakura) for the persistence of non-secular modes of thought at once more generally and more intensively than in the West.

Yet it is only relatively that even this rather nebulous abstraction is a common factor; and in practice rite and ceremony seem, to the outside observer, to be more potent in the life of many religious groups than more inward values. And to say that there is a common religiosity in Asiatic Asia may be true, but leaves out of the reckoning the enormous variety of particular beliefs, which is usually the important thing to the practitioner. As in Southwest Asia and the Indian sub-continent, 'Religion in danger' is a potent cry to rally group loyalties—but it is a specific religion that is implied, endangered by another specific religion. As in 16th-17th century Europe, political and economic groups express their conflicts in the language of religion, among the most powerful weapons known to combative man.

The Ultimate and the Universal may form a unity, but they are after all apprehended in divers specific formulations, and there is little unity in the human translation of these absolutes. The Buddhism of the Hinayana, beautiful and tender as it is, is tender in more than one sense, and survives (not unpenetrated by animist survivals) only in Burma, Siam, and Ceylon; in the sects of Tibet, China, and Japan it is scarcely recognizable as the non-theistic rational humanism of Gautama: the links are historical and go back to a distant and different age. The Confucian ethic again has a powerful rational validity; but, quite apart from the competitive or accretionary teachings of the Taoists and other sects, the course of Chinese history might suggest that its validity is not for all time, but for an age now dead. Japanese Shinto is hardly for export. Islam is of course in many ways a powerful unifying force—for Muslims; yet it too is subject to syncretic survivals and accretions, and it too has its sects, often bitterly hostile: the possession of a Book is a standing invitation to heretical inter-pretation. As for Hinduism, a religion in which the proffer of a cup of water may occasion ceremonial defilement, and in which caste is still a main determinant of social intercourse, is perhaps not the best foundation for the brotherhood of man.[1] It is certain, again, that the success of Christianity is in no way commensurate with the effort expended on its missions, and the value of its direct contribution to Asia is a matter for personal opinion; indirectly Christianity has doubtless aided in the laggard growth of a civic spirit in some areas, but here it is difficult to disentangle its role from that of Western secular humanism.

The impact of the 'materialist West' may have shaken the moral

---

[1] It is true that the notices of 'Hindu Pani' and 'Muslim Pani' on Indian railway stations have been replaced by the more catholic sign "Water for General"; but this is a very recent intervention of the State. It looks, incidentally, somewhat odd when the platform is occupied mainly by Other Ranks. Recent legislation on behalf of the 'Untouchables' has drawn the teeth of caste, but the monster may be an unconscionable time in dying.

foundations of Asian society, as the world market has shaken its economic; but if "by their fruits ye shall know them" be true, those foundations appear to have been rotten long ago. There is no basis for unity here. Despite the poignant lyricism and spiritual nobility of so many individual utterances, from the Vedic hymns three thousand years ago to Mohammed Iqbal's poems in our own day, many travellers in Asia have realized as never before the crushing force of the Lucretian epigram: *tantum religio potuit suadere malorem.*

INADEQUACY OF FEDERAL SOLUTIONS

It is hardly necessary to waste words in demonstrating the absence of political unity in Asia to-day. In effect only three or four areas are at present really stable politically, and they for very different reasons and on very different premises: Soviet Asia, Tibet, Saudi Arabia, Turkey. It is an odd list. Elsewhere the major components—Southwest Asia, India and Pakistan, Southeast Asia, the Far East—are themselves deeply divided by racial, linguistic, religious, and not least class cleavages, and these divisions are often so linked that language, class, and creed are distributed horizontally, with few cross-classifications. In such circumstances it is surely vain to look for a unified whole.

It has been suggested, notably by K. M. Panikkar in *The Future of South-East Asia*, that the way towards an admittedly distant unity lies through regional federations; in *The Revolt of Asia*, also, Payne sees the separate nationalisms of Asia as essentially immature and ephemeral surface phenomena on the more massive background of this exploited and oppressed half of humanity. Objectively there seems little solid reason for either view. In both Southwest and Southeast Asia the countries concerned are in a sense too similar for federation to be of much value in the economic sphere; they are competitive rather than complementary. The pluralism of society inhibits national unity even within individual states; while the fact that the larger shares of economic and technical power, skill, and initiative are in the hands of alien groups may exacerbate national feeling, but makes an autonomous industrial development exceedingly difficult, if not impossible.

Politically again competition rather than co-operation characterizes even states which proclaim the factitious unity of creed. The half-fledged state of Israel has defeated the Arab states in detail, both in arms and in diplomacy—the old story of the victory of cohesion over unorganized bulk. Yet Israel itself represents an uneasy alliance of potentially hostile elements—the old Zionist movement with the backing of capitalist circles in the U.S.A., and the strongly left-wing recent immigration from eastern Europe. Whichever may prevail, the mere existence and example of a régime so superior technically and administratively to its neighbours cannot but represent an insidious menace to the social and governmental systems of the Arab states. And even so their governing classes have been incompetent to achieve even the unity of short-term action. In Southeast Asia, on the other hand, there is no one common enemy; the translation of a general anti-imperialism into political action differs in each country with the particular imperialist power implicated, which also has as a rule local supporters not without influence, and influence not the less important because its role is cast in the *coulisses* of politics rather than upon the open stage. The situation is further complicated by the nascent or sub-imperialisms of the Indians and the Chinese.

As in other shatter-zones, it is not perhaps unfair to say that federalism provides in principle a splendid solution. Unfortunately all that is wrong is that the pre-requisite for the construction of stable federations is the ironing-out of the conflicts and problems which make it necessary to look for a federal solution. This circularity attaches to not a few of the arguments for Federalism as a panacea for the world's geopolitical problems.

THE EUROPEAN CONNECTION AS A FACTOR OF UNITY?

In so far as there is any unity in Asia, it is because the continent is, in Gunther's phrase, interlocked with Europe, and now with America. But this is the interdependence rather of Asiatic problems than of Asian peoples; and such as it is, this stage was reached long ago—certainly by 1902, when Russia dominated all the north, Britain all the south, and the Anglo-Japanese alliance linked the Far Eastern wings of both imperialisms; and soon the German infiltration into the Ottoman Empire provided another linking factor in the southwest. Then indeed a brawl in Bushire might have moved battalions in Manchuria; but in all this Asia was the passive victim of circumstance, not its active shaper.

Nationalism, indeed, was already stirring in many Asian countries when, as has often been noted, the Japanese victory of 1905 gave an impetus to spirited political actions whose simultaneity gave a spurious air of unity. The bringing of most of Asia into the world market meant some integration—the cultural landscape of the bazaar and the wharfside is strikingly similar through most of Asiatic Asia—but, as we saw most notably in Chapters I and III, the imperial powers pulled different ways, and in many respects actually increased the divergencies, and not only by dividing to rule; though that element was far from absent.

Economically it must be noted that, with the possible exceptions of India and of Soviet Asia, the resources for basic heavy industry are neither quantitatively sufficient, nor sufficiently well distributed in relation to each other and to the centres of economic activity, to enable Asia to build up industrial economies comparable in size to those of either western Europe or the U.S.A., although of course there is scope for very much more industrialization than exists. Asiatic Asia will remain dependent on the West, for some considerable time, for most of her needs in the heavier production goods, and probably also for technical and financial assistance. Continuous ties with Europe and America are also to the direct material and personal advantage of important groups in most countries—and often these are directing groups to which it is not easy to see an alternative, desirable as an alternative might sometimes be. Indeed, not merely the relative prosperity but the livelihood of many millions both in the East and the West will depend on a reasonable coming to terms between the new Asian states and the older powers of the West. In these circumstances, despite (or perhaps because of) the greatly weakened position of the old empires, it does not seem as if anti-imperialism in itself can be a source of fundamental unity, though it may of course lead to temporary tactical unity in action, e.g., that of India, Pakistan, and Ceylon in relation to Dutch 'police action' in Indonesia.

So far as anti-imperialism can play such a unifying role, it is probably as part of the greater doctrine of Communism. But this means that it is subsumed in a more positive programme, and one which is certainly interlocked with Europe and America, both in the immediate political sense that any countries where Communism is powerful are immediately brought into the front line of the cold war, or in the sense, which we may hope will prove more fundamental, that Communism, whatever else it may be, does represent the most thorough-going form of westernization in Asia, assaulting outright the social and land-tenure systems which stand in the way of agrarian reorganization, and theoretically repudiating as it does those religious bases to which the westernized urban bourgeoisies pay at least lip-service. Yet even here there are cross-currents: in practice it has obviously not been desirable to break the anti-imperialist front by a frontal attack on religion—whence some not unentertaining adjustments have been necessitated; and the emphasis on local nationalisms may well prove embarrassing when the conflicting welter of interests in Southeast Asia come onto the agenda of a Communist polity in the Far East. A Communist bloc might be much less monolithic in practice than in

26

theory. Here, obviously, China holds the key, and the outcome of the recent Communist successes is incalculable. It does not seem, however, that the general argument outlined above would be invalidated by Communist control of all China, since this would mean that some sort of *modus vivendi* with foreign traders would have to be attained, in order to secure the necessary technical equipment for economic rehabilitation.

THE PROBLEM OF LEADERSHIP

Further, if Asiatic Asia is to act together there must be some sort of organization, and if this is to be effective there must be some sort of leadership. It is fairly clear that the two congeries of small states in Southwest and Southeast Asia, even collectively, are too weak to stand alone in a world crisis. The problem is to secure leadership without imperialism. The Asian candidates are three: Japan, China, India.

It would be facile to assume that Japan having failed once is automatically out of the running. It is easy to point to the inadequacy of her material resources, and to the top-heavy industrial structure built upon them, which involved of necessity a particularly ruthless imperialism, an exploitation no less savage within Japan itself, and the suffering brought upon millions of Asia's peoples by the great gamble of the Pacific War. The Greater East Asia Co-Prosperity Sphere was at once an obvious fake and a fiasco, its grandiose sub-continental planning issuing only in a new economic localism (on a low plane of production) as Japanese shipping broke down beyond hope of repair. Politically also the structure was ramshackle; the Japanese were compelled to buy allies at the expense of other allies, e.g., by the cession of Burmese (Shan) and Malayan territory to Siam.

Asian views may differ: the idea of a pooling of the resources of the Far East and Southeast Asia is in itself a good one, and best carried out under the auspices of that Asian power which has admittedly the best natural position and technical equipment for the task; despite the brutalities of the Japanese occupation, without that great upheaval the hold of the European powers might have remained strong for decades: the world situation in 1941 compelled Japan to take what seemed the most favourable opportunity for action, and the resultant suffering was inseparable from a war in which the resistance of the other side was an unpredictable factor. To us the Japanese polity seems a bastard cross between the worst of both worlds, the grosser materialist elements of the Western machine age and the barbaric survivals of Oriental despotism. To Asia it may seem as if her fault was simply failure. And while the actual record of the Japanese conquerors in 1942-45 brought her moral (and material) prestige very low, the selection of an Asiatic nation as the guinea-pig for the atomic bomb may well seem to many Asian leaders, and their followers, to have reduced the moral claims of the West to nothing.

Moreover, especially since the Communist advance in China, there has been apparent a disposition on the part of the occupying régime in Japan to rehabilitate that country as a first line of defence—or deployment—against Soviet Asia. Since, however, 80 million people cannot well subsist on a cultivable area of 24,000 square miles merely by agriculture and fishing, this carries with it the corollary of rapid industrial reconstruction; and given the distribution of raw materials in the Far East, this might well result in a controlled Japanese sub-imperialism. It is obvious that this would not meet with Chinese approval; but the opinion of China, whether the Communist dominant or the Nationalist remnant, is not likely to count for much in this matter, except in so far as the need for Chinese raw materials and markets calls for special agreements. Australia also will be opposed to this policy of "restoring the material standing of Japan before any lasting psychological or spiritual adjustment can possibly have been made."[1]

As for China, it is likely, though not certain, that her internal troubles will put her out of court for an indefinite period. In any case, a Nationalist China would have had to face the difficulties caused by tactlessness in insisting on ancient but ineffective claims to territory or suzerainty (e.g. in northern Burma), and by the dislike of Malays, Siamese, and Indonesians both for the active trading elements and for the coolie who undercuts the relatively high standards which these southeast Asian peoples have long maintained. A Communist China would not, of course, be subject to quite the same disabilities, nor, presumably, would it have the same temptation to a forward policy, although it might develop the necessary military strength. Nevertheless its relations to the large numbers of Chinese in these areas would be delicate and difficult enough, since they include important elements not likely to support, nor to wish support from, a Communist China.

India is by far the largest, best-equipped, and best-administered Asian state (leaving aside Soviet Asia), and enjoys a magnificent strategic position in the Indian Ocean. Nevertheless neither its leadership nor that of China is likely to be willingly accepted by the smaller states, unless it is so vague as to be ineffective. As Wint sums it up, "It is not difficult to prove theoretically that the real interest of all concerned is to maintain the unity of South Asia. But to convince the inflammatory and insular

---

[1] C. A. Fisher, loc. cit., q.v. for a fuller discussion of this problem.

opinion of a dozen or more nationalist parties—that is a task indeed."[1]
The rapacities and economic dominance of the trading and money-lending classes in Burma and Ceylon, the drain of money remitted home by
labourers who would work for far less than the Burmese or Sinhalese
conception of the rate for the job, have given rise to bitter antagonisms
and understandable, if unjustified, suspicions of imperialist designs.
Indeed, when the export of much-needed rice from Burma is held up by
internal troubles, while the Burmese Government is expropriating at its
own rates of compensation large areas of land mortgaged to Indian
moneylenders and bankers, it must be admitted that the temptation is
strong and the descent from 'good offices' to a measure of control and
active interference all too easy. The subjectively anti-imperialist views of
Indian leaders might prove feeble bulwarks against the driving logic of
events.

It is not to the point to say that there is no important recent tradition of
expansion in India or China. There have been imperialist dynasties in
China—the Han and the Mongols—and historic imitation is a strong
factor in Chinese polity. Even in this century China has been uncon-
scionably tenacious of useless claims in the outer territories. India too had
her far-flung expeditions, as far as the east coast of Indo-China; admittedly in the distant past. More cogently, there is a very pertinent case to
hand. There seemed to be nothing presaging expansion in the history
of a country which, although archipelagic in character, for over two
centuries pursued a policy of isolation so strict that no vessel larger than
a fishing-smack could be built. Yet, within three-quarters of a century, a
short time in the life of a nation, Japan built up a power which, taking
advantage of a brief opportunity, overran in six months all the lands and
seas between the Arakan Yomas and the Solomon Islands, a land area of
about one and and a half million square miles with a population of about
150 millions.

It is true of course that any such development presupposes great advances in the industrial equipment of any of the three competitors. And
against it, above all, is the immense technological lead of the U.S.A.—a
lead of at least a century—and the increasing American interests in Southeast Asia, the obvious storm-centre where Indian, Chinese, and Japanese
interests converge and conflict.

It would certainly seem, however, that some co-ordinating power or
powers is a necessity if Southeast Asia and the Far East are not to be

---

[1] Guy Wint, *The British in Asia* (1947), p. 211. The whole book is an eloquent plea for
continued Indo-British co-operation in southern Asia, and ranks as one of the most thought-
provoking analyses of the contemporary Asian scene.

exposed to grave risks of anarchic disorder and social retrogression: already the interior of the Indo-Chinese peninsula bids fair to become for Europeans a *terra incognita* once more. Leaving aside the possibility of a Communist order of things (which depends more obviously on the entire world situation), can this co-ordination, and the technological and financial aid so necessary to the rehabilitation of trade, the reconstruction of agriculture, and the development of industry, be achieved without the material and psychological frustrations of a new imperialism, issuing inevitably in a new and bitterer, because more disillusioned, nationalism? Only the official optimist and the ardent or ill-informed romanticist would venture the affirmation.

These considerations were undoubtedly in the minds of the delegates to the Inter-Asian Relations Conference at New Delhi in 1947: many excellent generalities secured a wide measure of verbal assent, but, as Fisher points out, the real sting was taken out of such topics as racial conflicts and inter-Asian migration by Pandit Nehru's disclaimer that "care must be taken to avoid trespassing into the domestic problems of particular states"—as if much serious discussion of such matters were possible without such trespass. Agreement is easier to reach in an academic cloudland than on the geographical earth, whether of Asia or wherever; and this indeed is probably a pre-requisite of the holding of such conferences. Which does not mean that they are valueless, if rightly evaluated.

THE REAL UNITY OF ASIA

So far, then, the conclusion on all counts, seems to be that the unity of Asia is for Asians an illusion, and for Europeans a delusion which springs from the vivid perception of a difference between the West and the East and masks the deep differentiations within the East itself.[1] Even regionalism seems at a discount. Southeast Asia is weak in itself, and torn between the gravitational pulls of its greater neighbours to the north and the west; Southwest Asia fissiparous, and rendered more so by its poverty in men and technique and its wealth in oil, as well as its *damnosa haereditas* of an unrivalled strategic position—unrivalled, that is, for the purposes and manœuvres of outside powers—from which it has followed that "l'Asie Occidentale y a gagné l'histoire la plus attachante et la plus ancienne du monde, mais aussi de ne jamais connaître, sauf à des rares intervalles, le calme, la paix, et la prosperité."[2] The Far East could probably make a very workable block, but it too must look both ways,

---

[1] The converse fallacy pervades Eastern thought about the West.
[2] R. Blanchard, *Asie Occidentale* (Géographie Universelle T. VIII, 1929), pp. 233–34.

situated as it is in the distracted marchlands "between the pass and fell incenséd points Of mighty opposites."

There remains, however, one common denominator in Asiatic Asia, the most pervasive, the most standard of all: poverty, and especially agrarian poverty. Some small pockets of prosperity apart, throughout Asiatic Asia (including the southwest) the great bulk of men and women live in conditions of poverty, disease, and malnutrition not credible until they have been seen. Some of the economic results have been noted in our introductory survey—amongst others the inhibiting effects of low purchasing power on industrial development, the paralyzing illiteracy, the terrible loss of human energy through avoidable sickness and through lack of food. No easy solution of these problems can be envisaged; yet without a solution there can be no lasting peace and progress in Asia; and what are matters of theoretical discussion to us are matters of literal life or death to millions in Asia—nor is Asia insulated from the world.

It may indeed be held that no conceivable social system or technological advance (unless and until atomic energy is freely available for peaceful use) could ensure a humanly decent existence to the mass of the population in those areas with over 1000 rural population to square mile, such as eastern Bengal and much of the North China Plain. But beyond these relatively limited areas of concentration is a vast penumbra where the pressure of population on the soil is little less acute. Migration is practically ruled out—even could they adjust themselves to vastly different farming environments, there is literally nowhere to go for anything like the present increments (cf. above, pp. 35–38). Industrialization cannot do more, at the best, than take in the natural increase, leaving things no worse but no better; even this limited achievement is not very likely to be attained. All that is left is to check the increase; if not by the old and efficient Malthusian checks of war, pestilence, and famine, or by female infanticide and abortion, then by birth control. But though many, perhaps most, demographers who have studied Asian population problems would agree with this conclusion, few, if any, seem to have much hope of its application.

Although our general picture is drawn in dark shades, there is much in the contemporary changes in Asia to exhilarate the hearts of those who hold, with the Chinese proverb, that all men are brothers under the winds of heaven. The attainment of independence in much of Asia is a revolutionary event, an event still far from complete and subject to serious checks and limitations. Yet conceivably the release of psychological energies which normally accompanies great political revolutions may lead to a social revolution. It is difficult to see how this great and terrible common problem of agrarian crisis can be met without one, whatever the forms and expressions it might take. At best the way will be long and hard, and it is too early to say whether the revolt of Asia is mere revolt, whether it is the prelude to an Asian renaissance or to further social disintegration on the national and international scale. But, could such a recasting of the ancient moulds be secured without too catastrophic violence then, and then only, with scope for expansionist, probably collective, economies within national or regional limits, would the foundations of the true unity of Asia be laid; and the rise to its full stature of this great fraction of mankind might mean a real 'Third Force' compelling radical readjustments in current concepts of world power.

ASIA IN ITS WIDER SETTING

Thus far we have considered Asia from within outwards, finding no real unity as yet except in the obvious and purely formal locational sense; practically speaking, that usage attaches the word Asia to a large landmass. This is not, of course, a trivial or an unimportant sense. The power of the word, the idea, should not be underrated, and, however at variance in their internal affairs, many Asians would consciously think of themselves as such when confronted with the non-Asian world. It is, therefore, time to look at Asia from without inwards, to consider it as a part of the great globe itself.

Looked at from outside, Asia might at first appear an entity in international affairs and it is true that the swift contagion of political ideas and a certain community of needs and aspirations may from time to time induce a reaction and posture broadly common to the Asian peoples. Yet the relations between the peoples of Asia and extraneous states, as a result of modern history, are many and various. The so-called 'revolt of Asia' has scarcely so far achieved, even for parts of the continent, let alone the whole, that absolute degree of political independence which permits the immediate charting of new ways. Apart from the influence which springs from their economic and military strength, the 'great powers' still retain special political positions within the Asian world.

Soviet Asia and High Asia, the first an integral part of a federal Euro-Asiatic state, the second (apart from Tibet) under the tutelage of this great continental power, occupy a geopolitical position at once clear and stable. The political, agrarian, and industrial revolutions, which in many parts of Asia have yet largely to be consummated, have been in operation in Soviet Asia for more than twenty years.[1] No longer would it be true to

[1] Cf. Wint, *op. cit.*, pp. 153–157.

say of Soviet Asia, as Nansen once said of Russia, that it is 'a world still unborn'. Alone in Asia it possesses the sinews of modern industry and of war necessary for its defence. Alone in Asia it affords—in Siberia and Kazakhstan—the resources and space for colonization by Europeans. But it is a world apart; an iron curtain shuts it off from the outside world, apart from trade contacts at its Pacific ports.

In contrast, the Western powers retain financial, commercial, and political interests, and even some military bases, in the outer, seaward, lands from Southwest Asia to the Far East. The facts of geographical location and the distribution of oil resources, as we have seen, make Southwest Asia a sphere of primary interest to the Western powers. The retention of Malaya under the British Colonial Office and the continued adhesion of India, Pakistan, and Ceylon to the Commonwealth, suggest no immediate or abrupt cessation of British influence in the Indian Ocean. Economic bonds and commercial orientation may retain the independent Philippines within the orbit of the United States. And the French in Indo-China, the Dutch in Indonesia, strive to maintain their *points d'appui* in the face of nationalist pressure. Yet it would be short-sighted to conclude that geopolitically *plus ça change, plus c'est la même chose*. The revolt of Asia, along broadly socialist lines, may be arrested for a time, but like truth will out. Some Asiatic emplacements of the Western powers—notably the Philippines, Indo-China, and Indonesia—became liabilities and not assets after World War II.

It is the fashion to speak of the One World in which all the continents and their peoples are neighbours. Clearly this idea must not be allowed to obscure the high degree to which the world is compartmented along national, political, and cultural lines. Yet it is broadly true that for commerce, political ideologies, international affairs, and war, there is only one continuum—the whole world. Whatever Asian peoples may wish, the commercial peoples will not ignore their continent, and indeed cannot afford to do so. Although the march of modern science and technology may appear to threaten some of Asia's many valuable staples, it seems clear that these will and must draw the commerce of the Western, and even the Soviet, powers. Natural rubber, petroleum, wolfram, manganese, tin, copra, jute, Manilla hemp, sisal, tea, silk, sugar, spices, oilseeds and soya, and drugs—the most ancient and the most modern riches of Asia—all these will be sought, even though the production of synthetic rubber, nylon and other 'artificial silks', substitutes for quinine, and the like, may reduce dependence on Asia and introduce new elements of instability into its economy. Clearly, too, the outside world can serve the potentially vast Asiatic market and, if willing to forego political privileges and to conform to Asia's own assessment of its requirements, can profitably make an enormous contribution to the well-being of Asian peoples. But the Western powers, which have so much to offer that Asia needs, must recognize that the democratic ideas which they have spread in Asia have been learnt in their 20th and not their 19th century form. Many of the features of modern Asiatic society—the gearing of economy to alien commercial interests, the domination of privately owned plantations, the entrenchment of vertical monopolies responsible to shareholders in distant lands, the exportation of an unduly high proportion of the profits of local production—seem archaisms, incompatible with the development of a democratic society. As bad, or worse, are many indigenous forms of exploitation. Parliamentary liberalism is not enough. It should be more of a commonplace than it seems to be, that platitudes about defending a democracy which the Asian masses have hardly or never known are of little use against the appeal of the Communist slogan: *the land to the peasants*. Failure to realize this means the risk of being trapped in one's own propaganda; whence miscalculations, which might be fatal.

In international affairs and in strategy, as we have already tried to show, it is not Asia as a whole but certain of its major components which fix the attention of the outside world. It is no longer necessary to argue the thesis of the 'indivisibility' of world peace. The three 'great powers'—the United States, the Soviet Union, and the British Commonwealth and Empire—who by their co-operation or discord hold peace precariously in their hands, have learnt by experience to discern storm clouds on the Asian no less than on the European horizon. Asia, it would appear, seeks only to fulfil its own destiny (whatever that may be) and views with equal distaste and suspicion the intervention of any one of them in its affairs. The three powers are at least agreed that Japan shall not again be permitted to make the Far East an armed centre of disturbance to world peace, but they are much less agreed on what should be the exact role of Japan in the days to come. Still less are they agreed on a common policy for the maintenance of world peace.

The attempt has accordingly to be made to seek and to maintain an equilibrium of political and military forces, and in this attempt factors of geography, alike stable and dynamic, must be taken carefully into consideration. The strategy of both peace and war must be related to a physically unitary, if politically sundered, world. In the short view, the leading countries of 'Asiatic Asia'—India and China—appear unlikely to divert their energies from urgent social problems to the fields of external adventure; but it must not be forgotten that a forward external policy has in the past been frequently used to relieve accumulated internal tensions. And the great powers are still entrenched in Asia; even if they were not, they would still have to keep watch and ward there, if only on each other.

Recent studies in the United States,[1] following the Nazi writings in *Geopolitik* and the much earlier analyses of Sir Halford Mackinder, underline the geographical aspect of the joint problem of world peace and world war. For the United Kingdom, with its economy based on world trade and its dominions and dependencies widely distributed in every continent, it remains necessary to secure full and free inter-accessibility by sea, and, to this end, to prevent a potentially hostile great power from establishing itself at points in Asia or elsewhere from which this inter-accessibility could be threatened or denied. The construction of the Panama Canal and the experiences of World War II in the Pacific have led to the formulation of a similar policy by the United States, which may well give relative permanence to its interventionist policy in the trans-Pacific theatre.

Having discarded as inadequate for its security a policy related solely to the Western hemisphere, the United States now professes a policy which springs from a new realization of its 'encirclement' (*Fig.* 34). The encirclement which gives it constant concern is not, of course, that merely geographical encirclement which, as maps can be drawn to show, characterizes every area of the earth's surface. It is geopolitical encirclement which is in question; that is, encirclement by areas whose concentrations of population and of economic resources are great enough to make them potential bases for a bid for world mastery. The same arguments, in reverse, are of course ever present to the minds of Soviet leaders. Three such areas within the seaward zone of Euro-Asia are Western Europe, southern Asia, and the Far East. The degree of success attained by Nazi Germany and by Japan in the exploitation as power bases of Western Europe and the Far East—similarly placed at the oceanic extremities of Euro-Asia—emphasizes for the United States, and for the Soviet Union, the prime importance of these two theatres in the strategy of peace. Just how long this consideration will induce the United States to remain in military occupation of Japan and formerly Japanese-held islands cannot yet be foreseen. Nor is it yet clear what relationship will be formed between the Western powers and the new régime of Mao Tse-tung, which in itself should make for increased political stability in China.

If the gloomy prophets are right and a third world war comes, it might

[1] See, for example, N. J. Spykman, *The Geography of the Peace*, N.Y., 1944.

well put to the test for the first time the prediction, born of late 19th century Russophobia, which Mackinder publicized. Since the Napoleonic wars, Russia and Britain, the continental and the sea power, have fought together against continental power in Europe, though arrayed against each other by conflicting interests in the continent of Asia. A war in which the Soviet Union, already master of Eastern Europe and of the Heartland, challenged the maritime power of the United States and of Western Europe, must involve, as indeed its prevention must also involve, a careful evaluation, *inter alia*, of the geography of changing Asia: the greatest and the most diversified of the continents, the mother alike of most ancient civilizations and most primitive tribes, containing within its borders well over half of mankind, and possessing incalculable potentialities for the advance or the retrogression of its own peoples and of the world.

INDEX

Abadan, 70, 75
Abqaiq Oilfield, 70
Abu Dibis depression, 115
Addis Ababa, 93
Aden, 10, 20, 58, 60, 93, 161, 162
Aegean Sea, 53, 109, 110
Afghanistan, 17, 20, 51, 53, 127, 128, 157,
    162, 163, 172, 352, 353
Aghajari Oilfield, 70
Agra, 13, 123, 124
Agriculture, 99, *135–41*, *253–7*, 275, 278,
    284–5, 290, *291–2*, *325–7*
Ahmedabad, 131, 144
Ahmed, N., 169
Airways, 11–12, 39, 41, 65, 66, *90–93*,
    342, 377, 381
Akaba, 81, 83, 90, 102
Akita Oilfield, 293
Alaska, 17, 342
Albuquerque, Afonso de, 14
Aldan River, 309, 310, 334
Aleppo, 54
Alexandria, 90
Allen, G. C., 300
Alma Ata, 312, 333, 348, 353, 381
Al Qantara, 87
Altai *Krai*, 326, 328, 339, 345, 380
Altai, Plateau of, 309, 311, 315, 365
Altyn Tagh, 368
Aluminium, 275, 286, 324
Alward River, 69
Ambarchik, 355
Amman, 83
Amnok (Yalu or Oryoku) River, 282
Amritsar, 129, 144
Amu Darya (Oxus), 312, 326, 340, 353
Amur Province, 17
Amur River, 16, 271, 273, 308, 317, 319,
    334, 340, 341
Anatolia, 16, 51, 52, 63, 81, 104, 110
Andamans, 180
Andijan, 312
Angara River, 309, 317
Angkor, 187
Anglo-Egyptian Treaty, 1936, 81
Anglo-Japanese Alliance, 16
Anhwei, 250, 254, 258
Ankara, 54, 81, 84, 85, 93
Annam, 18, 195, 196, 215, 234
Annamites, 186, 189
Anshan, 275, 277
Anstey, V., 169
Anti-Taurus Mts., 52
Antonius, G., 116
Antung, 286

Arab, Arabian, 10, *55–6*, 63, 65, 66,
    95–103, 126, 187, 190, 202, 389,
    390
Arab Empire, 54
Arabia, 2, 20, 52, 53, 56, 58, 59, 74, 77,
    80, 81, 90
Arabian Sea, 122
Arab League, 63, 93, 96, 233
Arakan, 17, 126
Arakanese Buddhists, 128
Arakan Mts., 195, 223
Arakan Yoma, 126, 180
Aral-Caspian depression, 2, 308, 316
Aral Sea, 10, 312, 316, 320, 340
Ararat, Mount, 51, 105, 107
Aravalli Hills, 120
Archangel, 342
Arctic Ocean, 307, 308, 334, 340, 341
Arctic Routeways, 41–42
Arctic U.S.S.R., 315, 328, 342, *355–7*
Ardahan, *107–109*, 352
Armenia, Republic of, 305, 328, 345,
    349, 351
Aryan, 123
Ashkhabad, 82, 88, 312, 316, 321
Asia, Climate, 3
Asia, Diversity of, 5, *385–97*
Asia, Major divisions, 6–8
Asia, Name of, 4
Asia, Political, 39–49
Asia, Population, 5
Asia, Social Aspects, 12–14, 21–9
Asiatic Asia, 4, 6, 20, 29, *385–7*, 388, 390,
    391, 392, 396, 399
Asia, Vegetation, 3–4
Assal, 71
Assam, 129, 132, 135, 136, 137, 142, 143,
    160
Astara, 105
Asterabad, 53
Atjeh (Achin), 194
Atomic Power, 46, 142, 299, 324, 393
Attock, 143
Azerbaijan, 65, *105–7*, *349*, 351, 352

Baba Gurgur, Oilwell, 69
Baghdad, 44, 54, 58, 69, 76, 83, 84, 85,
    86, 87, 89, 91, 93, 115
Baghdad Railway, 85, 87, 90
Bahawalpur, 129, 157
Bahrein, 11, 20, 43, 71, 72
Bahr-el-Milh depression, 115
Baikal-Amur Railway (B.A.M.), 334,
    338, 339
Baikal, Lake, 17, 309

402

PRINTED IN GREAT BRITAIN BY
EBENEZER BAYLIS AND SON, LTD., THE
TRINITY PRESS, WORCESTER, AND LONDON